The Impact of Social Media in Modern Romantic Relationships

Studies in New Media

Series Editor: John Allen Hendricks

This series aims to advance the theoretical and practical understanding of the emergence, adoption, and influence of new technologies. It provides a venue to explore how New Media technologies are changing the media landscape in the twenty-first century.

Titles in the Series

The Impact of Social Media in Modern Romantic Relationships

Edited by Narissra M. Punyanunt-Carter and Jason S. Wrench

LEXINGTON BOOKS
Lanham • Boulder • New York • London

Published by Lexington Books
An imprint of The Rowman & Littlefield Publishing Group, Inc.
4501 Forbes Boulevard, Suite 200, Lanham, Maryland 20706
www.rowman.com

Unit A, Whitacre Mews, 26-34 Stannary Street, London SE11 4AB

British Library Cataloguing in Publication Information Available

Library of Congress Cataloging-in-Publication Data
The hardback edition of this book was previously cataloged by the Library of Congress as follows:

Names: Punyanunt-Carter, Narissra M., editor. | Wrench, Jason S., editor.
Title: The impact of social media in modern romantic relationships / edited by Narissra M. Punya-nunt-Carter and Jason S. Wrench.
Description: Lanham : Lexington Books, [2017] | Series: Studies in new media | Includes bibliographical references and index.
Identifiers: LCCN 2017006787 (print) | LCCN 2017013820 (ebook)
Subjects: LCSH: Man-woman relationships. | Social media. | Social networks. | Dating (Social customs)--Technological innovations. | Love.
Classification: LCC HQ801 (ebook) | LCC HQ801 .I57 2017 (print) | DDC 306.7--dc23 LC record available at https://lccn.loc.gov/2017006787

ISBN 978-1-4985-4448-1 (cloth : alk. paper)
ISBN 978-1-4985-4450-4 (pbk. : alk. paper)
ISBN 978-1-4985-4449-8 (Electronic)

Printed in the United States of America

Table of Contents

ONE

From the Front Porch to Swiping Right

The Impact of Technology on Modern Dating

Jason S. Wrench and Narissra M. Punyanunt-Carter

In 1989, Beth Bailey published her book, *From the Front Porch to the Back Seat: Courtship in Twentieth-Century America*. In her book, Bailey examines how courtship in the United States evolved over the years, from the earliest instances of courtship, when men went "calling" on potential mates with their calling cards. In the ninetieth and early twentieth centuries, the upper middle class engaged in strict rules related to calling upon someone at their house. If an individual was going to see a friend or relative, he would ring the doorbell, a servant would appear holding a silver tray, the caller would place his card on the tray, and the servant would deliver the card to the head of the household. For dating purposes, a gentleman caller would engage in the same behavior, but he would hand the servant his card and then leave, hoping that the woman who caught his eye would send her own card in return. These courtship behaviors were very public and strictly overseen by the female's family. Over the course of the twentieth century, dating changed from the calling card and meeting in one's parlor, to public places like dance halls, movie theaters, restaurants, bars, etc. As Bailey noted, "[I]t removed couples from the implied supervision of the private sphere—from the watchful eyes of family and local community—to the anonymity of the public sphere. Courtship among strangers offered couples new freedom" (24).

When Bailey published her book in 1989, she had no way of envisioning how courtship would continue to radically change as we entered into

1

the twenty-first century. In the same year when Bailey published her book, a software engineer working for Conseil Européen pour la Recherche Nucléaire (CERN) named Tim Berners-Lee was inventing the World Wide Web. Although the Internet had been around since 1969, the invention of the World Wide Web increased usability and created a common language for the creation of Internet content, HyperText Markup Language (html) (Berners-Lee 1999). The purpose of the current book is to examine how technology has changed dating and mating in the twenty-first century. To start us on this journey of discovery, we will first examine the history of online dating and how it has evolved over time.

ONLINE DATING—A BRIEF HISTORY

Although not an exact precursor to modern online dating, to many people, the 1700s and the creation of newspaper personal advertisements as the logical first step in our brief history (Cocks 2009). The first known personal advertisement occurred in 1692 in the agony column of the *Athenian Mercury*. For hundreds of years, the modern dating industry took many circuitous routes, from newspapers to their own brand of magazine. Of course, the popularity of newspaper personals varied with time. By the nineteenth century, personal ads proliferated in the Western world. In the United States, *The Wedding Bells*, *The Correspondent*, and *The Matrimonial News* are three examples of papers that were exclusively devoted to the publication of personal ads. Although personal ads were popular, the *New York Times* stopped publishing them by the 1870s (Schafer 2003). The interest in personal ads definitely changed with the decades. The 1930s to the 1950s represented fairly lean years for personal ads, but with the 1960s there was once again a resurgence in their popularity.[1] Personal ads remained an integral part of the dating landscape through the end of the twentieth century. The *New York Times* would actually bring back personal ads in the early twenty-first century as the paper started to look for new advertising streams (Kilgannon 2001). However, as Kilgannon (2001) reported, all proposed personal ads would be sent to the "advertising acceptability department, which will accept only ads 'in line with the integrity of the rest of our classified advertising section,' Ms. Park said. 'Any language or phrasing that is suggestive or in questionable taste in the opinion of *The Times* will be declined'" (para. 7). As of the writing of this chapter, personal ads are still alive and well at the *New York Times* (see http://www.nytimes.com/classifieds/personals/).

After personal ads, there was not a major leap in the change of dating patterns until the telephone. Admittedly, there are documented cases of people dating using the telegraph or radio, but these occurrences did not have the wide popularity or accessibility that personal ads had in the past (Standage, 1998). In 1981, we see the development of the telephony-based *chat line*. Individuals would call a 1-900 (or 976) number and could talk to psychics, or just to get the time and temperature. By 1985, there were a number of chat lines specifically devoted to helping men and women date, along with specific outlets for gay men. By 1999, some of these chat lines even started integrated web-cameras.

Also during the 1980s and into the 1990s came the proliferation of companies that helped match couples through video dating. Men would record video personals in which they would attempt to sell themselves to potential mates, who would then watch the videos and determine whom they would like to go on a possible date with in the future (Mulshine 2015). The notion of matchmaking was hardly a new one, but the incorporation of technology into these services took on a new life with the invention of VHS. Of course, video dating sites quickly grew more and more passé as the 1990s started to usher in new technology.

Although the Internet had been invented in 1969, access and utility was generally focused on the military and academic researchers. Even as computer technology became a more normalized household item during the 1980s and the early 1990s, most people did not own a modem because computers did not come with them. During this same time period, the U.S. Federal Government started a process that would give the general public access to the Internet. As modems became standard parts of a personal computer, people started using them to connect with Bulletin Board Services and eventually Internet service providers like America Online (AOL), Prodigy, and CompuServe in the early 1990s. However, these early experiences connecting online were quite expensive, because online access was charged by the hour. During these early years, those who had access to Internet relay chat (IRC) would often use chatrooms as a way of meeting people locally and globally. Then, as people accessed companies like AOL, Prodigy, and CompuServe, people moved to chatrooms and eventually instant messaging. In 1998, the idea of meeting people anonymously online became so ingrained in the American psyche that Hollywood released a movie based on *Parfumerie* by Hungarian playwright Miklós László. In *Parfumerie*, a man and a woman who have a negative working relationship find out that the person they have been falling in love with via an anonymous romantic letter service is really their coworker. The modern retelling, *You've Got Mail*, is named for the sound that AOL makes when you first log in to their service and there is e-mail waiting to be read.

The real change to online access came in 1996, when AOL changed its business model from a charge-by-the-hour system to a flat monthly fee of $19.95. This simple change lowered the cost of Internet access for the first time, allowing a broader base of people to become connected. Before the switch to a flat fee, many people would meet in chatrooms online that were arranged by interests, similarities, or geographic location.

Not surprisingly, over the last five years of the twentieth century, the proliferation of Internet dating occurred within the general public. In 1995, Match.com was founded, making it the first major player in the online dating world. At first, Internet dating was considered taboo and was marginalized, but over time Internet dating became normalized. In the decade following the founding of Match.com, Internet dating became very normalized and a number of different services were created. Table 1.1 shows a brief history of online dating and many of the key early websites are shown.

The next major technological change that really changed how the world dates was the release of the iPhone in 2007. Although smartphones and Palm Pilots had previously existed, the rich application infrastructure created by the iPhone would go on to revolutionize how people connected. Most of the major online dating players (e.g., Match.com, eHarmony, JDate, PlentyofFish, OkCupid, etc.) embraced the new cellphone technology, creating applications that took their web-based experiences to a mobile-based experience. In addition to the creation of the iPhone in 2007, Skout became the first software that enabled users to meet others based on a cell phone's global positioning services. Although Proxidating had tried doing this through Bluetooth technology, Skout really was the first major player in the GPS based mobile dating game. In 2009, the gay dating application Grindr took the idea of GPS dating and formalized it into an iPhone application that changed modern dating practices for gay men. Instead of going online to meet other gay men, gay men could look at their iPhones and see all of the other gay men connected in their geographic area.

In 2012, a new dating application, Tinder, added a new touch to the dating world. Instead of just seeing all of the available people around someone geographically, people would be presented with the images and profiles of potential dating partners. If someone was not interested in an individual, he or she could swipe her or his finger left across the screen of the phone. If someone was interested in another individual, he or she could swipe the person's image right across the phone. If Person A swiped right on Person B and if Person B also swiped right on Person A, the two individuals would be matched and could then message one another.

Over the past few pages, we have attempted to create a succinct history of the changes of hundreds of years of dating practices into a few short paragraphs. We know we have left out many details along the way in order to create a short narrative history. This history clearly demonstrates how humans have always adapted technology, from the newspaper in the 1600s to the smartphone of the twenty-first century, to find romantic love.

WIRING COMMUNICATION AND DATING

For our purposes, computers and computer technology ranging from earliest incarnations to the most recent revolution in cell phone technology is a clear case of mediatization. Jansson (2013) coined the concept of mediatization or "how other social processes in a broad variety of domains and at different levels become inseparable from and dependent on technological processes and resources of mediation" (289). For the purposes of this book, we are interested in how this technology has been used to impact dating in modern romantic relationships.

In 1993, Rose and Frieze proposed a simple script that most first dates follow. In their research, the authors found that first dates included the following: dress, be nervous, pick up (date), leave (meeting place), confirm plans, get to know, evaluate, talk, laugh, eat, attempt to make out and accept or reject, take (date) home, kiss, and go home. Klinkenberg and Rose (1994) further noted that dating scripts differed only slightly between heterosexual and gay (discussed plans, was nervous, groomed/dressed, picked up date [or was picked up]/met at a prearranged location, left one location for another, evaluated date, talked/laughed/joked, talked to other friends, went to movie/show/etc., had a meal, drank alcohol/used drugs, initiated physical contact, made out, had sex, stayed over, made plans for another date, and went home) and lesbian (discussed plans, was nervous, groomed/dressed, prepared for date, picked up date [or was picked up], evaluated date, talked/laughed/joked, went to movie/show/etc., had a meal, experienced positive feelings, drank alcohol/used drugs, initiated physical contact, kissed/hugged goodnight, took date home, and went home) couples. When looking at either the heterosexual or gay and lesbian scripts of the early 1990s, it's easy to see where parts of this script are not always in play with the mediated relationship. For example, where exactly does "stalking someone on Facebook to find out all of their likes and dislikes" fit into this script? Of course, as researchers Rauch, Strobel, Bella, Odachowski, and Bloom (2014) found, Facebook stalking before a first date is probably not a very good idea, because it actually increases arousal in individuals with high levels of social anxiety. The script from 1993 to the present has clearly evolved as a result of the technology.

While dating relationships have clearly changed over the course of the last thirty years, so has our understanding of the relationship between communication and technology. In 1989, Chesebro and Bonsall published *Computer-Mediated Communication: Human Relationships in a Computerized World*, which was the first real project to examine the intricate relationship between humans and computers from a communication perspective. In it, they wrote, "When a computer is used only to convey messages, human beings dominate the computer system. The computer does not directly manipulate the content of the user's message. . . . For all practical

Table 1.1.   A Brief History of Online Dating

1959	Jim Harvey and Phil Fialer, students at Stanford University, conducted a computerized matchmaking project using punch cards and an IBM 650 Mainframe.
1965	Jeff Tarr and Vaughan Morrill, students at Harvard University, conducted a study attempting to match people based on similarities using an IBM 1401.
Early 1970s	James Schur creates the first computerized dating company called Phase II.
1984	Jon Boede and Scott Smith created the Matchmaker Electronic Pen-Pal Network, which allowed users to meet using bulletin boards (BBS).
	Members of CompuServe's CB Simulator meet face-to-face, noting the first real gathering of people who met in a virtual environment.
1986	Gregory Scott Smith releases a BBS that allows individuals to find others in their geographic location. This is ultimately the precursor that becomes MatchMaker.com, which is the longest running online dating service.
Early 1990s	The United States sees a proliferation of online service providers like America Online (AOL), CompuServe, and Prodigy, among others.
1994	Kiss.com is registered by Terrence "Lee" Zehrer and becomes the first picture personals dating site to have 1 million users.
1995	Gary Kremen starts Match.com.
1996	In an unprecedented move, AOL switches its pay-per-hour model to a flat monthly rate of $19.95. This pricing change opens the Internet to the general public in a way unlike ever before.
1997	JDate is launched aimed at Jewish singles.
1998	The Tom Hanks and Meg Ryan movie *You've Got Mail* is released, demonstrating the potential of online portals like AOL for dating to a broader audience.
1999	Craig Newmark incorporates Craigslist.org, which he originally started working on in 1995, and allows people to publish free personals.
2000	eHarmony is founded by psychologist and relationship author Neil Clark Warren and his son-in-law Greg Forgatch.
	James Hong and Jim Young create a popular website called Hot or Not, where users can upload their images and then be rated by other members.
2002	Ashley Madison, a site designed for married individuals seeking extramarital affairs, is launched by Darren Morgenstern.
2003	PlentyofFish (POF) is founded by Markus Frind, becoming one of the first free dating sites.
	Proxidating is launched, allowing users to match and connect with other users nearby using Bluetooth technology.
	IAC/InterActiveCorp acquires Kiss.com, which is merged with their other major dating website, Match.com.

2004	OKCupid is launched by Chris Coyne, Christian Rudder, Sam Yagan, and Max Krohn, who were also the people behind TheSpark and Spark Notes.
	Mark Zuckerberg and his college roommates, Eduardo Saverin, Andrew McCollum, Dustin Moskovitz, and Chris Hughes, launch Facebook.
2005	Three employees of PayPal, Chad Hurley, Steve Chen, and Jawed Karim, set out to create a video dating website, but scrapped that idea and eventually created YouTube instead.
2006	MatchMaker.com is bought by Avalanche, LLC.
2007	Skout is launched by Christian Wiklund and Niklas Lindstrom as the first SNS that uses a cell phone's global positioning system to help members find others around them within their geographic location.
	Apple releases the first iPhone, ushering in a new generation of smartphone technology.
2009	Grindr is launched by Joel Simkhai and his company Nearby Buddy Finder, which enables gay and bisexual men to use GPS to locate other men.
2011	OkCupid is acquired by IAC/InterActiveCorp, the same company that owns Match.com.
2012	Tinder is founded by Sean Rad, Jonathan Badeen, Justin Mateen, Joe Munoz, Dinesh Moorjani, Chris Gylczynski, and Whitney Wolfe as a method for individuals to see potential matches in their geographic area and make decisions to swipe right (for interested) or swipe left (for not interested). The title of this chapter takes its name from this swiping action.
2015	Ashley Madison's website is hacked and twenty-five gigabytes of data is released, including customer information.

Table created by Punyanunt-Carter and Wrench.

purposes, the human being controls the computer's functions, and the computer is merely a kind of elaborate typewriter and delivery system" (97). In 1989, it was hard to imagine how computers would eventually impact how we communicate. In fact, most of the interpersonal communication discussed by Chesebro and Bonsall (1989) stemmed from earlier work by Chesebro (1985), in which he examined interpersonal interactions on bulletin boards, which found that 30 percent of messages on the bulletin boards were interpersonal in nature. At the time, Chesebro did argue five major distinguishing characteristics between online and face-to-face (FtF) friendships developed in bulletin boards. First, Chesebro noted that computer-mediated communicative (CMC) interactions were completely verbal, whereas FtF interactions contained both verbal and nonverbal behavior. Second, Chesebro argued that the differences in discursive differences in verbal communication were also important. CMC interactions were completely dependent upon text, so issues related to grammar, spelling, and typing ability would impact people's perceptions, whereas FtF interaction perceptions are often based on the intermixing of both verbal codes and nonverbal messages simultaneously.

Third, CMC interactions were usually asynchronous, whereas FtF inter-actions were always synchronous. Fourth, the social roles of participants differed. In CMC interactions, people had the ability to exert control over what sociological factors they told others (e.g., ethnicity, gender, socioeconomic status etc.), whereas in FtF interactions people had less control over sociological factors because others looked at them and used a range of information to make these judgments (rightly or wrongly). Lastly, Chesebro (1985) pointed out the difference in the use of time. Bulletin boards were inherently text-based, and people logged in and interacted with each other at all times of the day. As such, people could spend more time thinking about the messages they would send prior to sending them. People could also post messages that would get read at a later point by others. FtF interactions, on the other hand, were very much governed by time. As Chesebro (1985) wrote, "The moment at which a verbal utterance is made, it is conveyed to another. Likewise, the moment at which a nonverbal signal is initiated, it is received by another. Time itself cannot be manipulated in a face-to-face exchange. When something occurs, it is automatically transmitted to others" (210).

Of course, Chesebro's (1985) differences play less (or no) role in modern CMC interactions. First, today people have the option of engaging in interactions online that contain both verbal and nonverbal cues (e.g., Skype or Facetime). Second, discursive differences still play a role in a text-only interaction, but again, these are now optional and not necessarily the only way people interact. Third, although FtF interactions are still synchronous, we can now choose between asynchronous and synchronous CMC interactions. For online daters, this ability to create a first message asynchronously and then turn those messages into synchronous forms of communication is why many people desire online dating. Fourth, people can still hide behind the anonymity of the Internet, but some have argued that privacy and the ability to stay private in the digital age is increasingly more difficult (Mills 2008). As such, we have started seeing a blurring of public and private in a dating context. People tweet or text about their dates while they're on them, or they post pictures to Facebook or Instagram. Finally, modern CMC has opened the issue of time more broadly. Sure, people can swipe right at 3:00 a.m. and then receive a message that they're a match the next day (or even many days later), but people also have the ability to go on computer-mediated dates. The documentaries *Life 2.0* and *Second Skin* show couples meeting and dating in virtual worlds like *Second Life*, *Ever Quest*, and *World of Warcraft*. If anything, technology has opened up the possibilities of dating in ways not possible or imaginable even a decade ago.

PREVIEW OF THE BOOK

Now that we've looked at the evolution of dating and our understanding of dating within a communication framework, the rest of this chapter is a preview of what will come in this book. This book is broken down into four major sections: Understanding Social Media and Romantic Relationships, Different Contexts and Variables, Turbulence, and Dissolution.

Understanding Social Media and Romantic Relationships

In chapter 2, Liesel Sharabi and John Caughlin report on an original study conducted examining the use of technology as relationships progress. In their study, the researchers find that social media remains a constant form of technology within the modern dating relationship across its life cycle.

In chapter 3, Brianna L. Lane and Cameron W. Piercy examine the various sensemaking tools people utilize when deciding to make their relationship status "official on Facebook." In this original research study, the searchers found five primary reasons for why people take this step: 1) their value of privacy, 2) expectations from others, 3) the significance of the decision, 4) the consequences of defining the relationship, and 5) technical issues.

In chapter 4, Terri Manley uses Blumler and Katz's (1974) Uses and Gratifications Theory in an attempt to understand why millennials decide to engage in online dating. In this review of existing literature on the subject, the five basic themes explored are: 1) new technology, 2) validation, 3) casual sex versus love, 4) social connections, and 5) excitement.

In chapter 5, Jayson L. Dibble examines Rusbult's (1980) investment model of relationships in light of modern technology. This chapter examines the historic use of the model along with some shortcomings as a result of the changes in technology. The chapter ends with some specific guidance on where research in this area should go next.

Different Contexts and Variables

In chapter 6, Nathian Shae Rodriguez and Jennifer Huemmer examine how modern mobile dating applications impact relationships among men who have sex with men. Specifically, the chapter examines the intersection between virtual/physical spaces and hegemonic masculinity, and how this is played out in dating applications.

In chapter 7, Derek R. Blackwell performs a qualitative close reading of the "Dating over 45" discussion board on PlentyofFish.com. Using the Uses and Gratifications Theory, the study finds three overarching themes for why older people are dating online: 1) lack of offline dating partners,

2) as an outlet for engaging in peer interactions, and 3) as a learning outlet for those getting back into the dating scene after a death or divorce.

In chapter 8, Amy Janan Johnson, Eryn Bostwick, and Megan Bassick examine the literature surrounding social media use and long-distance relationships. The authors examine relevant CMC and interpersonal communication theories that can help explain this phenomenon. Finally, the authors examine what is known about geographically close relationships and social media, proposing that this information can further elucidate how long-distance relationships could be using social media.

In chapter 9, Hua Su reports on her research with forty-four single Chinese college students who use social media, in an attempt to draw implications of new media in romantic relationships. The chapter examines participant dating-seeking behavior, romantic displays, and gender expressions while discussing the interplay between social and personal spaces (both CMC and FtF).

In chapter 10, Catalina L. Toma and Jonathan D. D'Angelo show how individuals present themselves and form impressions of others through online dating profiles. The authors examine existing literature to further understand how users create an idealized version of themselves while generating perceptions of others in this mediated environment.

Turbulence

In chapter 11, Jennifer L. Bevan explores the expressions of romantic jealousy through social networking sites. Specifically, the chapter examines the literature around three basic themes: 1) types and correlates of SNS jealousy experience and expression, 2) interrelationships with intimate partner violence, and 3) the use and application of multiple theories.

In chapter 12, Jesse Fox and Jessica Frampton examine the intersections of social media, stress, and negative romantic experiences. The chapter specifically addresses issues surrounding social networking and impression management, technological incompatibility, and romantic jealousy.

Dissolution

In chapter 13, Hinda Mandell, Gina Masullo Chen, and Paromita Pain examine Facebook posts related to the #happywife, #sadwife, #happyhusband, #sadhusband hashtags. The authors look for patterns of understanding related to these hashtags and conclude that everyday chores (laundry, dishes, childcare) and stresses (finances, marital disputes, familial relationships, resentments) are depicted realistically in the comments on Facebook.

In chapter 14, Leah E. LeFebvre tackles the emerging problem related to ghosting. In this chapter, a theoretical perspective on ghosting emerges and its relationship to existing research to relationship dissolution. The purpose of this chapter is ultimately to encourage other scholars to initiate research lines into this unique phenomenon.

In chapter 15, Nicholas Brody, Leah E. LeFebvre, and Kate G. Blackburn examine post-relationship dissolution and social networking site surveillance. In this original study, the authors attempt to find the predicates of interpersonal electronic surveillance (IES) following a breakup. Ultimately, the authors offer an initial explanation for IES and its relationship specifically with social media.

PREVIEW OF THE BOOK

Over the last two decades, dating has evolved in unexpected ways as a result of technological advances. Some of these changes were expected, but many of these changes could not have been anticipated because of how technology evolved. For example, in 2005, PayPal employees Chad Hurley, Steve Chen, and Jawed Karim decided to enter into the video dating arena. Their original concept was a dating website that would allow subscribers to upload videos from the privacy of their own homes, which was similar in concept to the old-fashioned VHS video dating phenomenon. Ultimately, that dating website idea turned into YouTube. As a perfect example of Web 2.0 technologies, YouTube has enabled millions of users to create content and upload it for the world to see. Some YouTube content creators have even gone on to become real-world celebrities.

In the same way that YouTube changed how people shared and consumed media content, dating applications are changing how people look for love in the twenty-first century. Although traditional dating methods like meeting someone at school, the office, church, a bar/club, etc. still exist, more and more, dating is more similar to mail-order catalogs. People can flip through hundreds of online dating profiles to search for someone who meets their physical and personal ideals. According to Smith (2016), 15 percent of American adults have used online dating websites or applications. This number has tripled for since 2013 for the 18–23 age group and doubled for the 55–65 age group. We are only now starting to understand some of the long-term effects that this change in dating is having on interpersonal communication and dating relationships.

NOTE

1. Gay men started discreetly using the *Hobby Directory* for personal ads in 1946.

REFERENCES

Bailey, Beth L. 1989. *From Front Porch to Back Seat: Courtship in Twentieth-Century America.* Baltimore, MD: Johns Hopkins University Press.

Berners-Lee, T. 1999. *Weaving the Web: The Original Design and Ultimate Destiny of the World Wide Web by Its Inventor.* New York: Harper-Collins.

Chesebro, James W. 1985. "Computer-Mediated Interpersonal Communication," in *Information and Behavior,* ed. Brent D. Ruben, 202–22. New Brunswick, NJ: Transaction Books.

Chesebro, James W. and Donald G. Bonsall. 1989. *Computer-Mediated Communication: Human Relationships in a Computerized World.* Tuscaloosa: University of Alabama Press.

Cocks, H. G. 2009. *Classified: The Secret History of the Personal Column.* London: Random House.

Jansson, André. 2013. "Mediatization and Social Space: Reconstructing Mediatization for the Transmedia Age." *Communication Theory* 23: 279–96. doi: 10.1111/comt.12015.

Kilgannon, C. 2001. "The Times Will Publish Personal Ads." *New York Times,* March 31, accessed on November 26, 2016, http://www.nytimes.com/2001/03/31/nyregion/the-times-will-publish-personal-ads.html/.

Klinkenberg, Dean and Suzanna Rose. (1994). Dating scripts of gay men and lesbians. *Journal of Homosexuality* 26, 23–35.

Mills, Jon L. 2008. *Privacy: The Lost Right.* London, Oxford University Press.

Mulshine, Molly. 2015. "The 80s Version of Tinder was 'Video Dating'—And It Looks Incredibly Awkward." *Business Insider,* December 2, accessed on November 26, 2016, http://www.businessinsider.com/found-footage-awkward-80s-video-dating-2015-12.

Rauch, Shannon M., Cara Strobel, Megan Bella, Zachary Odachowski, and Christopher Bloom. 2014. *Cyberpsychology, Behavior, and Social Networking* 17: 187–90. doi: 10.1089/cyber.2012.0498.

Rose, Suzanna and Irene Hanson Frieze. 1993. "Young Singles' Contemporary Dating Scripts." *Sex Roles* 28, 499–509. doi: 10.1007/BF00289677.

Schafer, Laura J. 2003. "Looking for Love, Online or on Paper. *New York Times,* February 14, accessed on November 26, 2016, http://www.nytimes.com/2003/02/14/opinion/looking-for-love-online-or-on-paper.html.

Smith, Aaron. 2016. "15% of American Adults Have Used Online Dating Sites or Mobile Dating Apps." Pew Research Center, February 11, accessed on November 27, 2016, http://www.pewinternet.org/2016/02/11/15-percent-of-american-adults-have-used-online-dating-sites-or-mobile-dating-apps/.

Standage, Tom. 1998. *The Victorian Internet: The Remarkable Story of the Telegraph and the Nineteenth Century's On-Line Pioneers.* New York: Walker and Co.

I

Understanding Social Media and Romantic Relationships

TWO

Usage Patterns of Social Media Across Stages of Romantic Relationships

Liesel Sharabi and John P. Caughlin

With the widespread adoption of social network sites (SNSs) has come a proliferation of social media use in personal relationships. Today, more than half (65 percent) of adults are on SNSs (Perrin 2015), the most popular of which continues to be Facebook, with over 1 billion active users (Facebook 2016). One of the fundamental questions of research on social media and relationships involves the use of social media in relationship development. A number of studies have concluded "that users are more interested in maintaining ties with existing offline contacts rather than forging new ones" (Tong and Walther 2011, 106), but there is also evidence that people sometimes do use social media to establish close personal relationships (Bryant, Marmo, and Ramirez 2011). Indeed, others have found social media to be a crucial component in the ways relationships are developed across the entire trajectory, from initiation (e.g., Sprecher 2009) to maintenance (e.g., Ellison, Steinfield, and Lampe 2007), and even dissolution (e.g., Tong 2013).

Given that social media are important at the beginning and throughout many relationships, it is important to understand the role of social media vis-à-vis other means of communicating in developing relationships. Scholars have recently begun to explore how different types of communication technologies, including SNSs, are being used for relationship development (Fox, Warber, and Makstaller 2013; Yang, Brown, and Braun 2014), but the literature has yet to reach a consensus on precisely how patterns of media use change as relationships progress. This chapter examines such associations between social media use and the stages of relationship development, focusing on romantic relationships, a particularly important type of relationship in which social media use has become ubiquitous. Drawing upon data from a study of individuals who reported on their use of social media and other communicative modes with a romantic partner or interest, we discuss how social media become a consistent part of the interaction patterns of people in developing romantic relationships. We begin our investigation of this topic with a more thorough analysis of the most pertinent theories and empirical work.

SOCIAL MEDIA AND TECHNOLOGY USE IN ROMANTIC RELATIONSHIP DEVELOPMENT

Existing research and theorizing suggest two very different models for the role of social media and other communication technologies in romantic relationship development. The first is a *phase or stage approach*, which would assume a systematic progression from one mode of communication to another as relationships evolve over time. This perspective can be seen in the case of a hypothetical couple who moves from chatting online, to text messaging, to talking on the phone before finally transitioning to face-to-face (FtF) conversation as their primary form of contact. The second, a *multiplexity approach*, would imply that relationship development starts with relatively few modes of communication, but that more are added as relationships progress. This perspective is captured by a would-be couple who finds that their communication grows from one or two channels to several as their relationship becomes exceedingly more intimate.

Both of these perspectives on the integration of social media and other communication technologies into romantic relationships are theoretically plausible; indeed, recently scholarship has provided evidence in support of each perspective. Yet the distinctions between these two frameworks are important, as they suggest alternative roles for social media in the contemporary development of romantic relationships. To further elucidate the differences between these two approaches to understanding relational development and communication technologies, each is discussed in more detail below.

A Phase or Stage Approach to Social Media in Relationship Development

Relational stage models, such as that originally proposed by Knapp (1978), contend that relationship development is a sequential process characterized by a series of stages, or phases, on the path toward greater intimacy. Knapp, Vangelisti, and Caughlin (2014) described the five stages of escalation in the model as follows. The first stage, *initiating*, occurs when partners make judgments about each other's attractiveness and begin to engage in conversation. Next, in the *experimenting* stage, conversation is furthered through small talk and the exchange of superficial information. During the *intensifying* stage, the relationship becomes more intimate, with partners sometimes divulging deeply personal information or expressing their love for each other, while in the *integrating* stage, their lives continue to become increasingly enmeshed. Relationship escalation culminates with *bonding* in the final stage, which typically involves a formal commitment to the relationship. Of course, couples can also come apart, and the model depicts five separate stages of the deterioration and subsequent termination of relationships. The relational stage model has utility for the present study because it allows for broad comparisons of the communication modes that people choose to use at different points in the development of their romantic relationships and because previous scholarship has suggested that social media in particular are systematically related to the stages originally described by Knapp (Fox, Warber, and Makstaller 2013).

Indeed, there is empirical evidence from qualitative interviews that has supported the notion that social media and technology use is related to specific stages of relational development. In one study of thirty-four college students, Yang, Brown, and Braun (2014) reported that interactions via social media were primarily restricted to phases early in the development of relationships. Yang and colleagues concluded that there was "a sequence of media use tied to stages of relationship development—from Facebook in early stages to instant messaging and then cell phones as a relationship progressed" (5). Such findings are consonant with Ruppel's (2015) recent theorizing that the proportion of communication through asynchronous and reduced-cue technologies decreases as relationships develop because such affordances become less vital to users as they become more intimate with their relational partner.

It is important to note, however, that suggesting that Facebook and other social media may decline in importance as relationships progress does not mean social media will become unimportant in more developed stages. In fact, some research (e.g., Fox and Warber 2013) taking a stage perspective has pointed to different functions that social media may play early and later in the relational life cycle. For instance, Fox, Warber, and Makstaller (2013) asked undergraduate students in a series of focus groups about the role of a particular social medium (Facebook) across the stages of development in their relationships. Fox and her colleagues' participants reported that early in relationships, social media are frequently used to anonymously seek information about a prospective partner, and that people also value social media in newly forming relationships because they offer "a variety of convenient ways to interact with the target" (Fox, Warber, and Makstaller 2013, 778), such as posting on someone's timeline, commenting on pictures, or sending private messages. Interaction via Facebook was so prominent in the formative stages of relationships that participants often reported that "Facebook interactions have replaced the role of phone calls" (Fox, Warber, and Makstaller 2013, 777), although texting remained prominent along with Facebook. Although Fox and her colleagues' work suggested that Facebook is extremely prominent early in romantic relationships, they also found that it may be used in the later stages, although in more specific ways, such as by indicating exclusivity with a dating partner (that is, becoming "Facebook official").

Although different studies using a stage perspective vary in their specifics, stage studies all suggest changing uses of and preferences for social media and other communication technologies as relationships develop. For example, despite the differences in specific findings and focus, both the Yang, Brown, and Braun (2014) and Fox, Warber, and Makstaller (2013) studies imply that the use of one mode of communication can (and does) replace others, and that there are different frequencies of usage and preferences for usage for social media over the course of a developing relationship. That is, a core assumption of stage models is the expectation that the frequency (and preference) of some communication technologies would be going up and others going down over the course of relationship development. Specifically, taken together, the stage-based studies suggest that social media usage is a particularly prominent way for people to interact with each other in the early relational stages of romantic relationships, and it may be less so (albeit not absent) in closer stages of relational development.

A Multiplexity Approach to Social Media in Relationship Development

In her seminal work on multimodality, Haythornthwaite (2005) used the term *media multiplexity* to describe the tendency for people who are strongly linked to utilize more of their available modes of communication than do weak ties. That is, rather than positing strict phases or stages in which certain modes of communication are prominent at some times and not others, media multiplexity theory (MMT) suggests that as people become closer, they communicate through a more diverse range of channels (Haythornthwaite 2005). MMT provides a useful lens for understanding mixed-mode relationships (Walther and Parks 2002), which involve using both online and offline modes of communication, as is common for many developing romantic relationships. From a multiplexity approach, partners in the early stages of relationship development would be expected to use fewer, but not necessarily different, modes of communication than those in the later stages. The development of a relationship would therefore be seen as coinciding with an increase in the number of channels used to communicate.

MMT has its roots in an organizational setting and as such has not been studied extensively in romantic relationships, but work in other types of relationships suggests that this perspective is plausible. Baym and Ledbetter (2009), for example, found that members of Last.fm, a common interest social network site for music fans, communicated with their friends through a more robust number of channels as their relationships developed. Friends in the most intimate and interdependent relationships have also been shown to engage in more frequent interactions through multiple channels rather than relying on just one to communicate (Ledbetter 2009; Ledbetter and Kuznekoff 2012). Additionally, Ramirez and Broneck's (2009) research on everyday maintenance in a variety of relationship types suggests that different modes of communication do not always replace or crowd out others as relationships become closer; indeed, they found that instant messaging, e-mailing, talking on the phone, and talking in person tended to be positively correlated. That is, there is evidence that more communication by one mode can lead to more by other modes without any modes replacing the others (as would be suggested by at least some stage models). Such results suggest that romantic relationships may develop such that various modes of communication, including social media, may be used more frequently as relationships develop.

In fact, emerging research indicates that much like friends, close romantic partners may broaden their channel usage as their relationships progress. For instance, in their study of technology use in romantic relationships, Coyne et al. (2011) observed that romantic partners relied on multiple channels to communicate, but to varying degrees. Coyne et al. concluded that cell phones and text messaging were used the most frequently, but that there was still "evidence of a high amount of media use specifically to contact romantic others, although some forms (cell phones) are used more frequently than others" (158).

Moreover, there is evidence that in romantic relationships, rather than one mode of communication replacing others as the relationship develops, relational closeness is related to the extent that partners make connections among the various ways they can communicate (Caughlin and Sharabi 2013; Pusateri, Roaché, and Wang 2015). For example, in addition to posting to each other on social media, close partners may also text or talk about what they have written. Such possibilities are consistent with a key implication of MMT: that relational communication is not a zero-sum activity. Even if some forms of social media are crucial early in the development of romantic relationships, that does not necessarily mean that the importance of social media would decline as people incorporate other modes of communication into their romantic relationships. Instead, MMT would predict that modes of communication that are important in relationships (including social media) would remain important, but also that there would be general increases in terms of the number of channels that partners use across the stages of romantic relationship development. Hence, unlike the rises and falls predicted by the stage perspective, a multiplexity approach would suggest that closer relational stages are associated with more overall usage of all modes of communication.

Summary and Research Questions

The stage and multiplexity approaches offer alternative accounts of precisely how social media and other communication technology use changes as relationships develop. The present study explores usage patterns and preferences for social media from the perspective of both models, with the goal of clarifying the connection between media use and the progression of romantic relationships. Despite the tendency for previous research to view technology use as independent of FtF contact, our examination of how communication modes are utilized at different points in relationship development also includes the possibility that FtF contact may remain important throughout relationships. That is, rather than focusing only on communication technologies, we include FtF communication as a potential medium in developing relationships. To that end, we pose two questions about how social media and other communication modes map onto the developmental trajectory:

RQ1: How do people actually use social media and other communication modes in different stages of romantic relationship development?

RQ2: How do people prefer to use social media and other communication modes in different stages of romantic relationship development?

METHODS

Participants and Procedures

As part of a larger data collection effort (see Caughlin and Sharabi 2013), undergraduate students ($N = 317$) completed an online survey about their technology use with a current romantic partner or interest. Romantic interests were included so that participants would be reporting across the full developmental trajectory and not just the later stages of relationships. Students received extra credit in an introductory communication course for their participation. The final sample contained more women (63.4 percent) than men (36.0 percent), who ranged in age from 18 to 27 years ($M = 19.83$, SD = 1.12). The sample was predominantly Caucasian (69.4 percent), followed by Asian (12.0 percent), African American (8.8 percent), Hispanic (5.0 percent), other (2.5 percent), and Pacific Islander (0.3 percent). Participants described their romantic partner or interest as a serious dating partner (41.3 percent), casual dating partner (30.6 percent), friend (21.8 percent), acquaintance (3.2 percent), coworker or classmate (2.2 percent), and fiancée or marital partner (0.6 percent). Most reported knowing this person for one year (20.5 percent) or less (32.5 percent). All percentages may not sum to 100 percent due to missing data.

Measures

Relationship Stage Descriptions

Participants self-selected their stage of relationship development from Welch and Rubin's (2002) Relationship Stage Descriptions. The measure included descriptions of five stages of relationship escalation: (a) initiating (n = 50, 15.8 percent), (b) experimenting (n = 73, 23.0 percent), (c) intensifying (n = 78, 24.6 percent), (d) integrating (n = 75, 23.7 percent), and (e) bonding (n = 23, 7.3 percent). Because our focus was on relationship development, we collapsed the five stages of relationship de-escalation into one category: (a) de-escalating (n = 18, 5.7 percent). The language in the relationship stage descriptions was slightly modified for clarity.

Modes of Actual Communication

Participants responded to the stem, "How often [do] you use various channels to communicate with your romantic partner or interest . . ." (1 = *Never* and 7 = *Always*). We selected the channels based on a focus group study that examined the breadth of people's communication mode usage in their romantic relationships (Caughlin and Sharabi 2013). The measure captured the frequency of participants' communication through seven distinct modes: (a) FtF (M = 5.85, SD = 1.26), (b) private e-mail and social media messaging (PESMM; M = 3.66, SD = 1.72), (c) public social media messaging (PSMM; M = 3.38, SD = 1.69), (d) Internet chat (M = 3.24, SD = 1.90), (e) video chat (M = 2.82, SD = 1.94), (f) text messaging (M = 5.99, SD = 1.48), and (g) phone calls (M = 4.49, SD = 1.89).

Preferred Modes of Communication

Participants responded to a similar prompt about "Your preferences for various communication channels within your romantic relationship . . ." (1 = *Strongly Disagree* and 7 = *Strongly Agree*). Preference for each communication channel was tapped with two items that were averaged together to produce one composite score. The overall measure assessed participants' partiality for seven modes: (a) FtF (M = 6.34, SD = 1.11), (b) PESMM (M = 2.55, SD = 1.40), (c) PSMM (M = 2.58, SD = 1.31), (d) Internet chat (M = 2.42, SD = 1.35), (e) video chat (M = 3.07, SD = 1.51), (f) text messaging (M = 4.52, SD = 1.56), and (g) phone calls (M = 4.23, SD = 1.32).

RESULTS

Actual Usage Patterns in Relationship Development (RQ1)

The first research question actually implied two interrelated matters: one concerning whether particular modes of communication were used more or less frequently in different relational stages, and the second concerning the relative frequency of mode usage within each stage. We addressed the first issue of how frequently people used social media and other communication modes across the stages of romantic relationship development using a series of between-groups analyses of variance (ANOVAs). The amounts of communication through five of the seven modes were significantly different across stages: Internet chat, $F(5, 308) = 2.31$, $p = .04$, $\eta^2 = .04$; text messaging, $F(5, 310) = 8.90$, $p < .001$, $\eta^2 = .13$; phone calls, $F(5, 307) = 18.53$, $p < .001$, $\eta^2 = .23$; video chat, $F(5, 310) = 7.98$, $p < .001$, $\eta^2 = .11$; and FtF, $F(5, 309) = 5.03$, $p < .001$, $\eta^2 = .08$. Fisher's protected LSD post-hoc comparisons were used to identify the modes of communication used the most frequently at each stage of development (see the columns in Table 2.1). In general, some of the most frequent usage of Internet chat was in the earliest stages of relationship development. Meanwhile, participants in closer stages engaged in significantly greater amounts of text messaging, phone calls, video chats, and FtF communication compared to those in less-developed relationships. During de-escalation, Internet chat, text messaging, phone calls, and video chat were frequent. Interestingly, neither of the social media variables were significantly different across the stages of relational development: PESMM, $F(5, 310) = 1.13$, $p = .34$; and PSMM, $F(5, 309) = 1.28$, $p = .27$. This pattern suggests that the amount of social media usage was fairly consistent rather than being linked to specific phases of relationships.

To examine the other issue implied by the first research question, we also considered the relative frequency of communication mode usage within each relational stage using a succession of repeated measures and multivariate analyses of variance (MANOVAs) with the communication mode as the repeated factor (see the rows in Table 2.1). The amounts of communication were significantly different within stages: initiating, $F(6, 42) = 22.32$, $p < .001$, partial $\eta^2 = .76$; experimenting, $F(6, 66) = 48.57$, $p < .001$, partial $\eta^2 = .82$; intensifying, $F(6, 70) = 45.26$, $p < .001$, partial $\eta^2 = .80$; integrating, $F(6, 67) = 51.06$, $p < .001$, partial $\eta^2 = .82$; bonding, $F(6, 17) = 15.89$, $p < .001$, partial $\eta^2 = .85$; and de-escalating, $F(6, 11) = 19.16$, $p < .001$, partial $\eta^2 = .91$. Simple contrasts with FtF communication as the comparison group were used to identify the modes that participants used the most frequently within each stage. FtF communication was used significantly more than all the other modes in the initiating stage ($p < .05$), and significantly less than text messaging but significantly more than the other modes in the intensifying stage ($p < .05$). Similar amounts of FtF communication and text messaging were used in the experimenting, integrating, and bonding phases (that is, there were no statistically significant differences), yet the frequency of FtF communication was still significantly higher than the other modes ($p < .05$). FtF communication and phone calls did not significantly differ in the de-escalating stage, although FtF communication was used significantly less than text messaging and significantly more than the remaining modes. Thus, FtF communication was used more frequently than most modes, with the exceptions of text messaging and, during the de-escalating stage, phone calls.

Preferred Usage Patterns in Relationship Development (RQ2)

We approached the second research question about people's preferences for social media and other modes of communication in different stages of romantic relationship development using a set of between-groups ANOVAs. Participants statistically differed across stages in their preferences for five of the seven modes: PSMM, $F(5, 307) = 3.32$, $p = .01$, $\eta^2 = .05$; PESMM, $F(5, 308) = 5.69$, $p < .001$, $\eta^2 = .08$; Internet chat, $F(5, 309) = 2.71$, $p = .02$, $\eta^2 = .04$; phone calls, $F(5, 309) = 4.29$, $p < .01$, $\eta^2 = .06$; and FtF, $F(5, 309) = 4.50$, $p < .01$, $\eta^2 = .07$. Fisher's protected LSD post-hoc tests were used to determine which modes of communication participants favored at different stages of relationship development (see the columns in table 2.2). Social media (i.e., PSMM and PESMM), as well as Internet chat, were more preferred in the beginning stages of relationships than in later stages. In contrast, participants in closer relationships expressed a stronger affinity for phone calls and FtF communication than did those in less developed relationships. Preferences for PESMM and phone calls were

Table 2.1. Modes of Actual Communication Across the Stages of Relationship Development

Stage	Mode of Communication						
	PSMM	PESMM	Internet Chat	Text	Phone	Video Chat	FtF
Initiating	3.84	4.00	3.63^a	5.22^{abcd}	3.60^{abcd}	2.52^{abc}	5.82^a
Experimenting	3.24	3.50	2.69^{abc}	5.43^{efgh}	3.28^{efgh}	1.81^{adefg}	5.39^{bc}
Intensifying	3.49	3.69	3.48^b	6.28^{ae}	4.78^{aei}	2.94^d	5.72^{de}
Integrating	3.25	3.79	3.11	6.48^{bf}	5.55^{bfi}	3.48^{be}	6.25^{bd}
Bonding	2.96	3.22	3.22	6.35^{cg}	5.35^{cg}	3.65^{cf}	6.48^{ace}
De-escalating	3.35	3.22	3.83^c	6.61^{dh}	5.17^{dh}	3.44^g	5.83

Note: Means with like superscripts within columns were significantly different at the .05 level (using two-tailed tests). PSMM is public social media messaging; PESMM is private e-mail and social media messaging.

among their lowest during the de-escalation phase relative to other stages. Neither text messaging nor video chat were significantly different across the stages of development: text messaging, $F(5, 309) = .76$, $p = .58$; video chat, $F(5, 310) = 1.75$, $p = .12$. Overall, participants were generally more inclined to communicate through social media in order to form a new romantic relationship.

A slightly different portrait emerged when we compared the relative preferences for different communication modes within each relational stage using several repeated measures MANOVAs, with the communication mode again serving as the repeated factor (see the rows in table 2.2). Significant differences were found in the preferred modes within each stage: initiating: $F(6, 43) = 23.34$, $p < .001$, partial $\eta^2 = .77$; experimenting: $F(6, 63) = 33.79$, $p < .001$, partial $\eta^2 = .76$; intensifying: $F(6, 71) = 78.62$, $p < .001$, partial $\eta^2 = .87$; integrating: $F(6, 66) = 127.66$, $p < .001$, partial $\eta^2 = .92$; bonding: $F(6, 17) = 21.38$, $p < .001$, partial $\eta^2 = .88$; de-escalating: $F(6, 12) = 19.72$, $p < .001$, partial $\eta^2 = .91$. Simple contrasts within persons revealed that FtF contact was significantly more preferred than the other six modes of communication ($p < .05$), with just one exception. In the experimenting stage, the difference between text messaging and in-person communication was only marginally significant, $F(1, 68) = 3.16$, $p = .08$. Regardless of stage, participants almost always regarded FtF conversation as the most preferred mode of communication in their romantic relationships.

DISCUSSION

The current study examined the reports of actual use and preferences for social media and other communication modes by people in varying stages of romantic relational development. The literature suggests two competing models for how social media may be implicated in the course of developing romantic relationships: stage models and media multiplexity theory (MMT). Interestingly, there were results that can be interpreted with reference to both models.

Overall, the results most clearly and closely align with the tenets of MMT (Haythornthwaite 2005). In general, the reports of actual communication showed a pattern in which all the modes of communication tended to be used in more intimate stages of relationships as much or more than during less intimate stages. This suggests that people generally add more communication by more modes as their relationships become closer rather than go through a progression of modes as suggested by stage perspectives on social media. There were some exceptions to the general pattern; most notably, Internet chat and video chat were lower in the second stage (experimenting) than in the first stage (initiating), but in both cases these modes were higher again in the third phase (intensify-

Table 2.2.   Preferred Modes of Communication Across the Stages of Relationship Development

Stage	PSMM	PESMM	Internet Chat	Text	Phone	Video Chat	FtF
			Mode of Communication				
Initiating	3.48[ab]	3.10[abcd]	2.92[ab]	5.08	3.94[a]	2.32	6.26[a]
Experimenting	3.68[cd]	2.85[efg]	2.44	5.28	3.64[bc]	2.17	5.89[bc]
Intensifying	3.09	2.44[ah]	2.52[c]	5.15	4.15[d]	2.77	6.45[b]
Integrating	2.65[ac]	1.97[be]	2.07[ac]	4.77	4.77[abde]	2.80	6.80[ac]
Bonding	2.52[bd]	1.70[cfh]	2.04[b]	4.78	4.48[c]	2.91	6.39
De-escalating	2.78	1.94[dg]	2.67	5.33	3.72[e]	2.33	6.33

Note: Means with like superscripts within columns were significantly different at the .05 level (using two-tailed tests). PSMM is public social media messaging; PESMM is private e-mail and social media messaging.

ing), suggesting that they are not replaced as stage models would suggest but instead are reincorporated as relationships progress.

Also in contrast to a phase or stage approach, we found no evidence that social media usage was especially characteristic of particular stages or that social media were being abandoned for other channels as relationships progressed. Instead, both aspects of social media usage (PSMM and PESMM) were reported at moderate levels for people of all relationship stages. That is, social media appear to remain a constant in all of the stages of developing romantic relationships. Obviously, these findings leave open the possibility that the precise way that social media are used changes over the course of relationships (Fox, Warber, and Makstaller 2013), but these data suggest that the frequency with which romantic relational partners use social media to interact with each other remains fairly stable across the stages of relational development.

Even though the reported patterns of usage were generally consistent with media multiplexity, the findings reported here also provide some evidence that is consistent with studies that have associated social media use with the early phases of relationships. In terms of actual usage, social media are relatively flat across the various stages, whereas a number of other modes increase. Thus, as a proportion, social media are a relatively larger portion of the relational communication early in relationships than they are later. Such findings are consistent with Ruppel's (2015) suggestion that certain modes of communication (e.g., social media) become proportionally less prominent as relationships get closer. This obviously does not mean that social media are being phased out at later stages, but rather that as other modes of communication become increasingly more central to a dyad's repertoire, social media becomes a smaller portion. It makes sense, then, that people would associate social media more with earlier phases of relationships, even though it appears that communication via social media remains moderately frequent in all phases. Additionally, the preference data (see table 2.2) shows a trend for people to have stronger preferences for social media in earlier stages of relationships than in later ones. This suggests that even though usage may be fairly consistent, individuals' sense of norms for social media may reflect their preferences rather than the amount of usage. Taken as a whole, this evidence most strongly supports media multiplexity, but the findings also provide some glimpses into why the notion of stages may resonate with people as they reflect on the development of their romantic relationships. Although it may not be strictly accurate that social media are primarily used early in relationships, for example, these technologies do appear to play a relatively more prominent role early in relationships and are valued more highly early in relationships. Thus, from a perspective that considers the relative prominence of social media in romantic relationships, a stage or phase perspective makes sense.

Although the main focus of the current chapter was on understanding social media and other communication technologies in developing relationships, the prominence of FtF communication throughout the developmental process is worth noting. A great deal has been written about this technologically savvy generation of college students and their heavy use of new media (Mcmillan and Morrison 2006; Smith, Rainie, and Zickuhr 2011), yet even they used and preferred FtF communication for establishing and enacting romantic relationships. That people still enjoy talking FtF with their romantic relationship partners is perhaps not surprising, but the strong preference for FtF implies an interesting question with respect to the role of social media in romantic relationships. Given that people report a strong preference for FtF communication, especially at more advanced stages of relationships, and presumably most of them in such stages have ample opportunity to interact FtF, why do social media remain a moderately frequent mode of communicating for romantic partners in all of the stages?

The current study obviously cannot answer this important question, and it is therefore important for more research to seek to understand the functions of social media during the closer stages of romantic relationships. Previous work does explain why social media are important early in romantic relationships, as people seek information about each other and use social media as a convenient way to interact (Fox, Warber, and Makstaller 2013). Yet such functions do not seem to adequately explain why social media would remain prominent when partners are seeing each other in person consistently; for instance, are social media really as useful for finding out about a partner once one reaches the integrating phase? Granted, social media may still be partly about information seeking at any phase of a relationship (e.g., surveilling; Tokunaga 2011), but it seems unlikely that information seeking would remain as prominent in closer stages. Additionally, at some point during the integrating stage, people may use social media to publicly demonstrate their commitment to their relationship to others (Fox, Warber, and Makstaller 2013), such as when people change their profiles to make themselves "Facebook official" (Papp, Danielewicz, and Cayemberg 2012). Yet such events seem like discrete moments and do not seem to explain why interacting via social media remains fairly frequent at later stages of romantic relational development.

Clearly, more work needs to be done to explain what the functions of social media are in more intimate romantic relationships. The current study suggests that understanding such functions will require considering the other modes of communication available to relational partners as well; for instance, it probably means something different to post a publically visible affectionate message to a social media site than it does to send the same message via private text or in person. In short, there are good reasons to believe that social media serve functions in ongoing, intimate romantic relationships and that these functions are not yet fully understood. This should be an important focus for future work.

Of course, as with any study there were limitations. The most obvious one is that the data are self-reports, which may, of course, have biases. Although it would be difficult to do a study in which all modes of communication were directly observed, it would be useful to do a diary study that could help reduce some of the reporting biases. Also, although we can make some inferences about relational development based on the various stages of development that the participants reported, this is not the same as actually having data over time about relationships. Future work should augment the current study with longitudinal data. Furthermore, this study is descriptive and cannot speak to why people use and prefer certain modes or what effect that may have on relationship development. Additional scholarship should explore how social media and technology use are linked to specific outcomes at different points in romantic relationships. For example, whereas the current study examined average usage and preferences, there is undoubtedly variation in the patterns of social media usage in developing relationships, and future work should assess whether such variations are predictive of satisfying and enduring relationships.

In conclusion, our study addressed questions in the literature having to do with the role of social media and other communication technologies in different stages of relationship development. Importantly, the study suggests that social media are not associated only with a particular phase of romantic relationships, but instead become a consistent part of couples' communication repertoire, along with other modes of communication. Such findings highlight the importance of further work that seeks to understand the association between social media use and other modes of communication in intimate romantic relationships.

REFERENCES

Baym, Nancy K., and Andrew Ledbetter. 2009. "Tunes That Bind? Predicting Friendship Strength in a Music-Based Social Network." *Communication and Society* 12: 408–27. doi: 10.1080/13691180802635430.

Bryant, Erin M., Jennifer Marmo, and Artemio Ramirez, Jr. 2011. "A Functional Approach to Social Networking Sites." In *Computer-Mediated Communication in Personal Relationships*, ed. Kevin. B. Wright and Lynn. M. Webb, 3–20. New York: Peter Lang Publishing.

Caughlin, John P., and Liesel L. Sharabi. 2013. "A Communicative Interdependence Perspective of Close Relationships: The Connections between Mediated and Unmediated Interactions Matter." *Journal of Communication* 63: 873–93. doi: 10.1111/jcom.12046.

Coyne, Sarah M., Laura Stockdale, Dean Busby, Bethany Iverson, and David M. Grant. 2011. "'I luv u :)!': A Descriptive Study of the Media Use of Individuals in Romantic Relationships." *Family Relations* 60: 150–62. doi: 10.1111/j.1741-3729.2010.00639.x.

Ellison, Nicole B., Charles Steinfield, and Cliff Lampe. 2007. "The Benefits of Facebook "Friends": Social Capital and College Students' Use of Online Social Network Sites. *Journal of Computer-Mediated Communication* 12: 1143–68. doi: 10.1111/j.10836101.2007.00367.x.

Facebook. 2016. "Facebook Newsroom." Accessed November 15, 2016. http://newsroom.fb.com.

Fox, Jesse, and Katie M. Warber. 2013. "Romantic Relationship Development in the Age of Facebook: An Exploratory Study of Emerging Adults' Perceptions, Motives, and Behaviors." *Cyberpsychology, Behavior, and Social Networking* 16: 3–7. doi: 10.1089/cyber.2012.0288.

Fox, Jesse, Katie M. Warber, and Dana C. Makstaller. 2013. "The Role of Facebook in Romantic Relationship Development: An Exploration of Knapp's Relational Stage Model." *Journal of Social and Personal Relationships* 30: 771–94. doi: 10.1177/0265407512468370.

Haythornthwaite, Caroline. 2005. "Social Networks and Internet Connectivity Effects." *Information, Communication and Society* 8: 125–47. doi: 10.1080/13691180500146185.

Knapp, Mark L. 1978. *Social Intercourse: From Greeting to Goodbye*. Boston: Allyn and Bacon.

Knapp, Mark L., Anita L. Vangelisti, and John P. Caughlin. 2014. *Interpersonal Communication and Human Relationships* 7th edition. New York: Pearson Publishing.

Ledbetter, Andrew M. 2009. "Patterns of Media Use and Multiplexity: Associations with Sex, Geographic Distance and Friendship Interdependence." *New Media and Society* 11: 1187–1208. doi: 10.1177/1461444809342057.

Ledbetter, Andrew M., and Jeffrey H. Kuznekoff. 2012. "More Than a Game: Friendship Relational Maintenance and Attitudes toward Xbox LIVE Communication." *Communication Research* 39: 269–90. doi: 10.1177/0093650210397042.

Mcmillan, Sally J., and Margaret Morrison. 2006. "Coming of Age with the Internet: A Qualitative Exploration of How the Internet Has Become an Integral Part of Young People's Lives." *New Media & Society* 8: 73–95. doi: 10.1177/1461444806059871.

Papp, Lauren M., Jennifer Danielewicz, and Crystal Cayemberg. 2012. "'Are We Facebook Official?' Implications of Dating Partners' Facebook Use and Profiles for Intimate Relationship Satisfaction." *Cyberpsychology, Behavior, and Social Networking* 15: 85–90. doi:10.1089/cyber.2011.0291.

Perrin, Andrew. 2015. *Social Media Usage: 2005–2015*. Washington, DC: Pew Internet and American Life Project. http://www.pewinternet.org/2015/10/08/social-networking-usage-2005-2015/.

Pusateri, Kimberly B., David J. Roaché, and Ningxin Wang. 2015. "The Role of Communication Technologies in Serial Arguments: A Communicative Interdependence Perspective." *Argumentation and Advocacy* 52: 44–60. Accessed November 15, 2016. https://www.questia.com/library/journal/1G1-443059657/the-role-of-communication-technologies-in-serial-arguments.

Ramirez, Jr., Artemio, and Kathy Broneck. 2009. "'IM me': Instant Messaging as Relational Maintenance and Everyday Communication." *Journal of Social and Personal Relationships* 26: 291–314. doi: 10.1177/0265407509106719.

Ruppel, Erin K. 2015. "The Affordance Utilization Model: Communication Technology Use as Relationships Develop." *Marriage and Family Review* 51: 669–86. doi: 10.1080/01494929.2015.1061628.

Smith, Aaron, Lee Rainie, and Kathryn Zickuhr. 2011. *College Students and Technology*. Washington, DC: Pew Internet and American Life Project. http://www.pewinternet.org/2011/07/19/college-students-and-technology/.

Sprecher, Susan. 2009. "Relationship Initiation and Formation on the Internet." *Marriage and Family Review* 45: 761–82. doi: 10.1080/01494920903224350.

Tokunaga, Robert S. 2011. "Social Networking Site or Social Surveillance Site? Understanding the Use of Interpersonal Electronic Surveillance in Romantic Relationships." *Computers in Human Behavior* 27: 705–13. doi: 10.1016/j.chb.2010.08.014.

Tong, Stephanie T. 2013. "Facebook Use during Relationship Termination: Uncertainty Reduction and Surveillance." *Cyberpsychology, Behavior, and Social Networking* 16: 788–93. doi: 10.1089/cyber.2012.0549.

Tong, Stephanie T., and Joseph B. Walther. 2011. "Relational Maintenance and CMC." In *Computer-Mediated Communication in Personal Relationships,* ed. Kevin B. Wright and Lynn M. Webb, 98–118. New York: Peter Lang Publishing.

Walther, Joseph B., and Malcolm R. Parks. 2002. "Cues Filtered Out, Cues Filtered In: Computer-Mediated Communication and Relationships." In *Handbook of Interpersonal Communication* 3rd edition, ed. Mark L. Knapp and John A. Daly, 529–63. Thousand Oaks: Sage.

Welch, Susan A., and Rebecca B. Rubin. 2002. "Development of Relationship Stage Measures." *Communication Quarterly* 50: 24–40. doi: 10.1080/01463370209385644.

Yang, Chia-chen, B. Bradford Brown, and Michael T. Braun. 2014. "From Facebook to Cell Calls: Layers of Electronic Intimacy in College Students' Interpersonal Relationships." *New Media and Society* 16: 5–23. doi: 10.1177/1461444812472486.

THREE

Making Sense of Becoming Facebook Official

Implications for Identity and Time

Brianna L. Lane and Cameron W. Piercy

Facebook use has become a source of identity for emerging adults with many averaging one to two active hours on the site each day (Kalpidou, Costin, and Morris 2011). In fact, Facebook is the most popular social networking site, with more than 1.71 billion active monthly users and 1.13 billion daily users as of 2016 (Facebook Statistics 2016). Facebook has become the new tool for displaying a relationship status online, replacing the traditional "going steady" with a class ring or letterman's jacket. The public commitment of displaying one's relationship online has become known as becoming "Facebook official" (FBO). Making a relationship public has become an online communicative act directed at a broader social network, not just to those they encounter in face-to-face situations. The public declaration is communicated to one's entire computer mediated social network, which averages between 200 and 250 Facebook friends (Kalpidou et al. 2011).

Facebook is not simply the vehicle to communicate that one is in a relationship. It also allows users to specify the type of relationship they are in and with whom. For example, users can indicate they are in a relationship, engaged, married, in a civil union, in a domestic partnership, in an open relationship, or even declare their relationship is "complicated." Users can link their profile to their partner's profile by "tagging" one another, thereby increasing the size of the social network that has access to the public declaration. Individuals within the social network can then "like" or comment on the public display of attachment. Additionally, through the "share" feature, users within the social network can post the event of their friends' relationship status on their own timelines, thereby increasing the potential audience. Even though these affordances are not all equally adopted, Facebook has many channels through which users can share their relationship status with their social network.

However, a social declaration of the relationship comes with some potential consequences. The Relational Turbulence Model (RTM) proposed by Solomon and Knobloch (2004) describes how a relational transition, such as moving from casual to serious dating, can lead to tumultuous experiences, which the authors label "relational turbulence." Relational turbulence is a product of ambiguity and uncertainty of one's self, partner, and relationship. In mediated contexts, individuals must address this uncertainty by either avoiding the ambiguity and publicly declaring their relationship or by embracing the uncertainty and keeping their relationship private. This decision is determined by individuals' sensemaking. Simply stated, sensemaking describes how "once people begin to act (enactment), they generate tangible outcomes (cues) in some context (social) and this helps them discover (retrospect) what is occurring (ongoing), what needs to be explained (plausibility) and what should be done next (identity enhancement)" (Weick 1995, 55). In sum, sensemaking is an action-based decision-making perspective applicable to many contexts (Mintzberg and Westley 2010). Through this process of sensemaking, individuals come to understand, justify, and determine their decision to become FBO.

The purpose of this study was to understand how individuals made sense of their decision to become FBO in their relationship. There is limited research on what this relationship declaration can mean to participants and for the relationship. A recent study quantitatively assessed the meaning of being FBO and found that young adults perceived the announcement as a display of commitment, relational intensity, and social response (Fox and Warber 2013), but research has not yet uncovered how Facebook users interpret this decision through their sensemaking. In the following chapter, we first discuss the ambiguity surrounding the decision to be FBO. Next, we discuss the sensemaking process as it relates to this decision. Third, we describe the methods along with results, and finally, offer a discussion of the findings.

AMBIGUITY AND BECOMING FBO

Solomon and Knobloch (2004) proposed that the transition from casual dating to a more serious relationship creates relational turbulence. Relational turbulence is marked by relational uncertainty and interference from partners. The Relational Turbulence Model (RTM) describes the contributing factors that lead to relational turbulence stemming from a transitioning relationship. The transition is typically characterized by emerging intimacy which leads to relational uncertainty (Fox and Warber 2013). Relational uncertainty is defined as the degree of confidence a person has in their perception of involvement within their relationship (Knobloch and Solomon 1999, 2002a). Relational uncertainty is comprised of three sources of uncertainty: self, partner, and relationship. *Self-uncertainty* is defined as questioning one's own involvement in a relationship; *partner uncertainty* is defined as questioning one's partner's involvement in the relationship; and lastly, *relationship uncertainty* is defined as questioning the relationship itself. Berger and Bradac (1982) explained that relationship uncertainty is more abstract than self and partner uncertainty because it conceptualizes both partners as a cohesive unit. Relational uncertainty arises when the relationship has not yet been defined but has moved beyond relationship initiation scripts (Theiss and Solomon 2006).

Becoming FBO can be labeled as a conflict-laden, transitional period from a seemingly casual relationship to a more committed relationship (Papp, Danielewicz, and Cayemberg 2012). According to the RTM, this transitional period is accompanied by greater ambiguity and uncertainty. Individuals must first decide if they want to make that transition, and if they do, they must make sense of its implications. Previous research has shown that less uncertainty about one's partner is associated with relationship escalation (Berger and Calabrese 1975), but a relationship transition raises questions about the relationship itself (Knobloch and Solomon 2002b). Knobloch and Solomon (2002b) examined judgments of uncertainty versus general relational doubts and found that relational uncertainty was highest at moderate levels of intimacy. Uncertainty influences relational turbulence during transitional periods. Additionally, research has shown that people may choose to remain in an ambiguous situation if they anticipate information seeking will lead to negative consequences (Theiss and Solomon 2006).

Knobloch and Donovan-Kicken (2006) demonstrated that relational turbulence is related to social networks. In fact, network analyses demonstrate that at moderate levels of intimacy, social networks were more discouraging and less encouraging of courtship. Above the median level of intimacy, social networks become more helpful and less harmful for the relationship. Thus, research from the relational turbulence model suggests that the process of disclosing relationship information to interpersonal networks is meaningful to relational function. The uncertainty surrounding becoming FBO is inherent in the interpretation of the meaning of this public commitment. Individuals must assess what the decision means to themselves, to their partner, and to the public. The simple act of clicking a button on the website can be an interpersonally significant experience that affects how individuals interpret the intensity and commitment within their romantic relationships (Fox and Warber 2013).

Fox, Warber, and Makstaller (2013) interviewed focus groups to assess the personal and social implications of becoming FBO. Results revealed that individuals use FBO as a means of reducing uncertainty during initial stages of relationship formation. In short, to declare FBO indicates the relational partners are in an exclusive dating relationship and therefore the relationship is considered stable. In a quantitative analysis of what it means to be FBO, researchers found that women believed more strongly than men that FBO implied exclusivity and seriousness (Fox and Warber 2013). Fox and her colleagues (2013) also sought to determine how users within and outside of the relationship interpreted a couple's decision to go public, and whether the interpretation had consistent meanings in terms of portrayals of commitment. Ultimately, members of the focus groups indicated that FBO was a social and interpersonal statement about commitment and this statement reduced uncertainty within the social circle (Fox et al. 2013). Therefore, couples must determine how to define their commitment to one another as well as to their social network.

Conversely, if the relationship deescalates, an online public declaration like becoming FBO has implications as well. Research has shown that individuals attributed meaning when a person's relational status changed in terms of relationship entry, exit, and even when the information becomes unavailable (Fox et al. 2013). Specifically, "if an individual goes from single to not having a status, it is assumed that the person is in the beginning stages of a relationship but not necessarily ready to publicize it. Alternatively, if a person is listed as "in a relationship" but the status disappears, this is taken as a sign that a couple is in the process of breaking up but wishes to avoid a public spectacle" (Fox et al. 2013, 783). While becoming FBO can communicate commitment, reversing that decision can communicate relationship dissolution. Individuals commented that relational partners must have a mutual understanding of FBO and that defining the relationship online will also define the relationship offline (Fox et al. 2013).

Clearly the decision to become FBO can have both positive and negative relational implications. FBO can communicate commitment and exclusivity, but this decision can also be restrictive and cause relational turbulence. Relational uncertainty increases during this transitional period and necessitates individuals to make sense of the decision to become FBO. The following paragraphs detail Weick's (1995) sensemaking process theory.

SENSEMAKING AND BECOMING FBO

In his theory of sensemaking, Weick (1995) described seven properties of sensemaking. Sensemaking is retrospective, social, grounded in identity construction, ongoing, enactive of sensible environments, focused on and extracted by cues, and driven by plausibility. Weick, Sutcliffe, and Obstfeld (2005) stated that sensemaking is about asking what an event means. When people encounter an indecipherable event, they must interpret it, and that simple action of inquiring about the occurrence brings the event and its meaning into existence. This process of sensemaking allows them to act in the future or continue to act (Weick et al. 2005). Sensemaking is triggered by feelings of ambiguity. To manage ambiguity, interdependent people must "search for meaning, settle for plausibility, and move on" (Weick et al. 2005, 419). To make sense of a situation, individuals must connect the abstract with the concrete, starting with immediate context and cues. Though sensemaking is not often applied to close interpersonal relationships, this decision-making model is ideal for understanding retrospective decision justifications (Mintzberg and Westley 2010). DiMicco et al. (2009) utilized a sensemaking information organization approach to describe the usage of a social networking site. Unlike DiMicco et al.'s approach, Weick et al. (2005) formalized the sensemaking process.

Weick's sensemaking approach is grounded in identity construction; that is, sensemaking simply begins with the sensemaker (Weick 1995; Weick et al. 2005). Identity-related sensemaking involves questions of who we are, what we are doing, and why it matters (Weick et al. 2005). Identities are also formed out of interaction. Weick (1995) claims that an individual's identity is formed from an ongoing and continuously updated processing of cues from others and oneself. In constructing identity, the individual takes social action to test plausible interpretations of the situation relative to the self (Weick et al. 2005). Essentially, identity is formed through interaction with others.

To become FBO is an interactive statement of both the individual's identity and the relationship's identity. Relational partners must interact to become FBO and mutually agree on the decision, but becoming FBO is also an interaction with one's social network. Both the discussion about and the enactment of relationship status disclosure are instances when partners ask, "How can I know what I think until I see what I say?" (Weick et al. 2005, 412). Weick (1995) contended that individuals learn about their identities by projecting and testing identity claims in an environment and assessing the consequences. Individuals who are anticipating becoming FBO can examine others' FBO relationships and project themselves into that context to assess potential consequences.

Sensemaking is also retrospective, in that creation of meaning involves attention to that which has already passed. Individuals who make sense of their decision to become or not to become FBO will reflect on their past decision and rationalize it through retrospective accounts. Weick (1995) theorized that order, clarity, and rationality are goals of sensemaking, and when they have been achieved, the retrospection will cease. That is, though sensemaking is a continuous process, individuals only take note of the process when there are disruptions to the routine. Certainly, choosing to make one's relational status public represents a disruption in the otherwise usual process for relational partners. This disruption causes individuals to consider the past in order to make sense of the present.

Additionally, according to Weick (1995), sensemaking is social. Simply put, interacting with and anticipating the reactions of others can aid in sensemaking. To study sensemaking, one must pay attention to discourse. The decision to become FBO implies a discourse between relational partners. Each partner must give permission to be "tagged" in their partner's relationship status. Salancik and Pfeffer (1978) argued that social context was critical for sensemaking because it constrained people to actions they must justify, affected the saliency of information, and provided norms and expectations that can constrain explanations. Additionally, sensemaking is social when individuals focus not on shared meaning but on shared action. Individuals must consider the social implications and reactions when making sense of their decision to be FBO.

The ongoing continuous process of sensemaking is well-suited for examining relational status disclosure because in the process of becoming FBO, individuals engage in sensemaking before, during, and after the act, both privately and with partners. Weick (1995) said that a person cannot avoid acting, and those actions affect both the situation and the individual, necessitating sensemaking. Sensemaking also is driven by plausibility in that individuals do not need to emphasize accuracy, but rather believability. Weick et al. (2005) claimed that individuals do not need to perceive their situation accurately to make sense of it. They can simply act effectively by making sense of the situation in ways that focus on the goals of order, clarity, and rationality. Therefore, the act of publicly declaring or not declaring one's relationship status has meaning for the individuals involved, but it may not be perceived as accurate by the social network.

The decision to be FBO is burdened by uncertainty and ambiguity regarding the individuals involved, the state of the relationship, and the consequences of the decision. Relational partners must decide whether they will embrace ambiguity by not becoming FBO, allowing for speculation from their social network, or if they will avoid ambiguity and declare a relationship. Individuals must decide whether defining their relationship is more uncomfortable than the ambiguity of not defining it. They must therefore make sense of this decision by considering the consequences for their identity, social network, and the future. Therefore, the following research questions are posed:

RQ1. What are the reasons relational partners decide to be or not to be FBO?

RQ2. In what ways do relational partners make sense of their decision to be or not to be FBO?

METHOD

Participants

A sample of 192 undergraduate students participated in this study. To be eligible to participate in this study, participants were required to be in a relationship and have an active Facebook account. Fifty-seven participants were male and 135 were female, and the average participant age was 20.22 years (SD = 2.19; range = 18 to 34).

Design and Procedure

The data were collected as part of a larger project on relationship status disclosure. Participants were recruited through a communication department research pool and received extra credit for their participation. An online survey was conducted to assess the relationship among relational quality, being FBO, and relational characteristics such as satisfaction and commitment. Participants were asked about their relationship status on Facebook and their response determined the open-ended questions they received.

Participants who indicated their relationship status was "Facebook official" were asked the following question in their survey:

1. Did you and your partner ever discuss the choice to display your relationship status online? How did you decide to disclose your relationship status online?

Participants who indicated their relationship status was not "Facebook official" were asked the following questions:

1. There are many reasons why you may have chosen not to display your relationship status: Please describe why you choose not to display your relationship status online.
2. Have you and your partner ever discussed the choice to display or not display your online relationship status? Please describe that discussion, be as specific as possible.
3. Please describe any other reasons you choose to display or not display your relationship status.

Of those who shared their relationship status (n = 110), only five did not complete the open-ended question (4.5 percent). Of those who did not share their relationship status (n = 82), all but two (2.4 percent) completed at least one of the open-ended questions.

Data Analysis

A modified constant comparative analysis was used for this study. Glaser and Strauss established a systematic method-inductive data analysis that does not use an *a priori* scheme for coding (Glaser and Strauss 1967). Each participant response was treated as a single unit. If more than one reason was stated, each reason given was treated as a separate unit yielding 288 codable units. If no reason was given, the data were not coded. First, the data were coded according to whether or not the participants had discussed the decision to be FBO with their partners. In a process akin to open coding, responses were then compared and contrasted with each other and categorized by similar features. During the open coding process, the researcher moved inductively between the data set and categories, comparing data to data to find the most succinct categorization (Lindlof and Taylor 2010). This process was iterative and continued until all data were coded into categories. Once categories were determined, each category was compared and contrasted with the other categories. Finally, the categories were examined to find the interrelationships between them.

RESULTS

Data were first coded as to whether or not participants discussed the decision to become FBO with their partners. Of those who were FBO, fifty-one participants said they did discuss the decision with their partners and fifty-four said they did not. Of those who were not FBO, thirty-nine said they had discussed the decision and thirty-nine said they did not. Overall, ninety participants discussed the decision and ninety-three did not. Equal proportions did and did not discuss decisions for both those who were FBO and those who were not. Of the total 185 participants who responded to the open-ended items, only two individuals did not answer the question about discussing the decision to be FBO with their partners.

Participants' sensemaking resources for their decision regarding becoming FBO fell along two dimensions: time orientation and identity target (see table 3.1). Identity target deals with who is affected by the consequences of becoming FBO, the individual or the relationship. The time-orientation category involves considerations of the timing of the consequences of becoming FBO, either immediate or sometime in the future. Participants accounted for their decision to become or not to become FBO through (a) their value of privacy (33 percent), (b) expectations from others regarding the relationship (31 percent), (c) the significance of the decision on the relationship (18 percent), and (d) the consequences of defining the relationship (11 percent). Additionally, participants also cited technical issues (7 percent) as a reason not to become FBO. The most common reason reported for participants who were not FBO was privacy, and for participants who were already FBO it was the expectations of others (see table 3.2).

Value of Privacy

The desire to maintain privacy was the most common reason for participants not to become FBO, accounting for 41.41 percent of the total responses from those not FBO. On the other hand, those who were FBO claimed they wanted to share their relationship with the world and privacy was not as much of an issue, accounting for 14.44 percent of the total responses from those who were FBO. Participants citing privacy as a reason maintained that their relationship was "no one's business" and "a personal issue." Frequently identified was that relationships are too private and should not be shared in a public forum: "I like to keep my private life private" and "I don't think the status of my relationship should be shown on a social network." Additionally, participants cited reasons such as "I do not think it's necessary for the public to be involved in my personal relationship." Individuals who did not have a concern for privacy indicated, "We both enjoy others seeing our relationship," and "We wanted everyone to know that we were together."

Individuals who decided to become FBO also had concern for privacy, but their ambiguity avoidance was stronger than their concern for privacy: "We were both sort of reluctant to put our business online for everyone to see, but after briefly discussing it, we decided to go ahead and do it anyway." Privacy was used as a reason to avoid immediate consequences of declaring a relationship FBO. For example, one participant cited that if they became FBO "[people] treat you differently." This reflects on the identity orientation of "self" as well. Privacy was cited as a

Table 3.1. Sensemaking resources of becoming FBO

Identity	Time			
	Immediate		Future	
	FBO	Not FBO	FBO	Not FBO
Self	Value of privacy (32.99%; n = 95)		Defining the relationship (11.46%; n = 33)	
	13.68%; n = 13	86.32%; n = 82	33.33%; n = 11	66.67%; n = 22
Relationship	Expectations of others (30.90%; n = 89)		Significance of decision (18.05%; n = 52)	
	55.06%; n = 49	44.94%; n = 40	32.69%; n = 17	67.31%; n = 35

n = 288

Table 3.2. Total responses within each group

	FBO (*n* = 90)	Not FBO (*n* = 198)
Privacy	14.44% (*n* = 13)	41.41% (*n* = 82)
Expectations of others	54.44% (*n* = 49)	20.20% (*n* = 40)
Defining the relationship	12.22% (*n* = 11)	11.11% (*n* = 22)
Significance of decision	18.89% (*n* = 17)	17.68% (*n* = 35)
Technical reasons	N/A	9.60% (*n* = 19)

Table created by Punyanunt-Carter and Wrench.

personal matter, not a relational issue by frequently citing *"my* personal life" and "who *I* am dating" (emphasis added).

Expectations from Others Regarding the Relationship

Expectations regarding becoming FBO was the second-most popular reason overall for making sense of the decision and the number-one reason for those who were FBO, accounting for 54.44 percent of their responses. For those who were FBO, the decision was just what was expected of them and it was what they were supposed to do. Individuals who were FBO cited such reasons as becoming FBO was "just expected, as it is the norm for the day" and the decision was "just assumed." Another participant stated, "It was just the normal procedure at our high school." Many participants stated that they and their partner changed their status together. Frequently, expectations came from outsiders such as friends and family. One participant cited, "A friend changed [my status] and sent the request to him," and another claimed, "Our friends kept asking us when we were going to make it 'Facebook Official.'"

For individuals who were not FBO, common reasons for the decision were that people would not approve and that it would complicate things. Expectations of others accounted for 20.20 percent of the total responses from those not FBO. One example shows, "People tend to ask too many questions and involve themselves in the relationship, during fights etc.," which indicates that the individual had expectations for how people would react to the decision. Many participants who were not FBO expected their families to react negatively: "We have decided not to display any relationship style posts, pictures, or statuses on Facebook as a means to avoid drama with my family. Her family is accepting of her and her sexuality; it is mine that poses a threat to my well-being and our relationship." Participants were frequently concerned with the immediate consequences for their relationship. Participants also cited expectations from their partner as reasons not to be FBO. For example, one participant claimed, "I didn't know if she wanted everyone seeing that kind of information," and another stated, "I didn't want to freak her out and make her think I was being protective or clingy."

Significance of the Decision on the Relationship

Significance of the decision is the first category in the future orientation dimension. The percentages accounted for by this category were pretty even, accounting for 18.89 percent of responses from FBO and 17.68 percent from those not FBO. Participants who were FBO claimed that it was necessary to become FBO because a relationship is not official unless it is Facebook official, and it is seen as a sign of commitment. This has implications for the relationship in the long term. Becoming FBO has consequences for the relationship in that it is a "sign of commitment," "a big step in our relationship," and that making a relationship public would "make our relationship official that way." Frequently cited was that relational partners would become FBO once they had declared themselves as "boyfriend and girlfriend."

For participants who were not FBO, they claimed that becoming FBO did not mean anything and was not a symbol of commitment. One participant claimed, "We decided that our relationship status on Facebook doesn't really mean anything in the real relationship," and another stated, "We do not believe that by posting our relationship status on Facebook, it will make our relationship any more intimate or official." The category of significance falls into the relationship-identity dimension because participants tended to indicate that becoming FBO might have meant something to them or their partner, but it did not mean anything for the relationship: "I asked him if he wanted to put our relationship on Facebook and he said no, putting our relationship on Facebook is not going to make it stronger or mean anything more."

Consequences of Defining the Relationship

The perceived consequences of defining the relationship included references to how the decision would affect the individual in the future, accounting for 12.22 percent of the responses from those FBO and 11.11 percent from those not FBO. Common themes included keeping options open, seeing whether the relationship would last, and keeping an undetermined relationship status. Individuals who were FBO claimed they only made that decision after assessing whether it was right for them and whether their relationship would last. Simply put, participants "decided to wait awhile before [they] put it online." Having an undetermined relationship status also influenced their decision to become FBO: "Our relationship was off and on in the beginning. We decided to put our relationship on Facebook after being 'on' for six months. We wanted to make sure our relationship would last before putting it on a public site." Participants showed concern for "moving too fast," waiting to see "how the relationship worked out before putting it on Facebook."

Defining the relationship by becoming FBO was perceived to have consequences for the individual in that their options would become limited. One participant described, "As we started having conflicts, she took off her relationship status, and as a result of that I did the same thing because I thought it was unfair, in terms of potential future relationships." Similarly, another participant described not being FBO because "I have more than one romantic relationship going on currently. So it is in my best interest to not show my current status," and another claimed, "I've been having second guesses on even being in a relationship at all," and another, "I did not really want to [put my relationship on Facebook] because I was already in a relationship with another girl from a different country." One participant elaborated on a previous response: "Your relationship status being so defined seems to cheapen the relationship. People can know you are together or not together without being involved with you personally." Participants viewed defining the relationship as a restriction to their individual identity and decided that defining the relationship would have future consequences.

Technical Issues

Technical issues were a reason cited only for those not FBO, accounting for 9.60 percent of their responses. From the participants' view, they included reasons such as not having a Facebook account or not accessing Facebook frequently. One participant claimed, "I do not get on Facebook much and when I do my first thought is not to go change my relationship status." Some participants claimed they simply hadn't taken the time to change the status. Others stated the reason for not being FBO was that their partner did not have a Facebook account, and sometimes it was a combination of these reasons: "I am not online enough for my relationship status to matter. They do not have an active Facebook [account]." This category does not involve long-term or short-term consequences, nor does it imply consequences for the identities of the individual or the relationship.

DISCUSSION

The objective of this study was to examine how individuals made sense of their decision to become FBO. Analysis of participant responses revealed individuals draw on two sensemaking resources to justify their decisions. The first dimension of time orientation focuses on Facebook users' perception of the immediacy of consequences. To become FBO can result in immediate consequences or delayed consequences (i.e., consequences that have implications for the future). Participants used the second dimension of identity to make sense of potential consequences, focusing on their own identity or the identity of the relationship. Those who justified their decision based their own self-identity indicated the consequences would reflect on them individually and the choice to display their relationship was a personal one. Those who justified the decision by utilizing the identity of the relationship resource indicated that the consequences would reflect on their relationship as a whole and that therefore the decision should be mutual. Discussing the decision with their partner was equally likely for those who were and were not FBO. This could imply that some individuals see the decision as a relational decision and others as an individual choice, as reflected in the identity dimension. A justification that did not fit along the dimensions of time and identity was technical reasons regarding Facebook. Participants only used this reason if they were not FBO, and they justified their decision by stating they did not access Facebook frequently enough to declare their relationship or their partner did not have a Facebook account.

These findings contribute to our understanding of the sensemaking process by illustrating that participants used time and identity resources as justification for avoiding the ambiguity surrounding their relational transition and declaring FBO. Alternatively, some partners embraced the ambiguity and chose not to publicly declare their relationship. In a time of relational turbulence, such as when moving from casual to a serious relationship, uncertainty is heightened (Solomon and Knobloch 2004), and individuals are faced with the decision to make their relationship public. These implications speak to previous research illuminating the role of social networks in the broader relational support process (Knobloch and Donovan-Kicken 2006).

For some, the uncertainty is tolerable, and they justify that decision not by explicitly stating they want their relationship to remain ambiguous, but by drawing on sensemaking resources outside of the relationship. For others, the uncertainty is intolerable, and they ease the tension by declaring their relationship on Facebook, making their commitment social. Though participants do not evoke the term "uncertainty," they do demonstrate the motivation to reduce uncertainty. Specifically, through their use of the sensemaking resources of time and identity (with specific reasons including valuing privacy, expectations of others, significance of the decision, and consequences of defining the relationship), it is clear that the sensemaking process explains the FBO decision. This research integrates the inherently social relational turbulence perspective with sensemaking as a means to explain a complex social decision-making process.

Theoretically, this research extends the claims made by Weick and colleagues to demonstrate the utility of a formalized decision process in interpersonal relationships (Weick 1995; Weick et al. 2005). Though it may seem incongruous to apply organizational theory to interpersonal relationships, the overlap between how one feels toward and/or about an organization and a relationship partner may well be predicated on the same processes (e.g. Farrell and Rusbult 1981). This study suggests that it is time for increased integration between other social theorizing and interpersonal processes. Additional research should seek to differentiate social, psychological, and interpersonal dimensions of the interaction and the sensemaking processes.

Limitations and Future Directions

There were a few limitations in this study, some of which can be addressed in future research. The first limitation was in the use of open-ended questions in an online survey. While only seven participants did not answer the open-ended questions, typically answers were brief, limiting the scope of analysis. In-depth interviews, possibly with both members of the dyad, would allow researchers to delve deeper into individuals' sensemaking resources. Also, only one question was asked of participants who were FBO, while three questions were asked of those in a relationship but not FBO. The data allowed for variation and the seeming saturation of codes between those who were FBO and those who weren't, but symmetry between groups in survey design controls for any extraneous factors that could influence participant responses.

An additional limitation was the use of a student population. Emerging adults are the most common users of social networking sites, averaging one to two hours per day (Kalpidou et al. 2011), and they attribute meaning to actions afforded by Facebook. However, a larger population could provide varying sensemaking resources. This is evidenced in one participant's elaboration of an earlier response: "I also choose not to display my status because I feel it is a practice valued by a school age generation. I do not refer to my significant other as "boyfriend" because he is not a boy, we are adults. Your relationship status being so defined seems to cheapen the relationship." There is a different perception of Facebook and its implications between generations who grew up using technology in their everyday lives and generations who learned to incorporate it, and future research should examine this difference in detail.

CONCLUSION

Relationships experiencing a transition in commitment have increased turbulence indicated by partners' greater uncertainty about themselves, their partner, and their relationship (Solomon and Knobloch 2004). To cope with the uncertainty, relational partners can decide to become Facebook official and declare their relationship publicly. To some, this declaration indicates greater commitment, but to others it is a violation of privacy. Utilizing a sensemaking process involving enactment and generating tangible outcomes in a specific context, this process helps them discover what is occurring, what needs to be explained, and what should be done next (Weick 1995). The results of this study inform us about the decision to become FBO and the perceived consequences of this decision.

REFERENCES

Berger, Charles R., and James J. Bradac. 1982. *Language and Social Knowledge: Uncertainty in Interpersonal Relations*. Vol. 2. London: E. Arnold.

Berger, Charles R., and Richard J. Calabrese. 1975. "Some Explorations in Initial Interaction and Beyond: Toward A Developmental Theory of Interpersonal Communication." *Human Communication Research* 1 (2): 99–112.

DiMicco, Joan Morris, Werner Geyer, David R Millen, Casey Dugan, and Beth Brownholtz. 2009. "People Sensemaking and Relationship Building on an Enterprise Social Network Site." In *Proceedings of the 42nd Hawaii International Conference on System Science.*, 1–10. Los Alamitos, CA: IEEE Computer Society Press.

Facebook Statistics. 2016. *Facebook Newsroom*. http://newsroom.fb.com/Key-Facts.

Farrell, Daniel, and Caryl E. Rusbult. 1981. "Exchange Variables as Predictors of Job Satisfaction, Job Commitment, and Turnover: The Impact of Rewards, Costs, Alternatives, and Investments." *Organizational Behavior and Human Performance* 28 (1): 78–95.

Fox, Jesse, and Katie M. Warber. 2013. "Romantic Relationship Development in the Age of Facebook: An Exploratory Study of Emerging Adults' Perceptions, Motives, and Behaviors." *Cyberpsychology, Behavior, and Social Networking* 16 (1): 3–7.

Fox, J., K. M. Warber, and D. C. Makstaller. 2013. "The Role of Facebook in Romantic Relationship Development: An Exploration of Knapp's Relational Stage Model." *Journal of Social and Personal Relationships* 30 (6): 771–94.

Glaser, Barney G., and Anselm L. Strauss. 1967. *The Discovery of Grounded Theory: Strategies for Qualitative Research*. Chicago: Aldine Pub.

Kalpidou, Maria, Dan Costin, and Jessica Morris. 2011. "The Relationship Between Facebook and the Well-Being of Undergraduate College Students." *Cyberpsychology, Behavior, and Social Networking* 14 (4): 183–89.

Knobloch, Leanne K., and Denise Haunani Solomon. 1999. "Measuring the Sources and Content of Relational Uncertainty." *Communication Studies* 50 (4): 261–78.

———. 2002a. "Information Seeking Beyond Initial Interaction." *Human Communication Research* 28 (2): 243–57.

———. 2002b. "Intimacy and the Magnitude and Experience of Episodic Relational Uncertainty within Romantic Relationships." *Personal Relationships* 9 (4): 457–78.

Knobloch, Leanne K., and Erin Donovan-Kicken. 2006. "Perceived Involvement of Network Members in Courtships: A Test of the Relational Turbulence Model." *Personal Relationships* 13 (3): 281–302.

Lindlof, Thomas R., and Bryan C. Taylor. 2011. *Qualitative Communication Research Methods*. London: SAGE.

Mintzberg, Henry, and Frances Westley. 2010. "Decision making: It's not what you think." In *Handbook of Decision Making*, Vol. 6, ed. Paul C. Nutt and David C Wilson, 73–81. Chichester, West Sussex, UK: John Wiley.

Papp, Lauren M., Jennifer Danielewicz, and Crystal Cayemberg. 2012. "'Are We Facebook Official?' Implications of Dating Partners' Facebook Use and Profiles for Intimate Relationship Satisfaction." *Cyberpsychology, Behavior, and Social Networking* 15 (2): 85–90.

Salancik, Gerald R., and Jeffrey Pfeffer. 1978. "A Social Information Processing Approach to Job Attitudes and Task Design." *Administrative Science Quarterly* 23 (2): 224–53.

Solomon, Denise Haunani, and Leanne K. Knobloch. 2004. "A Model of Relational Turbulence: The Role of Intimacy, Relational Uncertainty, and Interference From Partners in Appraisals of Irritations." *Journal of Social and Personal Relationships* 21 (6): 795–816.

Theiss, Jennifer A., and Denise Haunani Solomon. 2006. "A Relational Turbulence Model of Communication About Irritations in Romantic Relationships." *Communication Research* 33 (5): 391–418.

Weick, Karl E. 1995. *Sensemaking in Organizations.* Thousand Oaks: Sage Publications.

Weick, Karl E., Kathleen M. Sutcliffe, and David Obstfeld. 2005. "Organizing and the Process of Sensemaking." *Organization Science* 16 (4): 409–21.

FOUR

Millennials' Use of Online Applications for Romantic Development

Terri Manley

College campuses across the nation today are primarily comprised of millennials, a generation known for their desire to multi-task and stay plugged in to the technological world (Cooper 2012). The generation consists of those born between 1980 and 2002 (Hartman and McCambridge 2011). The millennial generation is the largest generation in the United States, recently passing the baby boomer generation (Fry 2016). Members of the millennial generation have witnessed the rise and advances of technology during their lives (Gibson and Sodeman 2014). Individuals of this generation consider technological devices to be an intricate part of their lives, and they play a vital role in their day-to-day tasks (Beckstrom, Manuel and Nightingale 2008). With this desire to stay constantly connected to the online world, interpersonal communication continues to change. For example, imagine yourself at a restaurant and ask yourself how many individuals are on their cell phones and engaged in outside conversations versus conversations with those who are with them in their immediate area. Keller (2013) states that social media's effect on an individual's ability to interact and communicate is visible throughout all areas of society, which shifts the overall way we communicate; rather than face-to-face interaction, individuals prefer mediated communication (e.g., individuals would rather e-mail than meet; or text than talk on the phone). Gibson and Sodeman (2014) suggest that millennials are easiest to connect with through an online medium, further proving this interpersonal communication evolution. The changes among interpersonal com-

munication and the millennial generation challenges many years of previous research in the field. Limited research has been done on millennials
and the change occurring as a result of this technologically dependent
generation. It is argued, however, that the mode through which we
choose to communicate is what is changing, and that the needs and content remain the same. This type of research seeks to explore how new
channels of communication change the conversation, and challenge previous communication norms.

Many fun and exciting trends are a result of technological advances;
one of these is online dating applications. Online dating applications can
be a fun and exciting way to find prospective partners and satisfy personal needs; however, the use of these online dating applications is unique to
the millennial generation. Perusing these social networking sites (SNSs),
"pinning" ideas, sending "friend" requests, or "swiping right" for a potential partner is easily accessible, all from smartphones. Social networks
are of high importance to millennials, and a Pew Research Center study
(Fry 2016) found that 83 percent of millennials are so dependent on their
phones and networking sites they sleep with their phones beside them.

This chapter looks at romantic relationship building on the following
application-based platforms: Tinder, Bumble, Snapchat, Twitter, Instagram, and Facebook. These platforms are currently being used by the
millennial generation for romantic relationship development (Manley
and Hair 2016). Recent research has indicated that approximately 90 percent of millennials are using smartphones and using them in a variety of
ways (Charrier 2016). This market allows this demographic a lot of consumer power; however, the way this segment uses SNS is contingent and
different based on use (Charrier 2016). Thus, this chapter focuses not on
why millennials use SNS in general, but how they use them based on
romantic development and when seeking romantic development situations.

Infinedo (2016) states that about 97 percent of university students (i.e.,
that current millennial generation) actively use SNS daily. Reports have
indicated that consumers integrate two or more SNSs as a part of their
daily activities and access these SNSs on mobile devices. They report that
students within the university use Facebook approximately six hours a
day. Facebook attracts 1.49 billion users monthly and is a ubiquitous part
of individuals lives. Facebook is typically used by individuals between
the ages of 18 and 34, and practitioners use this platform to engage audiences by being thoughtful and creative. Twitter is essentially the same
idea as Facebook; however, it is based on a microblogging system in
which users can only "tweet" in 140 characters. Through this medium,
the "hashtag" has boomed. The hashtag has come to comprise an important expression in popular culture and is generally associated with various dimensions of activities in the social media environment. The hashtag is an emergent convention for labeling the topic of a micro-post and a

form of metadata incorporated into posts. The functionality of this concept is the common practice of sorting and selecting thematically related information from a surge of messages within the context of social media platforms. Instagram is a fun and quirky way to share content with friends through a series of pictures. Users are encouraged to take photos on their mobile devices and then filter the photos into a memory to keep forever. The overall goal of this SNS is to connect the world through photos. This platform has 320 million active users. Snapchat is an image-messaging and multimedia mobile application (Betters 2015). Snapchat involves a mix of private messaging and public content. Individuals use this platform to chat, message, and send images. Snapchat has approximately 200 million active users.

Tinder and Bumble are online dating applications designed for the fast-paced lifestyle of its users. Tinder and Bumble are essentially the same concept; however, on Bumble women are encouraged to reach out to males first. The creators of Bumble chose to create this platform because of the aggressive nature of males approaching women on Tinder and to empower women. Tinder has at least 10 million active users a day (Sumter Vandenbosch and Ligtenberg 2017). This dating application is the first of its kind that is specifically designed as a smartphone application versus just an extension of an existing dating website. Users on Tinder log on to the application an average of eleven times daily and swipe on average for around 8 minutes per log-on (Flynn 2015). Tinder consists of geographic features that allow users to connect with singles around them. Swiping a certain direction indicates specified interest on a potential partner. In order to form a "match," both partners must swipe right or upwards. If a potential match does not show interest by swiping right, a match will not be formed. If and when a match is formed users are given the option to initiate conversation via private messaging. Bumble has the same features and functionally, and since its launch in December 2014 over 90 million matches have been made (Frankel 2015).

This chapter uses Blumler and Katz, (1974) Uses and Gratifications Theory (UGT), to investigate motivations behind the millennial generations desire to explore the online dating scene. UGT has primarily been applied in the mass communication sector, and it looks at the motivational usage behind mediums. The interactive and flexible nature of SNSs fits well with the underlying assumptions of the UGT framework (Park and Lee 2014). SNS provides a unique opportunity to extend the UGT approach in that they are developing into integrative online communities in how users engage in a wide range of activities (Park and Lee 2014). This chapter is unique in the sense that it takes current literature from interpersonal communication management and applies it to the mass communication sector. Interpersonal communication and mass communication are synergistic in the sense that social media today has interpersonal dimensions. This chapter will condense and combine literature that looks at the specific motivations regarding the millennial generation, online applications and its romantic developmental features, and the role that UGT plays.

USES AND GRATIFICATIONS THEORY (UGT)

Katz, Blumler, and Gurevitch's (1974) development of Uses and Gratifications Theory (UGT) examined how and why people used different forms of media (Quan-Haase and Young 2010). UGT is concerned with what preexisting needs of consumers motivate users to engage with specific communications channels (Sundar and Limperos 2013). For example, if a consumer has the need to communicate with a relative who lives abroad, they may choose to utilize e-mail or another form of online messaging. The consumer's need of communicating with their family member is met through the ability to connect via e-mail with someone far away. While media meets a wide array of needs, those needs are preexisting. The original development of UGT was also interested in how these forms of media had the potential to influence viewers (Quan-Haase and Young 2010).

There are five overarching assumptions for UGT that can be singled out for commentary. The first assumption is that communication behavior is goal-directed, purposive, and motivated (Rubin 2009). This assumptions rests on the assumption that the audience is an active consumer versus just a passive consumer as Bogart (1965) suggested (Katz, Blumler, and Gurevitch 1974). The second UGT assumption stems from the idea of audience members being an active participant; however, it suggests audience members actively initiate the selection and use of communication vehicles, typically to satisfy needs or desires (Rubin 2009). Katz et al. (1974) states that this process then places a strong limitation on theorizing about any form of straight-line effect of media content on attitudes and behavior. The next major assumption is that social and psychological factors guide, filter, or mediate behaviors, which means that individuals are not just blank slates (Rubin 2009). Thus, audience orientations are explored on their own terms (Katz, Blumler, and Gurevitch 1974). The fourth assumption of UGT suggests the media competes with other forms of communication, such as interpersonal interaction for selection, attention, and use to gratify our needs or wants (Rubin 2009). This means audiences are typically aware of the needs they seek to satisfy and can verbalize them and thus satisfy them through mass media consumption (Katz, Blumler, and Gurevitch 1974). Finally, the last assumption of UGT is individuals are typically more influential than the media in satisfying needs, but not always (Rubin 2009). UGT understands that while audiences are more active than passive, there are moments when they can be passive; thus, it is suggested that audiences are not necessarily a dichotomous active/passive unit, but more on a continuum.

UGT Typologies

Katz et al. (1974) states each major piece of UGT research yields its own classification scheme of audience functions. These typologies differ greatly based on the researcher's scope of study, levels of study, medium of study, and cultural setting. McQuail, Blumler, and Brown (1972) provided the most adequate and stable typologies that can be applied to majority of studies; which include: diversion (including escape from the constraints of routine and the burdens of problems, and emotional release), personal relationships (including substitute companionship as well as social utility), personal identity (including personal reference, reality exploration, and value reinforcement), and surveillance. With the development of new technology however, new motivations have been formed. The creation of UGT and these original typologies applied to traditional forms of media such as newspapers, radio, and televisions; however, the introduction of the Internet and the function of interactivity within technology has now called for new typologies within UGT research to be formed.

Sundar and Limperos (2013) concept explication on new media's role in UGT identified two main problems within major studies which is researchers are using old measures designed for old media to capture gratification and gratifications are conceptually and operationalized too broadly. Overall, this study, challenged the notion that all gratifications are born out of innate needs, and proposes that affordances of media technology can shape user needs, giving rise to new and distinctive gratifications (Sundar and Limperos 2013). Sundar and Limperos (2013) state the idea of an active audience is no longer an assumption, but an obvious reality and media has changed overtime and throughout the theory due to the plethora of devices. The researchers proposed UGT is more than just a social and psychological need focused theory and researchers should focus on the technology-driven needs as well. Thus, they identified new motivations based on a compilation of multiple studies of new technology and the sources of gratifications. The typologies identified are as follows: modality-based (i.e., realism, coolness, novelty, and being there), agency-based (i.e., agency-enhanced, community-building, bandwagon, filtering/tailoring, and ownness), interactivity-based (i.e., interaction, activity, responsiveness, and dynamic control), and navigability-based (i.e., browsing/variety-seeking, scaffolding/navigation aids, and play/fun).

Further research has identified different typologies of motives on why individuals seek media use (e.g., psychological reasons); these include: habit, relaxation, kills time, spice up daily life, cognitive needs/information purposive, communication, social identity, social integrated need (e.g., who am I?), escape needs (e.g., horror needs = tension release), and parasocial interactions. However, these are just a few typologies of motivations that recent research has identified. The following section will look specifically at a few studies that employed UGT within the SNS scope to identify motivations of users.

SNS Research

Recent research has examined UGT applied to modern technologies and social networking sites (SNS). Modern media examined by UGT includes but is not limited to: smartphones, tablets, computers, robots, social networking sites, and smartphone applications (Sundar and Limperos 2013). The expansion of Internet platforms has also allowed users to generate their own content online, creating another new aspect to UGT. This modern approach also examines features of technology, and how the features satisfy the consumer's needs (Sundar and Limperos 2013). While consumers utilize media to satisfy a certain need, there are certain features that enhance the ability to satisfy a specific need. Palmgreen, Wenner, and Rosengren (1985) and Rubin (2009) also suggest that modern aspects of UGT are concerned with psychological factors of consumers that determine their expectations of online platforms. The development of new and recent phone applications and other forms of media are a result of certain needs consumers seek to satisfy. Smartphones have the ability to download applications that meet certain needs ranging from weight loss, finding a partner, and having groceries delivered to your doorstep. The fast-paced society has generated a multitude of needs, and certain media has arisen in response to those needs. Thus, a multitude of researchers have looked at applications such as Facebook, Instagram, Snapchat, Twitter, Bumble, Tinder, etc. to identify users' motivations to employ these platforms.

Ifinedo's (2016) study sought to understand students' need to adopt social networking sites pervasively as a part of their lives. Results indicated positive impacts of students' pervasive adoption of SNS and cultural factors of individualism-collectivism on pervasive adoption of SNS (Ifinedo 2016). Main typologies identified included self-discovery, entertainment value, social enhancement, and the need to maintain interpersonal connectivity (Ifinedo 2016). With regard to campus capital, results indicated students showed more willingness to use SNS when they knew others in their social network group had the same values (Ifinedo 2016).

Hayes, Carr, and Wohn (2016) sought to understand the depths of clicking of "likes" and understanding the usage behind this act within multiple platforms such as Facebook, Instagram, Snapchat, and Reddit. The overarching question by the researchers was to understand what these "lightweight signals mean" both to the senders and those receiving the cues (Hayes, Carr, and Wohn 2016). The authors argue the same cues for the same activity could have vastly different valences and a single click may be sent and interpreted in a variety of ways. Main typologies discovered within this study of receiving PDAs included: emotional purposes, status gratification, and social gratification (Hayes, Carr, and Wohn 2016).

Besides just basic studies on users' usage of SNS, other researchers have specifically looked at the motivations behind the romantic use of these SNS. For example, Dainton and Strokes (2015) looked at college students' romantic relationships on Facebook. They sought to understand the linkage between the motivation of the usage of these platforms and its connection to relationship maintenance and jealousy. Dainton and Strokes (2015) looked at the maintenance of romantic relationships via Facebook and the positive and negative activities of significant others. These involved traits of the users, cognitive traits, emotions, and jealousy. The purpose of this study was to understand which types of jealousy were related to maintenance on Facebook (Dainton and Strokes 2015). Results of this study indicated that those who used Facebook for relationship maintenance were more likely to engage in assurances and monitoring. These two characteristics were related to four types of jealousy associated with cognitive jealousy; however, there was no relationship found between maintenance and experiencing jealousy (Dainton and Strokes 2015).

Separate studies have looked at dating applications such as Tinder, Bumble, and Grindr (Manley and Hair 2016; Sumter Vandenbosch and Ligtenberg 2017; Daalmans Cunningham and Van Ommen 2016; Van der Wurff 2011; Garcia Lopez and Gaona 2012) and users' usage and motivations of these applications. Daalmans et al. (2016) sought to look at the dating application Tinder and understand how the cultural shift of love and sexual intimacy does not always go together, especially in this medium. The other purpose of this article was to identify the motives and purposes of Tinder users, and how these motivations either match or differentiate with the expectations of other users on online dating websites (Daalmans, Cunningham, and Van Ommen 2016). Results indicated that Tinder breaks the taboo of online dating in two different ways: romance and social criticism. In a comparison of Tinder versus other dating websites, users found Tinder to be a less desperate form of dating, and a more casual and less pressured form of making connections (Daalmans, Cunningham, and Van Ommen 2016). The motives behind Tinder are much more ambiguous than traditional dating websites, and one respondent states, "It's a game" (Daalmans, Cunningham, and Van Ommen 2016). Although, the motivations are somewhat different, if you are to meet traditional love through Tinder, there becomes a stigma on that relationship. The application overall is superficially based, thus, it is hard for consumers to find true depth to it, unless they actually do. Also, most respondents stated that they could meet a potential partner on Tinder; however, they would still prefer to meet their partners offline. Overall, there are five different motivation (typologies) identified for Tinder usage in this study: entertainment, to enhance self-confidence, tool for arranging a sexual, or non-binding or friendly date (Daalmans, Cunningham, and Van Ommen 2016).

Daalmans et al.'s (2016) study looked particularly at college students within their sample and conducted in-depth interviews to obtain results. Very similar results were obtained in the qualitative focus groups obtained from Manley and Hair (2016), which found six motivations related to their sample of millennials' usage of Tinder and Bumble. Their typology included social connections, simplicity, amusement, instant gratification, validation, and online protection (Manley and Hair 2016).

Using a different sample selection (i.e., slightly older demographics) and a more quantitative method (i.e., survey), Sumter et al. (2017) found slightly different results. This article conducted an online survey of Dutch emerging adults and their usage and perception of the dating platform Tinder. This convenience sample consisted of 163 adults (83 males, 80 females) with an average age of 23.74 (Sumter, Vandenbosch, and Ligtenberg 2017). This study found six motivations for users use of Tinder: love, casual sex, ease of communication, self-worth validation, thrill of excitement, and trendiness (Sumter, Vandenbosch, and Ligtenberg 2017). Other interesting results indicated differences between age and gender regarding the emphases of motivation. The authors concluded the article by stating that the love motivation was stronger than the casual sex motivation, which is contrary to popular belief about the popular dating application; thus, public perceptions about the application should be reevaluated, and "Tinder goes beyond the hookup culture," for older demographics anyways (Sumter, Vandenbosch, and Ligtenberg 2017).

This is just a snapshot of some of the studies that have looked at SNS and application-based relationship-building typologies within UGT; there are a plethora of other studies. For the scope of millennials' usage of Facebook, Instagram, Snapchat, Twitter, Tinder, and Bumble for romantic development, the authors have complied a comprehensive list of typologies based on prior literature. These typologies include: new technology, validation, casual sex versus love, social connections, and excitement.

ROMANTIC DEVELOPMENT MOTIVATIONS ON APPLICATIONS

Understanding why and how individuals engage in choosing which application bests fits their needs is one of the main focuses of UGT. Gratifications have been conceptualized as need satisfactions and are typically obtained when a person's needs are met by certain types of media sources which match their expectations (Katz Blumler and Gurevitch 1974). The sub-themes that are identified as to why individuals use modern applications are multilayered and contingent on the individual. Each person is unique in their own way; thus, over-generalizations are hard to make for large populations. These typologies are applied only to millennials in the most delicate manner and based purely on theory and empirical research.

New Technology

Researchers suggest that millennials expect technology to be simple (Solomon 2015). This generation has grown up with technology in the home and in school; thus, naturally millennials embrace and align themselves with technology, especially mobile technology. All of these platforms on mobile technology, and even on the Internet, must be user-friendly, because of the demand from the generation. It must be simple, because this generation did not grow up with the blue screens of computers that other generations experienced (Solomon 2015). Thus, dating application sites must be simple, and the process that the participant gets from the action must be simple and user-friendly. This is found in both Tinder and Bumble, for example. Tinder and Bumble give users a simple interface to consume (Manley and Hair 2016). The simplistic nature of building a profile, finding a mate, and having low expectations overall for the platform, makes this medium the perfect application for the millennial generation (Manley and Hair 2016). Tapping into their technology savviness and their need for overall simplicity from technology allows for simplistic relationships to take place through the medium.

Quotes from studies have been stated saying, "I've never made a Match profile, but I know they're pretty extensive on asking hobbies and really get to know you so they can find an ideal match. Tinder is just like, swipe, nothing really that personal" (Manley and Hair 2016 p. 22). The whole concept of applications, in general, of just making a profile is just quick and simple, that this taps into users need of wanting simplicity within new technologies. For example, within Tinder or Bumble users can throw a couple of pictures up and then see singles in the area right away, thus making romantic relationships so much easier to obtain and access. Daalmans et al. (2016) stated their respondents liked that the application made it easier for people to get into touch with people to go out on a date with. Individuals expressed their concern for safety when building relationships online, and they liked the way new applications allowed for proximity, pictures, and chatting to be main features of the application to build relationships (Daalmans Cunningham and Van Ommen 2016). Next, people identified that trendiness was important within applications when adapting the use of relationship-driven applications.

Most respondents looked for the newness, the idea of "everybody does it," and coolness factors when deciding to use applications. Sumter et al. (2017) found validity in these statements with their survey, which looked at trendiness of dating applications. They used measures such as whether it was new, everyone used it, and it was "cool," and they found reliability within these scales.

Validation

As suggested by Tyler (2008) millennials are perceived as overconfident, and demanding of praise and attention; they typically expect to be praised for a job well done and acknowledged by others. This means typically they cannot handle criticism. This is prevalent in the workplace; however, it transcends over into the social media space as well. Researchers have looked at why individuals seek to be "liked" on sites such as Facebook, and state that millennials more than ever crave external validation, no matter how secure or confident they are (Daly 2015). This leads to the Generation Validation effect, which suggests that individuals begin to focus so much on Facebook or Instagram "likes" that they begin to expect the same amount of validation offline too (Daly 2015). Daly (2015) quotes Dr. Leahy a psychologist from New York, who suggests that when people get praise for even the most mundane things, such as posting a picture of a cupcake, it dilutes the "like" by making its value less special and makes the "like" less special, and individuals begin to expect "likes" in all facets of their lives.

Since millennials need validation on a daily basis, they have sought to use Tinder, Bumble, Snapchat, and Twitter to fill the void of validation. They use these platforms to get the attention that they need that other social media sites are not providing, or they use these sites to supplement what is already found on Facebook/Instagram. Gaining validation from others is a way that participants are able to gain more "likes" and "hearts" from a virtual space to increase their self-esteem. This correlates with millennial research that suggests this generation needs praise and acknowledgement, now not only in the workplace, but in the dating sphere as well (Manley and Hair 2016). The Generation Validation effect is prevalent within this generation and is being enhanced even more by the applications because they fosters the idea that individuals do not need to leave their houses to go to a bar to get hit on; now they can receive pick-up lines through their phone while in their pajamas and be validated constantly even though they are not in their best state (Manley and Hair 2016).

This idea of validation was seen with some respondents within the focus groups that Manley and Hair (2016) conducted. The researchers reported that one female participant suggested that she felt that some females use the applications to get attention from males, and all they do on the application is string guys along to get the attention; however, never really like the person. They also quote another participant who stated her friends just used the application to talk to males and act like they are interested, but they never pursues anything either. Another example that the authors highlighted was with one participant who suggested with the application just getting a swipe is a mental thing and boosts your self-esteem it's like being told your pretty, which boosts self-confidence. Daalmans et al., (2016) used focus groups as well to find motivations for why users used applications for romantic development. One of those motivations was also self-confidence. The authors stated respondents would use applications to measure how well they would actually do within the market at the time. Daalmans et al. (2016) quote one respondent as saying, "Tinder is a pastime and boost self-confidence, but is also used for sexual encounters" (p. 144).

These same types of statements were also echoed within quantitative data. Sumter et al. (2017) within their survey of Tinder users included self-worth/validation scales, which had strong reliability (i.e., factor loading). These measures included statements such as: to improve my self-esteem, to feel better about myself, to feel attractive, to feel less alone, and to get compliments about my appearance. The authors stated this scale motivation referred to using Tinder to receive positive feedback about one's appearance and feeling more confident and happy by receiving validation in general (Sumter Vandenbosch and Ligtenberg 2017). This whole idea of narcissism within the use of SNS is nothing new and Sheldon and Bryant (2015) looked at what role narcissism and validation played within Instagram in the context of relationships. They conceptualized narcissism as a personality trait that entailed a person as having an exaggerated self-concept, a high level of self-importance, and a desire to be admired. Sheldon and Bryant (2015) used a ten-item scale to measure narcissism and its correlation with Instagram use, relationship building, and life satisfaction. It was discovered that narcissism was highly correlated with surveillance of others and coolness. Within the context of new media platforms and relationship building, these results indicated that people (i.e., millennials) with greater amounts of validation needs sought applications for relationship building within the context not to necessarily have a real relationship, but just to monitor their own self-image and to maintain high levels of self-confidence.

Casual Sex versus Love

The next millennial characteristic is the idea of instant gratification. Researchers suggest that this generation needs to feel like what they are doing is important and that they are on the right track (Steinber 2013). Individuals from this generation cannot resist checking their phone when it buzzes and expect immediate responses on e-mails sent out. In a Pew

Research Center survey, it was reported that about 60 percent of 18- to 34-year olds sleep next to their cell phones just so they don't miss calls, texts or updates during the night (Smith 2016). This addiction to phones is how one researcher suggests social media sites have hooked millions of people; they provide instant gratification (Alsop 2016). This affects the classroom and the workplace; this generation constantly craves raises or promotions every few months. This trickles over into dating applications because people that are using Tinder/Bumble have short-term goals that they are seeking to meet. These platforms provide the perfect place for individuals to immediately meet someone and then pursue a relationship with another, in whatever manner that may be.

Daalmans et al., (2016) was the best to address this issue or irony of new media skewing the dating scene of real versus perceived relationships. They suggested there is much criticism of dating applications like Tinder, calling Tinder a "meat market," because the whole platform is based on external characteristics of a potential love partner. The authors state this focus on appearance counters classic romantic standards of love being based on inner qualities. Thus, new media dating applications are criticized for mainly arranging multiple and noncommittal sexual encounters (Daalmans et al. 2016). However, classical-romantic ideas of love still have a role within contemporary Western culture and popular culture. The problem with these two conflicting roles, though, is disappointment within relationships due to incompatible expectations, which can cause conflict. So, love and sexual intimacy do not have to go together always, and new media has created more practical forms of love (Daalmans et al. 2016).

Within the focus groups that Daalmans et al. (2016) conducted, they identified dual motivations for users engaging in dating applications which were: a tool for arranging a sexual or non-binding or friendly date. The problem that the majority of individuals, especially millennials, faced when accepting dating applications as a real means of finding a romantic partner was their stigma. Although online dating has become extremely popular since its initial conception, the stigma of online dating still lingers. Respondents of focus groups reported that they were ashamed or did not want to associated with the idea of "desperately looking for love" by using online dating. The introduction of online dating applications begins to help users break down these stigmatizations; however, they only foster superficial relationships and not classic romantic relationships. Tinder users are not the typical online dating users that are "desperate" or "pathetic"; their use is more socially acceptable and it is not perceived as a medium that can only be used in the search for a permanent relationship.

Respondents from focus groups stated the use of dating applications is just a game (Daalmans et al. 2016; Manley and Hair 2016). Due to Tinder's superficial functions of choosing a potential mate based on appearance, and the simplicity of setting up an account, it fosters the idea of an overall superficial relationship. This idea of superficial or temporary relationships was found prevalent when one respondent stated, "If you're on Tinder it's like you always have short-term goals, there is no long-term. Like I'm not going to find my wife or anything like that it's like you're trying to get from point A to point B whether that's trying to sleep with someone or you're trying to make conversation with someone because you're lonely or so on and so forth" (Manley and Hair 2016 p. 25). Although respondents did indicate that a stable relationship could occur from dating applications, they did contend that it did still seem to be taboo in this operating mode (Daalmans et al. 2016; Manley and Hair 2016). Participants in other focus groups echoed this perspective throughout the discussions and suggested that it was not very typical to get anything serious out of Tinder/Bumble, and that when you tell friends that you met someone through one of these platforms, the relationship is usually brushed aside because it's not typical to get a real relationship from this platform (Manley and Hair 2016).

Within a quantitative survey by Sumter et al. (2017) they included both love and casual sex scales to measures users' gratifications sought when employing dating applications. Both scales had immense reliability and loaded highly within the survey. The caveat the author explained to this difference between users was age and gender difference. The authors found correlations between those who sought love-based relationships on dating applications and older generations. Older generations are more reflective to be on regular dating sites and thus, a typical seeker of love based relationships in the online forum than younger generations (i.e., millennials).

Social Connections

The way males and females use the dating application is completely socially based and ultimately used to either make new connections or to strengthen an already established connection. Each person is unique in his or her own way; however, everyone seeks to have a social connection met through these mediums. This concept goes back to the research from UGT, which suggests that the Internet provides three main purposes. Of the three main purposes, one of those was a social purpose; users engage with the Internet to ultimately form and deepen social ties (Sundar and Limperos 2013). Many researchers have indicated that the base behind using any of these applications was to build relationships (Manley and Hair 2016; Sumter Vandenbosch and Ligtenberg 2017; Daalmans Cunningham and Van Ommen 2016; Garcia Lopez and Gaona 2012).

Manley and Hair (2016) state that besides making new friends or new connections, the users of Tinder/Bumble use the applications to strengthen already built bonds with friends. Typically, females would use the applications in social settings with their friends and download the application and "play" on the application together. One quoted participant talked about how at a wedding she and her friends downloaded the application and used it to find some potential mates for the next night for each other (Manley and Hair 2016). Another female participant talked about how her male friends have taken her phone and downloaded the application and spoke on her behalf to other mates to make their night more amusing (Manley and Hair 2016). A male participant in their study spoke about how he and his friends would use the application to compare pick-up lines with each other and/or compare "ugly" chicks and laugh with one another (Manley and Hair 2016).

Sumter et al. (2017) also identified with users a gratification of "ease of communication" that was sought while employing dating applications. This measurement within its scale reflected a psycho-social need (i.e., feelings of being more at ease making connections online than offline). It included statements such as online less shy than offline, online easier to open-up, it helps me to find friendships, etc. This psychosocial motivation matched findings that align with literature on the rich-get-richer perspective of online dating. It was reported that men were more likely to like the ease of communication than women, which again aligned with prior research that indicated that more men consider online communication an easier way to meet new people and potential partners than women (Sumter Vandenbosch and Ligtenberg 2017).

Excitement

Another characteristic that is prominent in millennial research is that this generation seeks to be entertained and wants new adventures. Researchers suggest that in the work culture, to keep millennials entertained, management should focus on the different perks and entertainment packages offered versus health packages. This generation cares more about the free happy hour every Friday than lower health premiums (Lass and Lindenberger 2016). This is because millennials put friends and their lifestyles above work and typically have stronger relationships with their parents and stay rooted in their youthful characteristics. This is relevant in their motivations for using dating applications sites, because if the site was mundane and did not provide any enjoyment, it would not have attracted the participants to the medium. It also taps into participants' lifestyles of amusement, since they are able to see how their friends perceive and use the application and apply that information to their own usage. Online dating applications make life not so mundane for individuals and cater to the entertaining lifestyles that are important for this generation.

Manley and Hair (2016) stated that majority of their focus group participants first heard of Tinder/Bumble because of their friends and the funny stories they would tell about their experiences on the platforms. They even stated that some of their participants talked about just having the applications for joking purposes, and to see who they knew on the platform to swipe and make a joke out of it (Manley and Hair 2016). One participant stated that they got the application just for entertainment purposes and to see what type of responses they would get (Manley and Hair 2016). Daalmans et al. (2016) stated one gratification sought by its participants within its focus group was also entertainment. These researchers stated Tinder was seen by a large part of the respondents as a "swipe-game." They also reported users used dating applications to prevent boredom, to encounter acquaintances, to have free contact with people, and to judge people of the opposite sex. The functionality of Tinder allowed for users to sit at the DMV and swipe away their boredom and to still be engaged in something exciting like dating, which can't necessarily be done at the DMV.

Sumter et al.'s (2017) quantitative survey echoed this idea of excitement and entertainment found within new media dating applications with its measurement statements (i.e., because it is exciting, and for the kick of it). This idea of excitement and entertainment was not different across age or gender, which is probably because users were interested in using the application because of its popularity and less interested in its functionality (Sumter Vandenbosch and Ligtenberg 2017). This study did indicate that those with higher levels of sensation-seeking gratifications were correlated with seeking to use the Internet or dating applications to find someone to have sex with. Thus, it is understandable that users (i.e., millennials) that have this uncontrollable need for excitement and entertainment are also seeking short term relationships.

REFERENCES

Alsop, Ronald. 2014. "Instant Gratification & Its Dark Side." *Bucknell Magazine*. Accessed October 15 2016. http://www.bucknell.edu/communications/bucknell-magazine/instant-gratification-and-its-dark-side.html.

Beckstrom, M., Manuel, J., and Nightingale, J. 2008. "The wired utility meets the wired generation." *Electric light and power*. Accessed October 15, 2016. http://www.elp.com/index/display/article-display/342495/articles/electric-light-power/volume-86/issue-5/news-analysis/the-wired-utility-meets-the-wired-generation.html.

Betters, E. 2015. "What's the point of Snapchat and how does it work?" *Pocket-Lint*. Accessed October 15 2016. http://www.pocket-lint.com/news/131313-what-s-the-point-of-snapchat-and-how-does-it-work.

Charrier, R. 2016. "Millennials and social media: It's more complicated than you think." *Social Media Today*. Accessed October 15, 2016. http://www.socialmediatoday.com/social-networks/millennials-and-social-media-its-more-complicated-you-think.

Cooper, R. 2012. "The millennial generation: Research review." *National Chamber Foundation*. Accessed October 15, 2016. https://www.uschamberfoundation.org/sites/default/files/article/foundation/MillennialGeneration.pdf.

Daalmans, S., Cunningham, C., and van Ommen, M. 2016. "Love at first swipe? Een kwalitatieve interviewstudie naar de motieven en doeleinden van gebruikers van de applicatie tinder." *Tijdschrift Voor Communicatiewetenschap*, 44(2): 134–49. (Translated).

Dainton, M., and Stokes, A. 2015. "College students' romantic relationships on Facebook: Linking the gratification for maintenance to Facebook maintenance activity and the experience of jealousy." *Communication Quarterly* 63(4): 365–83. doi:10.1080/01463373.2015.1058283.

Daly, Annie. 2015. "Generation Validation: Why Everyone Just Wants To Be Liked." *ELLE*. Accessed October 15, 2016. http://www.elle.com/life-love/a14618/generation-validation/.

Flynn, K. 2015. "How Many People Are On Tinder? Company Defends With 'Actual Data' In Vanity Fair Comeback." *IBT*. Accessed October 15 2016. http://www.ibtimes.com/how-many-people-are-tinder-company-defends-actual-data-vanity-fair-comeback-2050092

Frankel, T. 2015. "Whitney Wolfe, founder of dating app Bumble, has had quite the year. She just can't discuss parts of it." *The Washington Post*.

Fry, R., 2016. "Millennials overtake Baby Boomers as America's largest generation." *Pew Research Center*.

García Jiménez, A., Cruz López De Ayala Lopez, M., and Gaona Pisionero, C. 2012. "A vision of uses and gratifications applied to the study of internet use by adolescents." *Comunicación Y Sociedad*, 25(2): 231–54.

Gibson, L. A., and Sodeman, W. A. 2014. "Millennials and technology: Addressing the communication gap in education and practice." *Organization Development Journal*, 32: 63–75.

Hartman, J. L., and McCambridge, J. 2011. "Optimizing Millennials' Communication Styles." *Business Communication Quarterly* 74(1): 22–44. doi:10.1177/1080569910395564.

Hayes, R. A., Carr, C. T., and Wohn, D. Y. 2016. "One click, many meanings: Interpreting paralinguistic digital affordances in social media." *Journal Of Broadcasting & Electronic Media*, 60(1): 171–87. doi:10.1080/08838151.2015.1127248.

Ifinedo, P. 2016. "Applying uses and gratifications theory and social influence processes to understand students' pervasive adoption of social networking sites: Perspectives from the americas." *International Journal Of Information Management*, 36(2): 192–206. doi:10.1016/j.ijinfomgt.2015.11.007.

Katz, E., Blumler, J. G., and Gurevitch, M. 1974. "Utilization of Mass Communication by the Individual." In *The Uses of Mass Communications: Current Perspectives on Gratifications Research*, ed. J. G. Blumler and E. Katz, 19-32. Beverly Hills, CA: Sage.

Keller, M. 2013. "Social Media and Interpersonal Communication." *Social Work Today*, 13(10): 10.

Klass. T., Lindenberger. J. 2016. "Characteristics of Millennials in the Workplace." *Business Know How*.

Manley, Terri, and Richelle Hair. 2016. "Mating and Dating: Millennials' Use of Online Dating Applications." Paper presented at the annual conference for the National Commutation Association, Philadelphia, Pennsylvania, November 9–13.

Palmgreen, P. G., Wenner, L. A., and Rosengren, K. H. 1985. "Uses and gratifications research: The past 10 years." In *Uses and gratifications research: Current perspectives* By K. E. Rosengren, L. A. Wenner, and P. G. Palmgreen, 11–37. Beverly Hills: Sage.

Park, N., and Lee, S. 2014. "College students' motivations for facebook use and psychological outcomes." *Journal Of Broadcasting & Electronic Media*, 58(4): 601–20. doi:10.1080/08838151.2014.966355.

Quan-Haase, A., and A. L. Young. 2010. "Uses and Gratifications of Social Media: A Comparison of Facebook and Instant Messaging." *Bulletin of Science, Technology & Society* 30(5): 350–61. doi:10.1177/0270467610380009.

Rubin, A. M. 2009. "The uses-and-gratifications perspective on media effects." In *Media effects: Advances In theory and research, 3rd ed.*J. Bryant and M. B. Oliver, 165–84, New York: Routledge.

Smith, C. 2016. "By the Numbers: 37 Impressive tinder Statistics." *DMR Stats and Gadgets*.

Solomon, Micah. 2014. "2015 Is The Year Of The Millennial Customer: 5 Key Traits These 80 Million Consumers Share." *Forbes*. Accessed October 15 2016. http://www.forbes.com/sites/micahsolomon/2014/12/29/5-traits-that-define-the-80-million-millennial-customers-coming-your-way/#3b7228a92a81.

Sumter, S. R., Vandenbosch, L., and Ligtenberg, L. 2017. "Love me tinder: Untangling emerging adults' motivations for using the dating application tinder." *Telematics & Informatics*, 34(1): 67–78. doi:10.1016/j.tele.2016.04.009.

Sundar, S. S., and Limperos, A. M. 2013. "Uses and grats 2.0: New gratifications for new media." *Journal Of Broadcasting & Electronic Media*, 57(4): 504–25. doi:10.1080/08838151.2013.845827.

Tyler, Kathryn. 2008. "Generation Gaps." *SHRM*. Accessed October 15 2016. https://www.shrm.org/hr-today/news/hr-magazine/pages/1training agenda.aspx.

Van der Wurff, R. 2011. "Are news media substitutes? Gratifications, contents, and uses." *Journal of Media Economics*, 24(3): 139–57. doi:10.1080/08997764.2011.601974.

FIVE

Revisiting the Investment Model of Relationships in Light of Technologically Mediated Communication

Jayson L. Dibble

The most important relationship behavior is the decision to stay in the relationship or to leave it (Le and Agnew 2003). Thus, understanding people's commitment to their relationships is paramount in relationship research. Since its inception, Rusbult's (1980) investment model of relationships has been a workhorse that enabled relationship researchers to account for the commitment felt by relational partners and thus predict the likelihood that certain relationships would endure. And metaanalysis reveals that the investment model has fared well under widespread testing (e.g., Le and Agnew 2003).

At the same time, the investment model emerged during a time before cell phones, text messaging, and electronic mail (e-mail), to say nothing of social networking platforms like Facebook or computer-based dating platforms like Match.com, Tinder, or Grindr. Social media and similar technologies have become embedded in the current fabric of the culture and in many ways have influenced the norms and expectations associated with romantic/sexual relationships, dating, and relating (e.g., Clemens, Atkin, and Krishnan 2015; Ellison, Heino, and Gibbs 2006; Valkenburg and Peter 2007). For example, the social networking site Facebook.com facilitates the amassing of hundreds if not thousands of contacts to include strangers, acquaintances, family members, current romantic partners, past romantic/sexual partners, romantic/sexual prospects, and so on. Prior to electronic social mediums, reaching out to a long-lost romantic flame required steps like remembering that person exists, locating their phone number, dialing that phone number, and having a synchronous voice conversation.

Moreover, electronically mediated communication now enables relationships to begin without any face-to-face contact whatever. This is best seen in what is commonly called online dating. The typical online dating platform enables subscribers to scan through the profiles of potential prospects, then establish contact with a prospect of interest by sending an electronic message. The prospect may return communication via another electronic message, and the entire body of communication between these two can remain electronic without ever requiring a synchronous oral conversation either by phone or face-to-face. If the two users continue to communicate in this way over weeks or months (or even years, as was the reported case for now-NFL star Manti Te'o and the person he once claimed to be a girlfriend [Gutman and Tienabeso 2013]), we might refer to this as an online relationship.

It is clear that the landscape of relationship communication has changed since the investment model was developed. Importantly, new research studies that focus on these new forms of technologically mediated communication might be spelling trouble for the ordinarily stalwart investment model. For example, the investment model's prediction of a negative relationship between one's perceived quality of relational alternatives and one's felt commitment to their romantic partner did not bear out when the communication with one's alternatives happened via Facebook or text messaging (Dibble and Drouin 2014; Dibble et al. 2015).

Even long-held theories can require revision from time to time and for any combination of at least three reasons. First, better measurement might show the prevailing view to be false (e.g., geocentrism fell away as better telescopes were developed and evidence mounted that the earth travels around the sun). Second, a theory may not do a good job of accounting for the available data. This seems to be the case for cues-based theories of deception which hold that liars emit leakage cues that observers can perceive and then use to detect the lie. However, decades of subsequent testing have yet to uncover a leakage cue general to all liars and which can be used to detect deception with reliability. As newer research showed, studies that claimed an effect for cues were offset by studies that failed to find an effect for cues, resulting in an average effect of virtually zero (Levine 2015). Failures of the cues-based approaches led some deception researchers to rethink their theories and develop newer theories that got ahead of the data instead of having to play catch-up. One example is Levine's (2014) truth default theory, born in part as an alternative to the cues-based approaches. Third, changes in culture and/ or technology might leave the theory ill-equipped to address the new reality. We apply this third possibility with regard to the investment

model of relationships. Researchers will always owe a large debt of gratitude to the investment model, but like geocentrism and cues-based theories of deception, the time may have come for theorists to rethink the
investment model and revise it to better account for the communication
that gets done electronically.

This chapter will focus on the investment model of relationships (Rusbult 1980) and its current state in light of new research on electronically
mediated communication in relationships. Specifically, I will review the
investment model in its original formulation. Next, I discuss the communication landscape now dominated by social media and other electronically mediated ways of connecting, especially in contrast to how the
landscape appeared when the investment model was developed. Then
I'll review studies that appear to raise questions for the investment model. This chapter concludes by suggesting some ways forward based on
extant research and theory.

THE INVESTMENT MODEL OF RELATIONSHIPS

The investment model (Rusbult 1980) was not the first theory to address
commitment in relationships. In fact, the investment model is a direct
descendant of an earlier theory called interdependence theory (Kelley
and Thibault 1978). Rooted in social exchange perspectives, which view
personal relationships as economies based on exchanges of resources,
interdependence theory predicts relationship satisfaction and commitment, defined as the psychological feeling of staying in the relationship.
Satisfaction is determined to the extent that the outcomes one receives
from their partner (i.e., rewards minus costs) exceed their personal comparison level, or what they personally believe they deserve in general
from a relationship partner. Commitment is predicted when the outcomes one receives exceed their perceived quality of alternatives to their
current relationship, that is, compared to the outcomes one could receive
if they were with a different partner or no partner at all.

Building on this approach, the investment model (Rusbult 1980) re-
uses the concepts of satisfaction, quality of alternatives, and commitment,
and retains their conceptual meanings as in interdependence theory (Kelley and Thibault 1978). And as with interdependence theory, the decision
to stay or leave a relationship is predicated on the commitment one feels
toward their partner. More specific to the investment model, commitment to one's partner depends on (1) satisfaction and (2) quality of alternatives, and Rusbult identified a third predictor of commitment: (3) investment size. Investments are tangible or intangible resources such as
time and effort, emotional investment, mutual social networks, the presence of children, and so on, that make it difficult for partners to exit the
relationship. The theory's general predictions can be summarized thus:

Satisfaction and investment are each positive determinants of commitment; quality of alternatives is a negative determinant of commitment; and in turn commitment is a positive determinant of the likelihood of staying in the relationship.

Meta-analytic work by Le and Agnew (2003) showed the predicted associations to be stable and sizable, and largely invariant to moderation. The winner in predicting commitment was satisfaction, followed by quality of alternatives and investment in a roughly two-way tie for second place. The investment model also seemed to perform best when applied to personal relationships and romantic relationships (as it was designed to explain). However, the model has since been applied to predict commitment in a variety of non-interpersonal settings, to include health care recipients' commitments to follow a medical regimen (Putnam et al. 1994), commitment to participating in musical activities (Koslowsky and Kluger 1986), and even players' commitment to multiplayer online games (Uysal 2016). The model showed stronger effects when applied to dating couples than when applied to married couples (Le and Agnew 2003), probably because variance is generally restricted in long-standing married couples who have likely reached their ceiling in satisfaction and their floor in quality of alternatives.

In short, the investment model has been a boon to relationship researchers for going on four decades. Although it was developed to account for commitment to relationships that were largely face-to-face in nature, it has been applied successfully to explain commitment to nonhuman targets. Interestingly, the model has not been applied widely to human relationships wherein the bulk, if not all, of the communication occurs electronically. In order to understand how the investment model might apply, let us first review what we know about the communication landscape as it now exists, with its prevalence of electronically mediated communication.

ELECTRONIC COMMUNICATION AND RELATIONSHIPS

Technological changes have produced a culture of people who spend increasing amounts of time communicating via electronic and computer-mediated technologies. For example, 92 percent of adults in the United States own a cell phone of some kind (Rainie and Zickuhr 2015), and almost two-thirds (64 percent) of Americans own a smartphone (Smith et al. 2015). This relatively new emphasis on computer-mediated communication channels differs from more traditional communication channels (e.g., telephone, face-to-face contact) in several ways. First, the emergence of mobile phones and Internet-enabled smartphones has created something of an "always on" culture, wherein people increasingly expect immediate connectivity to others regardless of their location or surroundings (West 2013). For example, nearly 90 percent of adults surveyed said they used their cell phones during the most recent social gathering they attended, and younger adults aged 18–29 reported a particularly high tolerance for mobile phone use in public and social settings (Rainie and Zickuhr 2015). In short, the proliferation of personal handheld electronic communication technologies seems to be coinciding with social norms that are becoming favorable to their use in an increasing number of social settings.

A second way that electronic- and computer-mediated communication is different from traditional channels is that—especially with social media platforms like Facebook and Twitter—users can amass of hundreds (in some cases, thousands) of contacts, and these contacts can be reached simultaneously with ease by an *individual* messenger. One benefit of this ability is that individuals can mass-message a large number of contacts at once, for example, to let friends and loved ones know they are safe during an emergency. In fact, Facebook.com has set up a "safety check" feature, which enabled people in Charlotte, North Carolina, to signal whether they were safe in the aftermath of race-related protests and violence (Hautala 2016). In a sense, individuals have become their own agents of mass communication, and scholars have described this as mass–personal communication (Love et al. 2013).

Third, social and other electronically mediated channels create communication that is also more private than ever before. In the past, talking on the telephone required not only actual *talking* (i.e., out loud) but also using one of a limited number of phones that was typically located in a common area such as the kitchen. Teenagers in general might complain they never get enough privacy from mom and dad, but teenagers in the days before cell phones who wished to chat on the phone with their romantic flames had little option but to risk being overheard by anyone who wandered by. The same conditions applied to people in committed romantic relationships who might wish to connect with an extra-relational romantic/sexual interest. This contrasts sharply with modern times, when direct messaging and individual handheld devices virtually eliminate the need for oral communication and prying ears/eyes. A related effect of new computerized modes of communication is that people tend to detach their online wanderings from their offline relationships (Parker and Wampler 2003), leading social media users to view certain socially mediated exchanges as having little to do with their face-to-face relationships. In a related vein, nearly half of the young adults surveyed aged 18–29 said they deliberately use their smartphones to avoid others around them (Smith et al. 2015). Intentionality aside, there seems to be something of a psychic separation of one's online communication from one's offline dealings.

Regarding romantic relationships specifically, people continue to do what they have always done: make contact, flirt, woo, and communicate with potential and current romantic partners. However, now these activities are increasingly happening via computer-mediated channels. For example, although only 15 percent of American adults report having used online dating sites or mobile dating apps, this figure is trending upward (Smith 2016). Moreover, online dating seems to be gaining acceptability as a means for locating romantic prospects. Whereas earlier many people might have believed that online daters are desperate, today only 16 percent of online daters and 24 percent of those who've never used online dating think this (Smith 2016). Along with this, sexting—sending sexually explicit pictures and/or messages via text message—is on the rise. Of adults surveyed, 9 percent (up from 6 percent in 2012) have sent a sext message to someone else, and 20 percent of cell phone owners have received a sext from someone they know (Lenhart, Duggan, and Smith 2014). Finally, more and more teenagers are turning to social networking sites to locate romantic prospects. At least half of the teens surveyed said they signaled their romantic interest in another person by "friending" that person on a social media site like Facebook (Lenhart, Smith, and Anderson 2015). Teens also expressed their attractions by "liking," commenting, sharing something funny, making a music playlist, sending flirty or sexy pictures, or making videos to share—all through social media sites (Lenhart et al. 2015). Digital communication technologies are indeed ubiquitous, and their influence on personal and romantic relationships has become deeply rooted in the ways people go about the business of finding prospects, initiating contact with those prospects, and maintaining their relationships.

TROUBLING DATA

Whether it relates to the more private nature of the communication, the normalization of social media into people's lifestyles, a separation of online and offline, or something else, emerging research suggests that certain hypotheses generated in good faith under the investment model (Rusbult 1980) are not supported in situations where the relationship partners are using computer-mediated channels for the bulk of their communication. Although I do not believe this will be fatal to the investment model, to the extent that these studies signal an emerging trend, the time may be ripe to revise Rusbult's workhorse to accommodate the latest means by which people are relating to one another. This section focuses on the research that might be troublesome for the investment model.

Some colleagues and I launched a new area of study about back burners: potential sexual and/or romantic partners whom people communicate with in case their current relationship situation fails (Dibble and Drouin 2014; Dibble et al. 2015). Because a large number of people's communication with their back burners today happens electronically through text messaging and social media, we restricted our focus to back burners with whom people interacted using Facebook and/or text messaging (whichever channel they used most). We gave college students a definition of back burners, then asked them to report the number of contacts they had on their Facebook and/or text message contact lists whom they would consider back burners. We also measured whether or not the students were already in a committed relationship, and for those who were, we used Rusbult et al.'s (1998) well-established measures to assess their commitment to their current partner and their perceived quality of alternatives.

In the language of Rusbult's (1980) investment model, back burners should serve as a proxy for the quality of one's romantic alternatives, because by definition back burners are relationship alternatives. Moreover, the investment model stipulates that the quality of one's alternatives is a negative predictor of relational commitment. But would these predictions hold when the communication with one's back burners occurs over Facebook or text messaging? In the case of the former, we found that the number of back burners did correlate positively with the perceived quality of one's alternatives. And when using the Investment Model Scales (Rusbult et al. 1998), we also found that the students' self-reported quality of alternatives correlated negatively with commitment to their current partner, $r = -.46$, which is nearly identical to the estimate from meta-analysis ($r = -.48$; see Le and Agnew 2003). Score two hits so far for the investment model. However, when we tested our expectation that one's number of back burners would correlate (negatively) with commitment, we found rs close to zero (Dibble and Drouin 2014). We were puzzled by this finding, and we wondered whether it had anything to do with the computer-based channels through which the students were connecting to their back burners.

Other studies carry similar reports. A recent dissertation by West (2013) centered on relationship commitment and monitoring relational alternatives using Facebook. In line with our back burner research, West was interested in the extent to which people use social networking sites to seek out potential romantic partners, and whether this activity impacted commitment to their current partner. Straight to the point of this chapter, West noted (correctly) that most research on the investment model was done in the offline world, and he wondered whether the model's predictions would hold up in the face of online communication. Specifically, people may think about the quality of their alternatives differently depending on whether they are searching for these alternatives online or offline. And thinking about these alternatives differently may spell different effects on commitment to one's current partner. Experimenting on a sample of (non–college student) adults, West randomly assigned half of his participants either to look over the Facebook profiles of five friends with whom the participant would consider dating if single, or—in the control condition—to look over the Facebook pages of five organizations to which the participant was linked. Using the investment model, he predicted that those who were prompted to study their romantic alternatives on Facebook would show less commitment to their current partners. Although West found no relationship between the experimental condition and commitment to their current partner, he did find that people's self-reports of the extent to which they *generally* monitored alternatives on Facebook related to commitment to their partner.

Michelle Drouin, Daniel Miller, and I teamed up yet again to conduct a study that largely corroborated West's (2013) findings. We ran an experiment to determine whether priming people to notice relational and sexual alternatives (to their current partner) or simply generating those alternatives from memory would lead to worse relational outcomes (Drouin, Miller, and Dibble 2015). We instructed half of our participants to scan their Facebook friend lists and to estimate the number of Facebook friends they would (a) consider having a sexual relationship with if they were single, and (b) consider having a committed relationship with if they were single. The other half of the participants generated (a) and (b) from their memories alone. We also measured participants' satisfaction with and commitment to their current partner. To have a clean comparison, we included an offset third group of participants who completed the satisfaction and commitment measures without being prompted to think of their alternatives. Interestingly, commitment levels were no different between the groups who counted their alternatives using Facebook and those who didn't count their alternatives at all. However, participants who generated their lists of alternatives from memory showed lower commitment levels relative to the control group. The investment model (Rusbult 1980) would predict the latter. That is, thinking of high-quality alternatives from memory alone (i.e., offline) should associate with lower commitment. But the same prediction did not bear out when the alternatives were primed online. Thus, not only was Facebook not the villain in this scenario, but there seemed to be another snag for the investment model where the online situation was concerned.

Let us examine two final studies. First, Martins et al. (2016) specifically took on the task of separating face-to-face encounters from online ones in their study of infidelity in dating relationships. Specifically, they assessed two kinds of infidelity: emotional and physical/sexual, each over two modalities: face-to-face and online. These four combinations were tested against the investment model variables (Rusbult 1980) using the typical Investment Model Scale (Rusbult et al. 1998), and the usual predictions were made: Each of the four infidelity–modality combinations should be correlated such that the greater levels of each behavior should be associated with lower commitment, lower satisfaction, lower investment, and greater perceived quality of alternatives (i.e., 4 infidelity behaviors–modalities X 4 investment model variables). Of these sixteen individual associations, the data supported only nine. Moreover, consistent with what we've already seen, the only time commitment was implicated was in the situation of face-to-face (but not online) physical infidelity—and this effect held for women only. Second, in a study about online surveillance, i.e., using digital technologies to keep tabs on relational partners by spying or checking up on both their online and offline behaviors, Tokunaga (2015) used the investment model to reason that couples who were in dissatisfied, uncommitted, and unhealthy relationships would resort to negative relationship maintenance behaviors such as online surveillance more than would couples in otherwise healthy relationships. Thus, he predicted that commitment to one's partner (measured using Rusbult et al. 1998) would be negatively related to their online surveillance of their partner. The data did not support this hypothesis.

THE WAY FORWARD?

A central thread running through the bulk of the above studies is that they address relationships in the context of *computer-mediated communication*. Computers, smartphones, direct-messaging, and social networking apps have become status quo for connecting to others and for maintaining relationships, so we are right to expect that researchers will continue to examine the implications of these technologies for personal and romantic relationships. At the same time, whereas the investment model (Rusbult 1980) has reigned supreme when applied to face-to-face and other offline contexts, it seems to have trouble predicting commitment with its usual gusto when the communication is brought online.

As was the case with cues-based theories of deception detection, the time may have arrived to bring the investment model in for repairs, an update, a reboot, or an outright replacement. To put forth a fully realized replacement goes beyond the goal and scope of this chapter, and I am not certain that an outright replacement is necessary. On one hand, some of the investment model's "legs" seem to remain strong. In particular, the predictions involving satisfaction tend to be supported even in the online realm. And we should recall that—of satisfaction, quality of alternatives, and investment—satisfaction was the largest predictor of commitment anyway (Le and Agnew 2003). So maybe we don't need to throw out the baby with the bathwater. On the other hand, as pertains to the way people today communicate with each other using computer-mediated modes, the most glaring deficiency for the investment model seems to be the link between quality of alternatives and commitment. As we await further testing and theoretical refinement, scholars might consider the following ideas as guides.

First, we need more studies that intentionally probe the limits of the investment model with regard to electronically/computer-mediated communication ("online" communication). Specifically, online contexts need to be compared against appropriate offline contexts with the express goal of determining which of the investment model's predictions are problematic. Of the studies I reviewed here, Martins et al. (2016) came the closest, but their goal was more to shed light on extradyadic sexual and emotional involvement in online and offline contexts, and the investment model tests were secondary. Still, they were able to array sixteen different investment model predictions across both face-to-face and online modes. The studies that have extended the reach of the investment model into nonhuman contexts need not cease, but these should be augmented by more of a "return to testing" phase wherein more scrutiny is given to understanding how the investment model behaves with regard to human relational commitment in online contexts.

Second, researchers should look to what is already being written about differences between online and offline relational dynamics. West (2013) wrote about these a fair amount, and so did Michelle Drouin and I (e.g., Dibble and Drouin 2014). West addressed the alternative commitment tenet and suggested that people might think about their alternatives in the online arena in ways that are qualitatively different than they do in the offline arena. This seems reasonable based on the back burner research my colleagues and I have done. Smartphones and other handheld technologies have made communication with others more private than ever before, and using these technologies in public or other social spaces has become more acceptable and normalized. Add in the finding that people keep in touch with back burners whether or not they're already in a committed relationship (e.g., Dibble and Drouin 2014), and we might argue that the practice of maintaining back burners is fairly normal. So, if it's normal to keep back burners in general (even if people might outwardly reject the practice), and if technology makes communication with back burners so private, then people may very well compartmentalize their dealings with their back burners (i.e., thoughts, feelings, and behaviors) separately from their thoughts, feelings, and behaviors toward their committed relationship partners. This separation might be so strong that when completing a questionnaire asking about their commitment to a current partner, any impact of people's back burners does not register even when those back burners are recognized as relationship alternatives. As we already found, the number of back burners a person reported did not predict commitment to their current partner (Dibble and Drouin 2014), and commitment was not dented by reviewing their Facebook friends list for romantic/sexual prospects, but instead by generating those prospects from memory alone (Drouin et al. 2015). If the investment model worked as well in the online and offline environments, we would expect stronger relationships than we've seen between the various proxies for relationship alternatives (number of back burners, Facebook friends with whom people would consider dating if they were single, etc.) and commitment to a current partner.

The theory of hyperpersonal communication (Walther 1996) points to additional reasons that may contribute to a separation of the online from the offline, and it may be useful toward refining the investment model. For example, computer-mediated communication can be asynchronous, and people can take time to edit their words, select the most flattering photos, and construct a "best self" before they send the message. This contributes to an idealization of the target, because the target's unflattering qualities are not on display. High idealization may set up something of a fantasy mode in which people can go privately to communicate however they wish, and, importantly, that they don't have to share with their offline world. Furthermore, if people believe that their *computer-mediated* dealings with any romantic and/or sexual prospects count as "fantasy," then they might not associate these fantasy interactions with their commitment to their offline partner, all the while recognizing these prospects to be relational alternatives. This might explain the correlation we found between the number of back burners (*actual* relational alternatives) and a paper-and-pencil measure of perceived quality of alternatives, even though we found no association between number of back burners and commitment to the current partner.

Let me add a special acknowledgment. Astute readers might recall that Uysal (2016) employed the investment model to explain commitment in multiplayer *online* games. So why aren't we bringing these data to bear on the current section? Uysal was interested in the online gamers' commitment *to the game itself*, and not, for example, to the other players with whom they interacted online. In this sense, Uysal's study represents one of many where researchers have utilized Rusbult's (1980) investment model to predict commitment to things other than human relationship partners. Our intent in this chapter was to critique the investment model under the conditions in which it was developed—to predict commitment to a human relationship partner. Thus, although Uysal's study involved an online context, the target of the gamers' commitment made the study difficult to apply.

CONCLUSION

Of course, all of the ideas in the preceding section are speculative for the time being, and we must await new research to examine the investment model's (Rusbult 1980) ability to explain commitment to relationship partners in an environment of computer-mediated communication. There appear to be real empirical differences between the way the investment model performs in offline settings and how it performs when the communication is done electronically. This chapter is intended as a launching point for the important task of recruiting scholarship that revisits a massively influential relationship theory to bring it in line with communication via social media sites and other electronic channels.

REFERENCES

Clemens, Chris, David Atkin, and Archana Krishnan. 2015. "The Influence of Biological and Personality Traits on Gratifications Obtained through Online Dating Websites." *Computers in Human Behavior* 49: 120–29.

Dibble, Jayson L., and Michelle Drouin. 2014. "Using Modern Technology to Keep in Touch with Back Burners: An Investment Model Analysis." *Computers in Human Behavior* 34: 96–100.

Dibble, Jayson L., Michelle Drouin, Krystyna S. Aune, and Robert R. Boller. 2015. "Simmering on the Back Burner: Communication with and Disclosure of Relationship Alternatives." *Communication Quarterly* 63: 329–44.

Drouin, Michelle, Daniel A. Miller, and Jayson L. Dibble. 2015. "Facebook or Memory: Which Is the Real Threat to Your Relationship?" *Cyberpsychology, Behavior, and Social Networking* 18: 561–66.

Ellison, Nicole, Rebecca Heino, and Jennifer Gibbs. 2006. "Managing Impressions Online: Self-Presentation Processes in the Online Dating Environment." *Journal of Computer-Mediated Communication* 11: 415–41.

Gutman, Matt, and Seni Tienabeso. 2013. "Timeline of Manti Te'o Girlfriend Hoax Story." January 21. *ABC News*. Retrieved October 5, 2016, from http://abcnews.go.com/US/timeline-manti-teo-girlfriend-hoax-story/story?id=18268647.

Hautala, Laura. 2016. "Facebook activates safety check in Charlotte." September 22. *CNET blog*. Retrieved from https://www.cnet.com/news/facebook-activates-safety-check-in-charlotte/.

Kelley, H. H., and J. E. Thibault. 1978. *Interpersonal Relations: A Theory of Interdependence.* New York: Wiley.

Koslowsky, Meni, and Avraham Kluger. 1986. "Commitment to Participation in Musical Activities: An Extension and Application of the Investment Model." *Journal of Applied Social Psychology* 16: 831–44.

Lenhart, Amanda, Maeve Duggan, Andrew Perrin, Renee Stepler, Lee Rainie, and Kim Parker. 2015. "Teens, Social Media & Technology Overview 2015." Pew Research Center, Washington D.C. Retrieved October 4, 2016, from http://www.pewinternet.org/2015/04/09/teens-social-media-technology-2015/.

Lenhart, Amanda, Maeve Duggan, and Aaron Smith. 2014. "Couples, the Internet, and Social Media." Pew Research Center, Washington, D.C. Retrieved October 4, 2016, from http://www.pewinternet.org/2014/02/20/couples-the-internet-and-social-media-2/.

Lenhart, Amanda, Aaron Smith, and Monica Anderson. 2015. "Teens, Technology and Romantic Relationships." Pew Research Center, Washington, D.C. Retrieved October 4, 2016, from http://www.pewinternet.org/2015/10/01/teens-technology-and-romantic-relationships/.

Levine, Timothy R. 2014. "Truth-Default Theory (TDT): A Theory of Human Deception and Deception Detection." *Journal of Language and Social Psychology* 33: 378–92.

———. 2015. "Scientific Evidence and Cue Theories in Deception Research: Odd and Paradoxical Findings from Meta-Analysis and Primary Experiments." Paper presented at the annual meeting of the National Communication Association, Las Vegas, NV, November 21.

Love, Brad, Charee M. Thompson, Brittani Crook, and Erin Donovan-Kicken. 2013. "Work and 'Mass Personal' Communication as a Means of Navigating Nutrition and Exercise Concerns in an Online Cancer Community." *Journal of Medical Internet Research* 15(5): e102. doi:10.2196/jmir.2594.

Martins, Alexandra, Marco Pereira, Rita Andrade, Frank M. Dattilio, Isabel Narciso, and Maria C. Canavarro. 2016. "Infidelity in Dating Relationships: Gender-Specific Correlates of Face-to-Face and Online Extradyadic Involvement." *Archives of Sexual Behavior* 45: 193–205.

Putnam, Dana E., Jack W. Finney, Phillip L. Barkley, and Melanie J. Bonner. 1994. "Enhancing Commitment Improves Adherence to a Medical Regimen." *Journal of Consulting and Clinical Psychology* 62: 191–94.

Rainie, Lee, and Kathryn Zickuhr. 2015. "Americans' Views on Mobile Etiquette." Pew Research Center, Washington, D.C. Retrieved October 4, 2016, from http://www.pewinternet.org/2015/08/26/americans-views-on-mobile-etiquette/.

Smith, Aaron. 2016. "15% of American Adults Have Used Online Dating Sites or Mobile Dating Apps." Pew Research Center, Washington, D.C. Retrieved October 4, 2016, from http://www.pewinternet.org/2016/02/11/15-percent-of-american-adults-have-used-online-dating-sites-or-mobile-dating-apps/.

Smith, Aaron, Kyley McGeeney, Maeve Duggan, Lee Rainie, and Scott Keeter. 2015. "U.S. Smartphone Use in 2015." Pew Research Center, Washington, D.C. Retrieved October 4, 2016, from http://www.pewinternet.org/2015/04/01/us-smartphone-use-in-2015/.

Tokunaga, Robert S. 2016. "Interpersonal Surveillance over Social Network Sites: Applying a Theory of Negative Relational Maintenance and the Investment Model." *Journal of Social and Personal Relationships* 33: 171–90.

Uysal, Ahmet. 2016. "Commitment to Multiplayer Online Games: An Investment Model Approach." *Computers in Human Behavior* 61: 357–63.

Valkenburg, Patti M., and Jochen Peter. 2007. "Who Visits Online Dating Sites? Exploring Some Characteristics of Online Daters." *CyberPsychology & Behavior* 10: 849–52.

Walther, Joseph B. 1996. "Computer-Mediated Communication: Impersonal, Interpersonal, and Hyperpersonal Interaction." *Communication Research* 23: 3–43.

West, Adam R. 2013. "Relationship Commitment and Monitoring Alternatives Using Facebook in Unmarried Romantic Couples." PhD diss., The University of Texas at Austin.

II

Different Contexts and Variables

SIX

Male Same-Sex Dating in the Digital-Mobile Age

Nathian Shae Rodriguez and Jennifer Huemmer

Public opinion on same-sex intimacy has evolved over the years with national governments echoing the sentiments of its citizens. The Netherlands was the first country to legalize same-sex marriage at a national level in 2000, and since then dozens of countries have followed suit, with Italy being the most recent, passing national legislature in May 2016 (Povoledo 2016). The United States joined the growing list of pro-equality countries in June 2015 and a recent national Pew poll shows 63 percent of Americans stating that homosexuality should be accepted by society (Fingerhut 2016). The poll also revealed that those who support same-sex marriage tend to be younger, more educated, and less religious.

The adoption of same-sex marriage and national polls are but a few ways in which we can measure public sentiment about gay romantic relationships. Regardless of how others feel about the issue, the global practice of men having romantic relationships and same-sex intimacy will continue as it always has since the earliest days of man (Halperin 1990; Richlin 1993; Roscoe and Murray 1997; Smith 1991). There are many societal factors that are internalized by individuals and influence same-sex romantic relationships. Political ideologies, religion, gender roles, race/ethnicity, class, and age, among others, play an important role in same-sex intimacy (Rupp 2001). This chapter will focus on the intersection of same-sex romance, digital-mobile technology, and masculinity.

GAY DATING APPS

The Internet has radically influenced the ways in which people in general have been able to search for potential romantic partners. For men who have sex with other men (MSM), the Internet has provided a space for communication and interaction, away from the inauspicious judgment of others who frowned upon same-sex intimacy. As technology progressed, the Internet was made mobile through the integration of Wi-FI and smartphones. Thus, enabling MSM to communicate with others as they moved about via mobile applications. Referred to as geosocial networking apps (GSNs), these apps can only be accessed via smartphones and show others in nearby proximity to the user (Blackwell and Birnholtz 2014). Users are able to meet other users in a digital, online space and are then able to meet in person, in a physical space, as a result transcending the boundaries between virtual and real-world (Bumgarner 2013).

These apps serve as a modern matchmaker of sorts, forging and fostering romantic relationships (Quiroz 2013). At the time of this writing, there are more than fifty apps available to download for gay, bisexual, and bi-curious men. Among the most popular are Grindr, Bristlr, SCRUFF, GuySpy, Mr X, GROWLr, Hornet, BoyAhoy, Jack'd, u2nite, and Wapo (Mathews 2016). Users of these apps must create a profile in which they upload a picture, select predetermined physical categories, and describe characteristics of both themselves and their desired partners. It is a form of advertisement of sorts that can, arguably, promote a culture of superficiality and indulgence (Freeman 2014).

Previous research has found MSM-focused apps to be used primarily for fostering relationships (Blackwell, Birnholtz, and Abbott 2014; Dang, Cai, and Lang 2013). The types of relationships sought vary and are dependent upon user and context. Blackwell, et al. (2014) interviewed users of the gay dating app Grindr and found that users had different ideas about what the app was used for. For some it was a space for fostering conversation and friendships, whereas others saw it as a sexualized space to meet potential sexual partners. One common contention among both camps of users was that the complex intersection of virtual and physical spaces affected how the users presented themselves to others. The user is able to present himself in one manner in the physical space in which he uses the app, and in another way on the virtual space where only users who were logged in to the social app could see him. He has two audiences, and depending on the combination of physical space and other uses online, the user's behavior and impressions of others is contextual.

More recent research has looked at the effect of user profiles on other users (Miller and Behm-Morawitz 2016; Yeo and Fung 2016). The use of femmephobic language on the profiles of individuals utilizing mobile dating apps has been found to negatively impact others' perceptions of the user (Miller and Behm-Morawitz 2016). In fact, femmephobic text impacted the intelligence, sexual confidence, dateability, and desire to meet the users offline for friendship. What was not affected was the desire to meet for sex. In a study on Japanese MSM, the use of photos highlighting physical appearance gave the perception that an individual was looking for a causal sexual encounter, rather than forming friendships or long-term romances (Yeo and Fung, 2016). This ultimately left other users frustrated and affected the perceived quality and satisfaction of using the app.

ISSUES OF MASCULINITY

Gender is not an inherent trait, but an "accomplishment" that results from correctly "doing" the actions and interactions that society deems normative and acceptable for that gender category (West and Zimmerman 1987, 126). Specifically, West and Zimmerman argue, "Doing gender involves a complex of socially guided perceptual, interactional, and micropolitical activities that cast particular pursuits as expressions of masculine and feminine 'natures'" (126). Sexual interaction, particularly heterosexual sex, is one of the most readily identifiable "pursuits" of culturally acceptable masculinity (Connell 2005). As such, scholars have, at times, presumed that society's increasing acceptance of homosexuality indicates a decreasing restriction on socially acceptable expressions of masculinity (Anderson 2015). However, Connell (1992) cautions scholars not to conflate gender with sexuality because, "In our culture, men who have sex with men are generally oppressed, but they are not definitively excluded from masculinity" (737). In line with Connell's (1992) argument, scholars have examined the way gay men negotiate their gender identities and sexual identities in online environments.

Because it cannot be assumed that gay males are somehow insulated from the culturally constructed standards of masculinity, scholars like Ward (2008) and Rodriguez, Huemmer, and Blumell (2016) contextualize their studies of mediated gay male interactions within the broader social framework of gender. Connell's (1996) theory of hegemonic masculinity argues that the overaching social structure of gender positions males as dominate and females as subordinate. Although the expectations for "doing" masculinity vary across cultures, locations, and moments in time, masculinity's most enduring quality is that it must be distinguished from the routine patterns of "doing" femininity (Connell 1992). Social media and online communities provide an interesting environment for exploring how gay men construct their masculine identities because these platforms are frequently used to build relationships and provide users an opportunity to construct visual representations of self (Siibak 2010).

Ward's (2008) study of the "Casual Encounters" section of Craigslist did, in fact, indicate that the men who used this space to seek out sex with other men frequently pulled from "hetero-masculine archetypes" to establish their masculine identities. Specifically, men seeking sex with men on Craigslist used misogynistic and homophobic language in many of their advertisements. Rodriguez, Huemmer, and Blumell's (2016) analysis of gay dating app user profile content developed the term "mascing" as a way of conceptualizing the homophobic and mysoginistic presentations of masculinity that manifest in the self-presentations of men seeking sex with men. The authors define mascing as "a form of policing that reinforces a masculine elite within the gay dating app community, an elite that is predominately white, young, fit, and healthy" (260). This is further supported by Reynolds' (2015) analysis of the Craigslist advertisement forums of "straight men seeking homosexual sex," which found that the men often highlighted their heterosexuality and used phrases like "male bonding" to solicit sex with other men (213). Clarkson (2007) argues that, by presenting a gay male identity that mirrors the dominant and aggressive ideal of hegemonic masculinity, the men's mediated identities are subordinating women and "non-straight-acting men" and, ultimately, reinforcing the patriarchal gender hierarchy (197).

The Body

The body is, essentially, the tool individuals use to construct gender through action, interaction, and self-presentation (Connell, 1996). Scholars therefore recognize that the current "ideal" of Western masculinity incorporates sexuality as well as race and physique. In 2005, Eng et al. put forth a rallying cry for queer theorists to include a more holistic approach to queer theory that examined not only sexuality but gender, socioeconomic status, nationality, and religion (4). West (2014) also argues for an examination of citizenship as a site for negotiating both normalcy and equality. In fact, West (2014) rebukes queer theorists' tendencies to reject citizenship as normalizing and therefore unproductive and suggests that, instead of ignoring the role of citizenship, scholars must examine how citizenship is performed as a way of exercising agency.

Ferguson (2005) furthers the arguments put forth by Eng et al. (2005) and West (2014) through discussions of the implications of heteronormativity and race on the construction of standardized national citizenship. In his article "Race-ing Homonormativity," Ferguson (2005) argues that, in modern Western culture, gay and lesbian identities are already institutionalized as a "new category of normativity" (59). To achieve this normativity, discussions of sex were relegated to the private sector, while the gay and lesbian movement appealed to other normative standards of American citizenship, particularly those of being white and having middle class values. Ferguson (2005) claims that representations of gay men rarely address sexual object choice in order to present the appearance of cohesive American citizenship that is often established through displays of racial bias.

The white male body is often put forth as the standard of "ideal" U.S. masculinity (Connell 1992). The perception that a white male body is more greatly esteemed than a non-white male body is a common cultural construction of gender, and as such, this construction is perpetuated by men who have sex with women and men who have sex with men. For example, Ward's (2008) study of the Craigslist "Casual Encounters" community of men who have sex with men revealed that not only do men use homophobic and mysoginistic language to establish a type of masculine dominance, but they also use images, language, and style choices to construct identities as white men seeking sex with other white men. Ward (2008) argues that "despite the ways in which the emphasis on whiteness may be experienced as the absence of racial fetish, the erotic culture of 'Casual Encounters' was rife with white fetishism" (429). Rodriguez, Huemmer, and Blumell's (2016) study of gay dating application profiles found that not only is racial bias evident in the users' profiles, but that many of the gay dating applications included settings that allowed the user to block members of other racial categories from even viewing their profile.

Muscularity and able-bodiedness are also important characteristics of the "ideal" male body because they represent the power, athleticism, and virility that ensure a man's "right to rule" (Connell 2005). Social networking sites provide a particularly useful framework for examining the body as a tool for constructing male identities because these sites provide users with the ability to present the self through imagery (Siibak 2010). Siibak's (2010) analysis of male profiles on an Estonian social networking site revealed that user profiles highlight the male body through images that depict the entire body or the upper half of the body. The fixation with muscular male bodies is also found among the gay male community.

Levesque and Vichesky (2006) attempt to explain the preoccupation with muscularity, stating, "Within the gay community, muscularity may be an important signal of health, which may be especially important as the community deals with the impact of HIV/AIDS" (46). The Bear movement in the gay community provides a useful illustration of how masculinity is defined and expressed at the site of the body, much in the same way that it is constructed among heteronormative communities (Hennen 2005). The Bear movement is rooted in the "appeal of the husky man" that hearkens back to the more traditional notions of the "natural," outdoorsy man's man (Hennen 2005, 25). Not only do gay men desire to have a muscular body (Levesque and Vichesky 2006), but Rodriguez, Huemmer, and Blumell's (2016) study of user profiles found that men use phrases like, "looking for muscular, masculine guy" to indicate their desire to find a muscular male partner. These studies illustrate that, while men who have sex with men may desire a sexual object choice that is inconsistent with the tenets of hegemonic masculinity, the emphasis on whiteness, virility, and muscularity mirrors many of the hegemonic masculine standards.

Health and Risk

As mentioned above, while MSM-focused apps are utilized for a multitude of reasons, such as companionship, friendship, romantic relations, and casual sexual "hookups" (Holman and Sillars 2012; Roth 2015), more emphasis has been placed on the latter motivation. One reason is that these apps are convenient for immediate interactions. They reduce the time it takes to find potential partners by providing an instant and incessant pool of men (Freeman 2014). This convenience increases the chances of causal encounters among MSM.

There are many obvious health risks associated with using MSM-focused dating apps for anonymous sex (Holloway et al. 2013), and the majority of MSM are aware of them (Wilkerson et al. 2012). Users of these apps usually deal with HIV- and STI-status in one of two ways. For some users, communicating about their HIV status in a digital-mobile space eliminates the need to discuss the issue in person (Sheon and Crosby 2004). Personal characteristics, including health and well-being, are exchanged before meeting face-to-face, and physical interactions are premeditated. For other users, there is a preference to keep such issues private or unspoken. There is a risk associated with anonymous sex that, for some, is adventurous and indicative of being a "real man" (Sheon and Crosby 2004, 2116).

Both manners of approaching health and risk factors are directly related to masculinity. While the users want to engage in sexual intimacy, they also want to protect themselves and their physicality as described in the previous section. By being upfront about HIV and possible STDs, the user is ensuring his health while still accommodating his virility. For others, the possible risk is associated with going against the rules, an act of rebellion that proves masculinity to himself and others. The interjection of digital-mobile technology enables the users, regardless of approach, to achieve their goal of same-sex intimacy. The users negotiate encounters on the virtual space and then engage in contact in the physical space.

Anonymity

Because many MSM may not embody a gay identity, but still have sex with other men, there is a need for anonymity among the users. Sometimes referred to as remaining on the "down low," users demonstrate a reluctance to disclose their identity, possibly for fear of being labeled as gay (King and Hunter 2004). Partners are chosen based on how well they will help conceal one's sexual identity (McCune 2014). This discourse perpetuates the stigma of being gay as shameful and reinforces the stereotype that all gay men are sexually promiscuous (Freeman, 2014).

A recent study found sex-seeking on gay dating apps to be more intensified for males who were either more confused about their sexuality or were less "out" in society (Chan 2016). There has also been evidence to show that MSM who identity as heterosexual mask their identity online and avoid offline gay venues (Lemke 2016). These individuals use gay mobile dating apps to instigate sexual encounters in physical spaces as often and as quickly as MSM who are out and open.

Mobile dating apps are particularly suited to foster anonymity. The technology of the app allows users to either upload photos or leave their profiles blank. Profile pictures can be faceless, headless, or a picture of someone completely different from themselves. In a study conducted by Fitzpatrick, Birnholtz, and Brubaker (2015), out of 25,365 profiles from Grindr users, roughly 69 percent depicted the user's face, 18 percent displayed torsos only, 4 percent included other body parts, and 10 percent were images that weren't even human. Furthermore, the app allows users to still utilize the app without uploading a picture or completing any descriptive information. Blank profiles flood a majority of gay mobile dating apps.

FUTURE TRENDS AND CONCLUSION

Public opinion and public policy regarding the LGBTQ community have changed drastically in the United States and across the globe in the last decade (Fingerhut 2016). As local, national, and global representations and discussions of men who have sex with men change, a growing body of academic scholarship has emerged to explore the role of technology and digital space in MSM relationships. Scholarship on MSM in digital spaces reveals that presentations of masculine identity and sexuality on gay dating apps are complex, at times resisting and at other times incorporating common cultural templates of gender and sexuality. Gay dating apps provide a site for scholars to explore presentations of identity, masculinity, and the body among MSM, but there is a growing need for scholarship that explores presentations of masculinity, identity, body, and health among other communities and across a range of diverse digital spaces.

It is only recently that scholars have started to focus less on the elements that dichotomize men who have sex with men from men who have sex with women, and more on the cultural routines that are naturalized across varying communities (Ward 2008). Specifically, it is significant to investigate those elements in digital-mobile spaces such as MSM-focused apps. More research is also needed that focuses on the more subversive cultural constructions that often seem "natural" and therefore invisible to add to the body of literature that focuses more exclusively on the manifestation of difference.

Furthermore, there is a need for scholarship that considers the various intersections of identity including race, sexuality, gender, socioeconomic status, etc., as they occur in the lived experiences of men who have sex with men (Ward 2008). When considered in a digital-mobile space, these intersections may be heavily influenced by geopolitics. The virtual and the physical are intertwined, providing a more complex system of interactions than other social media that are primarily virtual in their use and application.

REFERENCES

Alvear, Mike. 2015. "83 Percent of Gay Men Have Sent a Dick Pic on Dating Apps, Says Survey." *Huffington Post*, March 18. Accessed May 12, 2016. http://www.huffingtonpost.com/mike-alvear/83-percent-of-gay-men-send-dick-pics-on-dating-apps-says-survey_b_6893316.html.

Anderson, Eric. 2015. "Assessing the Sociology of Sport: On Changing Masculinities and Homophobia." *International Review for the Sociology of Sport* 50 (4–5): 363–67.

Blackwell, Courtney, Jeremy Birnholtz, and Charles Abbott. 2014. "Seeing and Being Seen: Co-situation and Impression Formation Using Grindr, a Location-Aware Gay Dating App. *New Media & Society* 17 (7): 1117–36. doi: 10.1177/1461444814521595.

Bumgarner, Brett. 2013 "Mobilizing the gay bar: Grindr and the layering of spatial context." In *Conference of the International Communication Association, London, UK,* 17–21.

Bruchey, Stuart. 1996. *The Elderly in America.* New York: Garland Press.

Chan, Lik Sam. "The Role of Gay Identity Confusion and Outness in Sex-Seeking on Mobile Dating Apps Among Men Who Have Sex With Men: A Conditional Process Analysis." *Journal of Homosexuality.* doi.org/10.1080/00918369.2016.1196990.

Chesebro, James W. 2001. "Gender, masculinities, identities, and interpersonal relationship systems: Men in general and gay men in particular." In *Women and Men Communicating: Challenges and Changes,* edited by L. P. Arliss and D. J. Borisoff, 33–64. Long Grove: Wavel and Press.

Clarkson, Jay. 2006. "'Everyday Joe' versus "'Pissy, Bitchy, Queens': Gay Masculinity on Straightacting.com." *The Journal of Men's Studies* 14 (2): 191–207.

Connell, Robert William. 1992. "A Very Straight Gay: Masculinity, Homosexual Experience, and the Dynamics of Gender." *American Sociological Review* 57, no. 6: 735–51.

———. 1995. *Masculinities: Knowledge, Power and Social Change.* Berkeley: University of California Press.

Dang, Hao, Stephanie Cai, and Xuanning Lang. 2013. "Location-based Gay Communication: An Empirical Study of Smartphone Gay Apps Use in Macau." *Social Science Research Network.* doi.org/10.2139/ssrn.2257253.

Demetriou, Demetrakis Z. 2001. "Connell's Concept of Hegemonic Masculinity: A Critique." *Theory and Society* 30, no. 3: 337–61.

Eguchi, Shinsuke. 2009. "Negotiating Hegemonic Masculinity: The Rhetorical Strategy of 'Straight-Acting' Among Gay Men." *Journal of Intercultural Communication Research* 38, no. 3: 193–209.

Eng, David L., Judith Halberstam, and Esteban Muñoz. 2005. "What's Queer About Queer Studies Now?" *Social Text* 23, no. 3/4: 1–17. Harvard.

Fejes, Fred. 2000. "Making a Gay Masculinity." *Critical Studies in Media Communication* 17, no. 1: 113–16.

Ferguson, Roderick A. 2005. "Race-ing homonormativity: Citizenship, sociology, and gay identity." In E. Patrick Johnson amd Mae G. Henderson (eds.), *Black Queer Studies: A Critical Anthology*. Durham, NC: Duke University Press, 52–67.

Fingerhut, Hannah. 2016. "Support Steady for Same-Sex Marriage and Acceptance of Homosexuality." *Pew Research Center*, May 12.

Fitzpatrick, Colin, Jeremy Birnholtz, and Jed R. Brubaker. 2015. "Social and Personal Disclosure in a Location-Based Real Time Dating App." In *System Sciences (HICSS)*, 2015 48th Hawaii International Conference, 1983–92. IEEE.

Freeman, Cody. 2014. "Hook-Up Apps Are Destroying Gay Youth Culture." *Time*, October 16. Accessed June 22, 2016. http://time.com/3510261/hook-up-apps-destroying-gay-relationships/.

Halperin, David, M. 1990. *One Hundred Years of Homosexuality and Other Essays on Greek Love*. New York: Routledge.

Hennen, Peter. 2005. "Bear Bodies, Bear Masculinity Recuperation, Resistance, or Retreat?" *Gender & Society* 19, no. 1: 25–43.

Holman, Amanda, and Alan Sillars. 2012. "Talk About 'Hooking Up': The Influence of College Student Social Networks on Nonrelationship Sex." *Health Communication* 27, no. 2: 205–216.

King, James. L., and Hunter, Karen. (2004). *On the Down Low: A Journey Into the Lives of "Straight" Black Men Who Sleep With Men*. New York: Harlem Moon.

Lemke, Richard, and Mathias Weber. 2016. "That Man Behind the Curtain: Investigating the Sexual Online Dating Behavior of Men Who Have Sex With Men but Hide Their Same-Sex Sexual Attraction in Offline Surroundings." *Journal of Homosexuality*. doi.org/10.1080/00918369.2016.1249735.

Levesque, Maurice J., and David R. Vichesky. 2006. "Raising the Bar on the Body Beautiful: An Analysis of the Body Image Concerns of Homosexual Men." *Body Image* 3, no. 1: 45–55.

Mathews, Hayley. 2016. "25 Best Gay Dating Apps." *Dating Advice, May 18*. Accessed September 5, 2016. http://www.datingadvice.com/online-dating/best-gay-dating-apps.

McCune Jr., Jeffrey Q. (2014). *Sexual Discretion: Black Masculinity and the Politics of Passing*. Chicago: University of Chicago Press.

Miller, Brandon, and Elizabeth Behm-Morawitz. 2016 "'Masculine Guys Only': The Effects of Femmephobic Mobile Dating Application Profiles on Partner Selection for Men Who Have Sex With Men." *Computers in Human Behavior*, no. 62: 176–85.

Ocampo, Anthony C. 2012. "Making Masculinity: Negotiations of Gender Presentation Among Latino Gay Men." *Latino Studies* 10, no. 4: 448–72. doi:10.1057/lst.2012.37.

Payne, Robert. 2007. "Str8acting." *Social Semiotics* 17, no. 4: 525–38.

Povoledo, Elisabetta. 2016. "Italy Approves Same-Sex Civil Unions." *The New York Times*, May 11. Accessed September 4, 2016. http://www.nytimes.com/2016/05/12/world/europe/italy-gay-same-sex-unions.html?_r=0.

Quiroz, Pamela Anne. 2013. "From Finding the Perfect Love Online to Satellite Dating and 'Loving-the-One-You're Near': A Look at Grindr, Skout, Plenty of Fish, Meet Moi, Zoosk and Assisted Serendipity." *Humanity & Society* 37, no. 2: 181–85.

Reynolds, Chelsea. 2015. "'I Am Super Straight and I Prefer You be Too': Constructions of Heterosexual Masculinity in Online Personal Ads for 'Straight' Men Seeking Sex with Men." *Journal of Communication Inquiry* 39, no. 3: 1–19. doi: 10.1177/0196859915575736.

Richlin, Amy. 1993. "Not Before Homosexuality: The Materiality of the Cinaedus and the Roman Law Against Love Between Men." *Journal of History of Sexuality* 3, no. 3: 523–73.

Roscoe, Will, and Stephen O. Murray. 1997. *Islamic Homosexualities: Culture, History, and Literature*. NYU Press.

Roth, Yoel. 2015. "'No Overly Suggestive Photos of Any Kind': Content Management and the Policing of Self in Gay Digital Communities." *Communication, Culture & Critique* 8, no. 3: 1–19.

Rupp, Leila J. 2001. "Toward a Global History of Same-Sex Sexuality." *Journal of the History of Sexuality* 10, no. 2: 287–302. Harvard.

Scott, D. Travers. 2011. "Contested Kicks: Sneakers and Gay Masculinity, 1964–2008." *Communication and Critical/Cultural Studies* 8, no. 2: 146–64.

Sheon, Nicolas, and G. Michael Crosby. 2004. "Ambivalent Tales of HIV Disclosure in San Francisco." *Social Science & Medicine* 58, no. 11: 2105–18.

Siibak, Andra. 2010. "Constructing Masculinity on a Social Networking Site: The Case-Study of Visual Self-Presentations of Young Men on the Profile Images of SNS Rate." *Young* 18, no. 4: 403–25.

Smith, Bruce, R. 1991. *Homosexual Desire in Shakespeare's England: A Cultural Poetics.* Chicago: University of Chicago Press.

Tiggemann, Marika, Yolanda Martins, and Alana Kirkbride. 2007. "Oh to be Lean and Muscular: Body Image Ideals in Gay and Heterosexual Men." *Psychology of Men & Masculinity* 8, no. 1: 15–24. doi:10.1037/1524-9220.8.1.15.

Ward, Jane. 2008. "Dude-Sex: White Masculinities and 'Authentic' Heterosexuality Among Dudes Who Have Sex with Dudes." *Sexualities* 11, no. 4: 414–34. doi:10.1177/1363460708091742.

West, Candace, and Don H. Zimmerman. 1987. "Doing Gender." *Gender & Society* 1, no. 2: 125–51.

West, Isaac. 2014. *Transforming Citizenships: Transgender Articulations of the Law.* New York, NY: New York University Press.

Wetherell, Margaret, and Nigel Edley. 1999. "Negotiating Hegemonic Masculinity: Imaginary Positions and Psycho-Discursive Practices." *Feminism & Psychology* 9, no. 3: 335–56.

Wilkerson, J. Michael, Derek J. Smolenski, Richard Morgan, and BR Simon Rosser. 2012. "Sexual Agreement Classifications for Gay and Bisexual Men and Implications for Harm-Reduction HIV Prevention." *Health Education & Behavior* 39, no. 3: 303–14.

Yeo, Tien Ee Dominic, and Tsz Hin Fung. 2016. "Relationships Form So Quickly That You Won't Cherish Them: Mobile Dating Apps and the Culture of Instantaneous Relationships." In Proceedings of the 7th 2016 International Conference on Social Media & Society: p. 2. ACM.

SEVEN

"Love Isn't Just for the Young"

*Examining the Online Dating Experiences
of Older Adults*

Derek R. Blackwell

INTRODUCTION

On his 1964 studio album *Softly, as I Leave You*, popular crooner Frank Sinatra proclaims, "Love isn't just for the young / It's for all who may wish upon a star / Love isn't just for the young / For true love doesn't ask how old you are." This sentiment has perhaps never been more true than in the present moment, as a combination of cultural and technological developments has dramatically reconfigured the dynamics of romantic relationships. According to a recent report from Match.com, people aged 50 and older are the company's fastest growing demographic, making up nearly one-third of the site's current user base (Match Fact Sheet 2014). Further, Grant Langston (n.d.), senior director at eHarmony, identifies users 55 and older as "the fastest growing demographic in *all* relationship-oriented sites." As a result, online dating companies have come to see older adults as a highly valuable target audience and have begun devoting increasing amounts of attention to this population through specialized services for older singles. SeniorPeopleMeet.com, one of the leading dating sites in this genre, reportedly saw a growth of 400 percent between 2009 and 2011 (New Website n.d.), while OurTime.com, another niche dating service for singles who are 50+, was recently ranked seventh on Experian Hitwise's list of the top online dating sites in the United States (Internet Dating Rankings 2014).

Despite this shift, few scholars have actually taken the time to examine the online dating experiences of older adults (Malta 2007). Perhaps this is unsurprising, since the dating behaviors of this age group were overlooked by the academic community long before they went online (McElhaney 1992), supporting Couldry's (2000) critique that among cultural researchers, "there has been an assumption that the experiences of the old are just not worth studying" (59). Nevertheless, Karlene Lukovitz (2007) of MediaPost's "Marketing Daily" suggests that being single later in life is becoming increasingly common, pointing out that over 40 percent of Americans 45 and older were single in 2007 and that single baby boomers age 45 to 54 are as active in online dating as 18- to 24-year-olds. Thus, for researchers to continue to overlook this population in studies of online dating, or dating in general for that matter, would be an unfortunate oversight. In an effort to promote a more inclusive approach to online dating research, this study will apply uses and gratifications theory to an analysis of an online discussion forum specially designed for older online daters. Because so little research is currently available on this issue, this study will focus on the fundamental questions of why and how older adults use online dating sites.

LITERATURE REVIEW

Uses and Gratifications of Online Dating

Once described by Elihu Katz (1959) as "the single, most promising direction for mass communication research" (2), the uses and gratifications (U&G) approach can be traced back to Herta Herzog's (1941) study of radio soap opera listeners, which investigated "what these programs mean to [listeners], why they listen, and what they do with what they hear" (66). With an emphasis on the audience (or in today's media environment, the *user*), U&G research acknowledges that different people use media for different reasons and with different results. As Katz, Gurevitch, and Haas (1973) explain, U&G research assumes that "the selection of media and content, and the uses to which they are put, are considerably influenced by [one's] social role and psychological predisposition" (1973, 165). Generally speaking, U&G studies tend to focus on two areas: (1) motives for media use, and (2) consequences of media use (Palmgreen, Wenner, and Rosengren 1985; Papacharissi 2008, 139). Scholars sometimes refer to these two areas as gratifications *sought* and gratifications *obtained*, respectively (Raacke and Bonds-Raacke 2008; Wenner 1982). Given the current study's focus on why and how the older adult audience makes use of the online dating medium, the U&G approach seems well suited. Further, Thomas Ruggiero (2000) argues that U&G "has always provided a cutting-edge theoretical approach in the initial stages of each new mass communications medium" (27), contending that U&G theory has become especially relevant with the rise of computer-mediated communication. Although this approach has been applied to a number of Internet-related topics, including online news consumption (Kaye and Johnson 2002), social networking (Dunne, Lawlor, and Rowley 2010), and online gaming (Wu, Wang, and Tsai 2010), U&G has yet to be incorporated into the growing body of scholarship on online dating.

While at the time of this writing there are no known studies that have directly applied the U&G framework to the study of online dating, there are several scholars who have explored questions of why and how people use online dating sites. In one attempt to explain people's tendencies to use online dating, Valkenburg and Peter (2007) tested two competing hypotheses: the social compensation hypothesis and the rich-get-richer hypothesis. According to the social compensation hypothesis, people use online dating to make up for the shortcomings that exist in their offline dating lives. From this perspective, one would expect online dating to be especially appealing to people who experience shyness, anxiety, or other social hang-ups that make relationship initiation more difficult. On the other hand, the rich-get-richer hypothesis predicts that online dating will attract those who already possess the necessary social skills for dating and are "low in dating anxiety" (Valkenburg and Peter 2007, 850). For these individuals, online dating serves as just another tool in their repertoire of resources for finding a romantic partner. After conducting an online survey of single Dutch Internet users, the authors found support for the rich-get-richer hypothesis, as individuals low in dating anxiety were found to be the most active online dating users. Similar findings were discovered by Kim, Kwon, and Lee (2009), who analyzed survey data from a large U.S. sample and concluded that "people who are sociable are more likely to use Internet dating services than are those who are less sociable" (447). The authors go on to highlight the fact that these findings stand in stark contrast to the once-popular stereotype of online daters as socially awkward loners.

Despite support for the rich-get-richer hypothesis, there are other studies in this area that seem to give credence to the social compensation hypothesis. Scharlott and Christ (1995), for example, surveyed 102 users of an early online dating service called Matchmaker and looked at how online dating might mitigate certain relationship-initiation barriers, including shyness. They found shyness to be a key variable in explaining how and why some respondents used the site, stating, "Apparently, many shy users employ Matchmaker to overcome inhibitions that may prevent them from initiating relationships in face-to-face settings" (199). In a more recent study, Whitty and Buchanan (2009) used an online survey to examine the personality traits associated with participation in online dating and speed dating. The authors measured shyness using a scale similar to that of Scharlott and Christ (1995), and in the end, they found that respondents with higher shyness scores were more likely to have tried online dating and more likely to report a likelihood of using online dating in the future (Whitty and Buchanan 2009). Both of these studies support Valkenburg and Peter's (2007) social compensation hypothesis in that online dating is conceived as a tool to counteract, or compensate for, the disadvantages that are often associated with shyness in offline dating situations.

At first glance, these mixed findings concerning social compensation and the rich-get-richer hypothesis may seem problematic; however, this conflict is easily resolved by applying the U&G framework. While Valkenburg and Peter (2007) position social compensation and rich-get-richer as "two opposing hypotheses" (849), focusing on which of the two helps to better explain online dating behavior, U&G theory recognizes that "a host of social and psychological factors mediate people's communication behavior" (Rubin 1994, 420). In other words, *both* hypotheses can be seen as valid explanations from the U&G perspective. Not only that, but it is highly likely that there are other explanations for online dating behavior beyond just these two. For example, while the studies mentioned thus far focus on *psychological* factors that might motivate online dating use (e.g., introversion, extroversion), they fail to address the *social* factors that may also be at work. One example of a social factor that could potentially serve as a motive for online dating is a lack of access to potential partners. Drawing on survey data from a nationally representative longitudinal survey, Rosenfeld and Thomas (2012) conclude that singles who are in a *thin market* are more likely to participate in online dating. The authors define a thin market as one in which "the cost of identifying multiple potential partners who meet minimum criteria may be large enough to present a barrier to relationship formation" (524). They identify gays, lesbians, and middle-aged heterosexuals as groups that face thin dating markets.[1]

One thing that the online dating studies mentioned in this section share in common is that in each case the authors operated from a pre-developed set of characteristics that they believed might explain user behavior. After attempting to predict the social and psychological factors associated with online dating, these authors then utilized surveys to test their predictions. Yet, because these studies relied on questionnaires specifically designed to test the authors' pre-formed hypotheses, they may have overlooked other important variables related to online dating behavior. In an effort to overcome this shortcoming and account for the broad range of factors that might motivate online dating use (as well as the broad range of uses individuals might have for online dating sites), this study will forgo the hypothesis testing of previous studies and instead adopt a more inductive approach. Casting predictions aside, this study will focus on organic discussions occurring on an Internet forum about online dating. By applying an inductive qualitative analysis to the postings on this forum, I hope to provide a rich description of the uses and gratifications of online dating that offers deeper insights than can be gleaned from a rudimentary list of predictors for online dating behavior.

In addition, the previous studies mentioned here have conceptualized the online dating audience in fairly broad terms, looking at online daters as one largely undifferentiated group. Because U&G theory states that media use is largely driven by the audience's "felt needs or desires" (Rubin 1994, 420), and different types of people have both different needs and different uses for the media (Katz, Gurevitch, and Haas 1973), it is only logical that the more diverse an audience is, the more diverse its uses and gratifications will be. Seeing as online daters are a relatively large and diverse population (Smith and Duggan 2013), attempts to capture the uses and gratifications of this audience might be made more feasible by focusing not on the entire group, but on a smaller subset of users. While there are many ways this population could be broken down, for this study I have chosen to focus on age. Given the very wide age ranges that have been included in previous studies (see Whitty and Buchanan 2009, and Kim, Kwon, and Lee 2009, for examples), I argue that it is important to consider the vast differences that might exist between the relationship goals of a teenager and a senior citizen. For this reason, I have chosen to focus on the less-represented end of the spectrum by studying a group that is often neglected by online dating researchers — older adults.

Online Dating and Older Adults

Interestingly, online dating exists at the intersection of two domains — the *online* (a realm dominated by new technologies and the Internet) and *dating* (the realm of sex and romance) — that are often associated with youth and young people. In fact, commonly deployed stereotypes of older adults as "technophobic and asexual" may seem to undermine the importance of the current study (Malta 2008, 6); however, a combination of recent social and cultural shifts has introduced two key developments — (1) a rise in Internet use by older adults and (2) a growing population of single older adults — that make online dating among this population an increasingly important subject for analysis.

Popular stereotypes suggest that most older adults are either resistant or inept in the area of new technologies (sometimes *both*), but there is a growing body of evidence on Internet use that seems to suggest otherwise. Research findings from the Pew Internet & American Life Project indicate that between 2000 and 2004 there was a 47 percent increase in the number of seniors (aged 65 and older) who used the Internet (Fox 2004). According to this study, wired seniors are "just as enthusiastic as younger users" in their online activities and will soon "transform the wired senior stereotype" by embracing this new technology. More recent Pew data show that older adults have also begun to embrace the more social aspects of the Web, as the use of social networking sites nearly doubled — from 22 percent to 42 percent — between 2009 and 2010 for Internet users aged 50 and older (Madden 2010). Similarly, a 2009 report revealed that women over 55 were the fastest-growing demographic group on Facebook, showing a 175.3 percent increase over a four-month period (Fastest Growing Demographic 2009). With a number of educational organizations devoted to helping this population become more tech-savvy (e.g., Older Adults Technology Services, Project GOAL), it looks as though the presence of older adults online will only continue to increase with time. The notion that older adults are not actively involved in dating has also been called into question in recent years. In 2014, data revealed that for the first time since 1976 (the year the government began tracking these statistics), more than half of the U.S. adult population was listed as single (Schwarz 2014). This suggests that, at the very least, the majority of adults in this country are *eligible* for dating. With regard to older adults specifically, Cohn and colleagues found that nearly 40 percent of Americans aged 45 and older were unmarried (Cohn et al. 2011). Moreover, previous scholars have projected a nationwide shift toward a larger population of older adults who are either divorced or have never been married than in times past (Cooney and Dunne 2001). Support for this prediction is grounded in a number of key changes that took place during the twentieth century. One such change is an increase in life expectancy. In 2012, life expectancy in the United States reached an all-time high of nearly seventy-nine years (Copeland 2014). This, coupled with the coming of age of the baby boomer generation, has contributed toward what some have labeled "the graying of America" as older adults begin to make up an increasingly larger percentage of the population (Nelson 2005, 218).

As stated earlier, the online dating industry has clearly taken notice of the older adult population; however, the body of research on older adults and online dating is still fairly limited. According to a recent Pew survey on dating and relationships in the digital age, approximately 13 percent of Internet users aged 45–54 and 8 percent of users aged 55–64 have flirted online (Smith and Duggan 2013). Moreover, at least two studies have found online dating use to increase with age (Stephure et al. 2009; Whitty and Buchanan 2009). In both of these examples, the authors speculate that their findings may be due to older adults' dissatisfaction and/or discomfort with more traditional dating methods; however, Stephure and colleagues (2009) note that the reasons for this discontent have yet to be determined. Whitty and Buchanan (2009) point out that in the first author's earlier work, "Many of the individuals she interviewed said they felt too old to go about dating via more traditional methods and had it not been for the internet they would not have considered even hoping to find romance again in their lives" (80).[2] With regard to *how* older adults use online dating sites, few notable differences have been identified between the online dating habits of older adults and those of the rest of the population. Malta (2007), for example, conducted a series of online interviews in order to test common stereotypes that older adults "don't do computers" and "don't do sex," and found that not only were older adults using the Internet to meet romantic partners, but that sex, cybersex, and even cyber-cheating were all a part of her participants' sets of experiences. Further, in an examination of partner preferences across the life span, Alterovitz and Mendelsohn (2009) found that the preferences of both genders were largely consistent across the four age groups analyzed in their study (20–34, 40–54, 60–74, and 75+). Nonetheless, a study by McIntosh and colleagues did yield a few interesting findings regarding the usage of online dating among older adults. These authors did a content analysis comparing 100 Match.com profiles of older adults with 100 profiles of younger adults and found that older adults were more selective about potential matches and willing to travel substantially farther to meet a potential partner (McIntosh et al. 2011).

The current study seeks to build on these previous works by drawing on actual discourse from the population of interest (older adults) that focuses on the topic of interest (online dating as an older adult). Methodologically, this study takes a slightly different approach than previous works by examining a collection of online postings written by older adult users of a popular dating website. Through a textual analysis of these postings, this study will apply a U&G approach in an effort to uncover the gratifications that older adults seek and obtain from online dating use. By investigating the answers that emerge when older adults discuss these issues in an undisturbed social setting, I hope to help broaden the body of knowledge on online dating to include a long-overlooked population whose increasing presence within the online dating realm is slowly changing the landscape of digital romance.

METHODOLOGY

Data for this study were collected from an online discussion forum hosted by the website Plenty of Fish, a free dating service that was recently ranked number one on the aforementioned Hitwise list of the top Internet dating sites in the United States (Internet Dating Rankings 2014). In addition to the site's popularity, Plenty of Fish is also one of the few widely used dating sites that features an active collection of online discussion forums that are openly accessible to the public. The forum analyzed in this study, titled "Dating Over 45," is dedicated to users 45 and older,[3] and according to the forum's rules, all postings must meet the following criteria: "The only valid topics permitted in this forum are for issues and discussion topics THAT ARE SPECIFIC and EXCLUSIVELY experienced by members, Ages 45 and Over. In Other Words— IF the topic or issue can be experienced by any age group, then it does NOT belong in this forum—post it to one of the other general forums" (Over 45 Forum n.d.). These guidelines make the discussion that takes place on this forum especially relevant as a source of data for this project since they require participants to focus exclusively on issues that are unique to older adults.

The use of forum postings as data stands in contrast to the few previous studies that have been done on older-adult online dating, which have relied on surveys, in-depth interviews, and analyses of online dating profiles. Unlike surveys and interviews, this study takes a more naturalistic approach, analyzing subjects in an unobtrusive manner that removes the risk of subjects adjusting their behavior due to the research context (Hammersley and Atkinson 1995). As Christine Hine argues, the Internet "provide[s] a naturally occurring field site for studying what people do while they are online unconstrained by experimental designs" (Hine 2000, 18). Further, by looking at interactions on online forums, as opposed to the one-way communication of user profiles, this study is able to capture actual conversations between users about their online dating experiences.

At the time that this research was conducted, Plenty of Fish's "Dating Over 45" forum contained an archive of approximately 1,725 conversational threads, most of which were several pages long. As stated earlier, the "Dating Over 45" forum moderator had established strict criteria in order to keep the conversations relevant to the target age group; however, during the analysis it quickly became apparent that not all postings on the forum were focused on online dating. Many of the threads discussed other types of relationship issues that were not directly related to the Internet (e.g., "Women that wear too much makeup at our age . . ."), whereas others were not about romantic relationships at all (e.g., "I'm 45 and going back to school at night to finish my Bachelor's"). That being the case, I created the following list of search terms in order to focus my analysis on the discussion threads that were most relevant to my research questions: *Internet, net, online, POF* (acronym for Plenty of Fish), *site, profile, message, meet, seeking,* and *too old.*[4] After examining the results from each of these searches, I was only able to identify twenty threads (1,597 comments in all) that directly addressed the topics of interest for this study. The bulk of my analysis revolves around an investigation of these threads.

After identifying my sample of discussion threads, I captured screenshots of all of the corresponding web pages, and engaged in a close reading of the content from each thread. All user screen names have been replaced with pseudonyms in an effort to protect the privacy of those mentioned.[5] Taking an inductive qualitative approach, I manually coded the content in these forum postings in an attempt to shed light on the gratifications sought (i.e., motivations for use) and the gratifications obtained (i.e., actual experiences) by older adults in the online dating realm.

FINDINGS

My analysis of the Plenty of Fish "Dating Over 45" forum suggests that online dating can serve at least three basic functions for older adults: (1) as a solution for a lack of offline dating opportunities, (2) as a virtual community that fosters a wide range of peer interactions, and (3) as a learning environment to facilitate one's re-emergence into the dating scene. Collectively, these findings help to extend Valkenburg and Peter's (2007) social compensation hypothesis, adding a new sociological dimension, and illustrate the important role discussion forums can play in shaping the online dating experience. The data presented below also help to support the notion that not only are there many different uses and gratifications for these services, but age plays an important role in shaping these uses and gratifications, as many informants perceived their relationship with online dating as uniquely different from that of younger users.

Online Dating as Social Solution

One notable pattern in the "Dating Over 45" forum was that users frequently commented on the lack of offline dating opportunities for people in their age group. Assorted versions of the question, "Where *else* could we go to meet people?" were raised by numerous users, suggesting that many saw the Internet as one of the few viable dating options for people their age. This mindset seemed to stem, in part, from a frustration with offline dating methods. In particular, venues such as bars and nightclubs were depicted as poor places for finding romantic partners. Many informants appeared to have given up on dating in these spaces long ago: "I don't do the bar scene and haven't for nearly 20 years" (Communique-chik, female). In some cases, this aversion to bars and nightclubs seemed to be due to feeling out of place in these settings because of age: "There are not many places where I live that the social scene incorporates all ages. I don't go to clubs because I would feel uncomfortable among all the young clubbers. When I lived in London this would not even be a consideration because there are all ages and types out clubbing. For some reason I feel here [in Ireland] that you are not allowed to be out when you reach a certain age, which of course is ridiculous" (ParaShades, female). Several other users stated that they avoided the bar scene but did not elaborate on why this was the case. This motivated me to expand my data search in an effort to identify additional explanations. Looking beyond the initial sample, I was able to locate one thread in the "Dating Over 45" forum specifically dedicated to the bar/nightclub issue. The comments therein seemed to suggest that some of this reluctance had to do with the types of people some forum users associated with the bar scene: "If you meet someone in the bar you have to ask yourself the question how often is she in the bar? How many men does she meet in the bars? Is alcohol a problem for her? If so, the drama that goes with addiction my friend . . . drugs and alcohol go hand in hand, are you up for that?" (Dabble2cute, female). As seen here, some users held negative associations with the bar and nightclub scene, linking it to morally questionable people and behaviors. Although the concerns expressed above are not automatically eliminated by taking one's search online, users like MachoGreen (male) expressed the belief that one of online dating's major advantages is that it presents users with a more desirable set of potential partners. He stated, "It's far easier to meet people with similar interests, goals and values in a site like this than trying to find someone at a bar." Thus, for some, the preference for online dating may derive from the belief that it increases the likelihood of finding a more compatible partner.

While there are certainly other offline social contexts for dating besides bars and nightclubs (e.g., recreational groups, social events/gatherings), the availability of these alternatives tends to be much greater for young people, especially around the college years (Paumgarten 2011). Typically, the number of offline dating opportunities tends to dwindle over one's lifetime, as peers begin to marry and singlehood becomes statistically less common.[6] Several informants in this study expressed an awareness of this tendency and cited it as one of the major factors that drove them to online dating. For these users, the problem wasn't just that there weren't enough places to go and find romantic partners but that there weren't enough potential partners available for people in their age range: "Those of us who are 40, 50+ something and single (for whatever reason) do have to realize that there just plain and simple are not as many single and available members of the opposite sex as there were when we were 20somethings" (DressyJoanne, female). Although research cited earlier in this paper indicates that the number of single older adults is actually on the rise (Cooney and Dunne 2001; Lukovitz 2007), the perception among forum users seemed to be that older adults were at a severe disadvantage when it came to finding a dating partner. As SteveWzy (male) stated, "In real life, most of us can go for days, weeks, or months without meeting someone who is single and available." Despite evidence that suggests a growing number of older adults are not only single but actively dating (Lukovitz 2007), GodzillaJack (male) stated, "To be 'single and looking' at 60 years old [is] probably not a natural condition." This lack of awareness about the proliferation of older singles seems to have created a dismal outlook for some older adults, making online dating a way out of a seemingly hopeless set of circumstances.

These complaints about fewer places to go in search of romantic partners and fewer potential partners to go around suggest that many informants felt they were faced with a "thin dating market" (Rosenfeld and
Thomas 2012, 524). In actuality, this problem might better be described as
the *perception* of a thin dating market, as research shows that nearly 40
percent of Americans in this age demographic are, in fact, single (Cohn et
al. 2011). Even so, this perception greatly influenced the gratifications
sought by the POF users in this study. In looking at why older adults use
online dating, these findings suggest that some are motivated by the
belief that their age places them in a thin dating market. One forum post
even went so far as to suggest that some older adults might not even use
online dating if they were a few years younger: "[I]n my way of thinking
you/me the over-45 group has more reason [to be online dating] MAYBE
than the young beautiful people. . . . I ask my friends all the time if they'd
be here in their 20's [and] most say no" (702Sunny, female). From this
perspective, it is easy to see why older adults have been so eager to
embrace online dating over the past few years.

Online Dating as Virtual Community

Although online dating services sometimes brand themselves as communities,[7] the reality is that most dating sites function as communities
only in the loosest sense of the word. Many of the perceived benefits of
virtual communities—their ability to facilitate shared experiences, collective action, and the exchange of social and emotional support—are largely absent from online dating sites due to structural differences in their
interface design. As Masden and Edwards (2015) explain, "The pairwise
style of interaction afforded by [dating] sites prevents a robust online
community from forming" (535). In other words, because online dating
interactions are typically private, one-on-one encounters, there is little to
no group conversation or group dynamic, making it difficult to foster a
true sense of community. However, for the group of older adults in this
study, Plenty of Fish seemed to be an exception, as these users often
expressed feelings of fellowship, camaraderie, and mutual support for
their fellow members. As was stated earlier, many of the topics addressed
in this discussion forum went far beyond online dating,[8] and it was often
through these broader discussions that the "Dating Over 45" forum was
able to facilitate such a communal feel.

A number of informants made mention of the fact that the POF community helped to fill a void that existed in their offline social lives. For
example, Alpha55 (female) stated, "This place gives me that adult con-
nection/conversation that I lack in my day to day life." Several others
acknowledged that the social gratifications of the site were just as valuable as the site's matchmaking capabilities (if not more so): "To tell you
the truth, right now I'm not even worried about dating. It's fun just to

chat with other singles" (MasterAshley). For some users, the platonic friendships formed on the site appeared to be an *unintended gratification*, one they did not anticipate or deliberately seek out. As one (presumably heterosexual) female user commented, "I would NEVER have thought that when coming on to this site, a majority of my mail would be coming from women. LOL, not in a million yrs." Again, this illustrates how the site had become much more to her than just a place to find dates. Considering the discussions the over-45 group had about a lack of offline contexts for meeting dating partners, it seems feasible that these individuals may be faced with a lack of offline opportunities to foster *friendships* with their single peers as well, making the perceived social gratifications of online dating even greater for many older adults.

One of the most compelling examples of how uses of POF went beyond matchmaking and into broader forms of community-building was a thread concerning a user who had unexpectedly died from a heart attack. The thread, started by a member who had offline connections with the man, was met with numerous messages of sympathy and emotional support, with some users even reminiscing about their online interactions with this individual. A post by WillPenguin (male) stated, "This kind of thread brings home a reality that all of us 'matures' have to face. We really don't know how long we have . . . or anybody else for that matter. I realize, that this is generally true for everybody, no matter what the age group . . . however, it does become more statistically probable above the 45-year mark." Another comment from this same thread revealed the extent to which connections made through the site could carry real-world significance for these users: "I'm so sorry to hear of this news! I've often thought of my POF friends when I've been preparing for a trip or hospital [visit] that kind of thing where you really never know what is gonna happen. I'd like to see the administrators here be given permission from family to email all the people such a member may have on his/her favs list and let them know they were valued in this person's life" (NiteBanker). Here we see an example of a user proposing what is arguably an *unintended use* of the site, one that would further expand its boundaries and could potentially add to its community dynamic.

Yet perhaps the most common form of social support exchanged by POF's "Over 45" group came in the form of encouraging one another in the pursuit of romantic partners. Through its presence alone, this group may help to reassure discouraged individuals that there are others out there who are facing similar challenges as single older adults. As one female user expressed, "Most of our friends are married or coupled so [we have] no single friends hanging around"; however, as members of this site, these users are given access not only to potential dates but to a pool of peers who are "in the same boat." The "Dating Over 45" discussion forum often served as a space where these users could both commiserate and encourage one another not to give up hope. For example, DandyXO (female) consoled a fellow POF member who had recently been rejected by a potential partner, stating "Well sweetie! Definitely was his loss and your absolute gain! [. . .] Don't take this to heart darlin'. Nothing wrong with you!" She followed up these words of encouragement by sharing a personal story of her own recent failed attempt at romance. Because adults in this demographic may have fewer single friends in their offline social networks, online dating could provide a unique opportunity for them to make new friends who can relate directly to the experience of searching for love at this stage in their life course.

Online Dating as Learning Environment

Finally, it appears that a site like Plenty of Fish may also serve as a learning tool for its older users. This educational function has several dimensions. First, a number of users discussed how online dating had helped them to re-enter the dating scene after many years of being out of practice. As AuthenticHeart (female) stated, "What online dating has done is help me with the transition into dating. It has helped me to discover what I'm really wanting and looking for, and what I don't want. [. . .] I've learned a lot about attitudes and what people think now—30 years is a long time to be out of the dating pool." This gratification seemed especially useful for recent divorcées like KnicksFantastic (male) who confessed, "After a 30 yr marriage, I SO wanted to find someone I could begin another long-term relationship with. I was single for the 1st time in 30+ yrs & it was VERY uncomfortable for me." In some cases, feelings of discomfort like the ones described here may be alleviated by a phenomenon known as the "online disinhibition effect." As Suler (2004) explains, the online disinhibition effect is a process in which people "loosen up, feel less restrained, and express themselves more openly" in the online realm (321). Thus, for some older online daters, this phenomenon may remove the anxieties of learning to date again and help for a smoother transition. The social learning concept of *observational modeling* may further help to explain this finding. As Bandura (1977) explains, "From observing others one forms an idea of how new behaviors are performed, and on later occasions this coded information serves as a guide for action" (22). In short, people often learn by watching others. Yet, for generations, romantic relationships have operated primarily in the private sphere, making it difficult to learn about dating in this way. This seems to have changed with the advent of online dating. As Suler (2004) later points out, one of the principal mechanisms behind the online disinhibition effect is the ability to be invisible: "When people visit web sites, message boards, and even some chat rooms, other people may not even know they are present at all" (322). As it applies to this study, the online dating realm has opened up new opportunities for one to be a "fly on the wall" for certain aspects of the dating process. Specifically, online

dating appears to have created a safe space where informants could readily observe their peers, pick up on current dating norms, and learn from
other single people in their age group about dating. AuthenticHeart's
aforementioned ability to "[learn] a lot about attitudes and what people
think now" is facilitated by this very principle, as the simple act of browsing user profiles can provide a wealth of information in this area. The
ability to view other people's profiles also creates new opportunities for
social comparison, as these users can measure themselves against "the
competition" in terms of what they have to offer. One male user, for
example, admitted to studying a set of male profiles that his female
friends had identified as appealing in order to make his own dating
strategies more effective. The ability to carefully analyze the dating and
courtship habits of a complete stranger—and to do so in such a discreet
manner—is, I would argue, a phenomenon that is unique to the online
dating realm.

Several POF users also took advantage of the site's forum feature to
ask questions and get advice to assist them in their search for partners.
Queries such as "Over 45 Men, How should we dress?" and "What do
women over 50 find desirable and undesirable in a man's profile?" were
quite common throughout the forum. Many users expressed their appreciation for the insights available on the forums with statements such as, "I
am however learning a lot from these forums about people's wants and
needs and certainly attitudes that will be invaluable in a couple of years
when I might feel the need for companionship from the opposite sex"
(ThinkCy). As was mentioned earlier, it is sometimes more difficult for
people in this age group to find other people their own age who are
single, so the ability to consult such a large number of them with so little
effort is understandably of great benefit. Further, these public conversations contribute to the body of knowledge and experience that is available to this community. As a result, invisible "lurkers" who visit the
forum but do not post can still benefit from the information being shared.

IMPLICATIONS

Social Compensation

One important contribution of this study is that it helps to extend
Valkenburg and Peter's (2007) social compensation hypothesis, the notion that people use online dating to make up for shortcomings in their
offline lives. Whereas Valkenburg and Peter discuss social compensation
in relation to psychological deficits (e.g., shyness, anxiety, etc.), the current study adds a sociological dimension to the concept, as online dating
was used to compensate for informants' structural position/circum-
stances. In particular, it was used to compensate for a lack of offline

dating opportunities, what Rosenfeld and Thomas (2012) call a "thin market" (524). In addition, it appears that many informants also used online dating to compensate for a lack of opportunities to foster friendships with single peers. Recalling the data presented earlier on the growing population of single older adults in the United States, the problem these informants identify as a lack of opportunities may be less about the *existence* of single older adults than it is the ability to *identify* them—a characteristic that is sometimes referred to as "legibility" (Curry, Phillips, and Regan 2004). Before online dating, the ability to assess whether a person was single was typically based on one's ability to successfully interpret a series of social cues—cues that may or may not be easily discernible (e.g., displays of affection toward a co-present other, presence of a wedding ring). Online dating sites simplify this process greatly by identifying the "open persons" in a given region who are interested in dating and available for interaction (Goffman 1963, 126). As a result, not only can single older adults have a heightened awareness of the fact that there really are "plenty of fish in the sea" who are in their age range, but the technology of online dating also allows them to connect with those "fish" relatively easily. As Shirky (2008) has argued, one of the biggest benefits of the Internet is that it makes it significantly easier for people to find each other. Because, apart from online dating, many of my informants did not know where to go to find each other, they wrongly assumed that single older adults were in short supply. As a result, I would argue that the *perceived* social compensation described by these informants differs from the *actual* social compensation that seemed to be taking place. While informants perceived online dating as compensating for their seemingly thin dating market, in reality, online dating was compensating for a dating market that simply lacked legibility.

Affordances of Online Discussion Forums

Another important contribution of this study is that, in addition to the methodological opportunities the POF forums open up for conducting studies like this one, discussion forums may also play a central role in shaping—and perhaps even enhancing—the online dating experience. Many of the gratifications derived by the users in the study—the giving and receiving of advice, the ability to commiserate during times of frustration, and the chance to share personal dating experiences—were largely facilitated by the existence of the forums. Not only are these forums useful to those that are active participants in the discussion, but they may also benefit an invisible population of people who read them but choose not to post. For older adult users, many of whom may have insecurities about the dating process (both on- and offline), these forums can provide vicarious experience to help ease the transition into the dating scene. This vicarious experience can ultimately help to increase these users' self-efficacy, as Bandura (1977) explains: "Seeing others perform threatening activities without adverse consequences can generate expectations in observers that they too will improve if they intensify and persist in their efforts. They persuade themselves that if others can do it, they should be able to achieve at least some improvement in performance."[9] Because the Plenty of Fish forums are fully public, even non-users can attain these vicarious experiences; thus, the forums might also serve as a kind of recruitment tool, enticing people to register for these services. Finally, the barriers Masden and Edwards (2015) describe as inhibiting community formation on most online dating sites appear to be reduced (if not removed) by discussion forums. The informants in this study demonstrated a collective cohesion that is not typically associated with online dating sites, and their ability to achieve this kind of group dynamic was thanks, in large part, to the online discussion forums. That being the case, online dating companies might consider incorporating this kind of interactive component on sites where it is not available, especially when targeting populations like older adults, who may be longing for more opportunities for peer interaction.

LIMITATIONS AND FUTURE RESEARCH

In considering the limitations of this study, one area that must be acknowledged is the use of online forum postings as data. As Wysocki and Childers (2011) rightfully point out, this kind of research is subject to a self-selection bias. Not only have the informants self-selected into Plenty of Fish, a site whose user base may differ systematically from that of other dating sites, but they are also part of a special subset of users on this site (participants in the online discussion forum), making it more difficult to generalize their experiences to the online dating community more broadly. Future studies can address these shortcomings by examining other dating websites and using other forms of data collection that allow for random sampling in order to capture a more representative pool of users. Another limitation of this study is that because it relies on naturalistic data, I was not able to probe areas of interest or influence the direction of the discussion in any way. Future studies should incorporate more direct forms of inquiry to further explore the themes identified here. In addition, any analysis of online behavior must take into account the potential gap between one's online self and one's "real world" self. As Hine (2000) explains, "People using text-based environments have often exploited the potential for representing themselves in ways quite different from their offline personae" (19). However, as Goffman's seminal work on social interaction suggests, the concept of social performance is not unique to the online realm, and the ability to present different versions of oneself to different audiences is an integral party of everyday life, even in face-to-face settings (Goffman 1959). Another important consideration is the fact that Plenty of Fish has an international user base, making it more difficult to draw conclusions about the extent to which the patterns observed in this study reflect an American context. Despite this shortcoming, Plenty of Fish is among the top dating sites in the United States, which suggests that American users should be well represented (Internet Dating Rankings 2014). The decision to choose the site for this study was based not only on its large American membership, but also on the fact that unlike many of its competitors, Plenty of Fish features online discussion forums—the rich data sources that ultimately made this study possible.

Finally, the parameters of the community analyzed—online daters ages 45 and older—are still relatively broad and subject to in-group variation. While the selection of this group helps begin to address a long overlooked population in this research area, the 45-and-up community is far from a monolith. Future studies should attempt to investigate the diversity of perspectives that may exist among older adult online daters. Not only could this population be broken down into more refined age categories, but other factors such as relationship status (e.g., divorced vs. never married) and sexual orientation are likely to play an important role in shaping the gratifications sought and obtained through online dating.

CONCLUSION

As the results of this study have shown, the search for romantic partnership in later adulthood can be a complicated endeavor. Fortunately, online dating services have become a new avenue to ease this process, opening up a wealth of new romantic opportunities for the older adult population. Making use of online dating tools may assist this group in overcoming some of the obstacles previously encountered in the offline dating realm in a manner that is easy, convenient, and more in line with their lifestyle. This may help to explain the significant growth in online dating use among this population in recent years. Ultimately, the subjects in this study seemed to be looking for many of the same things that their younger counterparts seek in online dating, just with a few added challenges. While in times past, singlehood beyond a certain age may have seemed like a fairly immutable condition, the Internet has, in some ways, leveled the playing field for older adults seeking romantic partnership. With the help of new technologies, love really isn't just for the young anymore.

NOTES

1. The authors operationalize "middle-aged" as individuals who are in their thirties and forties.

2. Original study presented as Monica Whitty, "Shopping for Love on the Internet: Men and Women's Experiences of Using an Australian Internet Dating Site," (presentation, International Communication Association Annual Conference, New Orleans, LA, May 27–31, 2004).

3. Although much of the earlier discussion in this paper is centered around the 50 and older demographic, Plenty of Fish does not have a 50 and older discussion forum. Of the two age-oriented forums available on Plenty of Fish, "Dating Over 30" and "Dating Over 45," the 45-and-older forum is the one that best captures the older adult population that is the focus of this study.

4. These search terms were created based on both my research questions and a preliminary overview of the forum's topics.

5. Pseudonyms were created using the username generator tool at http://namegenerators.org/username-generator/. In some cases, an informant's gender is also reported. This information was collected from user profiles; however, not all forum users chose to link their postings to a user profile.

6. A recent study based on data from the years 2006–2010 found that the median age at first marriage for women in the United States was 25.8, while for men it was slightly older, at 28.3. See Casey E. Copen et al., "First Marriages in the United States: Data from the 2006–2010 National Survey of Family Growth." *National Health Statistics Reports* 49 (2012).

7. Match.com, eHarmony, and OurTime.com each use the term "community" on their respective homepages to describe and promote their services.

8. See p. 10 for previous discussion.

9. See also Albert Bandura and Peter G. Barab, "Processes Governing Disinhibitory Effects through Symbolic Modeling." *Journal of Abnormal Psychology* 82 (1973): 1–9.

REFERENCES

Alterovitz, Sheyna Sears-Roberts, and Gerald A. Mendelsohn. 2009. "Partner Preferences Across the Life Span: Online Dating by Older Adults." *Psychology and Aging* 24, no. 2: 513–17.

Bandura, Albert. 1977. "Self-Efficacy: Toward a Unifying Theory of Behavioral Change." *Psychological Review* 84, no. 2: 191–215.

———. 1977. *Social Learning Theory*. Englewood Cliffs, NJ: Prentice Hall.

Bandura, Albert, and Peter G. Barab. 1973. "Processes Governing Disinhibitory Effects through Symbolic Modeling." *Journal of Abnormal Psychology* 82: 1–9.

Cohn, D'Vera, Jeffrey Passel, Wendy Wang, and Gretchen Livingston. 2011. "Barely Half of U.S. Adults Are Married—A Record Low." Pew Research Center Social & Demographic Trends. Retrieved from http://media.al.com/bn/other/Marriage-report-Pew-Research-Center-Dec-2011.pdf.

Cooney, Teresa M., and Kathleen Dunne. 2001. "Intimate Relationships in Later Life: Current Realities, Future Prospects." *Journal of Family Issues* 22, no. 7: 838–58.

Copeland, Larry. October 9, 2014. "Life Expectancy in the USA Hits a Record High." *USA Today*. Retrieved from http://www.usatoday.com/story/news/nation/2014/10/08/us-life-expectancy-hits-record-high/16874039/.

Copen, Casey E., Kimberly Daniels, Jonathan Vespa, and William D. Mosher. 2012. "First Marriages in the United States: Data from the 2006–2010 National Survey of Family Growth." *National Health Statistics Reports* 49.

Couldry, Nick. 2000. *Inside Culture: Re-imagining the Method of Cultural Studies*. London: SAGE.

Curry, Michael R., David J. Phillips, and Priscilla M. Regan. 2004. "Emergency Response Systems and the Creeping Legibility of People and Places." *The Information Society* 20, 357–69.

Dunne, Áine, Margaret-Anne Lawlor, and Jennifer Rowley. 2010. "Young People's Use of Online Social Networking Sites—A Uses and Gratifications Perspective." *Journal of Research in Interactive Marketing* 4, no. 1: 46–58.

"Fastest Growing Demographic on Facebook: Women Over 55." February 2, 2009. *Adweek Social Times*. Retrieved from http://www.adweek.com/socialtimes/fastest-growing-demographic-on-facebook-women-over-55/217037.

Fox, Susannah. 2004. "Older Americans and the Internet." Pew Internet & American Life Project, Retrieved from: http://www.pewinternet.org/~/media//Files/Reports/2004/PIP_Seniors_Online_2004.pdf.

Goffman, Erving. 1963. *Behavior in Public Places: Notes on the Social Organization of Gatherings*. New York: Free Press.

———. 1959. *The Presentation of Self in Everyday Life*. Garden City, NY: Doubleday.

Hammersley, Martyn, and Paul Atkinson. 1995. *Ethnography: Principles in Practice*. 3rd edition. New York: Routledge.

Herzog, Herta. 1941. "On Borrowed Experience." *Studies in Philosophy and Social Science* 11, no. 1: 65–95.

Hine, Christine M. 2000. *Virtual Ethnography*. London: SAGE.

"Internet Dating Rankings—U.S.A." May 6, 2014. *Online Personals Watch*, Accessed October 30, 2014. http://www.onlinepersonalswatch.com/news/internet_dating_rankings.html.

Katz, Elihu. 1959. "Mass Communications Research and the Study of Popular Culture: An Editorial Note on a Possible Future for This Journal." *Studies in Public Communication* 2: 1–6.

Katz, Elihu, Michael Gurevitch, and Hadassah Haas. 1973. "On the Use of the Mass Media for Important Things." *American Sociological Review* 38: 164–81.

Kaye, Barbara K., and Thomas J. Johnson. 2002. "Online and in the Know: Uses and Gratifications of the Web for Political Information." *Journal of Broadcasting & Electronic Media* 46, no. 1: 54–71.

Kim, Mikyoung, Kyoung-Nan Kwon, and Mira Lee. 2009. "Psychological Characteristics of Internet Dating Service Users: The Effect of Self-Esteem, Involvement, and Sociability on the Use of Internet Dating Services." *CyberPsychology & Behavior* 12, no. 4: 445–49.

Langston, Grant. n.d. "Nine Online Dating Myths for Seniors." *eHarmony Advice*. Accessed September 18, 2011. advice.eharmony.com/dating/nine-online-dating-myths-seniors.

Lukovitz, Karlene. May 23, 2007. "Packaged Facts: Marketers Missing the Boat on Mature Singles." *Marketing Daily*. http://www.mediapost.com/publications/article/60803/packaged-facts-marketers-missing-the-boat-on-matu.html.

Madden, Mary. August 27, 2010. "Older Adults and Social Media." Pew Internet & American Life Project. http://www.pewinternet.org/~/media//Files/Reports/2010/Pew%20Internet%20-%20Older%20Adults%20and%20Social%20Media.pdf.

Malta, Sue. 2008. "Intimacy and Older Adults: A Comparison Between Online and Offline Romantic Relationships." In *Re-imagining Sociology, Proceedings of the Annual Conference of the Australian Sociological Association*. Melbourne: TASA, https://www.tasa.org.au/wp-content/uploads/2011/01/Malta-Sue-Session-1.pdf.

———. 2007. "Love Actually! Older Adults and Their Romantic Internet Relationships." *Australian Journal of Emerging Technologies and Society* 5, no. 2: 84–102.

Masden, Christina, and W. Keith Edwards. 2015. "Understanding the Role of Community in Online Dating." In *Proceedings of the 33rd Annual ACM Conference on Human Factors in Computing Systems*. Seoul: ACM.

"Match Fact Sheet." *Match.com*. Accessed October 26, 2014. http://match.mediaroom.com/download/Match Fact Sheet 2014.pdf.

McElhaney, Lori J. 1992. "Dating and Courtship in the Later Years: A Neglected Topic of Research." *Generations: Journal of the American Society on Aging* 16, no. 3: 21–23.

McIntosh, William D., Lawrence Locker, Katherine Briley, Rebecca Ryan, and Alison J. Scott. 2011. "What Do Older Adults Seek in Their Potential Romantic Partners? Evidence from Online Personal Ads." *The International Journal of Aging and Human Development* 72, no. 1: 67–82.

Nelson, Todd D. 2005. "Ageism: Prejudice against Our Feared Future Self." *Journal of Social Issues* 61, no. 2: 207–21.

"New Website Unites Online Dating for Older Adults." *Chicago Tribune.* Accessed December 13, 2011. http://www.chicagotribune.com/special/primetime/chi-prime-time-dating-060811,0,2043303.story.

"Over 45 Forum FAQ and Rules." *Plenty of Fish Online Dating Forum and Singles Chat.* Accessed September 29, 2011. https://forums.plentyoffish.com/dating-Posts6376753.aspx.

Papacharissi, Zizi. 2008. "Uses and Gratifications." In *An Integrated Approach to Communication Theory and Research*, edited by Don W. Stacks and Michael B. Salwen, 2nd edition, 137–52. Routledge Communication Series. New York: Routledge.

Palmgreen, Philip, Lawrence Wenner, and Karl Erik Rosengren. 1985. "Uses and Gratifications Research: The Past Ten Years." In *Media Gratifications Research: Current Perspectives*, 11–37. Beverly Hills, CA: SAGE.

Paumgarten, Nick. "Looking for Someone: Sex, Love, and Loneliness on the Internet." *The New Yorker.* July 4, 2011. http://www.newyorker.com/magazine/2011/07/04/looking-for-someone.

Raacke, John, and Jennifer Bonds-Raacke. 2008. "MySpace and Facebook: Applying the Uses and Gratifications Theory to Exploring Friend-Networking Sites." *CyberPsychology & Behavior* 11, no. 2: 169–74.

Rosenfeld, Michael J., and Reuben J. Thomas. 2012. "Searching for a Mate: The Rise of the Internet as a Social Intermediary." *American Sociological Review* 77, no. 4: 523–47.

Rubin, Alan M. 2002. "Media Uses and Effects: A Uses-and-Gratifications Perspective." In *Media Effects: Advances in Theory and Research*, edited by Jennings Bryant and Dolf Zillman, 417–36. Hillsdale, NJ: Lawrence Erlbaum Associates.

Ruggiero, Thomas E. 2000. "Uses and Gratifications Theory in the 21st Century." *Mass Communication & Society* 3, no. 1: 3–37.

Scharlott, Bradford W., and William G. Christ. 1995. "Overcoming Relationship-Initiation Barriers: The Impact of a Computer-Dating System on Sex Role, Shyness, and Appearance Inhibitions." *Computers in Human Behavior* 11, no. 2: 191–204.

Schwarz, Hunter. "For the First Time, There Are More Single American Adults than Married Ones, and Here's Where They Live." *The Washington Post.* September 15, 2014. https://www.washingtonpost.com/graphics/politics/2016-election/campaign-finance/.

Shirky, Clay. 2008. *Here Comes Everybody: The Power of Organizing Without Organizations.* New York: Penguin Books.

Sinatra, Frank. Vocal performance of "Love Isn't Just for the Young," by Bernard Knee. Recorded August 27, 1962—October 3, 1964, with Neal Hefti. On *Softly, as I Leave You*, Reprise FS 1030, 33 1/3 rpm.

Smith, Aaron, and Maeve Duggan. 2013. "Online Dating & Relationships." Pew Internet & American Life Project. http://www.pewinternet.org/~/media//Files/Reports/2013/PIP_Online%20Dating%202013.pdf.

Stephure, Robert J., Susan D. Boon, Stacey L. Mackinnon, and Vicki L. Deveau. 2009. "Internet Initiated Relationships: Associations Between Age and Involvement in Online Dating." *Journal of Computer-Mediated Communication* 14, no. 3: 658–81.

Suler, John. 2004. "The Online Disinhibition Effect." *Cyberpsychology & Behavior* 7, no. 3: 321–26.

Valkenburg, Patti M., and Jochen Peter. 2007. "Who Visits Online Dating Sites? Exploring Some Characteristics of Online Daters." *CyberPsychology & Behavior* 10, no. 6: 849–52.

Wenner, Lawrence A. 1982. "Gratifications Sought and Obtained in Program Dependency: A Study of Network Evening News Programs and 60 Minutes." *Communication Research* 9, no. 4: 539–60.

Whitty, Monica T., and Tom Buchanan. 2009. "Looking for Love in so Many Places: Characteristics of Online Daters and Speed Daters." *Interpersona: An International Journal of Personal Relationships* 3, no. 2: 63–86.

Whitty, Monica T., and Adrian N. Carr. 2006. *Cyberspace Romance: The Psychology of Online Relationships.* Basingstoke, England; New York: Palgrave Macmillan.

Wu, Jen-Her, Shu-Ching Wang, and Ho-Huang Tsai. 2010. "Falling in Love with Online Games: The Uses and Gratifications Perspective." *Computers in Human Behavior* 26, no. 6: 1862–71.

Wysocki, Diane Kholos, and Cheryl D. Childers. 2011."'Let My Fingers Do the Talking': Sexting and Infidelity in Cyberspace." *Sexuality & Culture* 15: 217–39.

EIGHT

Long-Distance versus Geographically Close Romantic Relationships

The Effects of Social Media on the Development and Maintenance of These Relationships

Amy Janan Johnson, Eryn Bostwick, and Megan Bassick

A line of research in the field of communication has compared long-distance versus geographically close romantic relationships. This research has found both similarities and differences between these relationships. For example, long-distance and geographically close romantic relationships have been found to be equal in satisfaction, but long-distance romantic relationships have been found to be more idealized and more stable (Stafford 2016).

However, recent research on social media has shown how these technologies and new ways of communicating with our romantic partners have changed the ways romantic relationships are developed and maintained. For example, some research suggests that social media increases opportunities for jealousy (already a potential problem for long-distance romantic partners, who are often not as updated about their partner's everyday life, at least before social media!) and the influence of one's social network (Muise, Christofides, and Desmarais 2009; Papp, Danielewicz, and Cayemberg 2012). Only two studies known to the authors have examined how long-distance and geographically close romantic relationships differ in terms of the influence social media has on their relationships. Billedo, Kerkhof, and Finkenauer (2015) found that individuals in long-distance romantic relationships report a greater use of Facebook to maintain their relationships and to engage in partner surveillance. However, Tokunaga (2011) did not find a significant difference between long-distance and geographically close romantic partners in relation to surveillance. In addition, Billedo et al. (2015) found that long-distance romantic partners reported higher levels of jealousy related to social networking sites.

This chapter will utilize the existing research related to the differences between long-distance (LDRRs) and geographically close romantic relationships (GCRRs) and the theories that have been applied to these relationships to analyze current research on geographically close relationships and social media, to surmise what differences might exist for long-distance relationships, and to extrapolate how social media might affect long-distance relationships.

SOCIAL MEDIA USE IN LONG-DISTANCE RELATIONSHIPS

Research comparing geographically close and long-distance romantic relationships has found more similarities than differences between LDRRs and GCRRs (e.g., Stafford 2005; Stafford 2010). Long-distance romantic relationships report relational satisfaction, intimacy, and commitment levels equal to or greater than geographically close partners (Billedo et al. 2015; Stafford 2010; Stafford 2016). Contrary to popular assumptions, both types of relationships have similar levels of stress (Stafford 2016). Additionally, LDRRs are found to be as stable or even more stable than GCRRs (Stafford and Merolla 2007). Where GCRRs and LDRRs differ are in the amount and type of interactions they engage in, and who are typically in LDRRs. According to Stafford (2016), young adults are more likely to be in geographically distant relationships than middle-aged and older adults. In fact, as many as 75 percent of college students have reported being in a LDRR at some point in their college careers (Stafford 2010), and about 3.1 percent of marriages in the United States are classified as long-distance relationships (Stafford 2016).

LDRRs have fewer face-to-face interactions than GCRRs (Stafford 2010; Stafford and Merolla 2007), so they may need to depend on more nonphysical ways of communicating security to sustain closeness and feel emotionally tied to their partners (Borelli et al. 2014). Additionally, geographically close romantic relationships use communication technologies to supplement face-to-face (FTF) interactions to maintain the relationship, while in LDRRs, computer-mediated communication (CMC) takes more precedence (Rabby and Walther 2003). LDRRs need to use communication technologies in order to sustain the relationship (Stephen 1986). According to Caughlin and Sharabi (2013), individuals who incorporate FTF and online communication report feeling closer to their partners. Thus, LDRR partners may use social networking sites (SNSs) to maintain their relationships with their geographically distant partners. In fact, the primary reason individuals use the SNS Facebook is to maintain relationships (Fox and Anderegg 2016).

While SNSs would seem to be an important resource for communication in LDRRs, there is little research on SNS use in LDRRs (Billedo et al. 2015). Most LDRR research examines private, direct, and interpersonal communication channels, such as e-mail, texting, phone calls, and video chats (Billedo et al. 2015; Jiang and Hancock 2013; Johnson et al. 2008; Lee, Bassick, and Wilson Mumpower in press). Since LDRRs interact FTF less often than GCRRs, but communicate through additional channels about as often as GCRRs, how LDRRs use communication technologies such as social networking sites to maintain their relationships is an important area of research. In fact, Billedo et al. (2015) found that LDRRs use Facebook to interact with their romantic partners more than GCRRs. Also, those in LDRRs convey more strategic and routine maintenance behaviors through Facebook than those in GCRRs (Billedo et al. 2015).

When contemplating how SNSs can uniquely impact LDRRs, considering SNSs' particular affordances is helpful (Fox and Anderegg 2016). Affordances are characteristics or capabilities of a communication medium (Treem and Leonardi 2012). Social network sites have many affordances such as connectivity, visibility, editability, permanence, and publicity that can either foster or harm romantic relationships (Fox and Anderegg 2016). *Connectivity*, or association, is the extent to which a channel allows network members to acknowledge others' presence and see one another's content or information through a shared node (or in the context of Facebook, "friend") despite distance (Fox and Anderegg 2016; Treem and Leonardi 2012). Additionally, SNSs are simple, handy, and fairly inexpensive, which permits romantic partners the ability to be constantly connected with one another, despite geographic separation (Billedo et al. 2015). In SNSs, *visibility* is the extent to which individuals have access to information about another person that would otherwise not be easily accessible (Treem and Leonardi 2012), such as their mundane daily activities (e.g., what an individual ate for dinner), or messages between an individual and one's past romantic partners. In SNSs, members can often *edit* the content shared: individuals can crop past romantic partners out of photos; remove images, posts, or videos; and even change the wording of posts. However, due to *permanence* and *publicity*, SNSs can store content originally posted (see Facebook's terms of agreement) and other SNS users can also store and share content before it is removed or edited, making this content potentially immortal.

Even with the affordances offered by different types of communication technology, geographic separation is a challenge to relationship maintenance (Billedo et al. 2015). LDRR partners have adapted relational maintenance behaviors utilizing communication technologies that are commonly observed in FTF interactions of GCRRs. According to Billedo et al. (2015), connectivity and the public nature of SNSs offer a unique way for romantic partners, those in LDRRs in particular, to foster intimacy and maintain their relationships. Knapp's stages of coming together depict how two individuals become romantic partners (Knapp and Vangelisti 2005). The bonding stage, the last stage outlined, usually involves some sort of public display of unity, such as marriage, or in the SNS world, becoming "Facebook official" (FBO; Lane, Piercy, and Carr 2016). Because LDRR partners spend little time physically together, their ability to publicly communicate their relationships in more traditional ways (e.g., public display of affection) is lacking, but they can publicly communicate about their relationship through SNSs, such as posting a kissing emoji on their partners' Facebook walls, or tagging their partners in a post about how much they are looking forward to visiting them.

While SNSs have been among us for decades (e.g., Facebook started in 2004, MySpace started in 2003, and Six Degrees started in 1997), how they are used in romantic relationships is still a growing field of study. These websites bring people together despite geographic distance (Fox and Anderegg 2016), yet few have studied how LDRRs use or do not use these websites to maintain their relationships. The authors of this chapter encourage further research in this area and in the following sections outline theoretical approaches that have been used to study LDRRs and suggestions for future research involving LDRRs and SNSs.

THEORETICAL APPROACHES USED TO EXAMINE LONG-DISTANCE ROMANTIC RELATIONSHIPS

Although there are a variety of theories that examine romantic relationships, far fewer have been utilized to assess LDRRs. However, there are multiple theories that could help researchers explore LDRRs in more depth. These theories can also help explain the use of social media in LDRRs. Each of these theories will be briefly addressed below.

Social Exchange Theories

The first theoretical approach that is relevant to LDRR research is the social exchange approach. This group of theories proposes that individuals form, develop, and terminate relationships based on an examination of rewards and costs that a particular relationship brings. Out of this major group of theories, equity theory and the investment model are most directly related to LDRR research (Stafford 2005). According to equity theory, in an ideal relationship both individuals receive an equal amount of benefits and have an equal amount of costs brought on by the relationship, resulting in an equitable union. If a relational partner receives fewer benefits, and hence has more costs, he or she is likely to become dissatisfied over time and experience emotional distress, whereas those individuals in equitable relationships are more likely to be satisfied (Canary and Stafford 1994).

Oswald and Clark (2003) examined equity theory in the context of long-distance friendships and found that, contrary to their hypothesis, lack of proximity did not seem to increase the costs of an individual's long-distance friendships and did not impact their likelihood of maintaining that friendship. Although this research did not examine LDRRs specifically, it is easy to see how the theory could be applied to the romantic partner context. For example, does the use of social media change the frequency or types of costs those in LDRRs experience? Perhaps the ability to communicate via social media mitigates some of the issues associated with proximity by creating alternative avenues for individuals to feel connected. However, social media might also create additional costs not experienced in face-to-face contexts. For example, what happens when your relational partner posts pictures from a night out with friends on their social media account and you were not aware of his or her outing?

The second theoretical approach associated with the group of social exchange theories is Rusbult's (1980) investment model. According to this model, in order to determine whether a relationship is rewarding, and therefore worth maintaining, individuals compare their current relationships to (a) their expectations of what their relationship should be like and (b) alternatives to being in their current relationship (such as finding a different relational partner or being single). These comparisons should relate to one's commitment to their current relationship. For example, those who are less committed might find alternatives to their current relationship to be more rewarding than those who are highly committed.

The investment model has not been widely utilized in LDRR research. One example is Lydon, Pierce, and O'Regan (1997), in which they examined moral commitment in college LDRRs. The authors found that being morally committed to one's partner was positively associated with investment in one's LDRR. Additionally, moral commitment predicted the survival of one's relationship over time. Rusbult's (1980) model seems like a fruitful area for future research and provides an interesting set of questions for LDRRs in relation to social media. For example, how does social media impact one's investment in their LDRR? Facebook allows individuals to become "Facebook official," essentially announcing their investment to others in their social network. It would be interesting to see how expectations about the use of this feature impacts satisfaction in one's relationship and their likelihood to remain with their partner over time. Furthermore, what kind of role does social media play in the assessment of alternative relational partners, or the decision to end a relationship and be single? Social media can potentially introduce people to a wide range of others, which essentially increases the pool of alternative "others" from which they can choose. Perhaps this availability impacts one's decision to remain in their LDRR, especially if an alternative other is close in proximity. Such possibilities could potentially help explain why LDRRs report higher levels of Facebook jealousy than GCRRs (Billedo et al. 2015).

Uncertainty Reduction Theory

Uncertainty reduction theory (URT) was initially developed to help researchers understand initial interactions between individuals; however, since then it has been utilized to examine multiple points within the relationship cycle. According to the theory, when someone is unable to predict and/or explain another individual's behavior, he or she becomes uncertain, which is undesirable. The inability to cope with uncertainty about the other individual leads to a desire to reduce their uncertainty by gathering more information. The more information one gathers about that individual, the more they reduce their uncertainty about that person and the more comfortable they are said to feel (Berger and Calabrese 1975).

URT could be utilized in any relationship, but it could have noteworthy implications for LDRRs and social media use. For example, previous research by Stewart, Dainton, and Goodboy (2014) examined the use of social media from a URT perspective and found that individuals used social media to monitor the behavior of their partner, which was related to feelings of jealousy. Although the authors were not examining this process in a LDRR context, those in LDRR have less face-to-face interactions with their partners and therefore might rely on information posted online more than others. It would also be interesting to see whether those in LDRRs use social media to reduce their uncertainty more than those in GCRRs, and what kind of implications that monitoring might have for their relationships. Additionally, it would be useful to study the uncertainty reduction process for those LDRRs that initially develop online versus those that initially develop face-to-face. Do individuals within those contexts experience different levels of uncertainty? Furthermore, do they manage their uncertainty differently in relation to SNS?

The Hyperpersonal Model

The hyperpersonal model was first developed based on research by Walther (1996) and addresses the differences between relationships developed in a CMC context and face-to-face context. According to Walther and Parks (2002), relationships initiated online are different from those initiated face-to-face, particularly because individuals communicating online have fewer cues to rely on. Because of this, when individuals communicate online, they have the opportunity to strategically present themselves to others. This gives communicators the opportunity to present optimized versions of themselves, which can lead to idealization. Additionally, because of certain attributes associated with computer-mediated communication, relationships developed online might have greater levels of intimacy and liking than those developed face-to-face. In fact, research by Walther and Parks (2002) suggests that engaging in computer-mediated communication could lead to even more satisfaction than sending letters to a relational partner or talking on the phone.

The link between CMC and idealization outlined by hyperpersonal theory is of interest to LDRR researchers, because previous research has found a link between being in an LDRR and being prone to idealization of one's romantic partner (Stafford and Merolla 2007). This research has linked idealization to a heavier focus on intimacy, love, and relational issues in the talk of LDRR couples; therefore, the link between strategic presentation and idealization is highly relevant to LDRR, especially those initiated and maintained online. For example, social media provides individuals ample opportunity to strategically present themselves, which could then lead to more idealization for those who use social media as their main communication channel.

Attachment Theory

Another theoretical approach that has been useful to LDRR researchers is attachment theory (e.g., Pistole, Roberts, and Chapman 2010). According to this theory, when infants are separated from their mothers, they go through a predictable series of emotional reactions. These experiences during infancy then inform their expectations concerning the availability and responsiveness of attachment figures throughout one's lifetime (Bowlby 1973). Attachment itself takes the form of any sort of behavior that is associated with someone attaining or retaining proximity to another close individual (Bowlby 1973), and therefore is inherently tied to being physically and geographically close to other individuals. Furthermore, many researchers contend the attachments individuals form throughout infancy continue throughout their lives and impact their romantic relationships as adults (Hazan and Shaver 1987).

Research by Morey et al. (2013) found that attachment avoidance was negatively associated with young adults' use of the phone and texting in order to contact their relational partner, while an anxious attachment was negatively associated with the use of the phone and positively associated with the use of e-mail. Additionally, recent work by Lee, Bassick, and Wilson Mumpower (In Press) found that those in an LDRR with a preoccupied attachment style were likely to use texting to initiate conflict with their partner. With this in mind, it would be useful to know if attachment style impacts the ways those in LDRRs and GCRRs use social media specifically. There might be times when the easiest and best way to contact one's partner is through social media, but perhaps one's attachment style would impact the use of social media for relational purposes. For instance, are those with a preoccupied attachment style more likely to use certain social media outlets to initiate conflict with their partners? Additionally, more work needs to be done concerning the relationship between attachment style, social media use, and relational implications (i.e., satisfaction, likelihood of relational dissolution, etc.) for those in LDRRs. For example, is the use of certain social media sites for communication considered more appropriate for those with preoccupied attachment styles than other attachment styles, and what kind of relational impact would that use have for those in LDRRs versus GCRRs? The relationship between attachment style, social media use, and relationship status (LDRR versus GCRR) seems like a fruitful area of research.

Relational Dialectics Theory

Relational dialectics theory (RDT) was originally conceptualized by Baxter and Montgomery (1996) and suggests that every relationship experiences contradictory forces that work to simultaneously pull it together and push it apart. These forces occur between the relational dyad, and also between the dyad and the outside social network, and couples must try to balance these forces over time. In the most recent iteration of the theory, Baxter (2011) focuses on the discursive nature of these tensions, saying relationships themselves become meaningful through the interplay of multiple, competing discourses that exist. As time passes some of the discourses that exist become normalized, called centripetal forces, while others become marginalized, called centrifugal forces. Both centripetal and centrifugal discourses are legitimized through utterances, which can either be voiced by relational partners or reflected in sociocultural norms.

RDT is relevant to LDRR literature because there might be certain struggles that LDRRs experience that those in geographically close relationships do not. For example, if a couple meets online and maintains a LDRR, the social view that relationships are maintained face-to-face might place a strain on their relationship and cause conflict. Additionally, those in LDRRs should use different strategies for balancing the tensions they experience than should those in geographically close relationships. Fox, Osborn, and Warber (2014) suggest that simply the existence of social media causes a struggle for romantic relationships. Their research found the use of social media in romantic relationships to be associated with the dialectics of integration–separation, expression–privacy, and stability–change. The authors suggest that these issues are most likely associated with the ease with which social media allows people to connect and integrate their networks, which could impact their ability to maintain privacy and independence (Fox et al. 2014). Some of these dialectics might be heightened in LDRRs. For example, how do individuals in LDRRs handle the expression-privacy dialectic? As previously mentioned, if information that you would rather keep from your partner ends up on social media and your partner sees it, the post itself could cause conflict. Additionally, are there any tensions those in LDRRs experience because of social media that might not be experienced in geographically close relationships?

These theoretical approaches suggest issues that are relevant to the use of social media in both long-distance and geographically close romantic relationships. However, most of the research on social media has only examined geographically close romantic relationships, or it has not distinguished between the two types of romantic couples. The next section will examine factors that have been found to relate to the use of social media in romantic relationships and consider more specifically whether these factors may have different implications for geographically close and long-distance romantic relationships.

REANALYZING CURRENT RESEARCH ABOUT GEOGRAPHICALLY CLOSE ROMANTIC RELATIONSHIPS AND SOCIAL MEDIA

Benefits of Being a Long-distance Couple

Previously, this chapter has touched on the relevance of relational dialectics theory to LDRRs. This theory is also relevant to the benefits that individuals may perceive in being a long-distance couple. For example, Sahlstein (2004) talks about the benefits of having a long-distance relationship in terms of relational dialectics theory. When long-distance partners are apart, they can focus more on the autonomy dialectic, and when they visit each other, they can focus more on connection. However, research on social media has suggested that men find the amount of maintenance women expect them to engage in on Facebook as higher than they prefer (Fox, Osborn, and Warber 2014). Male long-distance romantic partners would not be exempt from this expectation, potentially lowering the advantage of being able to focus more on autonomy when physically separated from their romantic partner.

Another benefit of being a long-distance couple could involve potentially less conflict resulting from social media use with other individuals while engaging with one's partner face-to-face. For example, Hand et al. (2013) found that time spent on Facebook was negatively associated with intimacy level between romantic partners. Prior research has discussed conflicts that arise in romantic relationships due to social media use (Fox, Osborn, and Warber 2014) and the need to establish rules related to cell phone use (Miller-Ott, Kelly, and Duran 2012). Due to less day-to-day contact among long-distance partners, one's daily use of social media may not lead to as much potential conflict in long-distance relationships relative to GCRRs, providing a benefit for LDRRs. However, social media use during special times of face-to-face contact, such as during visits, might be especially conflict-inducing if individuals wish their partner to focus completely on them during these times. Fox and Moreland (2015) discuss the belief among one's social network that one should always be available through mediated means. These potential effects for long-distance couples relate to how individuals negotiate the dialectic of connection and autonomy in their particular relationship (Sahlstein 2004).

Commitment and Jealousy

Another example of extending current social media research to LDRRs would relate to the research on becoming "Facebook official" (FBO) (Fox and Warber 2013). Having each individual designate the other person as the one he or she is in a relationship with and linking their profiles has been found to be an important turning point in young adults' romantic relationships, noting exclusivity and a move toward a committed relationship (Mod 2010). Lane et al. (2016) found that couples who were FBO reported that their relationships were more committed and stronger than those couples who were not FBO. Because LDRRs tend to be more idealized than GCRRs, is it more or less important to individuals in these relationships to become "Facebook official"? Men and women have been found to interpret the social desirability of being FBO differently (Papp et al. 2012). Does this difference (and the potential for conflict that such a difference causes) occur equally for both long-distance and geographically close romantic partners?

As discussed earlier, prior research has also shown that the use of Facebook can relate to feelings of jealousy in romantic relationships (Muise et al. 2009; Utz and Beukeboom 2011). Such findings are not without basis, as Drouin, Miller, and Dibble (2014) found that romantic partners with lower levels of commitment were more likely to accept Facebook friend offers from romantic interests even while in a relationship. Utz and Beukeboom (2011) claim that there are three features of social network sites that can increase jealousy in romantic partners: 1) they allow partners access to more information about each other; 2) they allow individuals to monitor their partner in a way that is socially acceptable; and 3) the amount of information about their partner that is publicly available increases. Facebook allows a romantic partner another channel to see with whom their romantic partner is interacting, reducing one's privacy (Fox and Moreland 2015). Billedo et al (2015) examined how those in LDRRs utilize these features to monitor their partners and found that LDRRs reported more surveillance of their romantic partners through the use of Facebook than GCRRs.

In addition, social media can increase opportunities for jealousy due to the increased potential contact with ex-partners (Muise et al. 2009). Relationships may continue after a breakup if partners remain friends on Facebook, but these relationships might have ceased without this communication channel. Additionally, individuals may not know all of their partners' social media network members, increasing this uncertainty. This may be especially true for long-distance romantic partners whose relationship began online. Romantic partners in Muise et al. (2009) linked accessibility of information and lack of message context to jealous feelings related to Facebook. Long-distance partners may be even more susceptible to these jealousy-causing factors, given increased uncertainty in these relationships due to less daily face-to-face contact and the possibility of less overlap in their social networks. In fact, Billedo et al. (2015) found that LDRRs reported more jealousy related to Facebook than GCRRs. Future research should continue to examine factors regarding commitment and jealousy issues in LDRRs related to social media use.

Idealization and Social Media

As stated previously, research has shown LDRRs and GCRRs to be equally satisfied and committed (Stafford 2016). Stafford and Merolla (2007) suggest that this may be due to idealization. Hyperpersonal theory (Walther 1996) can also explain this, by outlining how characteristics of computer-mediated channels can lend themselves to overly positive views of the interactants. Stafford and Merolla (2007) go so far as to recommend that long-distance romantic couples make no long-term commitment, such as marriage, until they take steps to reduce this idealization.

However, features of social media may already be decreasing this idealization. As Muise et al. (2009) discuss, social media allows romantic partners more access to their partners' actions with other members of their social network, not just with their partner. Dainton and Aylor (2001) found that long-distance romantic couples who saw each other face-to-face less often report lower levels of trust. Whether social media allow LDRRs to go longer between face-to-face visits without a decrease in trust is an interesting question for future research. Mediated devices continue to decrease the differences between face-to-face and mediated interaction: Individuals can even use mediated devices to kiss their partner, and one new device even communicates the amount of force and the shape of a kiss (Saadatian et al. 2014). In addition, Mod (2010) suggests *all* romantic partners use Facebook as a way to present their romantic partner as an ideal partner, potentially decreasing any difference in idealization between GCRRs and LDRRs.

The Power of Social Networks

In general, research has found overlapping social networks to increase the stability of romantic couples (Parks and Adelman 1983). In the past, long-distance romantic couples might be expected to have a lesser degree of overlap in their social networks, especially if they met while they lived far away from each other or met online. However, by joining a social media site, one can immediately have access to many of the individuals that comprise a person's social network and observe their interactions.

This accessibility to former romantic partners has led to some individuals wondering if they should "unfriend" their ex-romantic partners (LeFebvre, Blackburn, and Brody 2015).

Fox and Moreland (2015) also found that individuals were likely to use information they gathered on Facebook to compare themselves to their romantic partners' former mates. Both LDRRs and GCRRs can have equal access to this information about former romantic partners, which might have been more available to GCRRs in the past.

Thus, social media potentially decrease the different degree of influence that one's social networks have for geographically close and long-distance couples, in that both types of couples can have access to each other's social networks and potentially both individuals' social networks have the ability to comment on their relationship and their actions concerning their relationship through the use of these media. Fox and Moreland (2015) discuss how one's social network can comment on one's romantic relationship through Facebook, for example. Therefore, this reasoning suggests that social networks should have more influence on long-distance romantic relationships than before social media developed.

The previous section has noted areas for future research focused on potential aspects of social media use that may be particularly relevant to LDRRs. These areas include how social media affects the benefits of being a long-distance couple, how it relates to feelings of commitment and jealousy, how social media affects idealization among romantic partners, and the increased power of social networks through the use of social media by romantic partners. The final section of this chapter will focus on several methodological and theoretical implications for future research on LDRRs and social media given the literature reviewed in this chapter so far.

METHODOLOGICAL AND THEORETICAL IMPLICATIONS

Methodological Implications

One clear methodological implication from this chapter is the need to focus on more types of social media other than Facebook. The great majority of research in this chapter focuses on this social media platform, which is potentially appropriate given that it is the most widely used SNS. However, research on other media suggests that the implications for both long-distance and geographically close relationships may differ based on the type of social media utilized. For example, Pittman and Reich (2016) found that different types of social media platforms affect loneliness in various ways. Visual images, such as Instagram and Snapchat (and presumably Facebook), were more important than text-based, such as Twitter and Yik Yak, in reducing loneliness. Research on Snapchat in particular has illustrated that individuals perceive Snapchat as a particularly personal channel of communication (Vaterlaus et al. 2016). One can send images and texts targeted to a certain person that then disappear in a certain time frame. This unique affordance of Snapchat could suggest that its use might potentially increase the influence of jealousy because the messages disappear quickly and romantic partners may not have access to their partner's interactions in this medium. In fact, research by Utz, Muscanell, and Khalid (2015) did find that Snapchat seemed to elicit more jealousy than Facebook. However, Vaterlaus et al. (2016) found that young adults believe Snapchat can both enhance and harm romantic relationships. For example, participants indicated believing that Snapchat could be used to cheat on one's partner, but that it also helps them feel more connected to others.

Additionally, some research has suggested active use of the social media platform Twitter is associated with poorer relational outcomes. For example, Clayton (2014) found a positive relationship between how often one utilizes Twitter, Twitter-related conflict in his or her romantic relationships, and the likelihood of infidelity, breakup, and divorce. Similarly, research on Instagram has found a connection between the pictures one posts and relational outcomes. Specifically, Ridgway and Clayton (2016) found the more selfies people post on Instagram, the more likely they are to experience Instagram-related conflict. Together, this research suggests that some of the patterns researchers have found on Facebook might translate to other social media platforms; however, more research is needed to understand the similarities and differences that exist.

Another methodological implication is that more research needs to be concerned with relational *development* via social media. Dating applications such as Tinder have changed the mate selection process in recent years; however, very little academic research testing its implications for romantic relationships exists. The usefulness of dating applications in a LDRR context is unclear. One implication these applications could have for LDRRs is in terms of how likely individuals are to utilize them in order to initiate and maintain LDRRs in the first place. Additionally, how does the use of a dating application impact relational satisfaction and the likelihood that the relationship will continue? For example, perhaps if a LDRR was initiated on a dating application, people might be more likely to worry about their partner using the same app to find alternative partners.

Theoretical Implications

One clear theoretical implication based on the research reviewed throughout the chapter is that theories associated with romantic relationships need to be extended to a LDRR context. One reason why extending previous work to a LDRR context is important is that research has shown that those in LDRR have experiences that differ somewhat from those in geographically close relationships (Stafford 2016). These differences suggest researchers cannot simply assume the theoretical implications related to geographically close relationships are similar in LDRRs. Therefore, it is important that researchers continue to use theories available to them to both examine how their theoretical components work in a LDRR context and to compare relational processes in LDRRs to those in GCRRs. Additionally, as social media continues to be an important factor in romantic relationships, researchers should seek to apply more media-specific theories to LDRRs in order to explain the role social media plays in LDRR development, maintenance, and dissolution. Because of its focus on mediated contexts, Walther's (1996) hyperpersonal model would provide valuable insight on this aspect of LDRRs. Overall, this chapter presented a variety of theories that might be useful to help scholars better understand LDRRs and how they function in regard to social media, and we believe tackling the questions suggested by these theoretical approaches represent a promising start.

CONCLUSION

The influence of social media use on romantic relationships is a new but expanding area of research. Continuing to consider how both geographically close and long-distance romantic partners utilize and are affected by social media is a very important area for current and future scholars. This chapter has summarized the current research on long-distance romantic partners and social media, has offered theoretical lenses useful for this research, and has suggested many fruitful research questions that could be addressed. A clear need to expand beyond the almost exclusive focus on Facebook is apparent.

REFERENCES

Baxter, Leslie A. 2011. *Voicing Relationships: A Dialogic Perspective*. Thousand Oaks, CA: Sage.
Baxter, Leslie A., and Barbara M. Montgomery. 1996. *Relating: Dialogues and Dialectics*. New York: Guilford Press.

Berger, Charles R., and Richard J. Calabrese. 1975. "Some Explorations in Initial Inter-action and Beyond: Toward a Developmental Theory of Interpersonal Communica-tion." *Human Communication Research* 1: 99–112. doi:10.1111/j.1468-2958.1975.tb00258.x.

Billedo, Cherrie J., Peter Kerkhof, and Catrin Finkenauer. 2015. "The Use of Social Networking Sites for Relationship Maintenance in Long-Distance and Geographi-cally Close Romantic Relationships." *Cyberpsychology, Behavior, and Social Network-ing* 18: 152–57. doi:10.1089/cyber.2014.0469.

Borelli, Jessica L., Hannah F. Rasmussen, Margaret L. Burkhart, and David A. Sbarra. 2014. "Relational Savoring in Long-Distance Romantic Relationships." *Journal of Social and Personal Relationships* 31: 1–26. doi:10.1177/0265407514558960.

Bowlby, John. 1973. *Attachment and Loss: Vol. 2. Separation: Anxiety and Anger.* New York: Basic Books.

Canary, Dan J., and Laura Stafford. 1994. "Maintaining Relationships through Strate-gic and Routine Interaction." In *Communication and Relational Maintenance*, ed. Dan Canary and Laura Stafford, 3–22. San Diego, CA: Academic Press.

Caughlin, John P., and Liesel L. Sharabi. 2013. "A Communicative Interdependence Perspective of Close Relationships: The Connections between Mediated and Unme-diated Interactions Matter." *Journal of Communication* 63: 873–93. doi:10.1111/jcom.12046.

Clayton, Russell B. 2014. "The Third Wheel: The Impact of Twitter Use on Relationship Infidelity and Divorce." *Cyberpsychology, Behavior, and Social Networking* 17: 425–30. doi:10.1089/cyber.2013.0570.

Dainton, Marianne, and Brooks Aylor. 2001. "A Relational Uncertainty Analysis of Jealousy, Trust, and Maintenance in Long-Distance Versus Geographically Close Relationships." *Communication Quarterly* 49: 172–88. doi:10.1080/01463370109385624.

Drouin, Michelle, Daniel A. Miller, and Jayson L. Dibble. 2014. "Ignore Your Partners' Current Facebook Friends: Beware the Ones They Add!" *Computers in Human Behav-ior* 35: 483–88. doi:10.1016/j.chb.2014.02.032.

Fox, Jesse, and Courtney Anderegg. 2016. "Turbulence, Turmoil, and Termination: The Dark Side of Social Networking Sites for Romantic Relationships." In *Contexts of the Dark Side of Communication*, ed. Eletra S. Gilchrist-Petty and Shawn D. Long, 269–80. New York: Peter Lang.

Fox, Jesse, and Jennifer Moreland. 2015. "The Dark Side of Social Networking Sites: An Exploration of the Relational and Psychological Stressors Associated with Facebook Use and Affordances." *Computers in Human Behavior* 45: 168–76. doi:10.1016/j.chb.2014.11.083.

Fox, Jesse, Jeremy L. Osborn, and Katie M. Warber. 2014. "Relational Dialectics and Social Networking Sites: The Role of Facebook in Romantic Relationship Escalation, Maintenance, Conflict and Dissolution." *Computers in Human Behavior* 35: 527–34. doi:10.1016/j.chb.2014.02.031.

Fox, Jesse, and Katie M. Warber. 2013. "Romantic Relationship Development in the Age of Facebook: An Exploratory Study of Emerging Adults' Perceptions, Motives, and Behaviors." *Cyberpsychology, Behavior, and Social Networking* 16: 3–7. doi:10.1089/cyber.2012.0288.

Hand, Matthew M., Donna Thomas, Walter C. Buboltz, Eric Deemer, and M. Buyanjar-gal. 2013. "Facebook and Romantic Relationships: Intimacy and Couple Satisfaction Associated with Online Social Network Use." *Cyberpsychology, Behavior, and Social Networking* 16: 8–13. doi:10.1089/cyber.2012.0038.

Hazan, Cindy, and Phillip Shaver. 1987. "Romantic Love Conceptualized as an Attach-ment Process." *Journal of Personality and Social Psychology* 52: 511–24. doi:10.1037/0022-3514.52.3.511.

Jiang, L. Crystal, and Jeffrey T. Hancock. 2013. "Absence Makes the Communication Grow Fonder: Geographic Separation, Interpersonal Media, and Intimacy in Dating Relationships." *Journal of Communication* 63: 556–77. doi:10.1111/jcom.12029.

Johnson, Amy Janan, Michel M. Haigh, Jennifer H. Becker, Elizabeth A. Craig, and Shelley Wigley. 2008. "College Students' Use of Relational Management Strategies in Email in Long-distance and Geographically Close Relationships." *Journal of Computer-Mediated Communication* 13: 381-404. doi:10.1111/j.1083-6101.2008.00401.x.

Knapp, Mark L., and Anita L. Vangelisti. 2005. *Interpersonal Communication and Human Relationships*. 5th ed. Boston: Allyn and Bacon.

Lane, Brianna L., Cameron Wade Piercy, and Caleb T. Carr. 2016. "Making It Facebook Official: The Warranting Value of Online Relationship Status Disclosures on Relational Characteristics." *Computers in Human Behavior* 56: 1–8. doi:10.1016/j.chb.2015.11.016.

Lee, Sunny, Megan A. Bassick, and Stacie Wilson Mumpower. In Press. "Fighting Electronically: Long-distance Romantic Couples' Conflict Management over Mobile Communication." *Electronic Journal of Communication* 26.

LeFebvre, Leah, Kate Blackburn, and Nicholas Brody. 2015. "Navigating Romantic Relationships on Facebook: Extending the Relationship Dissolution Model to Social Network Environments." *Journal of Social and Personal Relationships* 32: 78–98. doi:10.1177/0265407514524848.

Lydon, John, Tamarha Pierce, and Shannon O'Regan. 1997. "Coping with Moral Commitment to Long-Distance Dating Relationships." *Journal of Personality and Social Psychology* 73: 104–13. doi:10.1037/0022-3514.73.1.104.

Miller-Ott, Aimee E., Lynne Kelly, and Robert L. Duran. 2012. "The Effects of Cell Phone Usage Rules on Satisfaction in Romantic Relationships." *Communication Quarterly* 60: 17–34. doi:10.1080/01463373.2012.642263.

Mod, Greg Bowe. 2010. "Reading Romance: The Impact Facebook Rituals Can Have on a Romantic Relationship." *Journal of Comparative Research in Anthropology and Sociology* 1: 61–77.

Morey, Jennifer N., Amy L. Gentzler, Brian Creasy, Ann M. Oberhauser, and David Westerman. 2013. "Young Adults' Use of Communication Technology Within Their Romantic Relationships and Associations with Attachment Style." *Computers in Human Behavior* 29: 1771–78. doi:10.1016/j.chb.2013.02.019.

Muise, Amy, Emily Christofides, and Serge Desmarais. 2009. "More Information Than You Ever Wanted: Does Facebook Bring Out the Green-eyed Monster of Jealousy?" *CyberPsychology and Behavior* 12: 441–44. doi:10.1089/cpb.2008.0263.

Oswald, Debra L., and Eddie M. Clark. 2003. "Best Friends Forever? High School Best Friendships and the Transition to College." *Personal Relationships* 10: 187–96. doi:10.1111/1475-6811.00045.

Papp, Lauren M., Jennifer Danielewicz, and Crystal Cayemberg. 2012. "'Are We Facebook Official?' Implications of Dating Partners' Facebook Use and Profiles for Intimate Relationship Satisfaction." *Cyberpsychology, Behavior, and Social Networking* 15: 85–90. doi:10.1089/cyber.2011.0291.

Parks, Malcolm R., and Mara B. Adelman. 1983. "Communication Networks and the Development of Romantic Relationships: An Expansion of Uncertainty Reduction Theory." *Human Communication Research* 10: 55–79. doi:10.1111/j.14682958.1983.tb00004.x.

Pistole, M. Carole, Amber Roberts, and Marion L. Chapman. 2010. "Attachment, Relationship Maintenance, and Stress in Long Distance and Geographically Close Romantic Relationships. *Journal of Social & Personal Relationships* 27: 535–52. doi:10.1177/0265407510363427.

Pittman, Matthew, and Brandon Reich. 2016. "Social Media and Loneliness: Why an Instagram Picture May be Worth More Than a Thousand Twitter Words." *Computers in Human Behavior* 62: 155–67. doi:10.1016/j.chb.2016.03.084.

Rabby, Michael K., and Joseph B. Walther. 2003. "Computer-mediated Communication Effects on Relationship Formation and Maintenance." In *Maintaining Relationships through Communication*, ed. Daniel J. Canary and Marianne Dainton, 141–62. Mahwah, NJ: Lawrence Erlbaum Associates.

Ridgway, Jessica, and Russell Clayton. 2016. "Instagram Unfiltered: Exploring Associations of Body Image Satisfaction, Instagram #Selfie Posting, and Negative Romantic Relationship Outcomes." *Cyberpsychology, Behavior, and Social Networking* 19: 2–7.
doi:10.1089/cyber.2015.0433.

Rusbult, Caryl E. 1980. "Commitment and Satisfaction in Romantic Associations: A
Test of the Investment Model." *Journal of Experimental Social Psychology* 16: 172–86.
doi:10.1016/0022-1031(80)90007-4.

Saadatian, Elham, Hooman Samani, Rahul Parsani, Anshul Vikram Pandey, Jinhui Li,
Lenis Tejada, Adrian David Cheok, and Ryohei Nakatsu. 2014. "Mediating Intima-
cy in Long-Distance Relationships Using Kiss Messaging." *International Journal of
Human-Computer Studies* 72: 736–46.

Sahlstein, Erin M. 2004. "Relating at a Distance: Negotiating Being Together and Being
Apart in Long-Distance Relationships." *Journal of Social and Personal Relationships* 21:
698–701. doi:10.1177/0265407504046115.

Stafford, Laura. 2005. *Maintaining Long-Distance and Cross-Residential Relationships.*
Mahwah, NJ: Lawrence Erlbaum Associates.

———. 2010. "Geographic Distance and Communication during Courtship." *Communication Research* 27: 275–97. doi:10.1177/0093650209356390.

———. 2016. "Long-Distance Relationships." In *International Encyclopedia of Interpersonal Communication* edited by Charles R. Berger and Michael E. Roloff, 1–8. Hobok-
en, NJ: Wiley.

Stafford, Laura, and Andy J. Merolla. 2007. "Idealization, Reunions, and Stability in
Long-Distance Dating Relationships." *Journal of Social and Personal Relationships* 24:
36–54. doi:10.1177/0265407507072578.

Stephen, Timothy D. 1986. "Communication and Interdependence in Geographically
Separated Relationships." *Human Communication Research* 89: 191–210. doi:10.1111/
j.1468-2958.1986.tb00102.x.

Stewart, Margaret C., Marianne Dainton, and Alan K. Goodboy. 2014. "Maintaining
Relationships on Facebook: Associations with Uncertainty, Jealousy, and Satisfaction." *Communication Reports* 27: 13–26. doi:10.1080/08934215.2013.845675.

Tokunaga, Robert S. 2011. "Social Networking Site or Social Surveillance Site? Understanding the Use of Interpersonal Electronic Surveillance in Romantic Relationships." *Computers in Human Behavior* 27: 705–13. doi:10.1016/j.chb.2010.08.014.

Treem, Jeffrey W., and Paul M. Leonardi. 2012. "Social Media Use in Organizations:
Exploring the Affordances of Visibility, Editability, Persistence, and Association."
Communication Yearbook 36: 143–89. doi:10.2139/ssrn.2129853.

Utz, Sonja, and Camiel J. Beukeboom. 2011. "The Role of Social Network Sites in
Romantic Relationships: Effects on Jealousy and Relationship Happiness." *Journal of
Computer-Mediated Communication* 16: 511–27. doi:10.1111/j.1083-6101.2011.01552.x.

Utz, Sonja, Nicole Muscanell, and Cameran Khalid. 2015. "Snapchat Elicits More Jealousy than Facebook: A Comparison of Snapchat and Facebook Use." *Cyberpsychology, Behavior, and Social Networking* 18: 141–46. doi:10.1089/cyber.2014.0479.

Vaterlaus, J. Mitchell, Kathryn Barnett, Cesia Roche, and Jimmy A. Young. 2016.
"'Snapchat Is More Personal': An Exploratory Study on Snapchat Behaviors and
Young Adult Interpersonal Relationships." *Computers in Human Behavior* 62:
594–601. doi:10.1016/j.chb.2016.04.029.

Walther, Joseph B. 1996. "Computer-mediated Communication: Impersonal, Interpersonal, and Hyperpersonal Interaction." *Communication Research* 23: 3–43.
doi:10.1177/009365096023001001.

Walther, Joseph B., and Malcom R. Parks. 2002. "Cues Filtered Out, Cues Filtered In:
Computer-mediated Communication and Relationships." In *Handbook of Interper-
sonal Communication,* edited by Mark L. Knapp and John A. Daly, 529–63. Thousand
Oaks, CA: Sage.

NINE

Love in Mediated Landscape

The Socio-Spatial Logic of Young Chinese
Lovers' Media Use

Hua Su

Social media have become an integral part of romantic relating in many parts of the world, but scholars have just begun to understand their influence on romantic relationship. Recent studies have mainly focused on a single type of social network site (SNS), specifically Facebook, leaving the romantic use of other SNSs largely unknown. These studies have generated rich findings about how Facebook use affects romantic relationship by influencing couples' relationship development (e.g., Fox, Warber, and Makstaller 2013), relational dialectics (e.g., Fox, Osborn, and Warber 2014; Zhao, Sosik, and Cosley 2012), and romantic jealousy and relational happiness (e.g., Mod 2010; Utz and Beukeboom 2011), etc. The characterization of the media affordances in these studies and the highlighting of specific media practices, such as posting relationship status, provide useful insights for examining other SNSs used by romantic partners.

However, this single-medium and often single-usage approach forecloses the possibility of understanding the diverse media practices in romantic relationships. Multiple media tend to converge in intimate relationships, hence the redundancy of media use in close ties (Broadbent and Bauwens 2008). Romantic partners have been found to use diverse media to interact with each other for various purposes (Coyne et al. 2011). To understand the impact of social media on romantic relationships, researchers will benefit from a holistic understanding of the mediated landscape of love, where couples select and combine channels of communication in their interactions with each other.

This chapter extends the single-medium approach to social media and romantic relationships by examining a wide range of SNSs used by young Chinese lovers. It adopts a holistic perspective on media use among young Chinese and highlights the logic of use behind the seemingly diverse media practices. Online activities, as boyd (2014) illustrated, often have to do with offline life worlds. Teens in boyd's research want to have a private space where they can hang out without the interference of adults, but such a place is not available in their physical environment. Thus they go to social network sites and form "networked publics," where various activities take place including cyberbullying and democratic campaigns. The "virtual" place afforded by online network sites holds various potentials and risks for their users, and the complex manifestations of those potentials reflect both the characteristics of the media and those of media users' offline life worlds.

In the same vein, this chapter examines young Chinese's romantic use of social media with an emphasis on the interaction between their online practices and offline social arenas. It is based on semi-structured in-depth interviews with a total of forty-four Chinese college students and urban youth in Beijing from 2011 to 2014, a time period characterized by changing social media popular among young Chinese, from Renren Network (a Facebook-like SNS) and QQ (an instant messaging service later expanded to include the SNS Qzone), to Weibo (a Twitter-like microblogging sites), and later to Wechat (which integrates instant messaging and social networking services along with other functions). The shifting "mediascape" offered a great opportunity to examine young Chinese's logics of media use across channels, and to explore the influence of recent communication technologies on their romantic relating despite the differences between specific social media.

Specifically, this chapter points out the socio-spatial logic of media use manifested in young Chinese lovers' narratives about seeking potential dates, displaying romantic affections, and exploring gender identities and relationships. It argues that young Chinese's uses of social media for romantic relating involve a complex interplay between social and personal spaces, both online and offline. For young Chinese lovers, privacy often means freedom from social control, but offline social networks also suggest trust and accountability. The double functions of the social circles largely shape how young Chinese relate romantically on and with social media.

NETWORKED MATCHMAKING: AMBIGUOUS FRIENDSHIP
AND PARTICULARIZED TRUST

Every romantic relationship has to start somewhere. Unlike some forms of arranged marriage, where parents take care of mate selection and matchmaking, couples that follow a do-it-yourself pattern of dating have to meet and get to know each other before starting a relationship. Online dating sites provide a convenient way of looking for potential partners, but traditional social networks still play an important role in locating dates for young Chinese individuals. SNSs that connect friends, acquaintances, and friends' friends combine the convenience of online dating and the resources of offline social connections, hence becoming popular matchmaking intermediaries for college students.

One common "how we met" narrative among college students has three parts. First, one party (the initiator) saw the other party (the initiated) in some student activities and learned the latter's name through other students. Then the initiator sent the initiated a friend request at popular SNSs, commented on the latter's postings, and started to interact on the online sites. After some initial interactions, the two parties shifted to private messaging channels, such as texting, QQ IM, or Wechat, and had more personal conversations until the time was ripe for one party to profess love for the other. There were, of course, variations. If they had already met offline, their interaction via SNSs started sooner. Or if they were circumspect about interacting in public, their initial interaction took place via private messaging services at the SNSs although they read each other's public and semi-public profiles. In many cases, online network sites were instrumental in helping young Chinese initiate interaction and get acquainted with potential romantic partners. SNSs, along with private messaging services, accelerated the couples' journey from strangers to romantic partners by offering them a quick means of getting connected, becoming acquainted, and exploring relationship opportunities.

For young Chinese lovers, SNSs are useful for matchmaking particularly because of two social-technological factors: the ambiguity of becoming "friends" at SNSs and the articulation of latent offline connections. To begin with, making friend requests or adding friends at SNSs has an ambiguous nature. It opens up opportunities for furthering the relationship, but it can be interpreted as "just a friend" if things do not work out. The usefulness of the ambiguity is similar to what Kaufmann (2012) said about dance as a dating game in the nineteenth-century France. Unlike asking for someone's hand, which signifies a formal commitment, asking someone to dance could be understood as "just a dance," hence preserving the option of leaving the temporary association established in the dance (Kaufmann 2012, 67–75). Likewise, becoming friends through SNSs starts a casual relationship between young Chinese, who may take the relationship further or withdraw from it after some chats via instant messaging.

Moreover, SNSs give the young Chinese a chance to screen potential dates by browsing pictures, reading postings, and interacting in an online space. Getting to know each other at the initial stage is expedited by users' public and semi-public profiles and postings. The description of Luojia, a male college student looking for a new date after ending a long-distance relationship, exemplifies how young Chinese use social media to identify and strike up a conversation with a possible match. He was attracted to a young woman in a campus event, and he searched her name on Renren Network. He read her postings at the site to see whether her tastes and interests matched his, and then studied her latest posts for possible topics to break the ice. SNSs webpages with profiles, interaction records, and shared links to music, videos, and articles provide young Chinese with rich information about potential dates.

The expedition of the acquainting process underlines the issue of trust because presentation at SNSs always involves selective exposure. Young Chinese are well aware of this while using SNSs as a channel to get to know each other. For instance, Hongyu, a female college student, described Renren Network as a field on which the game of "detection and anti-detection" was played out: She made judgments about others' personalities based on their postings but at the same time deleted her own that might expose her character.

Impression management notwithstanding, searching for potential dates through SNSs suggests matching in terms of social station and trust through interlinking personal ties. SNSs make visible users' offline social networks, thus facilitating exchanges between latent ties that share common offline connections (boyd and Ellison 2007). For Chinese students, browsing profiles and seeking matches though online network sites are often already delineated by their school associations along with the prestige of the colleges. In addition, shared personal networks hold individuals responsible for their online performances. If necessary, online identities can be verified by mutual friends and acquaintances in the offline world. The interweaving of online and offline networks extends to a wider social circle what sociologists call "particularized" trust, or trust formed in everyday interactions between people who know each other (Steinhardt 2011). The extension of trust through offline social circles constitutes an important characteristic of SNSs as a matchmaking ground for Chinese college students.

The importance of offline associations and particularistic trust to the matchmaking of young Chinese contrasts with their discretion about dating anonymous strangers outside their offline social circles. Some SNSs offer features that enable connection between strangers. For example, Qzone and QQ (instant messaging) both allow searches to be made based on users' location, zodiac signs, age, gender, etc. Compared to Renren

Network, where real names and school affiliations are normatively displayed, Qzone and QQ encourage interaction under pseudonyms. Many young Chinese had experience using these channels to interact with anonymous strangers, but they tended to frown upon using it for romantic purposes. In the narratives of the college students, it is not outlandish to look for dates among strangers at Renren Network, but it is at least unscrupulous to do the same through Qzone or QQ. For one thing, it is hard to obtain trust without real names and institutional affiliations; for another, looking for dates among strangers often carries erotic implications and the social stigma of sex hunting.

The erotic and sexual connotations of connecting with strangers are already implicated in the design of some social applications. QQ, for example, has an associated e-mail service with a feature called the "floating bottle" that allows users to write an up-to-140-word message and send it in a hypothetical "bottle" to an unknown stranger. There are various types of bottles, such as the "location bottle" that targets users at specific areas and the "dating bottle" that seeks romantic opportunities. The latter allows users to specify the gender and age group of desirable receivers by choosing from such erotically suggestive options as *Shota*, a slang term from Japanese anime denoting prepubescent or pubescent boys, and *Loli*, slang for young girls with reference to Lolita characters in Japanese anime.

The "floating bottle" feature was adopted in the design of Wechat as Tencent developed the mobile phone application, but Wechat enhances users' capacity to connect with strangers instantly with location-based plug-ins, such as "look around," enables users to check out people nearby and "shake" that connects users who are using the same feature to meet strangers. By integrating online encounters and offline locations, these Wechat features facilitate not only virtual but also physical meetings between strangers, including arranging sexual encounters and advertising sex services. Local news reports about sex solicitation with the applications raised public concerns, particularly when it came to underage students. The social risk and stigma attached to intimacy between strangers (as opposed to latent ties) have likely discouraged college students from seeking serious relationships with anonymous strangers, or at least from expressing enthusiasm in using social media for such purposes. Social boundaries in the offline world implicate boundaries of morality and trust, which influence how Chinese college students use social media for matchmaking.

The social organization of the Chinese society has likely contributed to the strong influence of offline social circles. Partly because Confucianism emphasizes civility in concrete personal relationships, Chinese society encourages particularized trust in dense personal connections while discouraging generalized trust among strangers (Fukuyama 1995). Fei (1947/1992) made a similar observation of the Chinese social structure and argued that morality only makes sense in personal connections. He described the social structure as the *differential mode of association*, a term that recalls Ferdinand Tönnies's (1957) term, *Gemeinschaft*. More recent research provides less pessimistic accounts of generalized trust in China due to trust in political institutions (Steinhardt 2011), but in private matters such as matchmaking, particularized ties formed with friends and acquaintances continues to shape the online dating experiences of Chinese college students. Seeking romantic partners among strangers becomes less morally questionable and risky with the endorsement of social circles. SNSs enlarge their opportunities to connect with "strangers" and increase their speed of becoming acquainted without the help of human intermediaries, while at the same time extending the particularized trust of offline social circles to online networks through interlinking personal connections.

NEGOTIATED TIE-SIGNS: SHOWING OFF LOVE IN MONITORING CROWDS

The trust of interlinking personal relationships does not come without price. Moral accountability generates trust but also entails control. SNSs that contribute to interpersonal trust in matchmaking also tend to exert pressure on lovers' romantic expression. The double edge of social networks gives rise to young Chinese lovers' negotiation within social circles over proper presentation of self in online social spaces.

Social control is particularly pronounced at Renren Network in the narratives of young college students. Renren Network mainly replicates and extends their social circles in colleges and previous schools. With the offline circle replicated in the online space, the subculture of that group also finds online manifestations. Public postings with romantic implication are fair game for spectatorship at Renren Network. The convenience of watching—only a few clicks away—amplifies social surveillance characteristic of the offline crowds of schools and colleges. For example, Hongchuan, a first-year college student, described how he deleted his postings on Renren Network as a response to his classmates' mischievous comments. In a status update, he expressed gratitude to a woman in his class, but the status immediately caught the attention of other classmates, who kicked up a terrible row with teasing comments. In the words of Hongchuan, postings of romantic nature were likely to be "besieged," and the siege often took the form of "making a scene," "messing about," and "gossiping." Rumors, rows, and taunts are all ancient ways in which social groups exercise pressure on individuals to enforce social norms and boundaries (Spacks 1985). These forms of discipline are conveniently practiced in the online social space of Chinese students to regulate their expressions and behaviors at the online sites.

Besides peers, the presence of seniors and acquaintances at SNSs also contributes to the perception of social surveillance and control among Chinese college students. Many first-year college students were ready to tell stories of how their high school teachers watched out for dating among students for fear that romantic love would distract students from study and disadvantage them in the fierce competition for college admissions. Similar to what boyd (2014) has found among American teens, Chinese high school students were followed by their teachers at popular SNSs, and the online presence of teachers often leads to changes in students' presentation of self. For college students who are less concerned about monitoring by seniors, their discretion may be encouraged by possible judgment from acquaintances. SNSs often congregate audiences of varying degrees of closeness with the users. While teasing and joking in close circles of friends may be understood according to the subculture of the group, doing so in the presence of less well-acquainted social circles may invoke different interpretations and judgments. Concerns about reputation and social image in large social networks tend to discourage college students from posting romantic expressions that are likely to induce teasing and joking on SNSs.

Perceived surveillance and judgment largely contribute to young Chinese lovers' discretion at SNSs. For some, this means avoiding displaying any romantic association with each other at the online sites, especially when couples were uncertain about their relationships. For others, this means negotiating with the watching crowds over acceptable forms of romantic expression, particularly when lovers are ready to publicize their relationships. In fact, sharing some information about one's relationship is both common and necessary for lovers. In face-to-face contexts, for example, wearing engagement rings and holding hands in public—what Goffman (1971) called *tie signs*—function to present a team identity to the co-present others. Young Chinese called this public display of couple identity and mutual affection, *xiu en'ai* or *showing off love*.

A common reason young Chinese cited for *showing off love* on SNSs is to make announcements of their relationships, similar to going "Facebook official." Publicity means legitimacy, as the logic goes, and illegitimate relationships often have to remain in the shadow. *Showing off love* on SNSs dispels ambiguity in couples' understandings of relationship status and commitment (Mod 2010). As Katz (1981, 94) rightly put it, "so long as the information is not published—that is, so long as it is not 'public'— there is flexibility open to all concerned in the assignment of meaning." That is, publicity of the relationship holds lovers accountable. In the words of Luojia, a third-year college student, *showing off love* at SNSs "enhanced the couple's sense of security." By making a relationship public, it tells others that the relationship partners are no longer romantically available. *Showing off love* affirms couples' relationships by constructing them as a team within their social circles.

The relational commitment entailed in *showing off love* was conveyed through the channel as much as the message of the postings. Public delivery itself constitutes a personal message. For instance, Shenjie, a thirty-ish professional woman, made a point of posting her engagement pictures on Sina Weibo, a microblogging site, as a gesture of commitment to her fiancé. In her own words, "he would feel happier when he sees me telling other people about us." Shenjie's engagement photos on Weibo hence involve a message with two layers of meanings for two groups of addressees: to her friends' circle, the message was the photos; to her fiancé, the message was her commitment. This layered structure of address, or "addressivity" to use Bakhtin's term as adopted by Baxter (2011, 31) in the study of interpersonal relationships, characterizes lovers' public display of romantic affection on SNSs. *Showing off love* sends a personal message by means of publicity.

However, excessive displays of romantic intimacy are often thought to violate sociality in online social spaces as in offline spaces. Jiajin, a college student in his early twenties, described scenarios of *xiu en'ai* that were likely to repel co-present others: a couple sat in the front row of a classroom, hugging, kissing, and making lots of noise while other students were studying in the same room, or a couple posted "selfies" every day on Renren Network and kept saying how happy they were as a couple on social media. Such behaviors are often negatively sanctioned among young Chinese, as illustrated by the popular saying *xiu en'ai, si de kuai* or *showing off love, love ending fast*. This idiom expresses a popular sentiment or aversion towards undue public display of romantic intimacy. How and how much to disclose of one's romantic relationship at SNSs are matters of etiquette, and they involve the negotiation between lovers and their social circles over boundaries between personal and social spaces.

Young Chinese lovers' concerns about etiquette give rise to creative ways of *showing off love*. Adopting implicit strategies and crafting funny messages were popular ways to *show off love* in online social networks. For example, Shifei and Qianqian, a couple at the same college, adopted mirror images of a Minion as their profile pictures on Renren Network, with one Minion looking to the left and the other to the right. The subtle connection between these pictures only became evident to their friends when the couple commented on each other's status updates and the two pictures were thus juxtaposed. The subtlety and playfulness of the tie signs made the mirror images a socially acceptable form of *showing off love* in the couples' social circles.

Another implicit form of *showing off love* involves tagging romantic partners in re-posted messages, such as messages about astrological compatibility. Tagging someone in a post—using @ or at-mention to notify that person of the posting—entails double address like Shenjie's engagement photos at Sina Weibo. Like talking to someone within the earshot of a third party, tagging involves two sets of audiences at the same time: a general audience of the social circles and a specific audience of the romantic partner. While discussing what a great match a couple makes on SNSs may be too personal for the social spaces, tagging a boyfriend or girlfriend in a post about their astrological compatibility is not because it only notifies a specific person of a publicly available message. Since tags or the at-mention symbols are visible to anyone who can see the posts on such SNSs as Renren Network, Sina Weibo, and Wechat, tagging the loved one to a post of romantic compatibility itself constitutes a *tie sign*.

Besides *showing of love*, young Chinese also engage in verbal teasing to present couple identities on SNSs. Teasing in public contrasts with plain forms of *showing off love* in that it displays lovers' "fighting" rather than "liking." However, lovers' performance of teasing puts onstage their closeness despite the absence of any apparent expression of affections. Friendly teasing is an indicator of relational intimacy (Baxter 1992). Wenjun, a female college student, described lovers' mutual teasing in public as *xiu husun* or *showing off mutual bantering*. Teasing and joking are rituals of smudging boundaries and trafficking identities from one socially acknowledged realm to another while acknowledging the boundaries as legitimate (Goffman 1967). Here, the boundaries have to do with the proper territory of romantic display. While too much lovey-dovey interaction incurs aversion among young Chinese social circles, bantering gives them license to present a sense of intimacy in social spaces.

Social spaces are not gender free. Negotiating gendered etiquette, especially women's gender performance, is an important aspect of young Chinese's media practices with the presence of social circles. Erotic and sexual references to female romantic partners tend to be avoided on SNSs. Even when couples *show off love* playfully, they tend to invoke women's conjugal and domestic roles to cover up erotic implications of their play. For example, Xiaoding, a female college student, liked to post her consumer goods on Renren Network, and her boyfriend liked to tease her in follow-up posts by calling her *baijia niangmen'er*, or "wasteful woman who is likely to ruin the household." This form of teasing presents an understanding of romantic relationship in terms of marriage and invokes women's role in managing households. A similar example comes from Yue Min, a female college student who described the mutual bantering in her relationship as a form of *showing off love*. Her boyfriend once teased her unhealthy diet by writing on her Renren front page, "Mother's body shape will affect the next generation," to which she responded "How ungrateful you are to despise me!" This teasing and bantering about women's consuming habits and body shapes are flirtatious but decked out in comments on wifely and motherly duties. Wife and mother are traditionally considered "proper" gender roles of Chinese women in public in contrast to an object and subject of erotic desires. Young Chinese couples' teasing and joking at SNSs about women's "proper" roles hence legitimate their public displays of romantic intima-cy by not only denying its seriousness—it is just play—but also dressing it up in socially acceptable gender terms.

Plays, double addresses, and implicit tie signs all function as ways in which young Chinese negotiate romantic expression and social decorum at SNSs. These forms of communication allow enough ambiguity for such negotiations. Especially teasing serves to both transgress and discipline the boundaries of romantic love when used by lovers and their social circles respectively. Online network sites as the congregation of audi-ences from young Chinese's social circles provide moral anchors for their romantic commitment while at the same time regulating their public dis-play of romantic intimacy.

MEDIATED PRIVACY: ANONYMITY IN PUBLIC AND MESSAGES CROSS BOUNDARIES

While romantic expression is regulated at SNSs where offline social circles have a presence, young Chinese couples create secret spaces in anonymous online venues where they articulate their feelings and rela-tionships quite extensively. Similarly, in their closely knit offline commu-nities, young couples use private messages to smudge social boundaries of gender relations and performances. For young Chinese lovers, a pri-vate space is largely defined as free from social constraints, which offers the key to understanding their media practices.

One place to find the online romantic alcoves is weblogs. Internet blogging sites have been noted for their various blends of "publicness" and "privateness." By controlling identity information and access to blog entries, bloggers can engage in a range of "publicly private" and "pri-vately public" behaviors (Lange 2008). Some young Chinese create "pub-licly private" spaces in weblogs by concealing their identity information. Anonymity, in the narratives of young Chinese, is a mechanism of priva-cy in public places. Social decorum that organizes romantic expression of young Chinese tends to be less binding when they are in the midst of strangers, whom Simmel (1950, 404) described as noncommittal to the group and hence able to view things with a sense of objectivity.

An example is the joint blog of Yawen, a professional editor in her late twenties, and Tongbin, a college teacher who later became her husband. Soon after they began to date, the couple started a collaborative weblog account, where they could log in with a shared password and write about their feelings and experiences. Yawen likened their joint weblog entries to their one-to-one interaction via instant messaging, both being "two people's conversation behind the door." The anonymous weblog was the couple's secret "turf" despite its theoretical visibility to whoever hap-pened to come across it. This contrasted with their use of Qzone, an SNS where they interacted with friends and acquaintances and made a point not to post anything suggestive of their romantic affections. Their discretion at Qzone and their boldness in the weblog illustrated etiquette in social circles and liberty in the anonymous public.

Although SNSs are often thought to entail collapsed contexts and multiple audiences (Marwick and boyd 2010), some young Chinese use SNSs to communicate exclusively with romantic partners. They may use one online networking site for romantic interaction only while dedicating others to communication with larger social circles. Or they may create *xiaohao*, or "minor accounts," with pseudonyms for romantic communication aside from accounts known by their friends. For instance, Qianqian and Shifei created their "minor accounts" on Renren Network for exclusive interaction with each other. They manipulated the private setting to allow only "friends" to see her profile and added each other as the only friend on the accounts. Qianqian kept their dating log at her account, posting pictures of things they did, places they visited, and food they shared, as well as their "selfies." Then both parties added narratives, comments, and responses to each other's comments. To use the couple's words, this online space contained their "joint memory" and recorded how they "grew together." More than recording their dating experiences, the couple explored and constructed their relationship and identities through chronicling, commenting, and reflecting upon the pictures, narratives, and conversations.

While young Chinese build intimate alcoves in online venues, they also use private messaging to create personal spaces in offline social crowds. Especially in Chinese universities, life is largely collective, with students sharing closely knit living quarters. A private physical space is hard to acquire for college sweethearts on campus; messaging services, such as those offered by texting, QQ, and Wechat, provide couples with the means to create a virtual private space. Importantly, message exchange between college student sweethearts transgresses the gendered institution of college dormitories. Chinese students generally live in same-sex dormitory buildings supervised by guardians. This residential arrangement recalls the principle of sex segregation in traditional Chinese thought, a principle that continues to be implemented in modern institutions of collective lives such as factories (Mann 2011, 27–49). Young Chinese lovers negotiate the socio-geographic boundaries as they exchange messages across the same-sex dormitories. By using private messages to communicate across the same-sex dormitories, they take what Goffman (1961, 99) called a "spiritual leave" from prescribed identities in the homosocial spaces. The spatial segregation of the sexes thus becomes ineffective in proscribing heterosexual romances.

Private messaging also enables women to negotiate with stereotypical gender roles in romantic relating. Popular discourses of dating among the Chinese tend to regard men as the suitors and women the suited, which often holds back young Chinese women from making romantic advances. Within such discourses of dating, there is a sense of shame or embarrassment attached to women pursuing men, and a kind of "moral leverage" to women who are pursued. Some young Chinese women find messaging media a useful means to negotiate these discourses and to obtain the moral leverage while taking the initiative. Qianqian's use of private messaging provides a good illustration. She fell in love with Shifei while working with him at a student organization, but he was unaware despite her frequent hints. She tagged her work e-mails to him with a paragraph or two about her personal life and feelings, and she sent him greetings via Wechat every night before sleep, but he still did not get the message. So she created an anonymous e-mail account and sent him a note telling him in third person that Qianqian was his secret admirer. These concealed revelations of love demonstrate her active pursuit of him while waiting for him to announce his love first. Messaging media in this case, including both e-mail and Wechat messaging, facilitated her negotiation with the culturally preferred role of women in romantic relating. In various forms of concealed revelation, young Chinese women are able to make romantic advances in "respectable" manners.

Since it is taboo to publicly display erotic desires for and of respectable women, young Chinese find private messaging particularly useful in initiating romantic relationship. Private messaging services at SNSs give young Chinese a private (one-to-one) way to interact flirtatiously in public (with a stranger). For example, Chengang, a male college student, initiated an interaction with his girlfriend at Renren Network with a private message that complimented her clothes. He explained his media choice by invoking gendered etiquette in public places: a young woman responding to a public compliment on her looks by an unacquainted young man indicated indiscretion and loose virtue. Chengang's concern recalls what Gardner (1989) has found about "street remarks," or evaluative commentary offered by unacquainted men to young and attractive women: Women often have no choice but ignore the "street remarks" to maintain their respectability, because responding to vulgar and intrusive compliments ratifies the remarks. Using private messaging for a flirtatious ice-breaker, Chengang was able to initiate a flirtatious relationship with the unacquainted woman while reconstructing the boundaries of her respectability.

Social decorum and gender norms pose obstacles to romantic intimacy. Young Chinese lovers use private messaging and anonymous online venues to redress the constraints of etiquette in social arenas, the difficulty of obtaining a physical space of their own, and the stereotype of gender performance. For young Chinese lovers, mediated privacy afforded by anonymous online venues and private messages mend the faulty ecosystem of romantic relating in their offline worlds.

CONCLUSION: THE LOGIC OF LOVERS' MEDIA USE

Young Chinese lovers' media practices are rich and varied. Their online practices demonstrate complex connections with their social contexts, cultural norms, and offline relations. On one hand, they look for potential dates at SNSs that articulate their latent offline ties and seek a moral anchor for commitment with romantic displays at these SNSs. Offline social circles hold promises of match in social station and provide sources of trust through interlocking interpersonal ties. On the other hand, young couples negotiate social etiquette and norms of gender performance with various forms of implicit and playful online communication. They also create virtual private spaces away from social control at online venues through anonymity and within offline social settings by means of private messaging.

The logic of young Chinese lovers' media use revolves around the dialectics between the social and the personal realms of life. While offline social circles provide a potential match and moral anchor for romantic relating, they also exert influence on young Chinese regarding whom to choose and how to behave. Young lovers engage their social circles to endorse personal commitment, but they also get away from social regulation to build intimacy in private spaces both online and offline. The social-personal dialectics resemble what Baxter and Montgomery (1996) described as the push and pull between relational partners and their community, particularly the tension between relational autonomy and community connections. More importantly, the ways in which young Chinese lovers manage the dialectical tensions in their media practices illustrate culturally informed ways of seeking match, building trust, expressing commitment, performing gender identities, and conducting gender relations.

The importance of offline social circles for "online" dating among the young Chinese puts into perspective claims about romantic liberation in the digital age. In his study of French weblogs and online forums, Kaufmann (2012, 74) argues that the Internet has accelerated the dating trend that dances had started in nineteenth-century France and that "the whole of society has become a huge dance hall where anyone . . . can ask anyone else . . . to dance." Specifically, online forums and weblogs offer endless opportunities of meeting and dating in a world temporarily cut off from established rules and normative expectations in the offline world. Kaufmann's analogy between dance halls and the Internet illuminates the dating trend in France towards more individual freedom and less social control as well as the quickening of that trend by the Internet. However, the online world is not a flattened space where offline social boundaries cease to play a role in dating practices. Not everyone can dance with everyone else when education, social status, and other categories of social stratification still matter in mate selection. Societies control love attachment in various ways, and an important way to do that is to control individuals' informal relationships so as to channel their focus of affection (Goode 1957). SNSs as a networked matchmaking ground for young Chinese illustrate the new ways in which offline social connections shape individuals' love choices as the Internet opens up their opportunities of meeting with strangers.

The online-offline connections of young Chinese's media practices also suggest the limitations of using the public-private dichotomy to understand lovers' communication on social media. Chinese lovers tend to differentiate two kinds of public visibility, each entailing different levels of social control and corresponding rules of communication. While the public of strangers suggests freedom of romantic expression, the public of family, friends, and acquaintances entails discipline of lovers' interaction. The contrast between the two "public" places resonates with the loose bonding between strangers and the particularistic ties in closely knit communities. The perception of different "public" places sheds light on the shifting of dating spaces in the last century: Young Americans moved their dating from the front porches of family houses to the back seats in the car (Bailey 1988), and Chinese lovers in rural areas went to the cities to have some privacy away from their families and social circles (Yan 2003). In both cases, a public of strangers means privacy for lovers more than a familiar social circle. Viewed from this perspective, Chinese lovers' intimate alcoves online and private messages within offline social settings are only recent manifestations of the same attempt of youths to seek freedom from social control.

The virtual spaces of romantic intimacy hold both promises and risks for romantic couples. Kaufmann (2012, 89) argued that the Internet holds possibilities for young people and women who are straitjacketed by traditions because the Internet offers "a world apart that exists parallel to worlds in which socialization is more firmly grounded." For young Chinese, and particularly young Chinese women, private messaging and anonymous social media offer a comparatively "cut off" world for them to negotiate conventional gender roles and gendered morality as well as exploring gender relationships. Privacy, as Yan (2003) noted, is a privilege of the rich and the elite groups traditionally in China rather than a legal right for everyone. The uneven distribution of physical space as a limited resource adds to the lure of digital media through lovers' "remediation"—in the sense of restoration of damaged ecosystems and of reform in social and political senses (Bolter and Grusin 1999). Digital media, and particularly private messaging, redresses the unequal access to physical space and the institution of collective lives. Where the much-coveted physical space is out of reach, digital media enable young Chinese to create their virtual private spaces.

On the other hand, the virtual private spaces shift the power of information control away from lovers themselves. The storage of data in clouds and server farms and the private settings out of users' control partly explain why private online spaces are not really "private." Keizer (2012) noticed the paradox of digital privacy by pointing out that social media gurus secure their own private space in multi-billion-dollar homes while cashing in on the private information of media users. In this sense, digital media create new dangers to personal privacy by affording "private" virtual spaces. This outsourcing of information control to mediating parties is not new to lovers—think of postmasters, mail censors, and delivery personnel. Nor is using media of mass delivery for romantic purposes new. Valentine greetings in local newspapers sent romantic messages to specific persons, while secret codes and anonymity kept the messages private (Duck, Pond, and Schnittjier 1991). What is new is the lovers' capacity to record an unprecedented number of lovers' messages, sometimes with extraordinary, if not graphic, details, with digital media, and the unmatched power of the Internet to spread the messages in case of user indiscretion, technological glitch, or corporate greed. Privacy achieved with digital media entails high risks for romantic couples.

REFERENCES

Bailey, Beth L. 1988. *From Front Porch to Back Seat: Courtship in Twentieth-Century America.* Baltimore: John Hopkins University Press.

Baxter, Leslie A. 1992. "Forms and Functions of Intimate Play in Personal Relationship." *Human Communication Research* 18 (3): 336–63.

———. A. 2011. *Voicing Relationships: A Dialogic Perspective.* LA: Sage.

Baxter, Leslie A., and Barbara M. Montgomery. 1996. *Relating: Dialogues and Dialectics.* New York: Guilford Press.

Bolter, Jay D., and Richard Grusin. 1999. *Remediation: Understanding New Media.* Cambridge, MA: MIT Press.

boyd, danah m. 2014. *It's Complicated. The Social Lives of Networked Teens.* New Haven: Yale University Press.

boyd, danah m., and Nicole B. Ellison. 2008. "Social Network Sites: Definition, History and Scholarship." *Journal of Computer-Mediated Communication* 13 (1): 210–30. doi: 10.1111/j.1083-6101.2007.00393.x.

Broadbent, Stefana, and Valerie Bauwens. 2008. "Understanding Convergence." *Interactions: Toward a Model of Innovation* 15 (1): 23–27. http://dl.acm.org/citation.cfm?id=1330536&picked=formats&CFID=371629308&CFTOKEN=31507144.

Coyne, Sarah M., Laura Stockdale, Dean Busby, Bethany Iverson, and David M. Grant. 2011. "'I Luv U :)!': A Descriptive Study of the Media Use of Individuals in Romantic Relationships." *Family Relations* 60: 150–62.

Duck, Steve, Kris Pond, and Sara Schnittjier. 1991. "On Public Display of Private Intimacy: A Communicative Analysis of Valentine's Day Messages." Paper presented at the Third Conference of the International Network on Personal Relationships. Normal-Bloomington, Illinois, May.

Fei, Xiaotong. 1947/1992. *From the Soil: The Foundations of Chinese Society.* Berkeley, CA: University of California Press.

Fox, Jesse, Jeremy L. Osborn, and Katie M. Warber. 2014. "Relational Dialectics and Social Networking Sites: The Role of Facebook in Romantic Relationship Escalation, Maintenance, Conflict, and Dissolution." *Computers in Human Behavior* 35: 527–34.

Fox, Jesse, Katie M. Warber, and Dana C. Makstaller. 2013. "The Role of Facebook in Romantic Relationship Development: An Exploration of Knapp's Relational Stage Model." *Journal of Social and Personal Relationships* 30 (6): 771–94.

Fukuyama, Francis. 1995. *Trust: The Social Virtues and the Creation of Prosperity*. New York: Free Press.

Goffman, Erving. 1961. *Asylums: Essays on the Social Situation of Mental Patients and Other Inmates*. Chicago: Aldine Publishing Company.

———. 1967. *Interaction Ritual: Essays on Face-to-Face Behaviors*. New York: Doubleday Anchor.

———. 1971. *Relations in Public: Microstudies of the Public Order*. New York: Harper Colophon Books.

Goode, William J. 1959. "The Theoretical Importance of Love." *American Sociological View* 24 (1): 38–47.

Katz, Elihu. 1981. "Publicity and Pluralistic Ignorance: Notes on the 'Spiral of Silence'." In *Public Opinion and Social Change*, ed. Horst Baier, Hans M. Kepplinger, Kurt Reumann, and Elisabeth Noelle-Neumann, 28–38. Wiesbaden: Westdeutscher Verlag.

Kaufmann, Jean-Claude. 2012. *Love Online*. Cambridge: Polity Press.

Keizer, Garret. 2012. *Privacy*. New York: Picador.

Lange, Patricia G. 2008. "Publicly Private and Privately Public: Social Networking on Youtube." *Journal of Computer-Mediated Communication* 13: 361-80. doi: 10.1111/j.1083-6101.2007.00400.x.

Mann, Susan. 2011. *Gender and Sexuality in Modern Chinese History*. Cambridge: Cambridge University Press.

Marwick, Alice E., and danah boyd. 2010. "I Tweet Honestly, I Tweet Passionately: Twitter Users, Context Collapse, and the Imagined Audience." *New Media & Society* 13: 96–113.

Mod, Greg B. B. A. 2010. "Reading Romance: The Impact Facebook Rituals can Have on a Romantic Relationship." *Journal of Comparative Research in Anthropology and Sociology* 1 (2): 61–77.

Simmel, Georg. 1950. *The Sociology of Georg Simmel*. Trans. Kurt H. Wolff. New York: The Free Press.

Spacks, Patricia M. 1985. *Gossip*. New York: Knopf.

Steinhardt, H. Christoph. 2011. "How is High Trust in China Possible? Comparing the Origins of Generalized Trust in Three Chinese Societies." *Political Studies* 60: 434–54.

Tönnies, Ferdinand. 1957. *Community and Society*. Trans. Charles P. Loomis. New York: Harper & Row.

Utz, Sonja, and Camiel J. Beukeboom. 2011. "The Role of Social Network Sites in Romantic Relationships: Effects on Jealousy and Relationship Happiness." *Journal of Computer-mediated Communication* 16 (4): 511–27. doi:10.1111/j.1083-6101.2011.01552.x.

Yan, Yunxiang. 2003. *Private Life Under Socialism: Love, Intimacy, and Family Change in a Chinese Village 1949–1999*. Stanford: Stanford University Press.

Zhao, Xuan, Victoria S. Sosik, and Dan Cosley. 2012. "It's Complicated: How Romantic Partners Use Facebook." *Proceedings of the SIGCHI Conference on Human Factors in Computing Systems*: 771–80.

TEN

Connecting Profile-to-Profile

How People Self-Present and Form Impressions of Others through Online Dating Profiles

Catalina L. Toma and Jonathan D. D'Angelo

Online dating has profoundly altered the landscape of romantic connections in the twenty-first century. Not only do people turn to the Internet in large numbers to find romantic partners, but they also experience significant success in doing so. One nationally representative survey of U.S. adults shows that 17 percent of the heterosexual couples and 41 percent of the same-sex couples who had met in the previous ten years did so online (Rosenfeld and Thomas 2012). For heterosexual couples, this made the Internet the second most popular venue for meeting a romantic partner, after meeting through friends. Another study shows that, among Americans who married or began long-term committed relationships between 2005 and 2012, more than one-third had met online (Cacioppo et al. 2013). The same study shows that relationships originating online had a lower rate of divorce and a higher rate of satisfaction than those originating offline, although effect sizes were small (Cacioppo et al. 2013). The biggest predictors of using online dating websites are being single and being an Internet user (Sautter, Tippett, and Morgan 2010), suggesting that online dating has become a mainstream method for attracting romantic partners, rather than a niche filled by a specific group.

Clearly online dating is a transformative technology for romantic relationships. But how does it work? Its very name might be a misnomer, because "dating" oftentimes happens face-to-face or through interpersonal media (phone, text), rather than on online dating websites. These websites simply facilitate romantic *introductions*. Users are typically asked to construct detailed profiles describing themselves and then are connected with other users in the system either by compatibility algorithms (e.g., eHarmony), by specifying their own search criteria (e.g., Match.com), or a combination of the two (e.g., OKCupid). If users like each other based on their respective profiles, they initiate contact and proceed to the "dating" stage of their relationship through mediated or face-to-face communication. Under these circumstances, we argue that *profile self-presentation*, or constructing a desired version of the self for potential partners to peruse, and *impression formation*, or evaluating potential partners based on their online profiles, are the single most vital elements of online dating.

The purpose of this chapter is to analyze these two fundamental aspects of online dating. Since deception is a frequently used self-presentational tactic and one that elicits great concerns in online dating (Cali, Coleman, and Campbell 2013), we pay particular attention to how it infiltrates profile self-presentation. We synthesize the state-of-the-art literature and discuss the main theoretical frameworks that have been proposed to explicate these phenomena, with an eye on how the technological affordances inherent to online dating (e.g., unlimited composition time, editability, audience access) intersect with psychological variables (e.g., users' relationship goals, gender) in the production and evaluation of profiles. We end with proposals for future research.

SELF-PRESENTATION AND DECEPTION IN ONLINE DATING PROFILES

Self-presentation is defined as the process of constructing a version of self in order to convey a desired impression to an audience (Leary and Kowalski 1990). This construction process involves emphasizing certain attributes of self, downplaying others, and strategically utilizing deception in order to either rectify perceived shortcomings or ascribe to oneself credentials not possessed in reality. Decisions about the content of self-presentation, including the use of deception, are made based on self-presentational goals (i.e., what do I want to achieve based on this self-presentational act?), perceptions of the values and preferences of the audience (i.e., what is likely to impress my particular audience?), and the constraints and capabilities of the medium in which the self-presentation takes place (see also Toma and Hancock 2011).

Profile Self-Presentation

The theoretical framework of *selective self-presentation* (Walther 1996; 2007) has been fruitfully used to explicate online dating self-presentation, precisely because of its emphasis on how media features affect online communicators' ability to convey a desired persona. Online dating profiles, as an interaction venue, are substantially different from face-to-face. At a basic level, claims about the self in an online dating setting take the form of written text (i.e., answers to open-ended questions, such as "about me," and close-ended questions, such as height and weight) and photographs, while face-to-face claims are oral and involve the entire embodied self. At a deeper level, online dating self-presentation is governed by a series of technological affordances that are typically unavailable face-to-face and that are theorized to substantially shape what gets presented online. The strength of the selective self-presentation framework lies in delineating these affordances, specifically:

- *Asynchronicity*, or the absence of real-time interaction, allows online daters unlimited time to think through and compose their self-presentational claims, unlike face-to-face daters, who often have to think on their feet to respond to potential partners' questions.
- *Editability* allows online daters to alter and refine their self-presentational claims until they are satisfied with them. Conversely, face-to-face daters cannot erase gaffes or undesirable statements and thus cannot improve upon their self-presentation once delivered.
- *The reallocation of cognitive resources* enables online communicators to invest the entirety of their attention and thought into the construction of their self-presentation, without interruption or distraction. For instance, online daters can easily retreat to a quiet space (e.g., office, bedroom, library) for a length of time of their choosing to craft their profiles. By contrast, face-to-face daters must field questions and deal with environmental stimuli (e.g., waiters, food, other diners, if at a restaurant) concomitantly with constructing their desired self; this leaves them with fewer mental resources to invest into their self-presentation.

The key proposition of selective self-presentation is that these affordances allow online communicators more control over their claims than is available to their face-to-face counterparts; as a result, online self-presentations should be highly strategic and in synch with self-presenters' goals. This claim received support on several online platforms: On Facebook, users reported constructing self-presentations that they believed strategically embellished the desirable aspects of their personalities, such as their sense of humor and sociability (Toma and Carlson 2015); on online discussion boards, users engaged in more editing behaviors and took more time to craft their statements when interacting with desirable than less desirable targets, indicating that they did, in fact, exploit technological affordances to make a good impression when motivated to do so (Walther 2007); when creating online avatars, participants presented more desirable images when given a dating than a blogging or gaming premise, suggesting, again, that they took advantage of technological affordances to create attractive personae (Vasalou and Joinson 2009).

To understand how the notion of selective self-presentation applies to online dating, it is necessary to identify online daters' self-presentational goals, since selective self-presentation simply means that online daters are highly apt to act on their goals. How do online daters wish to come across in their profiles? Ellison, Heino, and Gibbs's (2006) pioneering work on this topic revealed that online daters experience competing desires, or tensions, that they must reconcile when crafting their profiles. On the one hand, they wish to come across as attractive as possible in order to be admired and entice potential mates. This desire for self-enhancement—that is, presenting a better version of self than strictly warranted by reality—is exacerbated by the perceived competitiveness of online dating. With dozens or even hundreds of singles populating the same dating arena, online daters feel compelled to stand out by boosting their attractiveness. On the other hand, online daters experience a need for authenticity, or presenting their veridical selves, because (a) they anticipate face-to-face interaction with potential partners, who might then be able to detect these deceptions and reject them on their account; and (b) they wish to be liked and appreciated for who they truly are, rather than for an unrealistic version of themselves. The online daters interviewed by Ellison et al. (2006) reported reconciling these competing desires by presenting elements of their "ideal selves"—that is, attributes that they wished they embodied and that they *could* conceivably attain in the future. For instance, one dater reported presenting herself as thinner in order to motivate herself to lose weight and therefore truthfully embody the self she claimed online. Resorting to the ideal self allows online daters to enhance their attractiveness while not significantly deviating from reality, or deviating in ways that cannot be justified or amended later. Importantly, such strategic self-presentation was enabled by the affordances of computer-mediated communication outlined earlier, providing support to the framework of selective self-presentation.

A more granular approach to the issue of online daters' self-presentational goals was taken by Toma and Hancock (Toma and Hancock 2010; Hancock and Toma 2009), who considered how online daters' self-presentational goals might be specifically tied to their understanding of what their audience wants. Evolutionary theory (e.g., Barber 1995; Buss and Schmitt 1993; Daly and Wilson 1995; Gangestad and Thornhill 1997; Thornhill and Gangestad 1993) is a useful lens for delineating what heterosexuals value in romantic partners, and therefore provides a framework for understanding online daters' audience-specific self-presentational goals. Evolutionary theory proposes that men and women developed mate preferences that, in the environment in which humans evolved, increased reproductive fitness—that is, their ability to successfully pass on their genes through offspring. Specifically, women developed a preference for men who could provide and protect, as this was necessary for survival during the difficult pregnancy and child-rearing process, when women themselves were less able to fend for themselves and their babies. Men's ability to provide and protect was denoted by markers of physical strength (e.g., height) and, in the current environment, by social status indicators (e.g., job, income, education). Men developed a preference for youthfulness and physical attractiveness in female partners; the former because women's ability to get pregnant expires at a much earlier age than men's, and the latter because physical attractiveness denotes healthy genes that would increase an offspring's likelihood of survival. As strategic self-presenters, heterosexual online daters should mold their self-presentations to their audiences' preferences, as predicted by evolutionary forces. Research finds support for these claims. Women online daters posted more photographs (an average of about four) than men (an average of about two), especially if they were attractive, as a way to showcase their physical appearance (Toma and Hancock 2010). Women also posted older photographs of themselves (an average of seventeen months old) than men (an average of six months old). These older photographs display a younger version of self, thus presumably appealing to men's preferences for youthfulness (Hancock and Toma 2009). By the same token, men gave themselves more leeway for embellishing their social status indicators (i.e., income, education), by declaring it more acceptable to misrepresent these elements than women (Toma, Hancock, and Ellison 2008). Note that, as before, these strategic self-presentations are enabled by the technological affordances postulated by the selective self-presentation framework.

Profile Deception

Let us now turn our attention to deception as a specific self-presentational tactic utilized by online daters. As mentioned before, people are generally wary of online deception, and perceive it to be a particularly salient problem in online dating. In a recent survey, about half of online daters reported serious concerns about the extent of prevarication in online dating profiles (Smith and Duggan 2013). These fears are likely to stem from the disembodied nature of online self-presentation, whereby online daters get to make self-presentational claims in the absence of the corporeal self (see also Toma, Jiang, and Hancock 2016), and from the impossibility of capturing a dynamic, constantly evolving self, into a static, two-dimensional (i.e., using text and photographs) profile. Indeed, an interview study reveals that online daters don't expect their own and others' profiles to be an exact replica of the offline self, but merely a good enough approximation, precisely because of the medium's limitations (Ellison, Hancock, and Toma 2012).

A large project examining the prevalence of deception in a sample of profiles from online daters in the New York City area found that 80 percent of daters had lied about either their height, weight, or age. However, deviations from the truth were small and gender-driven. Men increased their height by about half an inch, on average, whereas women were relatively honest about their height; women subtracted about eight pounds from their weight, significantly more than men, who only subtracted about two pounds, on average; and age was relatively honestly presented, with only a few outliers deviating from the truth. Notably, these deviations were measured objectively, in order to avoid the problem of having to rely on liars to be honest about their deceptions when probed by researchers. Participants were asked to step on a scale in order to obtain weight measurements, to stand against a measuring tape for height assessments, and to produce identification for verifying their date of birth (Toma, Hancock, and Ellison 2008). In a follow-up study of photographic deception, researchers found that the daters themselves rated their photographs as quite accurate, but judges who evaluated daters' photographs against an everyday photograph, taken by the researchers, had a different view. Judges rated women's photographs as significantly less accurate than men's, due to the presence of inaccuracies related to physical characteristics such as age, hairstyle, and skin (Hancock and Toma 2009). Overall, this pattern of deceptive self-presentation provides support for the selective self-presentation theoretical framework once again. Online daters did not lie indiscriminately, embellishing themselves simply because it is easy to do so online. Rather, they took advantage of technological affordances to produce deceptions that were frequent (in order to give themselves an advantage in the dating arena), but small (in order not to alienate potential mates upon subsequent face-to-face meetings), and strategically placed, appealing to the known preferences of the opposite gender. Men lied about their height, because women prefer taller men, and women lied about their weight and photographs presumably in order to enhance their physical attractiveness, which men favor in romantic partners. This pattern is consistent with the claims of evolutionary theory. The fact that photographs were the least accurate element of the profile—according to judges, but not to the daters themselves—reflects perhaps the extent of embellishment that is possible to use face-to-face before going on a date. Surely most daters did not plan to show up on a date looking like they did when they came to the lab to have their photograph taken for a research study. Thus, photographic deception may not be as problematic as the judges' ratings indicate, but may instead be small and strategic, consistent with the selective self-presentation framework.

IMPRESSION FORMATION IN ONLINE DATING PROFILES

Once online dating self-presentations are constructed, they are subject to scrutiny and evaluation by potential mates. How do online daters form impressions of others solely based on profiles? Much of the research to date has been concerned with the impact of *profile cues*, or bits of information contained in the profile, such as photographs, textual self-descriptions, or system-generated cues (e.g., time stamps about a users' last login) on impression formation in online environments. Two main theoretical frameworks have been advanced on this topic: social information processing theory (SIPT, Walther 1992) and choice architecture (Thaler and Sustein 2009), which we discuss below.

Social Information Processing Theory

While this theory was originally developed to explain how individuals develop impressions through text-only interactions, it has been subsequently expanded to include the evaluation of multimodal (i.e., text and photographs) online profiles. On the topic of forming impressions about online strangers, SIPT makes one straightforward prediction: In interaction contexts characterized by high levels of uncertainty (such as evaluating online strangers), every bit of information takes on much more meaning than it would otherwise. In order to reduce uncertainty, observers actively utilize each cue to extract judgments about their target, and ascribe them substantial diagnostic value. For instance, grammatical ability, the setting of photographs, or sequencing of hobbies become interpreted as highly telling of an unknown target's personality, although such information may be insignificant when evaluating a close friend's personality. Simply put, small online cues carry big meaning in terms of impression formation. An extension of this notion proposes that some online cues matter more than others. These cues have been labeled "sticky cues" (D'Angelo et al. 2015; Van Der Heide and Schumaker 2013), because they grab perceivers' attention and influence impression formation more than other cues. Following the dictates of SIPT, the majority of research on online dating impression formation has been concerned with identifying sticky cues and unpacking their meaning. Two such cues have received empirical attention: photographs and warranting cues. We describe them below.

Simply reviewing online dating websites reveals that most of them depend on photographs as the main way to showcase and differentiate among daters, at least initially. When online daters are connected with their matches, they are presented with thumbnails of these matches' photographs, on which they must click if they wish to obtain more information about that person. The profile photograph is literally the gateway to a potential partner's profile. Unsurprisingly, most online daters indicate that they carefully attend to this photograph and make decisions about whom to pursue based on it (Couch and Pranee 2008). In fact, many refuse to even engage with profiles lacking photographs (Heino, Ellison, and Gibbs 2010). The photograph is ascribed such diagnostic value that it is often used as a benchmark against which the reliability of other profile information is gauged. Best and Delmege (2012), and Gibbs, Ellison, and Lai (2010), found that online daters utilize photographs as checks for textual self-disclosure, rating profiles as credible if the text was congruent with the photographs and the reverse if they were incongruent. For example, an incongruent online dating profile might provide textual self-disclosures of outdoor adventure, but photographs of bottle service at a club.

This is consistent with previous impression formation research on Facebook, which suggests that photographs carry greater impression formation weight than textual self-disclosures (D'Angelo et al. 2014; Van Der Heide, D'Angelo, and Schumaker 2012).

While online daters actively attend to photographs and seek out profiles with photographs, laboratory research suggests that the presence of photographs might not have the straightforwardly positive effect that daters believe it to have. In one study, profiles in which the photograph was removed by the experimenters were rated as more trustworthy than those that displayed a photograph, presumably because purely textual online information encourages observers to idealize the self-presenters—that is, to mentally fill in the blanks for unavailable information with positive information (Toma 2010). This could facilitate relationship development, provided, of course, that the trust is well-placed. Moreover, research finds that an especially attractive photograph can be problematic for women daters' perceived trustworthiness: Men perceived more attractive women online daters as less trustworthy, although women did not display the same bias for attractive men's photographs (McGloin and Denes 2016).

Warranting cues are defined to be pieces of information that are perceived to be as resistant to manipulation by the self-presenter, and are therefore deemed more credible (Walther and Parks, 2002). In the case of online dating, this includes system-generated cues (e.g., time of last login) or links to websites hosted by external organizations (e.g., companies where daters are employed). Wotipka and High (2016) showed that when online daters are sensitive to such cues, they do, in fact, ascribe higher credibility to profiles containing warranting cues. This is consistent with prior research on social networking sites showing that warranting cues are important determinants of online impression formation (De-Andrea et al. 2015; Hall, Pennington, and Lueders 2014; Fox, Warber, and Makstaller 2013; Utz 2010; Walther et al. 2009).

Choice Architecture

The second theoretical framework to inform research on impression formation in online dating is choice architecture (Thaler and Sustein 2009). Choice architecture refers to the manner in which choices are presented and arranged, either in physical spaces (e.g., grocery stores) or online spaces. Since online dating by definition operates by giving users choices between potential matches, so much so that many online daters view using these websites as akin to shopping (Heino et al. 2010), and since designers of these websites have substantial control over how these choices are presented to users (e.g., how many choices are given, when these choices are given, etc.), this framework seems to be especially relevant to online dating. Unbeknownst to online daters, the mere availability of choices may affect their impressions of potential matches.

Choice architecture can be conceptualized across several dimensions. The first is the sheer *amount of choice* available, an issue addressed by the choice overload theoretical framework (Iyengar and Lepper 2000). While people typically desire a greater amount of choice (see Patall, Cooper, and Robinson 2008 for review), research has shown that more options are not always better, as they paradoxically decrease satisfaction with the selected item (e.g., Arunachalam et al. 2009; Iyengar and Lepper 2000; Schwartz 2004). The second dimension is the *quality of choices*. Research suggests that having more attractive options also decreases satisfaction with the selected item (Scheibehenne, Rainer, and Todd 2009). The relationship between attractive options and choice satisfaction is so strong that a more attractive small set reduces satisfaction more than a less attractive large set (Scheibehenne, Rainer, and Todd 2009). The third dimension is the *complexity of choices*, conceptualized as the number of attributes each choice contains, and operationalized as the number of choices in a set multiplied by the number of attributes of each choice (Greifeneder, Scheibehenne, and Kleber, 2010). More complex choices reduce satisfaction with one's selection more than less complex choices (Mogilner, Rudnick, and Iyengar 2008). For instance, if individuals can place their choices into categories, they experience greater satisfaction with their choice, because this exercise simplifies the choice (Mogilner, Rudnick, and Iyengar 2008). The fourth dimension is the *reversibility of choices*, with the reversibility effect arguing that, when people can change their minds about a choice, they experience less satisfaction with that choice than when they are locked into it (e.g., Gilbert and Ebert 2002; Frey 1981; Frey et al. 1984). The final dimension is the *loss of options*. Research has begun to explore what happens when people are faced with a pool of choices that is likely to diminish over time through the disappearance of some of the choices. Findings indicate that in such a context, individuals who tend to explore more and exhaust all options before making a decision (i.e., maximizers), search less because they are concerned with losing the options that they have (Patalano et al. 2015). In sum, the dimensions of choice architecture enumerated earlier (amount, quality, complexity, reversibility, and loss of choices) have been shown to affect people's perceptions of their choices in predictable ways: Choices that are more numerous, higher in quality, more complex, reversible, and less likely to disappear tend to decrease people's satisfaction with the selected item. Importantly, all these dimensions are highly salient to online dating.

Research to date has focused on the effects of the amount of choice available to online daters. A series of initial studies applying choice overload theory have found conflicting evidence. When single women were asked to select a hypothetical match out of four, twenty-four, or sixty-four online dating profiles, there was no impact of choice set size on satisfaction with the selection (Lenton and Stewart, 2008). However, Wu and Chiou (2009) and Yang and Chiou (2010) found that online daters who were presented with more matches (30 versus 60 versus 90, and 40 versus 80, respectively) engaged in more searching behaviors (i.e., examined more profiles) and selected partners who deviated more from their pre-specified ideal list of qualities, suggesting that choice overload did, in fact, have a psychological effect on online daters.

Attempting find some remedy to these inconsistent findings, we (D'Angelo and Toma 2016) conducted the most extensive study to date on the effect of choice overload on online daters' satisfaction with selected partners. Using an experimental design, we combined a number of key elements previously missing in the application of choice overload theory in online dating. First, unlike Lenton and Stewart (2008), we used a real online dating website, rather than a hypothetical one. Second, we hypothesized that online dating is a context where time matters in the sense that decrements in satisfaction should only be observed over time, and not immediately after a choice of a potential partner is made. Unlike choices of consumer goods, choices of romantic partners are complex and may require deeper thinking that unfolds over time. Thus, we asked participants to rate their satisfaction after an initial selection and again one week later. Finally, we considered the role of choice reversibility in satisfaction with a potential romantic partner, because reversibility is the basic premise of most dating websites (i.e., people can and frequently do change their minds about whom to date).

Results show that choice overload effects do emerge in online dating, but only after the passage of time. Consistent with Lenton and Stewart (2008), we found that, immediately after making their selection, online daters matched with six versus twenty-four potential partners did not differ in their levels of satisfaction with their choice. However, after one week had elapsed, those daters who chose from the larger pool were less satisfied with their choice, and more likely to want to change it, than daters choosing from the smaller pool, consistent with the choice overload theory. Reversibility did not have an effect on choice satisfaction, with daters who were told they could change their minds about their selection registering the same levels of satisfaction as those who were told they couldn't change their minds, both initially and a week later. However, online daters paired with a larger pool of choices *and* given the ability to reverse their selection were the only ones to experience a drop in satisfaction with their choice over the course of the week, and they ended up being the least satisfied of all participants in the study at the end of the week (D'Angelo and Toma 2016). This nascent body of evidence therefore suggests that the choice architecture that most closely resembles that of popular dating sites (i.e., many choices and the ability to change one's mind) may, in fact, be detrimental to online daters' satisfaction with potential partners.

FUTURE RESEARCH

Online dating self-presentation and impression formation are two facets of the same coin, yet they have received different levels of academic attention and present distinct opportunities for future research. Let us consider first online dating self-presentation. As this review shows, there is a well-developed and theoretically grounded literature on (1) the psychological goals that animate online daters, and how these goals are sometimes in conflict with one another; (2) the construction behaviors that online daters engage in, such as the posting of photographs and text; and (3) the use of deception as a self-presentational strategy. We argue that each of these branches of the literature can be deepened by future research. On the issue of psychological goals, research can take a more granular look at the different types of relationships pursued by online daters (e.g., casual versus serious; monogamous versus non-monogamous) as these are likely to affect self-presentational decisions (see also Gibbs, Ellison, and Heino 2006). For instance, online daters looking for casual liaisons can be expected to invest less effort into their profiles and emphasize their physical appearance more than daters looking for serious relationships. On the issue of construction behaviors, future research should focus on the *content* of self-presentations by performing content analyses of both textual and photographic claims. This approach has not been undertaken yet, with extant research focusing on quantitative indicators such as the number of photographs posted (Toma and Hancock 2010) or the length of the profile (Toma and Hancock 2012). What do online daters say about themselves? How do they use humor? What aspects of themselves do they forefront and which do they obstruct? What kinds of photographs do they post (e.g., solo versus group, head shots versus full-body shots, with or without pets). Big data analyses and natural language processing can be leveraged to address these questions, given recent developments on these techniques (see Shah, Cappella, and

Neuman 2015). On the issue of deception, we recommend that future research replicate existing findings, given the constantly shifting nature of online daters' demographics and relational goals. Larger samples should also be used, although this is likely to be difficult if researchers choose to verify online daters' claims, a procedure that requires online daters to be interviewed in person. The detectability of online dating deception in face-to-face meetings with future partners should also be examined, as it is likely to shape the path of relationship development. Relatedly, we also recommend that future research pursue questions regarding the *outcome* of using various self-presentation and deception tactics in online dating profiles: Which of these tactics is successful in securing attention on the site, and in fulfilling online daters' relationship goals? To the best of our knowledge, there is no research on this topic, despite its practical and theoretical importance.

On the theoretical front, the framework of selective self-presentation has demonstrated much utility in explaining online self-presentation patterns, and we expect it to maintain its validity moving forward. Evolutionary theory has also received strong support, although this theory is unsuited for explaining same-sex dating. We recommend that future research utilize a gender socialization approach to explaining gender-based mate preferences and how these preferences shape self-presentational choices.

A slightly different picture emerges for the literature on online dating impression formation. Here, we find the literature to be underdeveloped theoretically, with much opportunity to grow. The SIPT framework provides a general overview of the importance of small cues online, yet it does not make specific predictions about how individual cues operate in the impression formation process. It is encouraging that research has begun to apply warranting theory to make more granular propositions about the judgments elicited by specific types of cues—in this case, those that are more or less amenable to manipulation by the self-presenter. We recommend that future research more comprehensively apply warranting theory to online dating. Other theories are also suitable. For example, research in impression formation has established a non-normativity effect (Carr and Walther 2014; D'Angelo and Van Der Heide 2016), whereby cues that are unexpected and violate conventional self-presentational practices carry more weight in the impression formation process than normative cues, because they draw more attention. We believe the non-normativity effect can be fruitfully extended to online dating. Finally, it bears noting that impression formation is a holistic process, and considering the impact of profile cues in isolation does not illuminate the full picture of how online daters evaluate potential partners. To have a full understanding of what cues are more "sticky," it is important for online dating impression formation research to continue to test different types of cues against each other. While there exists a rich line of research pursing this path of impression formation research via social networking profiles (D'Angelo and Van Der Heide 2016; Carr and Walther, 2014; Van Der Heide et al. 2012; Walther et al. 2009), an important extension exists in the application of this material to online dating.

Our own choice architecture framework needs to be expanded in substantial ways. First, there is no clear indication of what actually *causes a drop* in satisfaction with choice overload. Do individuals simply feel regret for options discarded (Iyengar and Lepper 2000) or is there a more complex process of expectation disconfirmation (Diehl and Poynor, 2010) in action? Beyond mechanisms, the concepts of quality of options and choice set complexity have not yet been applied to online dating despite their promise. For instance, do individuals like Tinder dates better because the platform presents simpler sets?

A final, yet important, area for ripe for exploration in online dating is the notion of loss of options. While consumer goods are likely to be perpetually available, online daters are not: Options can disappear quickly as people partner up and drop out of the site. Thus, it would be beneficial both for online dating impression formation research and for choice architecture research in general to explore the implications of loss of options in online dating.

CONCLUSION

Online dating challenges millions of users to construct versions of themselves and to carefully attend to others' in the hopes of forging romantic connections. Personal profiles on these sites have become veritable gateways to romance. Understanding the complex psychological and communicative dynamics that shape these profiles is a task of utmost theoretical and practical importance. This chapter highlights the important strides academic research has made towards this goal and outlines exciting avenues for future research.

REFERENCES

Arunachalam, Bharath, Shida R. Henneberry, Jayson L. Lusk, and F. Bailey Norwood. 2009. "An Empirical Investigation into the Excessive-Choice Effect." *American Journal of Agricultural Economics* 91: 810–25.

Barber, Nigel. 1995. "The Evolutionary Psychology of Physical Attractiveness: Sexual Selection and Human Morphology." *Ethology and Sociobiology* 16: 395–424.

Best, Kirsty, and Sharon Delmege. 2012. "The Filtered Encounter: Online Dating and the Problem of Filtering Through Excessive Information." *Social Semiotics* 22: 237–58.

Buss, David M., and David P. Schmitt. 1993. "Sexual Strategies Theory: An Evolutionary Perspective on Human Mating." *Psychological Review* 100: 204–32.

Cacioppo, John T., Stephanie Cacioppo, Gian C. Gonzaga, Elizabeth L. Ogburn, and Tyler J. VanderWeele. 2013. "Marital satisfaction and break-ups differ across on-line and off-line Meeting Venues." *Proceedings of the National Academy of Sciences* 110: 10135–40.

Cali, Billie E., Jill M. Coleman, and Catherine Campbell. 2013. "Stranger Danger? Women's Self-protection Intent and the Continuing Stigma of Online Dating." *Cyberpsychology, Behavior, and Social Networking* 16: 853–57.

Carr, Caleb T., and Joseph B. Walther. 2014. "Increasing Attributional Certainty via Social Media: Learning About Others One Bit at a Time." *Journal of Computer-Mediated Communication* 19: 922–37.

Couch, Danielle, and Pranee Liamputtong. 2008. "Online Dating and Mating: The Use of the Internet to Meet Sexual Partners." *Qualitative Health Research* 18: 268–79.

D'Angelo, Jonathan D., and Brandon Van Der Heide. 2016. "The Formation of Physician Impressions in Online Communities: Negativity, Positivity, and Nonnormativity Effects." *Communication Research* 43: 49–72.

D'Angelo, Jonathan D., and Catalina L. Toma. 2016. "There Are Plenty of Fish in the Sea: The Effects of Choice Overload and Reversibility on Online Daters' Satisfaction With Selected Partners." *Media Psychology*: 1-27. doi: 10.1080/15213269.2015.1121827

D'Angelo, Jonathan, Chong Zhang, Jens Eickhoff, and Megan Moreno. 2014. "Facebook Influence Among Incoming College Freshmen Sticky Cues and Alcohol." *Bulletin of Science, Technology & Society* 34: 13–20.

Daly, Martin, and Margo Wilson. 1995. "Discriminative Parental Solicitude and the Relevance of Evolutionary Models to the Analysis of Motivational Systems." In *The Cognitive Neurosciences*, ed. M. S. Gassaniga, 1269–86. Cambridge, MA: MIT Press.

DeAndrea, David C., Brandon Van Der Heide, Megan A. Vendemia, and Mao H. Vang. 2015. "How People Evaluate Online Reviews." *Communication Research*. doi:0093650215573862.

Ellison, Nicole B., Jeffrey T. Hancock, and Catalina L. Toma. 2012. "Profile as Promise: A Framework for Conceptualizing Veracity in Online Dating Self-presentations." *New Media & Society* 14: 45–62.

Ellison, Nicole, Rebecca Heino, and Jennifer Gibbs. 2006. "Managing Impressions Online: Self-presentation Processes in the Online Dating Environment." *Journal of Computer-Mediated Communication* 11: 415–41.

Fox, Jesse, Katie M. Warber, and Dana C. Makstaller. 2013. "The Role of Facebook in Romantic Relationship Development: An Exploration of Knapp's Relational Stage Model." *Journal of Social and Personal Relationships* 30: 771–94.

Frey, Dieter. 1981. "Reversible and Irreversible Decisions Preference for Consonant Information as a Function of Attractiveness of Decision Alternatives." *Personality and Social Psychology Bulletin* 7: 621–26.

Frey, Dieter, Martin Kumpf, Martin Irle, and Gisla Gniech. 1984. "Re-evaluation of Decision Alternatives Dependent Upon the Reversibility of a Decision and the Passage of Time." *European Journal of Social Psychology* 14: 447–50.

Gangestad, Steven W., and Randy Thornhill. 1997. "Human Sexual Selection and Developmental Stability." In *Evolutionary Social Psychology*, ed. J. A. Simpson and D. T. Kenrick: 169–95. New York, NY: Psychology Press.

Gibbs, Jennifer L., Nicole B. Ellison, and Rebecca D. Heino. 2006. "Self-presentation in Online Personals: The Role of Anticipated Future Interaction, Self-Disclosure, and Perceived Success in Internet Dating." *Communication Research* 33: 152–77.

Gibbs, Jennifer L., Nicole B. Ellison, and Chih-Hui Lai. 2010. "First Comes Love, Then Comes Google: An Investigation of Uncertainty Reduction Strategies and Self-disclosure in Online Dating." *Communication Research* 38: 70–100.

Gilbert, Daniel T., and Jane EJ Ebert. 2002. "Decisions and Revisions: The Affective Forecasting of Changeable Outcomes." *Journal of Personality and Social Psychology* 82: 503–14.

Greifeneder, Rainer, Benjamin Scheibehenne, and Nina Kleber. 2010. "Less May Be More When Choosing is Difficult: Choice Complexity and Too Much Choice." *Acta Psychologica* 133: 45–50.

Hancock, Jeffrey T., and Catalina L. Toma. 2009. "Putting Your Best Face Forward: The Accuracy of Online Dating Photographs." *Journal of Communication* 59: 367–86.

Heino, Rebecca D., Nicole B. Ellison, and Jennifer L. Gibbs. 2010. "Relationshopping: Investigating the Market Metaphor in Online Dating." *Journal of Social and Personal Relationships* 27: 427–47.

Iyengar, Sheena S., and Mark R. Lepper. 2000. "When Choice is Demotivating: Can One Desire Too Much of a Good Thing?" *Journal of Personality and Social Psychology* 79: 995–1006.

Leary, Mark R., and Robin M. Kowalski. 1990. "Impression Management: A Literature Review and Two-Component Model." *Psychological Bulletin* 107: 34–47.

Lenton, Alison P., and Amanda Stewart. 2008. "Changing Her Ways: The Number of Options and Mate-standard Strength Impact Mate Choice Strategy and Satisfaction." *Judgment and Decision Making* 3: 501–11.

Lueders, Allyn, Jeffery A. Hall, Natalie R. Pennington, and Kris Knutson. 2014. "Nonverbal Decoding on Facebook: Applying the IPT-15 and the SSI to Personality Judgments." *Journal of Nonverbal Behavior* 38: 413–27.

McGloin, Rory, and Amanda Denes. 2016. "Too Hot to Trust: Examining the Relationship Between Attractiveness, Trustworthiness, and Desire to Date in Online Dating." *New Media & Society*. doi: 10.1177/1461444816675440.

Mogilner, Cassie, Tamar Rudnick, and Sheena S. Iyengar. 2008. "The Mere Categorization Effect: How the Presence of Categories Increases Choosers' Perceptions of Assortment Variety and Outcome Satisfaction." *Journal of Consumer Research* 35: 202–15.

Patalano, Andrea L., Emma L. Weizenbaum, Sydney L. Lolli, and Alexandra Anderson. 2015. "Maximization and Search for Alternatives in Decision Situations With and Without Loss of Options." *Journal of Behavioral Decision Making* 28: 411–23.

Patall, Erika A., Harris Cooper, and Jorgianne Civey Robinson. 2008. "The Effects of Choice on Intrinsic Motivation and Related Outcomes: A Meta-analysis of Research Findings." *Psychological Bulletin* 134: 270–300.

Rosenfeld, Michael J., and Reuben J. Thomas. 2012. "Searching for a Mate: The Rise of the Internet as a Social Intermediary." *American Sociological Review* 77: 523–47.

Sautter, Jessica M., Rebecca M. Tippett, and S. Philip Morgan. 2010. "The Social Demography of Internet Dating in the United States." *Social Science Quarterly* 91: 554–75.

Scheibehenne, Benjamin, Rainer Greifeneder, and Peter M. Todd. 2009. "What Moderates the Too-Much-Choice Effect?" *Psychology & Marketing* 26: 229–53.

Schwartz, Barry. 2004. *The Paradox of Choice*. New York: Ecco.

Shah, Dhavan V., Joseph N. Cappella, and W. Russell Neuman. 2015. "Big Data, Digital Media, and Computational Social Science Possibilities and Perils." *The ANNALS of the American Academy of Political and Social Science* 659: 6–13.

Smith, Aaron, and Maeve Duggan. "Online Dating and Relationships," Pew Research Center. http://www.pewinternet.org/2013/10/21/online-dating-relationships-2/.

Thaler, Richard H., and Cass R. Sunstein. 2009. *Nudge: Improving Decisions about Health, Wealth, and Happiness*. New York: Penguin Books.

Thornhill, Randy, and Steven W. Gangestad. 1993. "Human Facial Beauty." *Human nature* 4: 237–69.

Toma, C. L., and J. T. Hancock. 2011. "A New Twist on Love's Labor: Self-Presentation in Online Dating Profiles," in *Computer-Mediated Communication in Personal Relationships*, edited by, Kevin B. Wright and Lynn M. Web, 41–55. New York: Peter Lang.

Toma, Catalina L. 2010. "Perceptions of Trustworthiness Online: The Role of Visual and Textual Information." In *Proceedings of the 2010 ACM conference on Computer supported cooperative work*, 13–22.

Toma, Catalina L., and Cassandra L. Carlson. 2015. "How Do Facebook Users Believe They Come Across in Their Profiles? A Meta-Perception Approach to Investigating Facebook Self-Presentation." *Communication Research Reports* 32: 93–101.

Toma, Catalina L., and Jeffrey T. Hancock. 2010. "Looks and Lies: The Role of Physical Attractiveness in Online Dating Self-Presentation and Deception." *Communication Research* 37: 335–51.

Toma, Catalina L., and Jeffrey T. Hancock. 2010. "What Lies Beneath: The Linguistic Traces of Deception in Online Dating Profiles." *Journal of Communication* 62: 78–97.

Toma, Catalina L., Jeffrey T. Hancock, and Nicole B. Ellison. 2008. "Separating Fact from Fiction: An Examination of Deceptive Self-Presentation in Online Dating Profiles." *Personality and Social Psychology Bulletin* 34: 1023–36.

Toma, Catalina L., L. Crystal Jiang, and Jeffrey T. Hancock. 2016. "Lies in the Eye of the Beholder Asymmetric Beliefs about One's Own and Others' Deceptiveness in Mediated and Face-to-Face Communication." *Communication Research*. doi: 0093650216631094.

Utz, Sonja. 2010. " Show Me Your Friends and I Will Tell You What Type of Person You Are: How One's Profile, Number of Friends, and Type of Friends Influence Impression Formation on Social Network Sites." *Journal of Computer-Mediated Communication* 15: 314–35.

Van Der Heide, Brandon, and Erin M. Schumaker. 2013. "Computer-Mediated Persuasion and Compliance: Social Influence on the Internet and Beyond." In *The Social Net: Understanding Our Online Behavior*, ed. Yair Amichai-Hamburger, 79–98. Oxford, Oxford University Press.

Van Der Heide, Brandon, Jonathan D. D'Angelo, and Erin M. Schumaker. 2012. "The Effects of Verbal Versus Photographic Self-Presentation on Impression Formation in Facebook." *Journal of Communication* 62: 98–116.

Vasalou, Asimina, and Adam N. Joinson. 2009. " Me, Myself and I: The Role of Interactional Context on Self-Presentation Through Avatars." *Computers in Human Behavior* 25: 510–20.

Walther, Joseph B. 1996. "Computer-Mediated Communication: Impersonal, Interpersonal, and Hyperpersonal Interaction." *Communication Research* 23: 3–43.

Walther, Joseph B. 1992. "Interpersonal Effects in Computer-Mediated Interaction a Relational Perspective." *Communication Research* 19: 52–90.

Walther, Joseph B. 2007. "Selective Self-Presentation in Computer-Mediated Communication: Hyperpersonal Dimensions of Technology, Language, and Cognition." *Computers in Human Behavior* 23: 2538–57.

Walther, Joseph B., Brandon Van Der Heide, Lauren M. Hamel, and Hillary C. Shulman. 2009. "Self-Generated Versus Other-Generated Statements and Impressions in Computer-Mediated Communication: A Test of Warranting Theory Using Facebook." *Communication Research* 36: 229–53.

Walther, Joseph B., and Malcolm R. Parks. 2002. "Cues Filtered Out, Cues Filtered In." in *Handbook of Interpersonal Communication,* ed. M. L. Knapp and J. A. Daly, 529–63. Thousand Oaks, CA: Sage.

Wotipka, Crystal D., and Andrew C. High. 2016. "An Idealized Self or the Real Me? Predicting Attraction to Online Dating Profiles Using Selective Self-Presentation and Warranting." *Communication Monographs* 83: 281–302.

Wu, Pai-Lu, and Wen-Bin Chiou. 2009. "More Options Lead to More Searching and Worse Choices in Finding Partners for Romantic Relationships Online: An Experimental Study." *CyberPsychology & Behavior* 12: 315–18.

Yang, Mu-Li, and Wen-Bin Chiou. 2010. "Looking Online for the Best Romantic Partner Reduces Decision Quality: The Moderating Role of Choice-Making Strategies." *Cyberpsychology, Behavior, and Social Networking* 13: 207–10.

III

Turbulence

ELEVEN

Liking, Creeping, and Password Sharing

Romantic Jealousy Experience and Expression and Social Networking Sites

Jennifer L. Bevan

Romantic jealousy is a cognitive, emotional, and/or behavioral/communicative response to the need to protect and defend a romantic relationship from the threat of a perceived (possibly actual) rival (Bevan 2013). As the number and usage of social networking sites (SNSs) have exponentially grown in the last decade, romantic jealousy experience and expression has accordingly migrated into this increasingly influential communication context. Specifically, romantic jealousy can arise in response to partner or rival behaviors on Facebook (e.g., Muise, Christofides, and Desmarais 2009) or Snapchat (Utz, Muscanell, and Khalid 2015) and is often indirectly expressed by engaging in surveillance (e.g., Tokunaga 2011, 2014). Indeed, 27 percent of teens who have relationship experience say that social media has made them feel jealous or uncertain about the relationship, typically via posts and photographs (Lenhart, Smith, and Anderson 2015). It is thus not surprising that jealousy consistently emerges as a primary Facebook stressor across age groups and cultures (Baker and Carreño 2016; Fox and Moreland 2015; Rueda, Lindsay, and Williams 2015; Van Ouystel et al. 2016).

A comprehensive review of research examining jealousy in mediated contexts, including SNSs, was last undertaken by Bevan (2013). Since then, this body of scholarship has grown in volume and significance, now encompassing such important topics as intimate partner violence. Thus, based on the ever-increasing growth and influence of SNSs, their consistent associations with jealousy in initial empirical research, and the advancement of this research area, this chapter will provide an updated, interdisciplinary review and synthesis of studies that have investigated romantic jealousy experience and expression on SNSs. Namely, this review will be organized around three major themes: (1) forms and correlates of SNS jealousy experience and expression, including individual and relationship characteristics and differences according to specific SNS elements; (2) intimate partner violence; and (3) relevant theoretical approaches. Updated suggestions for future research and applications, with an eye toward specific theoretical and methodological considerations, will also be offered.

ROMANTIC JEALOUSY EXPERIENCE AND EXPRESSION ON SNSs

Bevan (2013) compiled four reasons why SNSs are a prime online location for romantic jealousy to develop and grow: (1) they offer a centralized location for accessing relationship information that (2) is permanently, publicly viewable to others; (3) SNS content often lacks context and can thus be ambiguous and open to (mis)interpretation; and (4) there is an increased opportunity for contact with former romantic partners and potential rivals on SNSs. Across studies reviewed then (Cole 2010; Marshall et al. 2013; Muise, Christofides, and Desmarais 2009; Utz and Beukeboom 2011), increased SNS usage was consistently related to greater jealousy. Subsequent research continues to support this relationship (Hoffman and DeGroot 2014/2015; Hudson et al. 2015; Orosz et al. 2015), though Dainton and Berkoski's (2013) finding for emotional jealousy and time spent on Facebook is an exception.

Facebook Jealousy

More recent research has continued to examine jealousy experience and expression on SNSs in multifaceted ways. First, a number of studies have focused on Facebook jealousy (Muise, Christofides, and Desmarais 2009) as a specific jealousy experience component. Facebook jealousy occurs when romantic partners become jealous in response to SNS behaviors, such as seeing that a partner has added a new "friend" or connection who could be a potential rival or learning information after monitoring the partner's SNS activities. This concept has subsequently been successfully expanded by Utz, Muscanell, and Khalid (2015) to include the Snapchat SNS, which was found to elicit significantly more jealousy than Facebook. Utz, Muscanell, and Khalid (2015) explained that this difference is likely because Snapchat's increased privacy means that a partner interacting with a potential rival via that SNS poses a more significant relational threat.

Facebook jealousy experience has been linked to a number of individual characteristics. For example, Utz, Muscanell, and Khalid (2015) found that Snapchat and Facebook jealousy were positively linked to the need for popularity, but were unrelated to self-esteem. Interestingly, cumulative university GPA was positively associated with Facebook jealousy, possibly because conscientious students may pay attention to their SNS relationships as they do their schoolwork (Hudson et al. 2015).

Regarding biological sex differences, females responded to hypothetical Facebook jealousy scenarios or page content with more Facebook jealousy (Hudson et al. 2015) and general jealousy (Cohen, Bowman, and Borchert 2014; Fleuriet, Cole, and Guerrero 2014; Muise, Christofides, and Desmarais 2014; Muscanell et al. 2013) than males. Females were also more jealous than males when it came to the majority of specific Facebook jealousy components, such as jealous feelings, spying, and fear of mate poachers (McAndrew and Shah 2013). Males, in contrast, felt more threatened than females in response to an ambiguous Facebook message between a romantic partner and potential rival (Cohen, Bowman, and Borchert 2014). However, in three other studies, there were no sex differences for Facebook or Snapchat jealousy experiences (Brem, Spiller, and Vandehey 2015; Drouin, Miller, and Dibble 2014; Utz, Muscanell, and Khalid 2015). A fairly consistent pattern is beginning to emerge: Females tend to experience more Facebook-related jealousy than males. Understanding the degree to which this pattern extends to other SNSs besides Facebook or to SNS-related jealousy expressions should be a goal for future SNS jealousy research.

With regard to relationship characteristics, long-distance romantic partners experience greater Facebook jealousy than geographically close partners (Billedo, Kerkhof, and Finkenauer 2015). Greater Facebook jealousy is also related to higher romantic relationship commitment (Drouin, Miller, and Dibble 2014) and increased cognitive and emotional jealousy experience and expression (Bevan, in press). However, Facebook jealousy was unrelated to the quality of sexual and relationship alternatives in one's Facebook friends list (Drouin, Miller, and Dibble 2014), general romantic relational uncertainty (Stewart, Dainton, and Goodboy 2014), and relationship investment (Bevan, in press).

Finally, research on Facebook jealousy, relationship satisfaction, and Facebook relationship maintenance behaviors is thus far inconsistent. Though Stewart, Dainton, and Goodboy (2014) reported no link between Facebook jealousy and relationship satisfaction, Bevan (in press) observed a negative association. Further, in one study, Facebook jealousy was positively related to Facebook openness and online monitoring, but unrelated to assurances or positivity (Dainton and Stokes 2015). In another, Facebook jealousy was positively related to all four of these forms of Facebook maintenance (Stewart, Dainton, and Goodboy 2014). Overall, then, research continues to validate this new form of jealousy experience, and findings have accumulated to the point that adding Facebook jealousy to the multidimensional experience of jealousy, described in more detail below, is suggested in order to better reflect romantic jealousy in the digital age.

Jealousy Experience and Expression

The multidimensional experience of jealousy is divided into cognitive (i.e., thoughts or worries), emotional (e.g., fear, sadness, anger, etc.), and behavioral jealousy, which comprises actions and communicative responses to jealousy (CRJs). These CRJs include both direct and indirect messages. Guerrero, Hannawa, and Babin's (2011) revised CRJ typology includes four superordinate categories: (1) destructive, or partner-focused, direct, and hurtful messages such as violence; (2) constructive messages, which are partner-focused, direct, and beneficial, such as open discussion; (3) avoidant, or partner-focused, indirect, typically negative messages like denials; and (4) rival-focused messages that are indirect, harmful expressions directed at a third party, such as contacting the rival.

A number of studies have examined either these three dimensions of jealousy experience, or a general jealousy experience variable that combines one or more of these dimensions, in the SNS context. For example, Dainton and Stokes (2015) found that cognitive and emotional jealousy were positively associated with Facebook openness and monitoring, but only cognitive jealousy was inversely related to Facebook assurances and positivity. Further, general jealousy about friends interacting on an SNS was directly related to increased fear of isolation, and indirectly linked to greater motivation to socialize with others (Lee, Min, and Kim 2015).

With regard to jealousy expression, the most frequently examined SNS jealousy response is online surveillance, which involves conscious, furtive, and deliberate actions occurring "over communication technologies to gain awareness of another user's offline and/or online behaviors" (Tokunaga 2011, 706). Bevan (2013) noted that online surveillance falls under Guerrero et al.'s (2011) rival-focused CRJ category, but is distinct in that it provides the jealous individual with a monitoring method that: (1) is less likely to decrease relational trust, because access to this online information has already been granted; and (2) decreases the possibility of being "caught" due to geographic distance. Accordingly, SNS surveillance is viewed as more common and acceptable than traditional surveillance behaviors (Utz and Beukeboom 2011) and is now a culturally widespread practice known as "Facebook stalking," or "creeping" (e.g., Walker 2016).

Research determined that SNS surveillance is consistently related to both increased SNS usage and greater jealousy experience (e.g., Dainton and Berkoski 2013; Elphinston and Noller 2011; Tokunaga 2011). Tokunaga (2014) subsequently suggested that SNS surveillance is a technologically mediated form of negative relationship maintenance, in line with Dainton and Gross's (2008) surveillance strategy. SNS surveillance was predicted by decreased relationship satisfaction and increased quality of relational alternatives, but it was not significantly related to commitment, partner trust, investment, or relationship length (Tokunaga 2014). Dainton and Berkoski (2013) also observed a significant negative correlation between online surveillance and relationship satisfaction.

From his findings, Tokunaga (2014) argued that SNS surveillance likely grows out of a jealousy experience, rather than as a jealousy antecedent, as it was examined in prior research (Elphinston and Noller 2011; Muise, Christofides, and Desmarais 2009). Specifically, according to Tokunaga (2014), "it is rare that undesirable information is carelessly left on one's profile, so spontaneous provocation of jealousy and distrust from mere participation on social networking sites is unfounded" (185). This direct path from SNS jealousy experience to expression is logical and aligns with the vast majority of scholarly jealousy conceptualizations and models. However, Baker and Carreño's (2016) qualitative findings offer evidence that this may instead be a reflexive cycle, in which jealousy leads to surveillance, which then spurs further jealousy and monitoring. The exact nature of SNS jealousy experience and expression, and the extent to which both work together as an ongoing process should be investigated in future research.

Two unique monitoring-related forms of SNS jealousy expression that have emerged in recent research are: (1) time spent on a partner's SNS profiles; and (2) partner password requests. First, when viewing content in which a romantic partner interacted with an unknown person, participants spent more time searching the partner's Facebook page than if that person was identified as a mutual friend or a cousin in Muise, Christofides, and Desmarais's (2014) hypothetical scenario study. Time spent visiting a partner's SNS profiles was also positively predicted by SNS surveillance (Tokunaga 2014). Second, Van Ouystel et al.'s (2016) participants viewed a password request as a commonplace behavior in romantic relationships and "a mutual token of love and trust but also as a kind of insurance policy against unfaithfulness" (83). Yet, password sharing can backfire if the romantic relationship ends, or it could evolve into a controlling, sometimes abusive, relational tactic (Rueda, Lindsay, and Williams 2015; Van Ouystel et al. 2016).

Despite encouraging initial research (e.g., Cole 2010) that jealousy expression on SNSs included messages other than simply surveillance, only three studies are known to have examined a range of Facebook-related jealousy expressions since Bevan's (2013) review. In the first, Cohen, Bowman, and Borchert (2014) qualitatively examined open-ended approach-avoid SNS jealousy responses to a partner's hypothetical Facebook conversation with a former partner. Seventy-one percent of Cohen, Bowman, and Borchert's (2014) participants indicated that they would confront either their partner or the rival in this situation. Participants who experienced more emotional jealousy and threat perception were also more likely to confront their romantic partners (Cohen, Bowman, and Borchert 2014).

Second, Hoffman and DeGroot (2014/2015) adapted Guerrero et al.'s (1995) CRJs to jealousy upon viewing information about a romantic partner on Facebook. As with research trends for general jealousy expression (Bevan 2013) and Facebook jealousy (Cole 2010), constructive and avoidant messages were found to be the most frequently used Facebook-related forms of jealousy expression, followed by destructive and rival-focused responses (Hoffman and DeGroot 2014/2015). Facebook jealousy was also positively related to all Facebook-related CRJs except for integrative communication (Hoffman and DeGroot 2014/2015). However, usage of these Facebook-related CRJs were largely unrelated to time spent on Facebook (Hoffman and DeGroot 2014/2015).

In the third study, Hudson et al. (2015) coded qualitative participant behavioral responses to finding a Facebook message between a romantic partner and a rival. These responses ranged from ignoring the message to confronting or physically harming the partner or the rival, thus reflecting multiple examples in Cohen, Bowman, and Borchert's (2014) approach-avoid categories. Almost 68 percent of Hudson et al.'s (2015) participants indicated that they would discuss the message with their romantic partners. In addition, females reported being more likely to confront their partner or confide in another person about the message than males, who, in turn, were more likely to respond by getting back at the partner or rival, or acting aggressively (Hudson et al. 2015).

In sum, research examining Facebook jealousy has grown substantially in recent years, and findings have begun to clarify its relationships with a variety of individual and relational characteristics, such as biological sex. Studies also suggest that romantic partners will employ a variety of offline, online, direct, and avoidant jealousy messages to communicatively respond to their SNS-related jealousy experience. However, SNS jealousy expression messages within and across the studies reviewed here are piecemeal at best and, at worst, inconsistently worded, measured, or applied. It is thus crucial that future research attempts to formally identify and classify the different forms of SNS-specific jealousy expression in the hopes of creating an exhaustive, reliable, and valid SNS jealousy expression typology.

SNS Elements and Jealousy

Another emerging area of SNS jealousy research concerns experience and expression differences according to specific SNS elements. The first element is the Facebook relationship status, which is an SNS relationship marker that offers a context "clue" that varies in terms of its clarity and ambiguity. Namely, individuals in romantic relationships who indicated that they were "in a relationship" on Facebook were more jealous than those who did not state that they were in a relationship (Orosz et al. 2015). Orosz et al. (2015) noted that being "Facebook official" in this way is a public, digital tie sign that may assist jealous individuals in abating their insecurities. As the popularity and positive perception of this Facebook relationship marker has decreased in recent years, especially among young adults (e.g., Notopoulos 2015), future research should consider how the accompanying increase in romantic jealousy might actually play into the increasingly negative perception of this SNS element.

Facebook communication, either via public wall posts and/or private messaging, is a second SNS element that can be linked to jealousy. For example, message access exclusivity was examined via hypothetical scenarios that depicted either a public (on the partner's Facebook wall) or private (as a Facebook message) flirtatious exchange between a romantic partner and one of their former partners (Cohen, Bowman, and Borchert 2014). Though the private message was not viewed as any more or less threatening than the public one, it did generate a stronger emotional jealousy experience and a greater likelihood of confronting the partner about the message (Cohen, Bowman, and Borchert 2014). In addition, seeing that a romantic partner liked or commented on a potential rival's status update can spark jealousy (Rueda et al. 2015; Van Ousytel et al. 2016).

Third, a number of nonverbal Facebook message elements have been examined. Fleuriet, Cole, and Guerrero (2014) found that a hypothetical public wall post by a potential rival that featured an attractive profile photo and included a wink-face emoticon generated a more emotional jealousy experience, which did not vary according to the capitalization of the post or the inclusion of multiple exclamation points. However, Hudson et al. (2015) did not observe Facebook jealousy differences according to whether a wink-face emoticon was present or absent in a hypothetical private Facebook message to a romantic partner. This inconsistency might be due to the Facebook message access exclusivity differences in the two studies, which underscores the potential importance of this SNS message element in terms of jealousy experience.

Fourth, Facebook friend list content—both number of friends and the extent to which potential rivals are present—has been examined in relation to Facebook jealousy. Namely, though Facebook jealousy experience was unrelated to number of Facebook friends, it was positively associated with Facebook solicitation behaviors (Drouin, Miller, and Dibble 2014). These solicitation actions involve sending or accepting a Facebook friend request from a potential romantic interest while either single or in a relationship. Facebook jealousy also fully mediated the relationship between attachment anxiety and Facebook solicitation behaviors (Drouin, Miller, and Dibble 2014), further demonstrating the relationship between these variables.

A fifth and final set of studies have specifically examined SNS photos, including tagging and content. Three SNS photo elements in particular can elicit jealousy: (1) romantic partners' liking or commenting on an opposite sex other's photos, particularly if complimenting their appearance; (2) an opposite sex other's comments on or likes of a romantic partner's photos; and (3) romantic partners posting photos with someone of the opposite-sex (Van Ouystel et al. 2016). The final element could also be employed strategically to make a former or current partner jealous (Van Ouystel et al. 2016). For example, when a hypothetical romantic partner's Facebook photos were set to private and no couple photos were visible, participants were more jealous, angry, disgusted, and hurt than if their photos were public and couple photos were present (Muscanell et al. 2013). Additionally, an attractive person in a Facebook photo with their hypothetical romantic partner aroused more jealousy when described as an unknown person or a mutual friend compared to being identified as the partner's cousin (Muise, Christofides, and Desmarais 2014).

Thus, relationship markers, message access exclusivity, visibility, and identification of photo content are SNS elements that are related to varying levels of jealousy. Specifically, the experience of jealousy increases when the following Facebook elements are present: (1) use of the relationship status feature when in a romantic relationship, (2) a private message between a romantic partner and potential rival, (3) a public post to a romantic partner in which a potential rival uses the wink-face emoticon and has an attractive profile photo, (4) soliciting friendships with potential romantic interests, and (5) romantic partner photo behaviors such as liking or commenting on potential rivals' photos, being in publicly posted photos with a possible rival who was unknown to the participant, and failing to post publicly viewable couple photos.

One consistent theme running throughout the above findings is the public versus private nature of the SNS elements; as such, visibility and message access exclusivity seem to be particularly relevant to heightened experiences of general and Facebook jealousy. Further untangling these associations in relation to specific SNS elements should be a focus of future research. In addition, examining these specific relationships on SNSs other than Facebook, such as on Instagram, Kik, or Snapchat, should be a future research priority to determine whether or not they are Facebook-specific in nature.

INTIMATE PARTNER VIOLENCE

The ease and convenience with which individuals can meet and interact with potential rivals via technologically mediated communication (TMC) channels such as SNSs can contribute to romantic relationship instability that could then increase the likelihood of violence (Baker and Carreño 2016). The nature of these connections aligns with the fact that jealousy is a common predictor of multiple aspects of intimate partner violence (e.g., Roberts 2005; Wigman, Graham-Kevan, and Archer 2008), which includes sexual coercion, psychological and physical aggression, stalking, and control of a partner's sexual or reproductive health (e.g., Black et al. 2010). As such, an emerging and significant topic in the realm of SNS jealousy is how it is related to intimate partner violence (IPV). Four such studies are described below.

First, Brem et al. (2015) examined Facebook jealousy, online surveillance, and the specific use of jealousy and surveillance as a Facebook mate retention tactic in relation to psychological and physical relational aggression. Jealousy/surveillance was the second most commonly used Facebook mate retention tactic reported by males and females, and involves behaviors such as asking for the partner's password, requesting that they unfriend, block, or not friend or talk to romantic rivals on Facebook, and snooping through the partner's private and chat Facebook messages. Each of the three Facebook variables was positively correlated to both forms of aggression. Further, Facebook jealousy/surveillance was the only mate retention tactic to significantly predict increased psychological and physical aggression. Finally, Facebook jealousy indirectly predicted both types of aggression via the Facebook jealousy/surveillance mate retention tactic (Brem et al. 2015). This study is notable because it is the first to empirically link Facebook jealousy and online surveillance with psychological and physical aggression, thus extending the consistent link between jealousy and IPV to the SNS realm.

The remaining three IPV studies were qualitative focus group studies that examined adolescents (Baker and Carreño 2016; Lucero et al. 2014; Rueda, Lindsay, and Williams 2015). All three of these studies confirmed that jealousy was a significant SNS usage issue for adolescents. They also found that password sharing and account monitoring were normal, even accepted, forms of online surveillance in teen dating relationships. Further, though these types of behaviors would be classified as IPV because they represent psychological aggression and control, adolescents in all three studies did not perceive them as being abusive as long as the information accessed stayed between the dating partners and did not become extreme. The consistency of these findings is even more notable because the samples were from Hawaii (Baker and Carreño 2016), Mexico (Rueda, Lindsay, and Williams 2015), and Michigan (Lucero et al. 2014).

One common response to online surveillance behaviors was to proactively delete one's own text and SNS messages before a partner could "find" them (Lucero et al. 2014). Romantic partners also responded to jealousy by exerting control over adolescents' technology use in two ways: (1) preventing them from communicating with potential rivals; and (2) isolating themselves by not returning texts or phone calls. Such isolation TMC behaviors were sometimes then met with harassment by the ignored partner (Baker and Carreño 2016; Rueda, Lindsay, and Williams 2015). Social network posts and other forms of TMC could additionally alert individuals that their SNS connections might be experiencing unhealthy relationship behaviors or IPV (Rueda, Lindsay, and Williams 2015).

Together, these findings paint a stark picture of how SNS usage can heighten jealousy and contribute to—as well as normalize—multiple online and offline IPV behaviors. That these behaviors begin and proliferate in adolescence and seem to extend to early adulthood underscores the importance of developing early prevention and intervention messages. To this end, there are a number of methods of addressing this problem, including creating prevention messages that address and reframe healthy TMC and SNS boundaries (Lucero et al. 2014; Rueda, Lindsay, and Williams 2015) and that identify initial online monitoring behaviors that are abusive so they can be addressed before they escalate (Baker and Carreño 2016). Messages can also be developed and employed to educate teens about healthy relationships (Rueda, Lindsay, and Williams 2015). Additionally, parents could be encouraged to monitor their children's SNS messages for IPV behaviors by them or their romantic partners (Rueda, Lindsay, and Williams 2015), and children can be taught that support from others, particularly their parents, is beneficial (Baker and Carreño 2016). Future research that, for example, tracks how SNS jealousy and IPV interact longitudinally, or explores how older adults manage their SNS jealousy, is suggested as well.

THEORETICAL APPROACHES

Both romantic jealousy and SNS usage are empirically understood via a variety of interdisciplinary theoretical approaches. However, in Bevan's (2013) review, only attachment theory had been employed to examine SNS jealousy expression. Such a narrow theoretical focus was a limitation of this early SNS jealousy research. Subsequently, though SNS jealousy research has substantially grown, use of theory has remained fairly stagnant. Namely, a handful of studies have applied attachment theory, the investment model, and the communicative interdependence perspective (CIP) to the study of SNS jealousy. The success of these theoretical applications, described below, has thus far been hit or miss.

Attachment Theory

Bowlby's (1973) attachment theory was initially developed to under-stand how children bonded with a maternal figure, but was later success-fully expanded to adult romantic relationship processes. Attachment theory has been a frequent, useful framework for explaining romantic jealousy experience and expression, so it is logical that it would be ap-plied to SNS jealousy as well. With regard to specific attachment styles, Marshall et al. (2013) found that use of online surveillance behaviors and the experience of Facebook jealousy increased for those with an anxious attachment style (i.e., seeking relational closeness while fearing rejection, and being attentive to relationship threats) and decreased for avoidant attachment style (i.e., feeling discomfort with closeness and being dismis-sive of relational threats) individuals. Relatedly, a dismissive (i.e., low anxiety, high avoidance) attachment style was inversely related to nega-tive emotion upon viewing a potentially jealousy-inducing Facebook message, which was positively associated with the preoccupied (i.e., high anxiety, low avoidance) attachment style (Fleuriet, Cole, and Guerrero 2014). Fearful (i.e., high anxiety and avoidance) and secure (i.e., low anx-iety and avoidance) attachment styles were unrelated to negative emo-tion (Fleuriet, Cole, and Guerrero 2014).

Further, greater attachment anxiety was related to greater Facebook jealousy (Drouin, Miller, and Dibble 2014; Muise, Christofides, and De-smarais 2014) and increased use of antisocial SNS jealousy behaviors, such as blocking the partner's access to an SNS profile or criticizing them in posts (Cole 2010). Muise, Christofides, and Desmarais (2014) also found that attachment anxiety predicted partner monitoring behaviors on Facebook for females, but not for males. Taken together, these SNS jealousy findings are consistent with the bulk of previous research that shows that individuals with greater attachment anxiety are more prone to jealousy (Bevan 2013). As such, attachment theory has been successful-ly extended to the understanding of SNS-related jealousy experience and expression.

The Investment Model

Three SNS jealousy studies (Bevan, in press; Drouin, Miller, and Dib-ble 2014; Tokunaga 2016) have examined multiple elements of Rusbult's (1980) investment model, which is centered around the importance of relational commitment in understanding a relationship's progression and continuation. According to this model, three aspects of relationship qual-ity predict commitment — higher satisfaction and investment, and lower quality of relational alternatives — and commitment then predicts any number of constructive or destructive relationship outcomes. Though the investment model's utility in explaining a variety of relationship processes has been consistently validated, it is not a reliably useful framework for understanding romantic jealousy (e.g., Bevan 2008).

This uneven pattern extends to SNS jealousy experience and expression research. Namely, one's number of sexual and relationship alternatives in their list of Facebook friends was unrelated to Facebook jealousy, which was positively related to commitment (Drouin, Miller, and Dibble 2014). Neither commitment nor alternative quality is related to online surveillance behaviors (Tokunaga 2016). Investment is also unrelated to Facebook jealousy (Bevan, in press) and online surveillance behaviors (Tokunaga 2016). Relationship satisfaction is inversely related to SNS jealousy experience and expression in two (Bevan, in press; Tokunaga 2016) of three (Stewart, Dainton, and Goodboy 2014) known studies. As these studies have been largely incomplete applications of the investment model that have produced inconsistent findings, it is imperative that future SNS jealousy research conduct tests of the full investment model to better understand these relationships.

The Communicative Interdependence Perspective

Caughlin and Sharabi's (2013) CIP proposes that TMC and face-to-face (FtF) interactions are inherently interconnected and that romantic partners who can more easily integrate and transition between these two communication channels will have higher relational quality. Though initially proposed for general communication patterns, CIP has recently been applied to specific interpersonal topics, including jealousy expression. Namely, Bevan (in press) found that, though the FtF channel was most frequently used to express jealousy, more than half of study participants combined FtF and one or more TMC modes, including SNSs, for jealousy expression. Further, those who used only TMC modes for expressing jealousy experienced greater cognitive, emotional, and Facebook jealousy and responded to jealousy using more destructive and rival-focused messages than those employing only the FtF mode (Bevan, in press). However, only using TMC modes to express jealousy was associated with more decreased relationship quality than not exclusively using those modes, whereas combining TMC and FtF modes was unrelated to relationship quality (Bevan, in press). In essence, these findings suggest that FtF communication is likely still the best route for jealousy expression if relationship quality is important (Bevan, in press). The CIP received mixed support in this study and, as a relatively new framework, additional research that focuses on SNS jealousy is suggested.

FINAL THOUGHTS

Since Bevan's (2013) review, there have been substantially more studies, and additional concepts, contexts, and theories have been included. The result is a more informed research area, albeit one that is a bit jumbled at times. In fact, this growth is starting to border on "research sprawl," in that there is not as much consistency and cohesiveness as there ought to be at this point in this research area's evolution. Similar concepts are labeled and/or measured differently, predictions are not informed by previous findings, and theories are absent and/or their tenets are not fully applied. SNS jealousy researchers should thus strive to focus on particular concepts and replicate previous methods and measures to allow for much-needed patterns to emerge.

This research sprawl unfortunately also means that it is still too early to forward evidence-based recommendations for alleviating the experience of SNS jealousy and encouraging its constructive expression. However, three recommendations for future research can be offered. First, dyadic data studies that determine the extent to which romantic partners hold joint versus distinct expectations about how to display and depict their relationships on SNSs and how to interface with possible rivals on SNSs would likely assist in clarifying research on specific SNS elements and jealousy. Second, it is clear that relationship stage and relationship quality variables should be important correlates and moderators in future SNS jealousy research, as findings for most relational quality variables such as maintenance, commitment, satisfaction, and investment are inconsistent as well as limited. Finally, to truly understand the impact that SNS jealousy has on individuals and relationships, studies must include and compare both offline versus online instances of jealousy, and consider how romantic partners integrate these channels when negotiating their jealousy. In sum, the research topic of SNS jealousy is one that is developing and active, but it must work through its growing pains in order to offer substantive practical and theoretical contributions.

REFERENCES

Baker, Charlene K., and Patricia K. Carreño. 2016. "Understanding the Role of Technology in Adolescent Dating and Dating Violence." *Journal of Child and Family Studies* 25: 308–20. doi:10.1007/s10826-015-0196-5.

Bevan, Jennifer L. 2008. "Experiencing and Communicating Romantic Jealousy: Questioning the Investment Model." *Southern Communication Journal* 73: 42–67. doi:10.1080/10417940701815626.

Bevan, Jennifer L. 2013. *The Communication of Jealousy*. New York: Peter Lang.

Bevan, Jennifer L. In Press. "Romantic Jealousy in Face-To-Face and Technologically-Mediated Interactions: A Communicative Interdependence Perspective." *Western Journal of Communication*.

Billedo, Cherrie Joy, Peter Kerkhof, and Catrin Finkenauer. 2015 "The Use of Social Networking Sites for Relationship Maintenance in Long-Distance and Geographically Close Romantic Relationships." *Cyberpsychology, Behavior, and Social Networking* 18 (3). 152–57. doi:10.1089/cyber.2014.0469.

Black, Michele C., Kathleen C. Basile, Matthew J. Breiding, Sharon G. Smith, Mikel L. Walters, M. T. Merrick, J. Chen, and Mark R. Stevens. "The National Intimate Partner and Sexual Violence Survey (NISVS): 2010 Summary Report." *Control Centers for Disease Control and Prevention.* 2010. https://www.cdc.gov/violenceprevention/pdf/nisvs_report2010-a.pdf.

Bowlby, John. 1973. *Attachment and Loss: Separation, Anxiety, and Anger.* New York: Basic Books.

Brem, Megan J., Laura C. Spiller, and Michael A. Vandehey. 2015. "Online Mate-Retention Tactics on Facebook Are Associated with Relationship Aggression." *Journal of Interpersonal Violence* 30 (16): 2831–50. doi:10.1177/0886260514554286.

Caughlin, John P., and Liesel Sharabi. 2013. "A Communicative Interdependence Perspective of Close Relationships: The Connections Between Mediated and Unmediated Interactions Matter." *Journal of Communication* 63: 873–93. doi:10.1111/jcom.12046.

Cohen, Elizabeth L., Nicholas D. Bowman, and Katherine Borchert. 2014. "Private Flirts, Public Friends: Understanding Romantic Jealousy Responses to an Ambiguous Social Network Site Message as a Function of Message Access Exclusivity." *Computers in Human Behavior* 35: 535–41. doi:10.1016/j.chb.2014.02.050.

Cole, Megan. 2010. *Jealousy and attachment 2.0: The role of attachment in the expression and experience of jealousy on Facebook.* Unpublished master's thesis, University of Central Florida.

Dainton, Marianne, and Lauren Berkoski. 2013. "Positive and Negative Maintenance Behaviors, Jealousy, and Facebook: Impacts on College Students' Romantic Relationships." *Pennsylvania Communication Annual* 69: 35–50.

Dainton, Marianne, and Jamie Gross. 2008. "The Use of Negative Behaviors to Maintain Relationships." *Communication Research Reports* 25: 179–91. doi:10.1080/08824090802237600.

Dainton, Marianne, and Alexandra Stokes. 2015. "College Students' Romantic Relationships on Facebook: Linking the Gratification for Maintenance to Facebook Maintenance Activity and the Experience of Jealousy." *Communication Quarterly* 63 (4): 365–83. doi:10.1080/01463373.2015.1058283.

Drouin, Michelle, Daniel A. Miller, and Jayson L. Dibble. 2014. "Ignore Your Partners' Current Facebook Friends; Beware the Ones They Add!" *Computers in Human Behavior* 35: 483–88. doi:10.1016/j.chb.2014.02.032.

Elphinston, Rachel A., and Patricia Noller. 2011."Time to Face it! Facebook Intrusion and the Implications for Romantic Jealousy and Relationship Satisfaction." *Cyberpsychology, Behavior, and Social Networking* 14: 631–35. doi:10.1089/cyber.2010.0318.

Fleuriet, Christina, Megan Cole, and Laura K. Guerrero. 2014. "Exploring Facebook: Attachment Style and Nonverbal Message Characteristics as Predictors of Anticipated Emotional Reactions to Facebook Postings." *Journal of Nonverbal Behavior* 38: 429–50. doi:10.1007/s10919-014-0189-x.

Fox, Jesse, and Jennifer J. Moreland. 2015. "The Dark Side of Social Networking Sites: An Exploration of the Relational and Psychological Stressors Associated with Facebook Use and Affordances." *Computers in Human Behavior* 45: 168–76. doi:10.1016/j.chb.2014.11.083.

Guerrero, Laura K., Peter A. Andersen, Peter F. Jorgensen, Brian H. Spitzberg, and Sylvie V Eloy. 1995. "Coping with the Green-Eyed Monster: Conceptualizing and Measuring Communicative Responses to Romantic Jealousy." *Western Journal of Communication* 59: 270–304. doi:10.1080/10570319509374523.

Guerrero, Laura K., Annegret F. Hannawa, and Elizabeth A. Babin. 2011. "The Communicative Responses to Jealousy Scale: Revision, Empirical Validation, and Associations with Relational Satisfaction." *Communication Methods and Measures* 5: 223–49. doi:10.1080/19312458.2011.596993.

Hoffman, Trisha K., and Jocelyn M. Degroot. 2014/2015. "Communicative Responses to Perceive Facebook Jealousy." *Journal of the Communication, Speech and Theatre Association of North Dakota* 27: 15–22.

Hudson, Michael B., Sylis C. Nicolas, Molly E. Howser, Kristen E. Lipsett, Ian W. Robinson, Laura J. Pope, Abigail F. Hobby, and Denise R. Friedman. 2015. "Examining How Gender and Emoticons Influence Facebook Jealousy." *Cyberpsychology, Behavior, and Social Networking* 18 (2): 87–92. doi:10.1089/cyber.2014.0129.

Lee, Jung, Jinyoung Min, and Hee-Woong Kim. 2015. "Want-To vs. Have-To Scoializations in Social Network Sites: Fear of Isolation, Jealousy, and Tie Strengths." Paper presented at *Pacific Asia Conference on Information Systems*.

Lenhart, Amanda, Aaron Smith, and Monica Anderson. 2015. "Teens, Technology, and Romantic Relationships." Pew Research Center. http://www.pewinternet.org/2015/10/01/teens-technology-and-romantic-relationships/.

Lucero, Jessica L., Arlene N. Weisz, Joanne Smith-Darden, and Steven M. Lucero. 2014. "Exploring Gender Differences: Socially Interactive Technology Use/Abuse Among Dating Teens." *Affilia: Journal of Women and Social Work* 29 (4): 478–91. doi:10.1177/0886109914522627.

Marshall, Tara C., Kathrine Bejanyan, Gaia Di Castro, and Ruth A. Lee. 2013. "Attachment Styles as Predictors of Facebook-Related Jealousy and Surveillance in Romantic Relationships." *Personal Relationships* 20: 1–22. doi:10.1111/j.1475-6811.2011.01393.x.

McAndrew, Francis T., and Sahil S. Shah. 2013. "Sex Differences in Jealousy over Facebook Activity." *Computers in Human Behavior* 29: 2603–6. doi:10.1016/j.chb.2013.06.030.

Muise, Amy, Emily Christofides, and Serge Desmarais. 2009. "More Information than You Ever Wanted: Does Facebook Bring Out the Green-Eyed Monster of Jealousy? *Cyberpsychology and Behavior* 12: 441–44. doi: 10.1089=cpb.2008.0263.

Muise, Amy, Emily Christofides, and Serge Desmarais. 2014. "'Creeping' or Just Information Seeking? Gender Differences in Partner Monitoring in Response to Jealousy on Facebook." *Personal Relationships* 21: 35–50. doi:10.1111/pere.12014.

Muscanell, Nicole L., Rosanna E. Guadagno, Lindsay Rice, and Shannon Murphy. 2013. "Don't It Make My Brown Eyes Green? An Analysis of Facebook Use and Romantic Jealousy." *Cyberpsychology, Behavior, and Social Networking* 16: 237–42. doi:0.1089/cyber.2012.0411.

Notopoulos, Katie. January 6, 2015. "No One Wants to Admit They're in a Relationship on Facebook Anymore."*Buzzfeed News.* https://www.buzzfeed.com/katienotopoulos/the-demise-of-making-it-facebook-official?utm_term=.pe0m1Znqm#.ppm9rLpB9.

Orosz, Gábor, Ádám Szekeres, Zoltán G. Kiss, Péter Farkas, and Christine Roland-Lévy. 2015. "Elevated Romantic Love and Jealousy if Relationship Status is Declared on Facebook." *Frontiers in Psychology* 6: 2–6. doi:10.3389/fpsyg.2015.00214.

Roberts, Karl A. 2005. "Women's Experience of Violence During Stalking by Former Romantic Partners." *Violence Against Women* 11: 89–114. doi:10.1177/1077801204271096.

Rueda, Heidi Adams, Megan Lindsay, and Lela Rankin Williams. 2015. "'She Posted It on Facebook': Mexican American Adolescents' Experiences with Technology and Romantic Relationships Conflict." *Journal of Adolescent Research* 30: 419–45. doi:10.1177/0743558414565236.

Rusbult, Caryl E. 1980. "Commitment and Satisfaction in Romantic Associations: A Test of the Investment Model." *Journal of Experimental Psychology* 16: 172–86. doi:10.1016/0022-1031(80)90007-4.

Stewart, Margaret C., Marianne Dainton, and Alan K. Goodboy. 2014. "Maintaining Relationships on Facebook: Associations with Uncertainty, Jealousy, and Satisfaction." *Communication Reports* 27: 13–26. doi:10.1080/08934215.2013.845675.

Tokunaga, Robert S. 2011. "Social Networking Site or Social Surveillance Site? Understanding the Use of Interpersonal Electronic Surveillance in Romantic Relationships." *Computers in Human Behavior* 27: 705–13. doi:10.1016/j.chb.2010.08.014.

Tokunaga, Robert S. 2016. "Interpersonal Surveillance over Social Network Sites: Applying a Theory of Negative Relational Maintenance and the Investment Model." *Journal of Social and Personal Relationships* 32: 171–90. doi:10.1177/0265407514568749.

Utz, Sonja, and Camiel J. Beukeboom. 2011. "The Role of Social Network Sites in Romantic Relationships: Effects on Jealousy and Relationship Happiness." *Journal of Computer-Mediated Communication* 16: 511–27. doi:10.1111/j.1083-6101.2011.01552.x.

Utz, Sonja, Muscanell, Nicole, and Cameran Khalid. 2015. "Snapchat Elicits More Jealousy than Facebook: A Comparison of Snapchat and Facebook Use." *Cyberpsychology, Behavior, and Social Networking,* 18: 141–46. doi:10.1089/cyber.2014.0479.

Walker, Leslie. August 16, 2016. "What Does 'Creeping' Mean?" http://personal-web.about.com/od/socialmediause/fl/What-Does-Creeping-Mean-Ins-and-Outs-of-Facebook-Creeping.htm.

Wigman, Stefanie Ashton, Nicola Graham-Kevan, and John Archer. 2008. "Investigating Sub-Groups of Harassers: The Roles of Attachment, Dependency, Jealousy and Aggression." *Journal of Family Violence* 23: 557–68. doi:10.1007/s10896-008-9171-x.

Van Ouytsel, Joris, Ellen Van Gool, Michel Walrave, Koen Ponnet, and Emilie Peeters. 2016. "Exploring the Role of Social Networking Sites within Adolescent Romantic Relationships and Dating Experiences." *Computers in Human Behavior* 55: 76–86. doi:10.1016/j.chb.2015.08.042.

TWELVE

Social Media Stressors in Romantic Relationships

Jesse Fox and Jessica Frampton

Interpersonal relationships have often benefited from the introduction of new communication technologies. The telephone enabled synchronous communication across long distances and the immediacy of another's voice. E-mail provided people a much faster delivery system for written communication and enabled communication across time zones or when a phone call was not practical. Texting capitalized on the accessibility of mobile devices and presented the convenience of anytime, anyplace communication. Social media have also offered several benefits, such as the ability to reach a wide range of people quickly or connect people from different parts of one's life.

With these benefits, however, come drawbacks. Lacking other bodily nonverbals, the telephone requires a deeper attention to and decryption of vocal cues. E-mail communicators must be wary of grammar, style, and writing mechanics to avoid misinterpretation. Texting can be overly accessible to the point of being invasive and annoying. Similarly, social media can have a number of downsides for communicating in interpersonal relationships.

In this chapter, we review the existing literature on the stressful or negative experiences associated with social media use in romantic relationships. First, we identify the distinct features of social media, elaborating on how these features may influence romantic relationship processes. Next, we provide an overview of several areas in which social media have been considered detrimental to romantic relationships: self-presentation and impression management of romantic relationships; technological incompatibility between partners; romantic jealousy; partner monitoring via online surveillance; social comparison; and social network interference in romantic relationships. Finally, we conclude by discussing how users are adapting their behaviors in an attempt to avoid these pitfalls while still capitalizing on the conveniences social media provide.

AFFORDANCES OF SOCIAL MEDIA

Affordances are the properties of a technology that enable specific actions (Gibson 1979), and how people perceive these affordances influences their behaviors (Norman 1990). Social media, and particularly social networking sites (SNSs), have specific social affordances that enable the actions a user can take (Fox and Moreland 2015; Treem and Leonardi 2013). These affordances determine how social information is conveyed and transmitted throughout the network, which influences how users receive, interpret, and are affected by this information. Affordances are also the key to understanding how romantic relationship experiences with social media are distinct from or similar to how romantic relationships functioned before the advent of such technologies. Without examining these affordances and comparing them to face-to-face or traditional channels, researchers cannot make claims that social media have distinct effects or have changed relationship processes.

One draw of social media is their ability to link individuals in one common virtual space. The affordance of *connectivity* or *network association* enables network members, no matter how disparate or geographically distant, to recognize each other's presence and typically view each other's content through a common node or "friend" (Fox and Moreland 2015; Treem and Leonardi 2013). *Visibility* means that information that was not easily accessible or publicized previously is now shared among the network (Treem and Leonardi 2013). Network association and visibility enable individuals to view information about their romantic partners that they may not have regular access to, such as seeing pictures and posts from previous relationships.

Other affordances of digital communication are also relevant to SNSs. *Persistence, editability,* and *replicability* are tied to the digital nature of text, pictures, videos, and other content. Because digital material is easily captured, saved, duplicated, and recirculated, information shared online may be accessible long after the initial post and difficult to remove permanently (Treem and Leonardi 2013). For example, a private romantic message could be widely shared and circulated without the partner's consent or knowledge, causing anger and embarrassment. Persistence and replicability also make it difficult to hide transgressions, relational indiscretions, or otherwise suspicious behaviors if they are posted to an SNS. Even if the offending content is removed, others may have stored it or shared it among other networks. Furthermore, several tools enable digital information to be manipulated, from simple cropping to intensive reconfiguration using programs such as Photoshop. In this way, artificial or deceptive material could be created to cause turmoil in a relationship.

Individual sites also have specific affordances that may foster stressful relational experiences. One particular Facebook feature, the ability to go "Facebook official" or "FBO" (i.e., link to one's partner in the relationship status), affords partner-specific connectivity (Fox and Warber 2013; Papp, Danielewicz, and Cayemberg 2012). Although this opportunity may seem like a way to promote togetherness, partners often have differing perceptions of the meaning and timing of this relationship status (Fox and Warber 2013), which can lead to tension, uncertainty, and conflict (Fox, Osborn, and Warber 2014). Other social media sites are designed to afford *anonymity*. If posters feel they cannot be identified, they may be more likely to engage in dishonest or aggressive behavior (Wright 2014). The type of gossip and accusations that circulate on these sites could threaten a romantic relationship whether or not the posted information is accurate. Thus, it is important to consider that the same affordances that allow us to share experiences and memories among friends also have the potential to challenge, complicate, or damage romantic relationships. As the following sections will demonstrate, many studies have shown that SNSs can initiate, promote, and exacerbate the dark side of relationships.

RELATIONAL SELF-PRESENTATION AND IMPRESSION MANAGEMENT

One of the most popular areas of research on social media is self-presentation and impression management. Impression management theorists argue that as social beings, humans are faced with a constant pressure to maintain a positive image among others to achieve social goals (Goffman 1959; Leary and Allen 2011). The *asynchronous* nature of computer-mediated communication enhances interactants' capabilities to modify one's self-presentation by selectively revising messages before transmission (Walther 1996). According to the hyperpersonal model, this affordance of *editability* enables a more idealized version of the self to be presented online (Walther 1996). Thus, information presented on social media tends to be positively skewed and may create pressure for individuals in romantic relationships to self-present to their romantic partners or the broader network in a way that may be exaggerated or inauthentic. For example, studies have shown that romantic partners feel pressure to present the relationship in a positive or idealized manner, even when the relationship is in turmoil (Fox, Osborn, and Warber 2014; Fox and Moreland 2015).

On social networking sites, the *network association* of many different audiences—which may include close friends, acquaintances, family, co-workers, people from the past, or unknown second-degree network ties—creates *context collapse*, and users may feel pressured to maintain a certain image for this imagined audience (Litt 2012). On social media, romantic partners might find it difficult to disclose information to one audience while withholding the same information from undesired audiences; for example, they may want family and friends to know about an engagement or pregnancy, but they may not want to disclose that information to co-workers or ex-partners. Social media sites also afford *social feedback* in the form of comments and "likes," which may yield negative outcomes for the relationship. For example, disapproving friends could make snarky comments on a couple's photo, which could upset the couple or give others a bad impression about the relationship. Thus, individuals are faced with many impression management challenges when navigating how to disclose and present a romantic relationship on social media.

TECHNOLOGICAL INCOMPATIBILITY

Within the couple, there may be discrepancies in how they self-present on social media. For example, Joe may want to disclose every detail about the relationship online, whereas Amanda may prefer to keep things private. Problematic discrepancies in romantic partners' technology use, or *technological incompatibility*, can be a stressor in relationships. This incompatibility may be based on the amount or timing of use, the type of connections maintained, the nature of interactions with ties, perceived rules violations, or the range of content shared on a site (Fox, Osborn, and Warber 2014; McDaniel and Coyne 2016; Tokunaga 2014).

When technology-related behaviors or expectations do not match, these discrepancies may create conflict in relationships or diminish relationship satisfaction (Hall and Baym 2011; McDaniel and Coyne 2016). Indeed, negative perceptions of how a romantic partner uses social media can diminish feelings of relational intimacy (Hand, Thomas, Buboltz, Deemer, and Buyanjargal 2013). Some couples have divergent expectations for romantic relationship maintenance online, and different practices by partners can create conflict (Fox and Moreland 2015). Some romantic partners struggle to establish boundaries for privacy and argue about what is acceptable to post online; in extreme cases, this can lead to the termination of the relationship (Fox, Osborn, and Warber 2014).

One possible explanation for these discrepancies is differences in romantic partners' attachment style. Attachment theory suggests that our tendencies to be anxious or avoidant toward others has significant implications for how individuals experience, enact, and communicate within romantic relationships (Hazan and Shaver 1987; Simpson 1990). Several studies have found that attachment styles predict various negative relational behaviors on SNSs (e.g., Fox and Warber 2014; Marshall 2012; Marshall et al. 2013; Reed et al. 2015, 2016; Weisskirch and Delevi 2013). In general, those who are high in anxious attachment rely more on SNSs, put significant stock in their content, and experience more negative emotions as a result. Avoidant individuals typically prefer not to communicate with their partners via SNSs unless they can be used to create distance from the partner.

Differences in attachment style may lend themselves to technological incompatibility and lead to conflict if, for instance, an anxious individual anticipates interaction or public displays of affection on SNSs from his or her avoidant partner, who abhors the idea of attending to needy posts or publicizing the relationship. Some partners may feel "smothered" or stressed by obligations to meet the needs of anxious partners (Weinstein and Selman, 2016). Thus, it is important that couples assess their behaviors and relational expectations and negotiate social media practices that are acceptable to both parties.

ROMANTIC JEALOUSY

Jealousy is one of the most studied stressors in relation to SNSs and romantic relationships (e.g., Cohen, Bowman, and Borchert 2014; Dainton and Stokes 2015; Elphinston and Noller 2011; Muise, Christofides, and Desmarais 2009; Utz and Beukeboom 2011). Jealousy has been defined as a cognitive, emotional, and behavioral experience that involves the need to defend a valued relationship from the threat of a perceived third-party rival (Bevan 2013). Social media provide ample opportunity to perceive potential rivals due to affordances such as *visibility, network association,* and *persistence.* Because information about potential rivals and their interactions with one's romantic partner is so readily available on SNSs, jealousy may be more common now than ever before (Fox, Osborn, and Warber 2014; Muise, Christofides, and Desmarais 2009). Indeed, research has shown that higher levels of SNS use or involvement with SNSs predict greater romantic jealousy (Elphinston and Noller 2011; Muise, Christofides, and Desmarais 2009). Unfortunately, the jealousy triggered by social media content has the potential to negatively influence relationship satisfaction (Elphinston and Noller 2011).

Social media content is accessible to almost anyone with an internet connection. The sites are most often free to use and continue to grow in popularity (Van Dijck 2013). With just a few clicks, a wealth of information about one's romantic partner and potential rivals is displayed on a screen. SNSs such as Facebook and Instagram serve as digital scrapbooks of a user's personal life and relationships. Due to the affordance of *multi-*

modality (Tokunaga 2011), SNS profiles consist of a variety of media such as text, photos, and videos. Not only can users upload their own photos, videos, and statuses, but others can post photos and comments on a user's profile as well. For example, Fox and Anderegg (2014) noted that it is common for Facebook users in romantic relationships to tag romantic partners in photos and publicly post on their romantic partners' profiles. Thus, SNSs afford highly visible methods of interaction (Treem and Leonardi 2013) and provide more information about a partner's relationships than other means of communication (Muise, Christofides, and Desmarais 2009).

Visibility can contribute to romantic jealousy when a user is able to view ambiguous photos or interactions between a third-party rival and their romantic partner (Fox, Osborn, and Warber 2014; Muise, Christofides, and Desmarais 2009; Utz, Muscanell, and Khalid 2015; Van Ouytsel et al. 2016). Fleuriet, Cole, and Guerrero (2014) found that people are likely to experience negative affect when a rival with an attractive profile picture posts on a romantic partner's wall or when the rival uses flirtatious emoticons in the post. Likewise, Gershon (2010) described how people experience jealousy when others post photographs of their romantic partners at parties with potential rivals or photos of their romantic partners hugging rivals. Due to *network association*, a rival's SNS posts on a romantic partner's profile may be particularly threatening when they are visible not only to the jealous individual, but to the partner's entire network as well (Muscanell et al. 2013; Utz and Beukeboom 2011).

On the other hand, a lack of visibility may also evoke romantic jealousy. Private communication through social media is seen as more threatening and evokes more jealousy than public communication (Cohen, Bowman, and Bochert 2014; Utz, Muscanell, and Khalid 2015). Similarly, Muscanell et al. (2013) reported that privacy settings on photographs led to jealousy when participants discovered that photos of a romantic partner with a rival were hidden from view. People were especially jealous if there were no photos of themselves with their romantic partner on their romantic partner's profile. The authors speculated that participants perceived the lack of photos of the current relationship as their partner's attempt to hide the relationship from others in their network. However, Van Ouytsel et al. (2016) noted that hiding the relationship from other network members, such as parents and other family members, may actually be desired in some romantic relationships. Thus, it appears that jealousy is less likely to be evoked if there is mutual understanding between partners about the privacy of the relationship.

The affordance of *network association* (Treem and Leonardi 2013) allows for the exploration of a romantic partner's social network ties. Users' profiles are linked as "friends" or "followers," and these links allow for easy access to a potential rival's profile page. Once on the page, it is easy to make social comparisons to a rival that lead to jealousy. For example, if a person looks at photographs of a rival on SNSs and perceives the rival as more attractive or more physically dominant than they themselves are, they are likely to think that rival poses a threat to the relationship (Dijkstra and Buunk 2002). Van Ouytsel et al. (2016) described how some jealous individuals asked their romantic partners to disassociate with rivals on SNSs by "unfriending" them. In these cases, rivals were no longer able to fully view the romantic partner's page, and network members no longer saw a link between the romantic partner's profile and the rival's profile.

Jealousy About the Past

White and Mullen (1989) suggested that jealousy may occur in the absence of a current threat to the relationship itself. In these instances, jealousy is evoked because there is "a loss of a sense of uniqueness or specialness about the relationship" (White and Mullen 1989, 10). Thus, information about a romantic partner's past on SNSs can evoke jealousy if it makes a person feel that the current relationship is somehow less special. There are two types of jealousy directed at the past: retroactive jealousy and retrospective jealousy. *Retroactive jealousy* occurs when a person feels upset about a romantic partner's past romantic or sexual relationships that existed prior to the current relationship. For instance, Anne could become jealous when listening to her spouse Taylor describe a romantic date with an old girlfriend that occurred years before Anne and Taylor met. Taylor's ex-girlfriend never posed an active threat to the relationship itself, and Taylor is no longer in contact with the ex. On the other hand, *retrospective jealousy* occurs when a partner feels jealous in regard to a rival that once threatened the current relationship in the past. For example, Dan and Morgan are a couple that has been married for ten years. Dan might experience retrospective jealousy thinking about how Morgan had a one-night stand with Max while Dan was away on business five years ago. The one-night stand ended, but Max was once an active threat to the relationship in the past.

Anderson, Kunkel, and Dennis (2011) found that people often avoid discussing past sexual and romantic relationships with new romantic partners because this type of information may evoke jealousy, lead to comparisons with past lovers, and make people feel as if the current relationship is less special. Although the topic of exes may be easy to avoid in face-to-face contexts, it is often difficult for SNS users to avoid information about a romantic partner's exes due to the affordance of *persistence* (Treem and Leonardi 2013). Social media have the potential to evoke both retroactive jealousy and retrospective jealousy because they store historical user profile information (Tokunaga 2011). Information about ex-partners and old relationships is likely visible on a romantic partner's page long after the relationship ends. If photos of a romantic partner happy with an ex-partner are displayed on a user's computer screen, retroactive jealousy may ensue. Likewise, if a user sees an old flirtatious post from a rival who was attempting to steal the romantic partner in the past, retrospective jealousy may be evoked.

Individual Differences in SNS-Related Jealousy

It is important to note that social media affordances may not contribute to jealousy for all users. Several individual difference variables have been linked to the experience of jealousy (see Bevan 2013 for a review). Marshall et al. (2013) explored attachment styles as predictors of Facebook-related jealousy. They found that an anxious attachment style was positively associated with jealousy, and an avoidant attachment style was negatively related to the experience of jealousy. This finding was supported by Miller et al. (2014), who reported that people with a preoccupied attachment style expressed the most anger and fear when viewing photos of their hypothetical romantic partners touching a close friend. When anxiously attached SNS users feel jealous, they may respond in ways that harm the romantic relationship. For instance, Drouin, Miller, and Dibble (2014) found that anxiously attached individuals experiencing jealousy intentionally sent and accepted friend requests from other romantic interests. In turn, sending and accepting friend requests from other romantic interests was related to lower relationship commitment.

Additionally, research has shown that a user's sex is related to the experience of SNS-related jealousy. Several studies have observed that females are more jealous in response to SNS information indicating a threat from a third-party rival (Cohen, Bowman, and Borchert 2014; Dijkstra, Barelds, and Groothof 2010; McAndrew and Shah 2013; Muscanell et al. 2013; Rueda, Lindsay, and Williams 2015). Males seem to be more aware of these sex differences in SNS-related jealousy than females (McAndrew and Shah 2013). Researchers have also found that females tend to perform more jealousy-motivated behaviors overall than males (Bevan 2013; McAndrew and Shah 2013). Surveillance or partner monitoring is one such jealousy-motivated behavior that can serve as a unique stressor in romantic relationships.

PARTNER MONITORING

Romantic jealousy is often cited as a cause of *interpersonal electronic surveillance* (Tokunaga 2011), or online partner monitoring. Romantic partners often have ways of keeping up with—or keeping tabs on—each other's business, and several studies have shown that SNSs and other online channels facilitate this surveillance (e.g., Elphinston and Noller 2011; Fox and Anderegg 2014; Fox and Tokunaga 2015; Lyndon, Bonds-

Raacke, and Cratty 2011; Marshall et al. 2013; Tokunaga 2011; Tong 2013). In some ways, this monitoring behavior can have benefits to the relationship: asking questions, showing interest in the partner's activities, and interacting with their networks can serve positive relational maintenance functions. Romantic partner monitoring can also have a dark side rooted in mistrust, jealousy, or obsession, however. Typically, the nature and extent of online surveillance of a romantic partner varies by the individual's goals and the status of the relationship.

According to uncertainty reduction theory (Berger and Calabrese 1975) and other uncertainty management perspectives (Afifi and Weiner 2004; Brashers 2001), when people are experiencing negative feelings as a result of uncertainty, they may seek out information to reduce that uncertainty. If the partner's social media presence is accessible, there is little need to hire a private detective to figure out what one's partner is up to; the *visibility*, *network association*, and *persistence* of social media enable users to track their partners and their partners' network ties with unprecedented ease. The ability for users to share *multimodal* information on these platforms also provides not just text, but richer media such as photographs and videos that can be examined. Such monitoring can trigger jealousy, stress, and other negative emotions (Elphinston and Noller 2011; Marshall 2012).

Online surveillance is also used as a method of manipulating or controlling the partner (Van Ouytsel et al. 2016). An individual can monitor what the partner does and whom the partner interacts with, which may then be used as justification for controlling behavior. For example, the individual may see flirty comments from the partner's ex and demand that the ex be "unfriended." Online content may be cited as evidence that the partner cannot be trusted or allowed to engage in certain behaviors, such as going out with friends unsupervised. More direct forms of control are also common, such as demanding a partner's password to observe their private interactions on SNSs (Weinstein and Selman 2016).

Partner monitoring online can also reach levels that are unhealthy or obsessive (Chaulk and Jones 2011). The accessibility to so much information about or contact with the partner can lead to an expectation and growing dependence on it. Reed and colleagues (2016) note that this accessibility may lead to a "cycle of anxiety" about the relationship. Similarly, Su (2016) argues that because of this dependence, an absence of contact or information is perceived more negatively; anxious partners experience "ambiguity in silence" wherein they began to make negative attributions about themselves, the partner, or the relationship because of the lack of information. A constant preoccupation with the partner's activities and interactions with others can be a sign of distrust and deep insecurity. Thus, although online surveillance may enable some positive relationship maintenance behaviors and information seeking, it also has the potential to be a source of distress and conflict for couples.

SOCIAL COMPARISONS

When making self-assessments of experiences such as romantic relation-ships, social comparison theory suggests that we evaluate others, particu-larly our peers (Festinger 1954). The variety of information available via social media makes them prime grounds for social comparison (Hafer-kamp and Krämer 2011; Johnson and Knobloch-Westerwick 2014). Sever-al studies have found that SNSs are a common context for stressful or otherwise negative social comparisons, and they lead to diminished self-perceptions, negative emotions, and decreased life satisfaction (Chou and Edge 2012; Fox and Moreland 2015; Fox and Vendemia 2016; Frisson and Eggermont 2016; Haferkamp and Krämer 2011).

One form of social comparison for individuals in romantic relation-ships is to perceived romantic rivals, including ex-partners or attractive "friends" who are visible in the network even when they are never en-countered offline (Fox, Warber, and Makstaller 2013). A woman who feels insecure in her dating relationship may probe into her partner's romantic history by looking at old photo albums, posts about or ex-changes with the former partners, or other persistent markers of previous relationships. If the partner is still connected with an ex, the insecure individual could also probe the ex's current profile for other points of self-comparison.

According to interdependence theory, other comparisons play an im-portant role in the sustenance of relationships (Kelley and Thibaut 1978). Rusbult's (1980) investment model suggests that based on our levels of commitment and investment in our relationships, we may compare our current partner and relationship to others. We may assess our compari-son level by comparing our relationship to other couples who seem to have better relationships than ours due to their constant affection online or endless photo albums of exotic vacations. Additionally, various social media platforms, including online dating sites, enable us to assess our comparison level for alternatives to the relationship. Due to their *search-ability, network association,* and the *visibility* of information such as rela-tionship status, social media provide unprecedented access to relation-ship alternatives. These relationship alternatives may create imagined or real threats to the continuance of the relationship (Drouin, Miller, and Dibble 2014; Fox and Tokunaga 2015).

NETWORK INTERFERENCE

Regarding romantic relationships, perhaps one of the most understudied aspects of social networking sites is network interference. Family, friends, peers, and even ex-partners are very influential in the development and maintenance of romantic relationships (Eggert and Parks 1987; Hogerbrugge, Komter, and Scheepers 2013; Sprecher 2011). Social ties may determine who is acceptable to date, what behaviors are acceptable in a relationship, and whether a relationship is sustained or terminated.

The affordances of social networking sites provide prime opportunities for ties to monitor or become involved in an individual's romantic relationship. Information about the relationship that may be difficult to discover through traditional means may be visible on social media through a relationship status, posts, pictures, or exchanges with the partner or other ties on one's profile. Due to the affordances of *network association* and *social feedback*, other network members have unprecedented access to information, as well as the opportunity to "like" or comment on the relationship information. As a result of context collapse, disparate ties (such as family, friends, peers, and co-workers from both partners) are able to semi-publicly discuss, argue, or present a united front regarding a relationship. These affordances may maximize the network's influence on—or meddling in—a romantic relationship, as there is more fodder for gossip or speculation about the nature or health of the relationship. Ties that may not have met the partner offline have the ability to garner information about or interact with the partner, and ties from different domains that normally would have been unknown to each other may be able to collaborate or interact.

Research on the nature of network interference in romantic relationships via social media is rather limited at this time. One study noted cases in which individuals posted on their ex-partners' pages (e.g., flirting, sharing old pictures of the couple) to invoke jealousy from a new romantic partner (Fox, Osborn, and Warber 2014). Announcing a change in relationship status can result in disapproving comments or network members publicly taking sides to support or criticize the change (Fox, Warber, and Makstaller 2013). If users make negative comments about a relationship-related post, other network members perceive the relationship negatively, even if the original post reflected positively about the relationship (Ballantine, Lin, and Veer 2015). These perceptions could in turn affect network members' support for the relationship.

A specific form of interference may also occur on account of the network association afforded by SNSs. Regardless of a person's relationship status, others may see social media as an opportunity to connect with or poach someone's mate; alternatively, an individual in a relationship may flirt with or engage in online infidelity with others via SNSs (Drouin, Miller, and Dibble 2014; McDaniel, Drouin, and Cravens 2017). Ex-partners may use social media as a convenient way to re-establish contact, attempt to rebuild a relationship, or interfere with the current relationship (Fox, Warber, and Makstaller 2013; Ramirez and Bryant 2014). Thus, having a romantic relationship visible to a broad social media audience may ultimately affect the duration and quality of the relationship.

CONCLUSION

As this chapter has demonstrated, the very affordances of social media that facilitate relationships can also create pressure and stress within romantic relationships. As social media users become familiar with the affordances of these platforms, however, they are developing and refining strategies to cope with these stressors. Knowing that relationship status updates are publicized to the network, many users now hide their status on Facebook regardless of whether or not they are in a relationship. Due to the context collapse on sites like Facebook, many users have sought out pseudonymous accounts on sites like Instagram or Twitter and maintained a smaller network limited to close friends or peers. Snapchat has become popular because it affords private messaging similar to texts, and these messages disappear from view after they are received. As such, users believe their messages are not persistent and that the app affords them more privacy for romantic exchanges. As users become more familiar with these platforms and their affordances, they will continue to adapt their behavior to maximize the benefits and minimize the costs of social media to their romantic relationships.

REFERENCES

Afifi, Walid A., and Judith L. Weiner. 2004. "Toward a Theory of Motivated Information Management." *Communication Theory* 14: 167–90. doi: 10.1111/j.1468-2885.2004.tb00310.x.

Anderson, Mike, Adrianne Kunkel, and Michael Robert Dennis. 2011. "'Let's (Not) Talk About That': Bridging the Past Sexual Experiences Taboo to Build Healthy Romantic Relationships." *Journal of Sex Research* 48: 381–91. doi: 10.1080/00224499.2010.482215.

Ballantine, Paul W., Yongjia Lin, and Ekant Veer. 2015. "The Influence of User Comments on Perceptions of Facebook Relationship Status Updates." *Computers in Human Behavior* 49: 50–55. doi: 10.1016/j.chb.2015.02.055.

Berger, Charles R., and Richard J. Calabrese. 1975. "Some Explorations in Initial Interaction and Beyond: Toward a Developmental Theory of Interpersonal Communication." *Human Communication Research* 1: 99–112. doi: 10.1111/j.1468-2958.1975.tb00258.x.

Bevan, Jennifer L. 2013. *The Communication of Jealousy*. New York, NY: Peter Lang.

Brashers, Dale E. (2001). "Communication and Uncertainty Management." *Journal of Communication* 51: 477–97. doi: 10.1111/j.1460-2466.2001.tb02892.x.

Chaulk, Kasey, and Tim Jones. 2011. "Online Obsessive Relational Intrusion: Further Concerns About Facebook." *Journal of Family Violence* 26: 245–54. doi: 10.1007/s10896-011-9360-x.

Chou, Hui-Tzu Grace, and Nicholas Edge. 2012. "'They are Happier and Having Better Lives than I am': The Impact of Using Facebook on Perceptions of Others' Lives." *Cyberpsychology, Behavior, and Social Networking* 15: 117–21. doi: 10.1089/cyber.2011.0324.

Cohen, Elizabeth L., Nicholas D. Bowman, and Katherine Borchert. 2014. "Private Flirts, Public Friends: Understanding Romantic Jealousy Responses to an Ambiguous Social Network Site Message as a Function of Message Access Exclusivity." *Computers in Human Behavior* 35: 535–41. doi: 10.1016/j.chb.2014.02.050.

Dainton, Marianne, and Alexandra Stokes. 2015. "College Students' Romantic Relationships on Facebook: Linking the Gratification for Maintenance to Facebook Maintenance Activity and the Experience of Jealousy." *Communication Quarterly* 63: 365–83. doi: 10.1080/01463373.2015.1058283.

Darvell, Millie J., Shari P. Walsh, and Katherine M. White. 2011. "Facebook Tells Me So: Applying the Theory of Planned Behavior to Understand Partner-Monitoring Behavior on Facebook." *Cyberpsychology, Behavior, and Social Networking* 14: 717–22. doi: 10.1089/cyber.2011.0035.

Dijkstra, Pieternel, and Bram P. Buunk. 2002. "Sex Differences in the Jealousy-Evoking Effect of Rival Characteristics." *European Journal of Social Psychology* 32: 829–52. doi: 10.1002/ejsp.125.

Dijkstra, Pieternel, Dick P. H. Baraelds, and Hinke A. K. Groothof. 2010. "An Inventory and Update of Jealousy-Evoking Partner Behaviours in Modern Society." *Clinical Psychology and Psychotherapy* 17: 329–45. doi: 10.1002/cpp.668.

Drouin, Michelle, Daniel A. Miller, and Jayson L. Dibble. 2014. "Ignore Your Partners' Current Facebook Friends; Beware the Ones They Add!" *Computers in Human Behavior* 35: 483–88. doi: 10.1016/j.chb.2014.02.032.

Eggert, Leona L., and Malcolm R. Parks. 1987. "Communication Network Involvement in Adolescents' Friendships and Romantic Relationships." *Annals of the International Communication Association* 10: 283–322. doi: 10.1080/23808985.1987.11678649.

Elphinston, Rachel A., and Patricia Noller. 2011. "Time to Face It! Facebook Intrusion and the Implications for Romantic Jealousy and Relationship Satisfaction." *Cyberpsychology, Behavior, and Social Networking* 14: 631–35. doi: 10.1089/cyber.2010.0318

Festinger, Leon. 1954. "A Theory of Social Comparison Processes." *Human Relations*, 7: 117–40. doi: 10.1177/001872675400700202.

Fleuriet, Christina, Megan Cole, and Laura K. Guerrero. 2014. "Exploring Facebook: Attachment Style and Nonverbal Message Characteristics as Predictors of Anticipated Emotional Reactions to Facebook Postings." *Journal of Nonverbal Behavior* 38: 429–50. doi: 10.1007/s10919-014-0189-x.

Fox, Jesse, and Courtney Anderegg. 2014. "Romantic Relationship Stages and Social Networking Sites: Uncertainty Reduction Strategies and Perceived Relational Norms on Facebook." *Cyberpsychology, Behavior, and Social Networking* 17: 685–91. doi: 10.1089/cyber.2014.0232.

Fox, Jesse, and Jennifer J. Moreland. 2015. "The Dark Side of Social Networking Sites: An Exploration of the Relational and Psychological Stressors Associated with Facebook Use and Affordances." *Computers in Human Behavior* 45: 168–76. doi: 10.1016/j.chb.2014.11.083.

Fox, Jesse, Jeremy L. Osborn, and Katie M. Warber. 2014. "Relational Dialectics and Social Networking Sites: The Role of Facebook in Romantic Relationship Escalation, Maintenance, Conflict, and Dissolution." *Computers in Human Behavior* 35: 527–34. doi: 10.1016/j.chb.2014.02.031.

Fox, Jesse, and Robert S. Tokunaga. 2015. "Romantic Partner Monitoring After Breakups: Attachment, Dependence, Distress, and Post-Dissolution Online Surveillance via Social Networking Sites." *Cyberpsychology, Behavior, and Social Networking* 18: 491–98. doi: 10.1089/cyber.2015.0123.

Fox, Jesse, and Megan A. Vendemia. 2016. "Selective Self-Presentation and Social Comparison Through Photographs on Social Networking Sites." *Cyberpsychology, Behavior, and Social Networking* 19: 593–600. doi: 10.1089/cyber.2016.0248.

Fox, Jesse, and Katie M. Warber. 2013. "Romantic Relationship Development in the Age of Facebook: An Exploratory Study of Emerging Adults' Perceptions, Motives, and Behaviors." *Cyberpsychology, Behavior, and Social Networking* 16: 3–7. doi: 10.1089/cyber.2012.0288.

———. 2014. "Social Networking Sites in Romantic Relationships: Attachment, Uncertainty, and Partner Surveillance on Facebook." *Cyberpsychology, Behavior, and Social Networking* 17: 3–7. doi: 10.1089/cyber.2012.0667.

Fox, Jesse, Katie M. Warber, and Dana C. Makstaller. 2013. "The Role of Facebook in Romantic Relationship development: An exploration of Knapp's relational stage model." *Journal of Social and Personal Relationships* 30: 771–94. doi: 10.1177/0265407512468370.

Frison, Eline, and Steven Eggermont. 2016. "'Harder, Better, Faster, Stronger': Negative Comparison on Facebook and Adolescents' Life Satisfaction Are Reciprocally Related." *Cyberpsychology, Behavior, and Social Networking* 19: 158–64. doi: 10.1089/cyber.2015.0296.

Gershon, Ilana. 2010. *The Breakup 2.0: Disconnecting Over New Media*. Ithaca: Cornell University Press.

Gibson, James J. 1979. *The Ecological Approach to Visual Perception*. Boston: Houghlin Mifflin.

Goffman, Erving. 1959. *Presentation of Self in Everyday Life*. Garden City, NY: Anchor Books.

Haferkamp, Nina, and Nicole C. Krämer. 2011."Social Comparison 2.0: Examining the Effects of Online Profiles on Social Networking Sites." *Cyberpsychology, Behavior, and Social Networking* 14: 309–14. doi: 10.1089/cyber.2010.0120.

Hall, Jeffrey A., and Nancy K. Baym. 2012. "Calling and Texting (Too Much): Mobile Maintenance Expectations, (Over)dependence, Entrapment, and Friendship Satisfaction." *New Media & Society* 14: 316–31. doi: 10.1177/1461444811415047.

Hand, Matthew M., Donna Thomas, Walter C. Buboltz, Eric D. Deemer, and Munkhsanaa Buyanjargal. 2013. "Facebook and Romantic Relationships: Intimacy and Couple Satisfaction Associated with Online Social Network Use." *Cyberpsychology, Behavior, and Social Networking* 16: 8–13. doi: 10.1089/cyber.2012.0038.

Hazan, Cindy, and Phillip Shaver. 1987. "Romantic Love Conceptualized as an Attachment Process." *Journal of Personality & Social Psychology* 52: 511–24. doi: 10.1037/0022-3514.52.3.511.

Hogerbrugge, Martijn J. A., Aafke E. Komter, and Peer Scheepers. 2013. "Dissolving Long-Term Romantic Relationships: Assessing the Role of the Social Context." *Journal of Social and Personal Relationships* 30: 320–42. doi: 10.1177/0265407512462167.

Johnson, Benjamin K., and Silvia Knobloch-Westerwick. 2014. "Glancing Up or Down: Mood Management and Selective Social Comparisons on Social Networking Sites." *Computers in Human Behavior* 41: 33–39. doi: 10.1016/j.chb.2014.09.009.

Kelley, Harold H. and John Thibaut. 1978. *Interpersonal Relations: A Theory of Interdependence*. New York: Wiley.

Leary, Mark R., and Ashley Batts Allen. 2011. "Self-Presentational Persona: Simultaneous Management of Multiple Impressions." *Journal of Personality and Social Psychology* 101: 1033–49. doi: 10.1037/a0023884.

Litt, Eden. 2012. "Knock, Knock. Who's There? The Imagined Audience." *Journal of Broadcasting & Electronic Media* 56: 330–45. doi: 10.1080/08838151.2012.705195.

Lyndon, Amy, Jennifer Bonds-Raacke, and Alyssa D. Cratty. 2011. "College Students' Facebook Stalking of Ex-Partners." *Cyberpsychology, Behavior, and Social Networking* 14: 711–16. doi: 10.1089/cyber.2010.0588.

Marshall, Tara C. 2012. "Facebook Surveillance of Former Romantic Partners: Associations with Postbreakup Recovery and Personal Growth." *Cyberpsychology, Behavior, and Social Networking* 15: 521–26. doi: 10.1089/cyber.2012.0125.

Marshall, Tara C., Katherine Bejanyan, Gaia Di Castro, and Ruth Lee. 2013. "Attachment Styles as Predictors of Facebook-related Jealousy and Surveillance in Romantic Relationships." *Personal Relationships* 20: 1–22. doi: 10.1111/j.1475-6811.2011.01393.x.

McAndrew, Francis T., and Sahil S. Shah. 2013. "Sex Differences in Jealousy over Facebook Activity." *Computers in Human Behavior* 29: 2603–6. doi: 10.1016/j.chb.2013.06.030.

McDaniel, Brandon T., and Sarah M. Coyne. 2016. "'Technoference': The Interference of Technology in Couple Relationships and Implications for Women's Personal and

Relational Well-Being." *Psychology of Popular Media Culture* 5: 85–98. doi: 10.1037/ppm0000065.

McDaniel, Brandon T., Michelle Drouin, and Jaclyn D. Cravens. 2017. "Do You Have Anything to Hide? Infidelity-Related Behaviors on Social Media Sites and Marital Satisfaction." *Computers in Human Behavior* 66: 88–95. doi: 10.1016/j.chb.2016.09.031.

Miller, Michael J., Amanda Denes, Brianna Diaz, and Ross Buck. 2009. "Attachment Style Predicts Jealous Reactions to Viewing Touch Between a Romantic Partner and Close Friend: Implications for Internet Social Communication." *Journal of Nonverbal Behavior* 38: 451–76. doi: 10.1007/s10919-014-0196-y.

Muise, Amy, Emily Christofides, and Serge Desmarais. 2009. "More Information Than You Ever Wanted: Does Facebook Bring out the Green-eyed Monster of Jealousy?" *Cyberpsychology & Behavior* 12: 441–44. doi: 10.1089/cpb.2008.0263.

———. 2014. "'Creeping' or Just Information Seeking? Gender Differences in Partner Monitoring in Response to Jealousy on Facebook." *Personal Relationships* 21: 35–50. doi: 10.1111/pere.12014.

Muscanell, Nicole L., Rosanna E. Guadagno, Lindsay Rice, and Shannon Murphy. 2013. "Don't It Make My Brown Eyes Green? An Analysis of Facebook Use and Romantic Jealousy." *Cyberpsychology, Behavior, and Social Networking* 16: 237–42. doi: 10.1089/cyber.2012.0411.

Norman, Donald A. 1990. *The Design of Everyday Things.* New York: Doubleday.

Papp, Lauren M., Jennifer Danielewicz, and Crystal Cayemberg. 2012. "'Are We Facebook Official?' Implications of Dating Partners' Facebook Use and Profiles for Intimate Relationship Satisfaction." *Cyberpsychology, Behavior, and Social Networking* 15: 85–90. doi: 10.1089/cyber.2011.0291.

Ramirez Jr., Artemio, and Erin M. Bryant. 2014. "Relational Reconnection on Social Network Sites: An Examination of Relationship Persistence and Modality Switching." *Communication Reports* 27: 1–12. doi: 10.1080/08934215.2013.851725.

Reed, Lauren A., Richard M. Tolman, and Paige Safyer. 2015. "Too Close for Comfort: Attachment Insecurity and Electronic Intrusion in College Students' Dating Relationships." *Computers in Human Behavior* 50: 431–38. doi: 10.1016/j.chb.2015.03.050.

Reed, Lauren A., Richard M. Tolman, L. Monique Ward, and Paige Safyer. 2016. "Keeping Tabs: Attachment Anxiety and Electronic Intrusion in High School Dating Relationships." *Computers in Human Behavior* 58: 259–68. doi: 10.1016/j.chb.2015.12.019.

Rueda, Heidi Adams, Megan Lindsay, and Lela Rankin Williams. 2015. "'She Posted It on Facebook': Mexican American Adolescents' Experiences with Technology and Romantic Relationship Conflict." *Journal of Adolescent Research* 30: 419–45. doi: 10.1177/0743558414565236.

Rusbult, Carol E. 1980. "Commitment and Satisfaction in Romantic Associations: A Test of the Investment Model." *Journal of Experimental Social Psychology* 26: 172–86. doi: 10.1016/0022-1031(80)90007-4.

Simpson, Jeffrey A. 1990. "Influence of Attachment Styles on Romantic Relationships." *Journal of Personality & Social Psychology* 59: 971–80. doi: 10.1037//0022-3514.59.5.971.

Sprecher, Susan. 2011. "The Influence of Social Networks on Romantic Relationships: Through the Lens of the Social Network." *Personal Relationships* 18: 630–44. doi: 10.1111/j.1475-6811.2010.01330.x.

Su, Hua. 2016. "Constant Connection as the Media Condition of Love: Where Bonds Become Bondage." *Media, Culture & Society* 38: 232–47. doi: 10.1177/0163443715594037.

Tokunaga, Robert S. 2011. "Social Networking Site or Social Surveillance Site? Understanding the Use of Interpersonal Electronic Surveillance in Romantic Relationships." *Computers in Human Behavior* 27: 705-13. doi: 10.1016/j.chb.2010.08.014.

———. 2014. "Relational Transgressions on Social Networking Sites: Individual, Interpersonal, and Contextual Explanations for Dyadic Strain and Communication Rules Change." *Computers in Human Behavior* 39: 287–95. doi: 10.1016/j.chb.2014.07.024.

Tong, Stephanie T. 2013. "Facebook Use During Relationship Termination: Uncertainty Reduction and Surveillance." *Cyberpsychology, Behavior, & Social Networking* 16: 788–93. doi: 10.1089/cyber.2012.0549.

Treem, Jeffrey, and Paul Leonardi. 2013. "Social Media Use in Organizations: Exploring the Affordances of Visibility, Editability, Persistence, and Association." In vol. 38 of *Communication Yearbook*, ed. Charles T. Salmon, 143–89. New York: Routledge.

Utz, Sonja, and Camiel J. Beukeboom. 2011. "The Role of Social Network Sites in Romantic Relationships: Effects on Jealousy and Relationship Happiness." *Journal of Computer-Mediated Communication* 16: 511–27. doi: 10.1111/j.1083-6101.2011.01552.x.

Utz, Sonja, Nicole Muscanell, and Cameran Khalid. 2015. "Snapchat elicits more jealousy than Facebook: a comparison of Snapchat and Facebook use." *Cyberpsychology, Behavior, and Social Networking* 18: 141–46. doi: 10.1089/cyber.2014.0479.

Van Dijck, José. 2013. *The Culture of Connectivity: A Critical History of Social Media*. New York: Oxford University Press.

Van Ouytsel, Joris, Ellen Van Gool, Michel Walrave, Koen Ponnet, and Emilie Peeters. 2016. "Exploring the Role of Social Networking Sites within Adolescent Romantic Relationships and Dating Experiences." *Computers in Human Behavior* 55: 76–86. doi: 10.1016/j.chb.2015.08.042.

Walther, Joseph B. 1996. "Computer-Mediated Communication: Impersonal, Interpersonal, and Hyperpersonal Interaction." *Communication Research* 23: 3–43. doi: 10.1177/009365096023001001.

Weinstein, Emily C., and Robert L. Selman. 2016. "Digital Stress: Adolescents' Personal Accounts." *New Media & Society* 18: 391–409. doi: 10.1177/1461444814543989.

Weisskirch, Robert S., and Raquel Delevi. 2013. "Attachment Style and Conflict Resolution Skills Predicting Technology Use in Relationship Dissolution." *Computers in Human Behavior* 29: 2530–34. doi: 10.1016/j.chb.2013.06.027.

White, Gregory L., and Paul E. Mullen. 1989. *Jealousy: Theory, Research, and Clinical Strategies*. New York: Guilford.

Wright, Michelle F. 2014. "Predictors of Anonymous Cyberaggression: The Role of Adolescents' Beliefs About Anonymity, Aggression, and the Permanency of Digital Content." *Cyberpsychology, Behavior, and Social Networking* 17: 431–38. doi: 10.1089/cyber.2013.0457.

IV

Dissolution

THIRTEEN

#SadWife and #HappyHusband

The Performance of Unattainable Marital Ideals on Facebook

Hinda Mandell, Gina Masullo Chen, and Paromita Pain

The performance of marriage has a stronghold on Facebook. Anniversary messages, spousal birthday greetings, birth announcements, travel montages, spousal promotions at work, and photos of colorful floral bouquets—"just because my spouse loves me!"—fill news feeds as regularly as chores and marital gripes comprise the actual lived experience of conjugal life offline and at home. It is perhaps a coincidence, but it is also a testament to marriage's specific place within Facebook culture, that at the same time we began writing this chapter, a seven-day "Love Your Spouse Challenge" overran Facebook (Mooney 2016). The fact that the word "challenge" was part of the, well, *challenge*, gilded the trend with an ironic twist. Was it that hard to demonstrate love of one's spouse for a seven-day stretch? The online performance of this marital "love" sits at the core of this chapter, which explores the expression of unattainable marriage ideals performed on this social-networking site. The spousal coupling represents a bedrock of American society. And showboating— or at the very least "humble brags"—represent the cornerstone of social interactions on Facebook. This chapter examines the performance of marriage on Facebook through an examination of the #happywife, #sadwife, #happyhusband, and #sadhusband hashtags. What we've found through a screening of these hashtags is that a "sad" spouse and a "happy" spouse are very much the same thing: It's an individual who loves one's life partner with bursting pride, and is willing to sacrifice one's own happiness for another's contentment. In other words, these hashtags reveal the performance of an ideal spouse where the inconvenience of everyday chores (laundry, dishes, childcare) and stresses (finances, marital disputes, familial relationships, resentments) are absent from the rose-tinted world of marital performance on Facebook.

There are plentiful examples of Facebook users employing these hashtags in their social media posts on a regular basis. Indeed, a recent query in the search field showed that 100,000 people were "talking about" #sadwife at the moment and 99,749 people were talking about #happywife. Through a qualitative textual analysis of these posts, we will demonstrate the ways in which people perform marriage on Facebook. (We aimed to include both heterosexual and homosexual marriage in our analysis. Homosexual marriage holds particular relevance at this current moment, as the U.S. Supreme Court granted the right to same-sex marriage nationwide in 2016, broadening the definition of *marriage*. However, we did not find any overt instances of same-sex marriage use of these hashtags in our data. This may be because our sample includes only public Facebook pages, not private ones, or because these particular hashtags resonate more with opposite-sex couples.) Using narrative inquiry (Clandinin 2006) and impression management theory (Baym 2010; Bazarova et al. 2010), we will interpret these data, so we can better understand the performance of gender roles within a romantic, social media context.

FACEBOOK AND THE EXPRESSION OF MARITAL IDEALS

Storytelling sits at the center of this chapter. An analysis of hashtag use within the spousal context can help us better understand dynamics of power and gender within this space. What are the stories Facebook users tell as they update their social media networks about their performance of "wifeness" and "husbandry"? (Mandell 2015). What themes emerge through these stories (i.e. Facebook posts) based on the gender of the storyteller? Through the process of narrative inquiry, we have the opportunity to study lived experience of Facebook users who employ the aforementioned spousal hashtags. "It is commonplace to note that human beings both live and tell stories about their living," writes D. Jean Clandinin, a professor of education at the University of Alberta who has published extensively on the narrative inquiry method. "These lived and told stories and talk about those stories are ways we create meaning in our lives as well as ways we enlist each other's help in building our lives and communities" (Clandinin 2006, 51). Story, as a site for analysis, represents a portal through which a person interacts with her world and extracts meaning. "Narrative inquiry, the study of experience as story, then, is first and foremost a way of thinking about experience" (Connelly and

Clandinin 2006, 477). What's relevant and necessary about this narrative approach is that it takes an object of the everyday—such as a Facebook post—and upholds it as a masterful way to identify and understand life situations. In this case it's marital performance along gender lines. By shifting stories as a theoretical from the inconsequential periphery to the critical center, we are assured of their value to unlocking our understanding of lived experience. As Clandinin writes with powerful provocation: "The truth about stories is that that's all we are" (Clandinin 2006, 51).

Stories about marriage hold particular relevance because we know that Americans are fascinated with marriage and the pairings of two individuals, each with their own history and set of life experiences, who come together in a conjugal partnership (Swidler 2013; Udry 1971).

> No relationship is more personal and intimate than marriage. At the same time, no relationship is surrounded by so many cultural prescriptions, fables, myths, traditions, laws, and taboos. To be married is to be placed in a special relationship to another person—a relationship whose acceptable boundaries have already been established and whose general shape has already been determined (Udry 1971, 20).

The acceptable roles within this traditionally gendered institution of marriage are neither equal nor natural. But the expectations of the passively natured wife as caretaker, homemaker, and child-rearer, and the aggressively oriented husband as the breadwinner and decision-maker, are deeply rooted in shared norms across Western society (Blood and Wolfe 1965; Swidler 2013). Gender differences between men and women are normalized by rooting them in biology. "They are rendered normal, natural features of persons and provide the tacit rationale for differing fates of women and men within the social order" (West and Zimmerman 1987, 142). Through an analysis of Facebook posts we can determine the way that marital performance both bucks and bolsters the standard presentation of marriage.

In addition, our analysis will help illuminate how people represent themselves—or misrepresent themselves (Hall and Pennington 2013)—online through the lens of this valued societal institution of marriage. Even in the offline world, people are skilled at manipulating how others see them. As philosopher and gender theorist Judith Butler (1993, 1997) suggests, we perform our identity—often unconsciously—and create different versions of ourselves. Social media sites, such as Facebook, offer a particularly fluid platform for impression management because the online identity is not limited by geography, time, or space (Baym 2010; Bazarova et al. 2010). We are free to re-create a new identity for ourselves in the digital sphere in ways that we cannot offline. Or, we at least pad the identity that we have, making it more than it is. When people post on social media sites, they imagine an audience for their posts, a "mental conceptualization of the people with whom we are communicating" (Litt

2012, 330). With their audience in mind, people craft specific messages that create a virtual sense of identity that fits their needs and makes them appear more appealing to others. Part of the aim in this online work that people do is to foster a public *face*—a sense of how others view a person—that makes the person desirable to others (Goffman 1959).

In fact, research has found that people express fewer negative emotions in Facebook status updates than they do in private social media messages, offering support for the "gross national happiness" (Bazarova 2010; Kramer 2010) hypothesis on the platform. Moreover, status updates are "public displays" and "show that concerns about self-presentation are prominent in people's minds when they express positive emotions via status updates" (Bazarova 2010, 133). As such, status updates provide a powerful means to maintaining relationships (Walther and Ramirez 2010) and presenting them publicly. Specifically, research has shown that people who brag about their romantic relationships on Facebook are often mired by low self-esteem or fear about the health of their pairings (Marshall, Lefinghausen, and Ferenczi 2015). In fact, people are most likely to post relationship-relevant information on days when they feel most vulnerable (Emery et al. 2014). As a result, people may be using postings on Facebook as a "way of laying claim to their relationships when it feels threatened" (Marshall, Lefinghausen, and Ferenczi 2015, 38). In addition, Facebook offers a powerful means for people to understand and demonstrate their relationship through the context of others (Zhao, Sosik, and Cosely 2012). Based on these theoretical frameworks, our chapter will provide new knowledge about how people tell the story of their marriage relationships online and represent their own marital identities through the rich data of qualitative analysis.

MARRIAGE, AMERICAN STYLE

We did not limit the geobased locations of the Facebook updates culled for this chapter. Therefore, Facebook users who posted #sadwife, #happywife, and #sadhusband, #happyhusband, may be residing anywhere from Nebraska to Nairobi. Yet it's worth reflecting on the *American* institution of marriage. After all, we'd argue, the specific cultural breed of this institution is as much a consumer export and product as Hollywood blockbusters and popular American brands. J. Richard Udry, who writes extensively on conjugal couplings in his seminal book, *The Social Context of Marriage*, says that mass media represent prominent sites from which people extract information to learn about marital-role expectations, and American mass media is exported and consumed across the globe (Udry 1971). It is also worth noting that in these status updates, we easily see the same emergent themes of money, work, and sex that sociologists Philip Blumstein and Pepper Schwartz (1983) delineated as categories for study in their groundbreaking work, *American Couples*. It seems clear that our data mimic very American themes about marriage. It is obvious to the point of cliché and truism, but scholarly investigations into contemporary marriage say its basis is love. Love, at least, is where it begins. Intuitively, we also grasp that "[t]he couple is a basic unit of society" (Blumstein and Schwartz 1983, 11). The American family places primacy on the husband-wife dyad, which historically has cast sex-specific roles to husbands, who were expected to be in charge of the economic interests of the household; and to wives, who were expected to maintain childrearing, emotional responsibilities, and domestic duties relating to "'interior considerations'" (Blumstein and Schwartz 1983, 27). While such expectations may seem anachronistic in our high-tech and gender conscious world that is increasingly breaking down barriers of inequity in marriage and beyond, it's worth lingering on what appears to be this outdated gendered construction because we will see parallels in our analysis of these Facebook hashtags related to spousal performance.

A vibrant, strong marriage can translate into nothing less than an ideal life. "The notion of the 'good life' was comprised of the hardworking and prosperous husband, the nurturing wife and mother, and the small and happy troupe of children for whom she cared . . ." (Blumstein and Schwartz 1983, 27). Therefore, seeking, finding, and nurturing romantic love, which is the bedrock of this institution, is no small feat because it can lead to "the good life" that can only be obtained through marital ideals. "Thus, romantic love—in the *right* context and with the *right* type of person—is and has been glorified in our country" (Blumstein and Schwartz 1983, 28). We can understand love as "a strong emotional attachment, with at least the components of sex desire and tenderness" (Udry 1971, 241). It is institutionalized, because—like any social institution (Berger and Luckman 1967)—it features recognizable patterns, activities and behaviors, for those caught up in it (Udry 1971). The love at the heart of marriage may be romantic, but it's also supposed to be steadfast and lasting. "And Americans have always married 'forever.' . . . The American tradition is to hope for the best, which means a lifetime of loyalty to . . . one's marriage partner" (Udry 1971, 162). Of course the great irony is that couples typically get married when their romantic love for each other is strong and at its peak. It is quite literally a honeymoon phase. And then life sets in. "Gradually, or sometimes suddenly, they are presented with the realities of marital life," the marriage scholar Udry writes in his book. "The idealized pictures of one another from courtship crumble under the impact of sharing the same bathroom and listening to one another snore. The 'true selves' are revealed to one another in the harsh glare of marital reality" (Udry 1971, 241).

While optimistic love and its strong narrative function may be the basis for marriage, a powerful element that impacts all marriages on a much more practical level is a couple's economics. Issues relating to money tend to creep into, and can often define, every part of a marriage, from the day-to-day interactions between spouses, to power dynamics, sex, family planning, recreational activities, obligations outside the home, and relationships with children and extended family members. Even if money plays an integral role in conjugal dynamics, and can even become the defining element in a "good" or "bad" marriage,

> Americans are uncomfortable about the relationship between money and marriage. We believe that people should marry for love, not money. . . . For a "nation of capitalists" we are terribly romantic. Yet there are other sayings too that remind us that people can't live on love alone. . . . [I]t is obvious to newlyweds and relatives alike that money, job, and success are hard facts of life. From then on money matters. Promotions are big news. Bonuses are something to get excited about and bills something to worry about (Blood and Wolfe 1965, 80).

While it's true that money is a necessity in contemporary life, and a dearth of it makes for a subsistence existence that is both emotionally and physically grueling, there is something deeper at play when we probe money's role in marriage. We know that historically, "For the husband, the economic function is his main job in life" (Blood and Wolfe 1965, 80). Therefore, the primacy of money in a marriage, and by extension in life generally speaking for married couples, demonstrates a husband's traditional power in marriage. His success becomes the family's ability to lead the "good life." His professional and economic struggles can drag down a family. "In marriage, adherence to the male-provider philosophy grants greater power to husbands" (Blumstein and Schwartz, 1983, 56). (In their study of American coupling, sociologists Blumstein and Schwartz [1983] found that among gay men, the partner who makes the most money holds the balance of power in the relationship.) Therefore, even in more equitable households today, flaunting a financially sound "good life" — or a less fortunate, less cash-flush reality — can lead men to acutely feel pride or embarrassment, even as women work outside the home at historic rates. Even today, the deeply embedded social expectations tie men's worth to their financial success and ability to "provide" for their families. While the elements of love include sexual attraction, companionship, care, and affirmation, there is also what marriage scholar Robert O. Blood Jr. referred to as "pseudo loves," including infatuation and idealization. With infatuation we witness a lovelorn person engaging in an "extravagant or foolish passion," while with idealization we see a person who views his/her love interest as the picture of perfection "where the actuality does not exist" (Blood 1962, 11). The Facebook posts relating to our spousal hashtags embody the performance of pseudo loves to an audience of "friends."

PERFORMANCE OF THE SELF ON SOCIAL MEDIA

Decades before the Internet was created, sociologist Erving Goffman (1959) used the dramaturgical metaphor of a stage to explain how people "perform" themselves. He defined this performance as "all the activity of a given participant on a given occasion which serves to influence in any way any of the other participants" (Goffman 1959, 15). He saw this performance as a deliberate act as people express aspects of their identities to others intentionally, crafting an idealized public self. In contrast, Butler's (1993, 1997) concept of performativity (Papacharissi 2012) suggests that people perform themselves unconsciously. In essence, both saw identity as something that people perform, but Goffman believes people are aware they are doing it, while Butler suggests this performance happens outside of conscious thought. We embrace both approaches, suggesting that people may perform identity both consciously and unconsciously simultaneously. We select what parts of ourselves we want others to see, and we also unconsciously project parts of ourselves based on our own inner needs. Therefore, in our analysis we aim to uncover both of these aspects of performance through four marriage-related hashtags popular among Facebook users.

Goffman's (1959) dramaturgical metaphor suggests that people reveal their *backstage* identities when they reveal their private selves to others. In an online space, where privacy does not really exist (Chen and Mandell 2016), *backstage* is the means by which people "keep up appearances" (Hogan 2010, 378) in a public space, such as Facebook. In other words, in the digital world, private space becomes how individuals conjure their presentations in their own heads before they perform them in the public virtual space of the Internet. As such, hashtags such as #happywife, #sadwife, #happyhusband, or #sadhusband on Facebook may become a means by which people perform their identity to keep up these appearances.

On social media sites, such as Facebook, we are free to conjure a new identity for ourselves in the digital sphere in ways that we cannot offline, or at least tweak the identity that we have, making it more palatable than it might be. When they post on social media, people imagine an audience abstractly (without a particular person in mind) as well as in a targeted way (imaging specific people or groups of people, such as relatives, friends, or even others who share a common interest) (Litt and Hargittai 2016). However, a study that examined 119 Facebook accounts over two months, using observation, surveys, and interviews, found that a targeted audience is the more common approach, and this target audience may relate to a variety of social groups, most of which are homogenous (Litt and Hargittai 2016). So people may imagine they are posting for their church friends or their work colleagues, and these groups, of course, may overlap. With their audience in mind, people foster a virtual sense of identity that fits their needs and makes them appear more appealing to others by the messages they create. Part of the aim here is to foster a public *face*—a sense of how others view a person—that makes the person desirable to others (Goffman 1959).

With a malleable tool like the Facebook status update, people have great power to craft their public *face* to meet what they see as the expectations of this targeted imagined audience. In fact, research has found that people express fewer negative emotions in Facebook status updates than they do in private social media messages, offering support for the "gross national happiness" (Bazarova et al. 2010; Kramer 2010) hypothesis on the platform. Moreover, status updates are "public displays" and "show that concerns about self-presentation are prominent in people's minds when they express positive emotions via status updates" (Bazarova et al 2010, 133). As such, status updates provide a powerful means to maintain relationships (Walther and Ramirez 2010) and present them publicly. It is also important to note that hashtags—series of words prefixed with a hash symbol (#) (Bastos et al. 2013; Cunha et al. 2011)—provide a potent tool to communicate how people present their identities. Hashtags started as a way to sort information on Twitter but have evolved into a method to add emotion, sarcasm, or humor (Brock 2012) to posts on a variety of social media platforms. They add richness to computer-mediated communication that lacks the social cues—such as inflection or facial expression—of face-to-face speech (Baym 2010). As a result, our focus on specific hashtags taps in to the way the authors of these Facebook status updates intended to categorize or add context to their own content.

HASHTAG ANALYSIS

In our analysis, we looked at posts that appeared to be written by women (based on their screen name and physiological appearance) for #happywife and #sadwife, and men for #sadhusband and #happyhusband. Our reasoning was that we are most interested in how each gender plays out the constructed role of being a wife or being a husband through status updates. "Wifeness" has been conceptualized as acting out the practice and role of social norms related to societal expectations of being a wife (Mandell 2012; 2015). Although being a husband has been less conceptualized, we argue that men also conform to societal norms in how they play out this role, although they do so from a position of greater power and privilege than women. Our search yielded fifty-three #sadwife posts; 229 #happywife posts; eighteen #sadhusband posts; and 162 #happyhusband posts. Overall, we found more hashtagged posts related to wives than husbands. We suggest this may mean that women feel more pressure to perform their "wifeness" online by telling stories about themselves on the public stage of Facebook (Papacharissi 2015) than men do. If crafting a status update is a means to craft an idealized public self either consciously or unconsciously (Butler 1993, 1997; Goffman 1959; Papacharissi 2015), then those with less power in society have more to gain by creating this virtual reality. In the interest of realism, we retain misspellings or grammatical errors when quoting status updates that people posted.

#Happy Is More Prominent Than #Sad

There were more posts tagging #happywife and #happyhusband than #sadwife and #sadhusband. Again, this suggests that performing one's marriage on Facebook through these hashtags is mainly about presenting a positive or idealized view (Goffman 1959) of the relationship to others. We know that people in general tend to promote a sunnier view of their lives on social media than a more-gloomy reality (Bazarova et al. 2010). Therefore, it stands to reason that people would also do this when posting about their marriages. Either consciously or unconsciously (Butler 1993, 1997; Goffman 1959), they shape their own marriages—and their wifeness or husbandness—to fit the societal norms that they believe their imagined audience would favor. As a result, happiness gets more attention than sadness. But what does it mean to be a happy or sad spouse in the context of this chapter? Let's examine each of the four hashtags to determine the most prominent themes to emerge from each category.

#Sadwife

Misses Husband

The most prominent characteristic of a Sad Wife is one who misses her husband and who loves him so much that love hurts. We documented nineteen instances when a wife categorized herself as sad because she misses her husband, whether it was because of conflicting work schedules or out-of-town travel due to professional obligations. In these cases, the Sad Wife's identity is pronounced because the person who made her a wife is absent from her life on a temporary, and perhaps even fleeting, basis. In each of these instances, we clearly saw definitive heterosexual pairings, which we determined through the wife's photo sharing of a husband or the reference to a standard male name of her husband. "One thing I always hate about school starting back is that I very rarely see Jason #sadwife," wrote one woman (Waclawik 2016). And another: "I miss him even more now that he is my Husband!! #sadwife" (Jacobs 2013), indicating that their apparently recent marital status cements not only their bond to each other, but also the depth of feeling toward one another. A third woman helps her husband get ready for an upcoming trip: "Helping my Hubby pack to go back to Orlando for another week.

#sadwife" (Newman 2015), and a fourth wife declares, "I MISS MY HUB-BY!!! Hurry up an come home!!! #sadwife #workinghusband #sadface-blues" (Kilgore 2015). This subtheme demonstrates that when a wife and husband are removed from each other, the wife feels a sense of loss, incompleteness, and her sense of gravity is off-kilter. What is notable about this theme, however, is not just their feelings of loss and incompleteness but also how these women choose these emotions as part of how they perform their own identities of wifeness through social media. They are fitting a dominant female narrative of dependency and proclaiming it writ large through the computer-mediated public space of Facebook. In so doing, they are perpetuating the myth of emphasized femininity, in which women are seen as "fragile and weak" (Milestone and Meyer 2012, 20).

I Love Him So Much

A wife's overflowing love for her spouse objectively appears to be a positive force for one's marriage. But for some wives the sheer volume of their love turns them into a Sad Wife because the force of their feelings for their spouse is overwhelming. We counted this subtheme in seven posts. For instance, one wife wrote, "wish I could just take the pain from my husband so he could feel better!!! #sadwife" (Mason 2013), while another woman wrote: "I hate that my hubby is sick. I miss being around him and talking to him. This separate room thing is no fun. #sadwife #ihatetheflu" (Tate 2014). In other posts there was a blurred line between missing their husband and loving him. In these posts the wife expresses a sentiment that is more than "just" missing her husband. She misses him because the bounds of her love for him are so vast. One woman wrote: "Yay I get my bed to myself tonight <3 Yeah right I want my husband to come back home. I hate that he has to go out of town for a business trip! #sad wife" (Aguilar 2013). And in a related instance, another wife wrote: "A lot of people think its SO NICE to have there husbands or bf working in the oilfield. I don't I miss my hubby and I just want him home every night so he can hold me when I feel sad!! #sadwife" (Salinas 2013). This subtheme demonstrates that the flipside of love is vulnerability to the power of its emotion; that these wives are so committed, devoted and in love with their husbands that they feel sad when their spouses are unwell or away from them. Again, this theme illustrates women portraying an idealized identity that performs femininity in a way that conforms to regulatory norms, and the fact that they are performing for their own husbands is meaningful (Connell 1987).

#Sadhusband

The most prominent characteristic of a Sad Husband is one who misses his wife and who is a caregiver to an ailing wife. With this hashtag, men seemed to be both expressing sincere negative emotion but also defining their role as husband, as someone whose job it is to care for his wife. This taps in to a very hegemonic view of maleness, as the caretaker of the more fragile female. From advertisements to television shows, the media bombards society with a very narrow view of maleness that is normatively heterosexual; associated with self-reliance and individualism; and rigid in binary gender roles (Kluck 2015; Rademacher and Kelly 2016). Hegemonic masculinity is culturally idealized (Milestone and Meyer 2012) and constructed in relation to various views of masculinity as well as in relation to women (Connell 1987), creating a patriarchal hierarchy. Because men have more power in society, women have less. This is not to say that the men's sentiments are not heartfelt. Rather, we suggest that in proclaiming them on Facebook, they are creating an idealized masculine self through social media that fits society's hegemonic norms. We make a choice about what we share and what we withhold on social media, so by sharing these stories about themselves, men are choosing, perhaps subconsciously, to put forth a view of themselves that reinforces their masculine role as provider. Even though these men are performing hegemonic masculinity, it does not mean they are being unkind to women (Connell 1987). Rather, they are performing their own selves on Facebook in a way that maintains the practices of hegemonic masculinity, or the institutional dominance of men over women.

Misses Wife

Similar to the #sadwife trend, we documented more husbands expressing their "Sad Spouse" status because they missed their wives. This subtheme represents the most recurring theme under #sadhusband. There were seven instances of a husband who misses his wife. "Today is truly a sad day. My beautiful wife is headed to South Beach for a whole week! So I'm spending Christmas without my baby. #sadhusband" (Triplett 2015), writes one man. Another confesses: "I'm ready for my wifey to come back. #lonelyhusband #sadhusband #someonefeedme" (Kearney 2015). A third husband writes, "I have been out of town working all week and I'm not coming home till Monday night and it's killing me being away from my wife . . . and kids I love y'all so much and will be home soon . . . #SadDad #sadhusband" (Calhoun 2016). The use of the hashtag in this way again reinforces that "husbandness" is defined in contrast to the conceptualization of wifeness. In particular, the status update that suggested a man was ready for his wife to come back so that she would feed him, sets up a clear a division in their roles: Husbands are providers, while wives offer sustenance. So when wives are gone, husbands define that loss in relation to how it influences them. By choosing a status update that casts them as at a loss when their wives are gone, they are defining husbandness as the power position in a marriage, reifying hegemonic masculinity.

Caregiver

The second most recurring theme for a Sad Husband is husbands who take on a caregiver and protector role for an ailing wife. One husband wrote simply, "Belinda is ill #SadHusband" (Klassen 2014), and a second wrote, "Today my heart if heavy my beautiful wife . . . lost her uncle . . . So if you can keep her in your prayers it'll be greatly appreciated . . . I'm here Baby every second you need me . . . #SadHusband #safejourney" (Fasthorse 2015). These status updates offer touching tributes to wives, but they still place husbands as those whose job it is to provide for the women and be in control of the relationship. Because men cannot perform this role when their wives are ill—or have hit a deer when they are not around—their status updates communicate a cognitive dissonance (Festinger 1957) in which the reality clashes with their idealized sense of a masculine self. They may feel genuine loss, of course, at being away from their wives. But by sharing this loss on Facebook with this hashtag, they are exhibiting part of a performance of gender that involves repetition and reenactment of "meanings already socially established" (Butler 1999, 178). Thus, our focus is not on the fact that men are missing their wives. We are interested in what it means that they are sharing this story because it reinforce notions of what married life *should* be like. For both #sadwives and #sadhusbands we see recurring themes where husbands and wives miss their spouses overwhelmingly, and they also take on the emotional burden and responsibility during difficult personal times.

#HappyWife

The most prominent characteristics of a Happy Wife include one who posts photographs of herself with her husband, who posts selfies featuring truisms about love and marriage, who celebrates life events with her spouse, and who receive gifts from her spouse. These suggest a very idealized view of marriage that women are choosing to portray through the digital space of Facebook. Not only are these updates perpetuating norms of hegemonic masculinity (Kluck 2015; Rademacher and Kelly 2016) and emphasized femininity (Milestone and Meyer 2012), but they are communicating to others that their marriage is one to be envied. This suggests these women are keeping up appearances online by this strategic revelation of the *backstage* (Goffman 1959; Hogan 2010) of their lives to others.

Couples Photographed Together

We documented forty-two instances of wives posting celebratory photos of themselves posing with their husbands. Couples' photos featured everything from the mundane—they are just hanging out—to adventurous—they are traveling abroad in a foreign locale on vacation; from dining out together to cuddling at home. "I LOVE being spoiled, but not with gifts or money. Just time, attention and kisses #happywife #happywe #blessedsunday" (Lopez 2016), wrote one woman, whose post featured an up-close shot of the "happy" couple in bed, smooching, their eyes closed and their faces puckered. Another woman posted a photo of herself with her husband and their infant daughter: "#myfamily, mylife, #happywife" (Amorganda 2015). And a third woman posted a simple greeting of herself smiling alongside a husband wearing a neutral expression. She wrote, "Good Morning! #happyWife #happyLife" (Pilapil 2015). Photos of couples posing together highlighted spousal unity and cohesion, cementing the strong performative state of their marriage.

Selfies and Marital Clichés

Happy wives also regularly featured solo photographs of themselves, oftentimes with a trite sentence about love, marriage, or life. We documented thirty-six instances of wife selfies. "Going on a date with my husband! #simpleLife #happyWife," wrote one woman (Tejada-Batcheller 2016). Wrote another, as the poster sat smiling in the car—her hand resting casually against her face: "Thank you LORD you never fail me even though i know i fail you. #blessed #happywife" (Andren 2016). And another wife featured a series of shots showing off her décolleté in a halter top, her hair pulled back from her face: "A happy man marries the woman he loves; a happier man loves the woman he married. #happywife" (Jyn 2016). Another wife, posed with her body in profile outdoors in a fitted skirt suit with stilletos, her head coquettishly tilted to the side, instructs her friends, "Cherish every moment #happywife" (Alvarez-Thomas 2015). The solo-selfies category declare wives as strong women who are asserting their wife status through upbeat truisms about their life circumstances.

Life Events

Happy wives are also those who share posts relating to life events with their friends. We documented twenty instances in this category. Cheerful photographs feature couples dancing at weddings, celebrating birthdays at restaurants, and marking anniversaries at resorts. "Celebrated 6 months at the most romantic restaurant last night. It was so cozy! #happywife . . . #marriedlife" (Sazan 2015). The corresponding photo featured a patio lit with Christmas lights and place settings elegantly displayed. Another wife posted a photographic throwback to her wedding day: "Happy anniversary ... 2 years ago we had an amazing day! Still feel like yesterday! #happyhubby #happywife #happylife" (Balkestein-Grothues, 2016). The photo features a beaming bride and groom seated at their table, both dressed in white—as they are enjoying what is no doubt an amusing toast in their honor. And another wife posted a figure of herself posing with her husband in advance of a party. When wives post celebratory photos of life events, they are marking not only the occasion but also signaling that happy couples are those who reach life's milestones together.

Love, Gifted

What is love without the commercial tokens featuring appreciation and love for one's spouse? We documented seventeen instances each of Happy Wives receiving gifts and flowers from their husbands. One woman posted a vibrant yellow and red bouquet: "Fresh tulips on Sunday morning. #love #lovemyhusband #picoftheday #photooftheday #Sunday #happywife" (Eleganza 2016). Yet this poster was hardly alone in sharing her bouquet. Wrote another, with a corresponding photo of an assortment featuring white daisies with orange and yellow roses: "Special delivery! Feeling #loved #JustBecauseFlowers #Best #Hubby #HappyWife" (Orozco 2016). Wives who showcase gifts and flowers from their husbands highlight that they are adored and loved.

#HappyHusband

Unlike the #HappyWife category, which featured numerous subthemes, the #HappyHusband hashtag was dominated by food. Particularly, photos and posts about *good* food prepared by their wives and consumed at restaurants. We found sixty-six instances of the "good food" subtheme. The second most recurring theme was generic praise for the wife, at thirty-one instances. But due to space constraints we will only focus on the former theme. When husbands post about food, a gendered construction of marriage surfaces. Wives and husbands have clearly delineated roles in this construction of marriage, with men portraying themselves as the focus in the relationship—the person to whom food should be provided. In contrast, women are cast in the subordinate role in the private sphere (Milestone and Meyer 2012) of providing food as women have for centuries. Even the theme where men praise their wives furthers this gendered construction of marriage, because it portrays him as in possession of something worthwhile, thereby raising his value. The concept of mental models is illustrative here. Mental models (Lakoff 1990) are concepts, based on our experiences and the media, of what something—such as marriage—should be like. It is sort of the *best* version. So while most marriages hardly fit the societal norms of married life, people perpetuate that norm, perhaps unwittingly, through something as simple as a status update. And while many marriages today may be equalitarian, subconsciously people still compare their own roles to a societal norm that derives from a gendered society. They create their idealized idea of marriage by revealing the parts of their own marriage that fit societal norms by providing the *best* example of marriage and not sharing the parts that deviate.

Good Food

The maxim that the path to a man's heart is through his stomach was validated through this subtheme. It is clear without question that a Happy Husband is one who is well fed and gastronomically satisfied. "Homemade Potato Soup and salad . . . Mrs. Money . . . I love you . . . forreal forreal. #HappyHusband #HappyTummy #Ilovemywife" (Money 2014), wrote one man, featuring a photograph of his wife's culinary efforts. Another husband posted a close-up shot of his wife's cooking, including a huge head of broccoli. "Twice stuffed Shrimp & Cheese Baked Potato with broccoli & cucumber salad. #HappyHusband #WifeIsABeastInTheKitchen" (Jones 2015). And yet another husband featured his wife, in action, standing from afar at the kitchen countertop. "My wife is cooking dinner . . . #happyhusband" (Ferrer 2016). This status update was particularly telling because it suggested very clearly that it is not just good food that makes a happy husband; it is the wife in the act of cooking the food. In a very concrete way, the use of the hashtag in this way conjures a narrow view of wifeness that views women's place as in the domestic sphere. It reinforces emphasized femininity, which centers on women as "'naturally' kind and caring" (Milestone and Meyer 2012, 20) and predisposed to care for men, particularly their husbands. Even though the wife may have chosen to make the food, when he shared this picture, he sent a message about his own digital identity. At some level, he wanted the world to know that his identity is tied to having a wife who will do this for him. Much as a man of days gone by might trumpet his new wife's dowry of goats or sheep, this status update becomes a public digital proclamation of his worth in society.

Some posters even equated food with love. "My wife really loves me!" (Life in Japan 2015), wrote one with a close-up shot of Buffalo wings. Even more telling, another showed a pictures of what appeared to be steaks on a grill with the status update: "This is why I love my wife" (Mabilog 2015). This implies a troubling transactional relationship between spouses. *I will love you if* . . . And part of this *if* is that you meet my needs and perform wifeness in the way I believe it should be performed. This conjures a mental model of the *best* wife—caring, nurturing, putting others first. Though the wife may find the act of preparing her husband's food enjoyable or even empowering, a status update like this still performs marriage in a way that emphasizes women's hegemonic normative domestic role. Those who read it may feel the "unspoken invisible hand" (Chen 2013) of the "psychic operation of the norm" (Butler 1997), urging women to conform to this role. In another status update, the use of the hashtag even more clearly reinforced women's domestic role: "I have to brag on my wife! I came home from work to a baked ham, mashed potatoes, and corn on the cob!" (Stolte 2016). Not only does the man describe his wife's actions in a way that reinforces her role as family cook, but he takes credit for her actions in a sense by bragging about them. One man seemed to channel our own thinking in his critique of how the #happyhusband hashtag is being used. He wrote: "If the only way you can hashtag #happyhusband is because you cook him textbook picture perfect meals, do Zumba/workout, and sleep on his chest; I have no respect for him. Maybe he should be cooking you meals, or giving you a massage while You relax" (Dudding 2016).

MARRIAGE ON FACEBOOK IS GILDING PERFECTION

No relationship is more personal and intimate than marriage. At the same time, no relationship is surrounded by so many cultural expectations, myths, traditions, and proscribed behavior. To be married is to be placed in a special relationship to another person—a relationship whose boundaries have already been established and whose general shape has already been determined by powerful social forces that continue to shape the roles of husbands and wives even today (Udry 1971). The performance of marriage on Facebook reifies the traditional narrative of heterosexual marriage, in which the wife is dependent on her husband's presence and material support; and husbands rely on wives for good food and domestic care. Yet on Facebook, such gendered performances are not constricting but instead represent a clear path to a fulfilling life gilded by love and a sense of belonging. The narrative stories of these status updates depict a home life centered on the marital dyad as the basis for "having it all." In this way, wifeness and husbandness become conceptual, cognitive shortcuts for *peopleness*. To be married is to be a complete person, albeit one who has happy and sad moments. But, no bother, even in sad moments Facebook posters seem to cheer a marital perfection that undergirds their very essence—at least online.

REFERENCES

Aguilar, Neclo. 2013. "Yay I Get My Bed to Myself Tonight <3 Yeah Right I Want My Huband to Come Back Home. I Hate That He Has to Go Out of Town for a Business Trip! #Sad Wife." Facebook post, December 19.

Alvarez-Thomas, Daniellia. 2015. "Cherish Every Moment #HappyWife." Facebook post, December 29.

Amorganda, Jo An. 2015. "#MyFamily, MyLife, #HappyWife." Facebook post, March 14.

Andren, AiCa A. 2016. "Thank you LORD You Never Fail Me Even Though I Know I Fail You #Blessed #happywife." Facebook post, July 27.

Balkestein-Grouthues, Maret. 2016. "Happy Anniversary . . . 2 Years Ago We Had an Amazing Day! Still Feel Like Yesterday! #Happyhubby #Happywife #Happywife #Happylife." Facebook post, July 5.

Bastos, Marco Toledo, Rafael Luis Galdini Raimundo, and Rodrigo Travitzki, "Gate-keeping on Twitter: Message Diffusion in Political Hashtags." *Media, Culture & Society* 25: 260–70.

Baym, Nancy K. 2010. "Interpersonal Life Online." In *The Handbook of New Media*, ed. Leah A. Lievrouw and Sonia Livingstone, 35–54. Washington, DC: Sage.

Bazarova, Natalya N., Jessie G. Taft, Young Hyung Choi, and Dan Cosley. 2010. "Managing Impressions and Relationships: Self-Presentation and Relational Concerns Revealed Through the Analysis of Language Style." *Journal of Language and Social Psychology* 32, no. 2: 121–41.

Berger, Peter L. and Thomas Luckmann. 1967. *The Social Construction of Reality: A Treatise in the Sociology of Knowledge.* New York, NY: Anchor.

Blood, Robert O. 1962. *Marriage.* New York, NY: Free Press of Glencoe.

Blood Robert O., and Donald M. Wolfe. 1965. *Husbands & Wives: The Dynamics of Married Living.* New York: Free Press.

Blumstein, Philip, and Pepper Schwartz, 1983. *American Couples.* New York, NY: Morrow.

Brock, Andre. "From the Blackhand Side: Twitter as a Cultural Conversation." *Journal of Broadcasting & Electronic Media* 46: 529–49.

Butler, Judith. 1993. *Bodies That Matter: On the Discursive Limits of Sex.* New York, NY: Routledge.

Butler, Judith. 1997. *The Psychic Life of Power.* Stanford, CA: Stanford University Press.

Butler, Judith. 1999. *Gender Trouble: Feminism and the Subversion of Identity.* New York, NY: Routledge.

Calhoun, William. 2016. "I Have Been Out of Town Working All Week and I'm Not Coming Home Till Monday Night and It's Killing Me Being Away From My Wife . . . and Kids I love Y'all So Much and Will Be Home Soon . . . #Saddad #Sadhusband." Facebook post, March 17.

Chen, Gina Masullo. 2013. "Don't Call Me That: A Techno-Feminist Critique of the Term *Mommy Blogger.*" *Mass Communication and Society* 16, no. 4: 510–32.

Chen, Gina Masullo, and Hinda Mandell. 2016. "Predicting a New Scandal Environment in the 21st Century." In *Scandal in a Digital Age,* ed. Hinda Mandell and Gina Masullo Chen, 209–15. New York, NY: Palgrave Macmillan.

Clandinin, D. Jean. 2006. "Narrative Inquiry: A Methodology for Studying Lived Experience." *Research Studies in Music Education* 27, no. 1: 44–54.

Connell, Raewyn. 1987. *Gender and Power: Society, the Person and Sexual Politics.* Cambridge, MA: Polity.

Connelly, Michael F., and D. Jean Clandinin. 2006. "Narrative Inquiry." In *Handbook of Contemporary Methods in Education Research,* ed., Judith L. Green, Gregory Camilli, and Patricia B. Elmore, 477. Mahwah, NJ: Lawrence Erlbaum.

Cunha, Evandro, Gabriel Magno, Giovanni Comarela, Virgilio Almeida, Marcos Ande Goncalves, and Fabricio Benevenuto. 2011. "Analyzing the Dynamic Evolution of Hashtags on Twitter: A Language-Based Approach." *Proceedings of the Workshop on Language in Social Media,* 58–65.

Dudding, Clayton. 2016. "If the Only Way You Can Hashtag #Happyhusband is Because You Cook Him Textbook Perfect Meals, Do Zumba/Workout, and Sleep on his Chest . . ." Facebook post, January 29.

Eleganza, Nova. 2016. "Fresh Tulips on Sunday Morning. #Love #Lovemyhusband #Picoftheday #Photooftheday #Sunday #Happywife." Facebook post, July 31.

Emery, Lydia F., Amy Muise, Emily L. Dix, and Benjamin Le. 2014. "Can You Tell That I'm in a Relationship? Attachment and Relationship Visibility on Facebook." *Personality and Social Psychology Bulletin* 40, no. 11: 1466–79.

Fasthorse, Manny III. 2015. "Today My Heart if Heavy My Beautiful Wife . . . Lost Her Uncle . . . So If You Can Keep Her in Your Prayers It'll Greatly Appreciated . . . I'm Here Baby Every Second You Need Me . . . #SadHusband #Safejourney." Facebook post, August 4.

Ferrer, Albert. 2016. "My Wife is Cooking Dinner . . . #Happyhusband." Facebook post, August 8.

Festinger, Leon. 1957. *A Theory of Cognitive Dissonance.* Palo Alto, CA: Stanford University Press.

Goffman, Erving. 1959. *Presentation of the Self in Everyday Life.* New York, NY: Doubleday.

Hall, Jeffrey A., and Natalie Pennington. 2013. "Impressions Management and Formation on Facebook: A Lens Model Approach." *New Media & Society* 16, no. 6: 958-82.

Hogan, Bernie. 2010. "The Presentation of the Self in the Age of Social Media: Distinguishing Performances and Exhibitions Online." *Bulletin of Science, Technology, & Society* 30: 377–86.

Jacobs, Shantelle Harvey. 2013. "I Miss Him Even More Now That He is My Husband #Sadwife." Facebook post, April 8.

Jones, Gil A., Jr. 2015. "Twice Stuffed Shrimp & Cheese Baked Potato with Broccoli & Cucumber Salad. #HappyHusband #WifeIsABeastInTheKitchen." Facebook post, August 20.

Jyn, Jyn. 2016. "A Happy Man Marries the Woman He Loves; a Happier Man Loves the Woman He Married. #Happywife." Facebook post, April 7.

Kearney, Will. 2015. "I am Ready for My Wifey to come Back. #Lonelyhusband #Sadhusband #Someonefeedme." Facebook post, March 12.

Kilgore, Ebony Gunn. 2015. "I MISS MY HUBBY!! Hurry Up an Come Home!! #Sadwife." Facebook post, September 7.

Klassen, Joe. 2014. "Belinda is Ill #Sadhusband." Facebook post, June 14.

Kluck, Yannick. 2015. "'The Man Your Man Should Be Like': Consumerism, Patriarchy, and the Construction of the Twenty-First Century Masculinities in 2010 and 2012 Old Spice Campaigns." *Interactions: Studies in Communication and Culture* 6, no. 3: 361–77.

Kramer, Adam D.I. 2010. "An Unobtrusive Behavioral Model of 'Gross National Happiness.'" *Proceedings of the CHI 2010: Language 2.0*, April 10–15, Atlanta, GA.

Lakoff, George. 1990. *Women, Fire, and Dangerous Things: What Categories Reveal About the Mind.* Chicago, IL: University of Chicago Press.

Life in Japan. 2015. "My Wife Really Loves Me! Happy Sunday Everyone! #Buffalowings #Tomatobeer #Love #Happyhusband." Faceook post, February 15.

Litt, Eden. 2012. "Knock, Knock, Who's There? The Imagined Audience." *Journal of Broadcasting & Electronic Media* 56: 330–45.

Litt, Eden and Eszter Hargittai. 2016. "The Imagined Audience on Social Network Sites." *Social Media + Society* January/March: 1–12.

Lopez, Mary Grace. 2016. "I LOVE Being Spoiled, But Not With Gifts or Mondey. Just Time, Attention and Kisses #Happywife #Happywe #BlessedSunday." Facebook post, July 31.

Mabilog, Patrick. 2015. "The is Why I Love My Wife @Ces.mabilog #Happyhusband #Happyeater." Facebook post, October 24.

Mandell, Hinda. 2012. "'Stand By Your Man' Revisited: Political Wives and Scandal." In *Media Depictions of Brides, Wives, and Mothers*, ed. Alena Amato Ruggiero, Lanham, MD: Lexington.

Mandell, Hinda. 2015. "Political Wives, Scandal, and the Double Bind: Press Construction of Silda Spitzer and Jenny Sanford through a Gendered Lens." *Women's Studies in Communication* 38, no. 1: 57–77.

Marshall, Tara C., Katharina Lefinghausen, and Nelli Ferenczi. 2015. "The Big Five, Self-Esteem, and Narcissism as Predictors of the Topics People Write About in Facebook Status Updates." *Personality and Individual Differences* 85: 35–40.

Mason, Melody M. 2013. "Wish I Could Just Take the Pain From My Husband So He Could Feel Better!! #Sadwife." Facebook post, October 24.

Milestone, Katie, and Anneke Meyer. 2012. *Gender & Popular Culture.* Malden, MA: Polity.

Money, Kevin D. 2014. "Homemade Potato Soup and Salad . . . Mrs. Money . . . I Love you . . . Forreal Forreal. #HappyHusband #HappyTummy #Ilovemywife." Facebook post, September 22.

Mooney, Paul. 2016. "Love Your Spouse Challenge Fills Facebook with 7 Days of Photos—and a Bit of Backlash." *Inquisitr.com*, August 2. Accessed November 8, 2016, http://www.inquisitr.com/3376384/love-your-spouse-challenge-fills-facebook-with-7-days-of-photos-and-a-bit-of-backlash/.

Newman, Holly Johnson. 2015. "Helping My Hubby Pack to Go Back to Orlando For Another Week #Sadwife." Facebook post, November 8.

Orozco, Jackie. 2016. "Special Delivery! Feeling #Loved #JustBecauseFlowers #Best #Hubby #HappyWife." Facebook post, April 19.

Papacharissi, Zizi. 2012. "Without You I'm Nothing: Performance of the Self on Twitter." *International Journal of Communication* 6: 1989–2006.

Papacharissi, Zizi. 2015. *Affective Publics: Sentiment, Technology, and Politics.* New York, NY: Oxford University Press.

Pilapil, Lea. 2015. "Good Morning! #Happywife #HappyLife." Facebook post, March 14.

Rademacher, Mark A., and Casey Kelly. 2016. "'I'm Here to Do Business. I'm Not Here to Play Games': Work, Consumption, and Masculinity on *Storage Wars*." *Journal of Communication Inquiry* 50, no. 1: 7–24.

Salinas, Jessica Marie. 2013. "A Lot of People Think its SO NICE to Have There Husband or BF Working in the Oilfield. I Don't I Miss My Hubby and I just Want Him Home Every Night So He Can Hold Me When I Feel Sad!! #Sadwife." Facebook post, April 22.

Sazan, 2015. "Celebrated 6 Months at the Most Romantic Restaurant Last Night. It was so cozy! #Happywife . . . #MarriedLife." Facebook post, November 8.

Swidler, Ann. *Talk of Love: How Culture Matters.* 2013. Chicago: University of Chicago Press.

Stolte, Kase. 2016. "I Have to Brag on My Wife! I Came Home From Work to a Baked Ham, Mashed Potatoes, and Corn on the Cob! . . . #HappyHusband." Facebook post, May 2.

Tate, Ashely. 2014. "I Hate That My Hubby is Sick. I Miss Being Around Him and Talking to Him. This Separate Room Thing is No Fun #Sadwife. #Ihatetheflu. Facebook post, February 10.

Tejada-Batcheller, Jiesha. 2016. "Going on a Date With My Husband! #SimpleLife #HappyWife." Facebook post, July 30.

Triplett, Christopher. 2015. "Today is Truly a Sad Day. My Beautiful Wife is Headed to South Beach for a Whole Week! So I am Spending Christmas Without My Baby. #Sadhusband." Facebook post, December 21.

Udry, J. Richard. 1971. *The Social Context of Marriage.* Philadelphia, PA: Lippincott.

Waclawik, Tara. 2016. "One Thing I Always Hates about School Starting is That I Very Rarely See Jason #Sadwife." Facebook post, January 13.

Walther, Joseph B., and Artemio Ramirez Jr. 2010. "New Technologies and New Directions in Online Relationships." In *New Directions in Interpersonal Communication Research*, ed. Sandi W. Smith and Steven R. Wilson, 264–84. Thousand Oaks, CA: Sage, 2010.

West, Candace, and Don H. Zimmerman. 1987. "Doing Gender." *Gender & Society* 1, no. 2:142.

Zhao, Xuab, Victoria Schwanda Sosik, and Dan Cosely. 2012. "It's Complicated: How Romantic Partners Use Facebook." *Proceedings of the CHI' '12*, May 5–10, Austin, Texas.

FOURTEEN

Phantom Lovers

Ghosting as a Relationship Dissolution Strategy in the Technological Age

Leah E. LeFebvre

WHEN HAPPILY-EVER-AFTER NEVER COMES . . .

Dissolution, similar to initiation and maintenance, is shifting to incorporate more technology (Weisskirch and Delevi 2013). Individuals are likely to seek dissolution as often as initiation, so what happens when happily-ever-after does not happen—commonly referred to as relationship dissolution. Everyone from high school adolescents to hopeful mobile daters to famous Hollywood celebrities, such as Charlize Theron/Sean Penn, has experienced ghosting. In 2015, actress Charlize Theron and actor Sean Penn broke off their romantic relationship and long-time friendship. Rumors sprouted in the media about their dissolution, and the alleged ghosting by Theron. . . . She expressed that, "There is a need to sensationalize things . . . when you leave a relationship there has to be some f—ing crazy story or some crazy drama. And the f—ing ghosting thing, like literally, I still don't even know what it is. It's just its own beast" (Fisher 2016). Allegedly Theron cut off all communication and refused to answer any of Penn's attempts to reach her. She then engaged in the ultimate silent treatment (Safronova 2015), or ghosting, and Penn's happily-ever-after with Theron disappeared.

The rise in social media platforms advancing relational development calls for scholarship to investigate this burgeoning phenomenon. This chapter examines the recent emergence of ghosting as a phenomenon scholars have yet to thoroughly explore. Practices employing ghosting strategies have existed since the introduction of new interactive technologies. Furthermore, the terminology dates back nearly a decade, and is widely utilized in common vernacular in popular culture; therefore, this chapter initiates an investigation of ghosting in relation to interpersonal dissolution communication and behaviors.

CONCEPTUALIZING GHOSTING

I was told they were going to the bathroom and then they never returned.
(LeFebvre et al. 2017)

In 2006, a recent linguistic relational dissolution term, *ghosting,* gained traction on Urban Dictionary (Stevenson 2016). *Ghosting* refers to: "unilaterally ceasing communication (temporarily or permanently) in an effort to withdraw access to individual(s) prompting relationship dissolution (suddenly or gradually) commonly enacted via one or multiple technological medium(s)" (LeFebvre et al. 2017). Ghosting has emerged on the relationship dissolution forefront, and it emulates withdrawal or avoidance strategies, while simultaneously differentiating itself by being applied through technological mediums.

Commonly, ghosting occurs when one partner initiates disengagement, often without the non-initiating partner immediately knowing. The absence of interaction, irregularity in communication patterns, and sometimes abruptly ending communication causes non-initiators to then realize that they and their partner are no longer in a relationship. *Poof!* Into thin air, the partner disappears, as does the relationship. This relationship dissolution practice, *ghosting,* relies on technologically driven advancements in online and mobile dating applications (Whitbourne 2015). Commonly, there are no answers to any calls, text messages, or social media platform messages (e.g., Tinder, Facebook, Snapchat, Instagram, Twitter, etc.). Non-initiators are essentially cut off from all contact and communication from the initiator and totally removed from the relationship. Removing physical connections and closing communication refers to avoidance strategies (LeFebvre et al. 2017). Initiators, however, do not remove themselves from all those information communication technologies; they are present, except they are no longer communicating with their previous partners, the non-initiators. The previous partner is *ghosted* and becomes a figment of the past, without communication or closure for exodus from the relationship.

Relationship development commonly incorporates the use of contemporary technologies in initiation and maintenance to define, clarify, and communicate relationships (Stanley, Rhoades, and Fincham 2011). Breakup dissolution is increasingly shifting to accommodate technological advancements (Weisskirch and Delevi 2013). The least caring and compassionate, most indirect, self-oriented, and distancing strategies often involve the use of emerging information communication technologies and social media: texting, instant messaging, voicemail, e-mailing, or social networking sites (Sprecher, Zimmerman, and Abrahams 2010). Texting is utilized most frequently (Weisskirch and Delevi 2013). Breaking up via technology may emulate avoidance via distance communication, where individuals are separated physically and psychologically from their partner (Sprecher, Zimmerman and Abrahams 2010). While technology affords individuals the ability to ghost more easily through increased physical remoteness (Sciortino 2015) partners negatively endorse receiving technological dissolution (Gershon 2010; Starks 2007). Technological devices and social media platforms allow easy access as well as easy withdrawal. Ghosting is a technologically based practice of dissolution, where disengaging initiators avoid direct confrontation, and the discussion of the relationship state, and utilize technological absence to evidence their relationship exit.

Technology, especially social media and networks, create the opportunity to access others (LeFebvre et al. 2017); ghosting withdraws that technological affordance to maintain interaction. The ability to gather information can decrease, since contact commonly occurs via technology causing limited access, reducing face-to-face contact, or restricting social networking sites' connectivity. Relationship partners who do not have mutual friends and connections are left without the direct ability to monitor their previous partners. Non-initiators possess relational artifacts via their physical and virtual remnants (LeFebvre et al. 2017), and may observe or monitor their previous partners from afar. Non-initiators know that their previous relationship partners remain active in their typical social media and networking accounts, yet their communication remains severed without rationale for closure. Ghosting appears more challenging for non-initiators without social media overlap and no mutual friends or ties. They are left to manage the uncertainty of the ghosting alone without the ability to obtain closure.

Why Study Ghosting?

Ghosting encompasses the disappearance of a partner without explanation; this relationship development captures dissolution in a technologically initiated and dissolving landscape. Most people have scripts, or hypothesized cognitive structures that, when activated, organize and communicate event-based situational information (Abelson 1981). The sixteen-step ordered script for relationship dissolution, or blueprint, starts with one individual losing interest either in the partner and/or the relationship, or becoming attracted to alternatives (Battaglia et al. 1998). As partners begin to withdraw from the relationship, they become less communicative, increase physical distance, and employ avoidance. This script, produced prior to technological advancements, delineates the breakup process. Although the script emphasized that talking with the partner transpired throughout the dissolution process, ghosting illustrates an absence of communication (Battaglia et al. 1998). Online dating sites and mobile dating apps provide an ease of use never before seen in the dating arena, allowing ghosting to mutate (Samakow 2014) and become part of the dating dissolution script. As technological advancements continue to emerge in the relational development sphere, methods for dissolving relationships evolve simultaneously from colloquial practices.

EXAMINING RELATIONSHIP DISSOLUTION STRATEGIES

"I think people do it because it is a quick easy way out rather than taking the time to meet with someone face-to-face. And actually have a conversation that would probably be pretty awkward. I guess it takes the awkwardness out of it."
(LeFebvre et al. 2017)

Dissolution Process

Partners undergo multiple decisions affecting relationship trajectories. One decision may involve whether to disengage the relationship, and to what extent (LeFebvre et al. 2017). Utilizing the relationship dissolution process theory, the trajectories create a flow chart for disengagement delineating the dynamic, complex path when one or both partners makes the decision to exit the relationship.

Six features are identified in the relational dissolution process:

1. Gradual or Sudden Onset of Relationship Problems
2. Unilateral or Bilateral Desire to Exit the Relationship
3. Use of Direct or Indirect Actions to Accomplish the Dissolution
4. Rapid or Protracted Nature of Disengagement Negotiation
5. Presence or Absence of Relationship Repair Attempts
6. Final Outcome of Relationship Termination or Continuation

Onset of Relationship Problems

Initially, the partners determine whether the decision to exit a relationship derives from incrementalism or a critical incident. Incrementalism develops from several relationship problems or a stockpile of concerns accruing over time (e.g., laziness, lack of investment, forgetfulness, etc.), whereas a critical incident involves a specific negatively valence incident usually from a single-reported problem of major magnitude (e.g., infidelity, abuse, lying, etc.) (LeFebvre et al. 2017). The onset of relationship problems then spurs one or both partners to reconsider the relationship's existence.

Unilateral or Bilateral Initiation

In the next step, one or both partners may decide to initiate dissolving the relationship. Unilateral dissolutions, or one partner initiating, exist more frequently and the post-dissolution process reflects breakup roles (Doering 2010; Sprecher, Zimmerman, and Abrahams 2010). For bilateral dissolution, researchers found that individuals who share breakup responsibility experienced fewer regrets and more positive emotions in relation to the dissolved relationship (Wilmot, Carbaugh, and Baxter 1985). Although bilateral dissolution may appear to reduce negativity and individualistic responsibility, when researchers combined breakup accounts from both partners, often no consensus suggesting bilateral breakups, or mutual dissolution occurred (Hill, Rubin, and Peplau 1976). Relationship partners do not always accurately report their dissolution initiation; when both partners' accounts were collected, consensus did not suggest bilateral dissolution existed. Unilateral ghosting primarily encapsulates ghosting since the non-initiator experiences an obvious lack of communication or disappearance. Although bilateral dissolution may occur with technological assistance, the action does not create a non-initiator and therefore no trace or semblance of disappearance prevails.

Direct or Indirect Action

Initiators have the opportunity to utilize direct or indirect strategies when dissolving relationships. Directness refers to the extent the initiator communicates the desire to exit or has terminated the relationship with the partner. Direct strategies involve explicit, straightforward, and candid communication. Utilizing direct strategies for dissolution increases initial acceptances by non-initiators (Baxter 1984). Indirectness refers to unclear, implicit, ambiguous communication or behaviors that do not leave the non-initiators with a coherent or transparent understanding that the relationship is ending. Utilizing indirect strategies for dissolution decreases the initial acceptance of dissolution.

In another study, Baxter aligned dissolution strategies along two basic dimensions (x- and y-axis) (Baxter 1985). She combined indirectness-directness on the y-axis with self and other orientations on the x-axis. When considering dissolution strategies, initiators should consider or reflect on their and their partners' feelings. The x-axis indicates the degree to which the initiator protects the partner. The other-oriented approach attempts to decrease the hurt by avoiding embarrassment or manipulation of the partner, whereas the self-oriented approach displays concern for self at the partner's expense. The two dimensions combine to form four disengagement strategy categories (Baxter 1985; Regan 2017; Zimmerman 2009).

Timeliness of Dissolution

Ghosting utilizes primarily indirect dissolution strategies through social media and/or technologically associated mediums. The degree of self and other orientations may vary in ghosting applications. In a recent study, researchers extended Baxter's (1985) conceptual model and posited that indirect ghosting strategies operate in two dimensions (x- and y-axis within the indirect quadrants) applied through a specific medium or channel to form four indirect ghosting strategies (LeFebvre et al. 2017). This study further postulated the ghosting enacted indirect strategies and extended the lower two quadrants of Baxter's original model to include two distinct quadrants under indirectness. The two dimensions combine to form four indirect ghosting disengagement strategy categories (see Table 14.1).

Specifically, the conceptual extension aligned dissolution strategies along two basic dimensions (x- and y-axis) in the indirect quadrant. The y-axis represents short- and long-term, and the x-axis represents sudden and gradual orientations. The y-axis overlays the indirectness and directness; specifically, the y-axis represents the degree to which the initiator chooses to dissolve from sudden to gradual. The sudden strategy is closer to a direct strategy (although still indirect), whereby the initiator does not explicitly communicate to the non-initiator—yet the exit is quick. Contrarily, the gradual strategy applies an indirect approach by opting out of any confrontation, by slowly dissolving the quality and quantity of communication. This exit strategy is longer and more drawn out for both initiator and non-initiator. This extension parallels the rapid and protracted nature of disengagement negotiation originally articulated by Baxter; however, it specifically narrows the scope to ghosting.

Table 14.1. Indirect Ghosting Disengagement Strategies

	Sudden		
	Quickly disappears without notice and leaves opportunity to reinitiate communication.	Quickly disappears without notice and does not plan to reinitiate communication.	
Short-Term			**Long-Term**
	Slowly disappears over time and leaves opportunity to reinitiate communication.	Slowly disappears over time and does not plan to reinitiate communication.	
	Gradual		

Source: LeFebvre, Leah E. et al. 2017. "It's Not Me, It's Definitely You: Conceptualizing the Ghosting Phenomenon in Emerging Adult Relationships."

Additionally, in this recent study (LeFebvre et al. 2017), the x-axis represents permanency (short- to long-term), indicating the degree to which dissolution exists (i.e., termination or continuation). However, ghosting applies primarily indirect strategies; therefore, initiators operate below the x-axis (self- and other-orientation). Short-term, or temporary, ghosting appears to operate based on the initiators' desires (e.g., self-oriented), whereas in the long-term, initiators chose to terminate the relationship without lingering hope or leaving an opening to rekindle the relationship with the partner (e.g., other oriented).

Ghosting alludes to relationship temporality or permanent dissolution with a specific initiator to instigate the ghosting and a non-initiator to become aware of the previous interactions, communication, and connection. Temporary ghosting may resemble or imitate on/off relationships, or cyclical relationships. A salient characteristic in on-again/off-again relationship descriptions included multiple transitions of breakups and renewals (Dailey et al. 2016). Ghosting does not allow for further interaction with a previous partner (dissolved relationship), whereas haunting allows for persistent presence and continued interaction with less investment via technological interaction, ultimately enabling a relationship resurrection. Future research should examine the nuances between permanent dissolution, ghosting, and possible relationship resurrection, haunting, and the timeline for dissolution and reinitiation between non-cyclical and cyclical ghosting relationship communication in social media.

Positioning Ghosting

Ghosting clearly represents: indirect actions (commonly through technological mediums), typically a unilateral desire to exit the relationship (the withdrawal or absence of one partner), and often across a spectrum from absence to presence for relational repairs (no attempt at repair due to an apparent departure). The onset of relationship problems, nature of disengagement, and final outcome vary in ghosting, specifically regarding the relationship dissolution strategies that encompass directness-indirectness and other-self orientations (Baxter 1979, 1982, 1985). This chapter highlights the scholarship combining previous scholarship and emerging conceptualizations tying in social media and technological mediums altering dissolution strategies.

The indirect, self-oriented, and distancing strategies are perceived as the least compassionate actions, often involving emerging social media and mobile technologies (Sprecher, Zimmerman, and Abrahams 2010). The nuances afforded by emerging social media and networking technologies alter the means and methods for dissolution; since many relationships start via *technology*, the ability to dissolve via the same medium without obstruction is desirable and sought by those exiting the relationship (LeFebvre et al. 2017).

EMERGENCE AND OUTCOMES OF GHOSTING

While the ghosting phenomenon has recently gained heightened attention in popular press, empirical examinations have yet to catch up with current relational dissolution linguistic etymology. One recent study provided the conceptualization for ghosting offered in this chapter, as well as began to understand the rationalization for why and how ghosting is enacted by initiator and non-initiators. Otherwise, no academic literature on this phenomenon exists, and therefore, it has yet to be conceptualized. Since empirical investigation and evidence has yet to be explored, we speculate on the emergence of ghosting and specifically the outcomes that should be considered for initiators and non-initiators.

Originally posted in Urban Dictionary in 2006, the term *ghosting* gained popularity in verbiage and practice and continued to gain traction throughout 2014 and 2015 (Stevenson 2016). However, the rationale for why *ghosting* emerged in colloquial terminology likely stems from the ability to initiate, maintain, and dissolve relationships through social media and social networking sites. Although more traditional face-to-face breakups may have enacted indirect strategies, such as "Dear John" letters, the ability to further withdraw and avoid becomes easier with the assistance of common communication mediums, particularly the advent of social media and social networking sites on mobile phones.

Although, online dating sites existed decades before mobile dating applications, we conjecture that the accessibility to multiple people via a handheld private communication device enables relationship formation and maintenance and just as easily dissolution and evasion. Mobile phone platforms provide venues for interpersonal relationships, and would-be-applicants are exploring and utilizing them at increasing levels (Smith and Anderson 2016). Since 2005, the public's exposure to online dating and more recently mobile dating apps increased with many individuals knowing someone using medium platforms to initiate relational communication, which simultaneously corresponds with the emergence of ghosting. Therefore, we link the ability to readily communicate with and access people, and increasing social media and networking opportunities to meet people with the advent of ghosting—which calls attention to the divergent uses of mobile phones and exponential communication through disappearing or decreasing interactions.

Ghoster/Initiator

Individuals retain a certain amount of choice in how a relationship will be conducted (Duck 1994), including how the relationship will eventually end. Initiators choose to enact ghosting for several reasons (LeFebvre et al. 2017). If ghosters initiated the communication and interaction on online mediums, they thought it was also easiest to enact disappearing similar to emergence. Additionally, oftentimes after interaction had occurred through online, offline, or multimodal mediums, initiators determined both attraction and intimacy existed. Besides desired physical, emotional, and/or intellectual appeals, initiators chose ghosting because of boredom, negativity, safety, and most commonly, better alternatives, whether real or perceived. Nevertheless, initiators should consider discretion when applying direct strategies. Direct strategies indicate the desire to exit the interaction or relationship, despite the fact that they do not have to be honest about the specifics or lack of individual attributes exhibited by said partner.

As such, dissolution strategies vary in regard to purpose, where some are more compassionate and caring than others, particularly those that account for timeliness and directness. Initiators may choose to ghost as a way to save their face or save the non-initiators' feelings. In reality this leaves the ghoster in a predicament, and they are also affected by the non-closure. Ghosting does not employ communicating care when dissolving the relationship. Instead, direct and other-oriented strategies are the kindest and most compassionate, and they enable initiators to experience closure for both partners. Complete avoidance lacks any and often all communication that the relationship is over—although not communicating does become clear through time. Strategies used to exit the relationship vary in degree of distress felt by one partner (Sprecher, Zimmerman, and Fehr 2014). Nevertheless, if both partners remain upfront about their intentions, this in turn could help emerging adults better learn how to handle difficult conversations, provide closure for their current relationship, and enable skills to improve future relationships.

The initiator's decision to dissolve the relationship directly impacts the non-initiator, and simultaneously affects the initiator's "self." The broken or incomplete script alters their ability to account for relationship dissolution processes, such as accounting through grave-dressing and resurrections processes. Ghosters have to process and explain to themselves, and their social networks, how and why they performed those actions. They do not have the ability to provide justification as easily to others without direct termination; rather, they have to affirm their choices through self-affirmation. Since ghosting does not provide any cues or guidelines for the initiators, ambiguity is typical. Initiators may have to struggle with the surrounding guilt and/or relief with an open-ended departure. Initiators may want to consider whether they demonstrated an immaturity in relationship behaviors and etiquette, and as a consequence, ghosting may leave them unable to adequately perform these tasks in future situations, and it denies them the ability to experience personal growth in relationship development.

Ghostee/Non-Initiator

Since ghosting lacks adequate information gathering and reduces the ability to obtain more information, it does not allow for uncertainty reduction. Hence, non-initiators, or ghostees, maintain uncertainty and ambiguity. Uncertainty and ambiguity are utilized interchangeably and synonymously; since variations exist in literature and scope, both should be explored in association with the ghosting phenomena. As ghostees attempt to reduce uncertainty, they may internalize the relationship dissolution and induce self-blame, since that is the only information understood. Ghosting appears opposite to face saving and reduces partner self-image (Whitbourne 2015). Ghosting does not occur at a particular set point in the relationship; rather, ghosting is elusive because it can occur at any point in the relationship whether only after minimum communication or interaction on only asynchronous mediums, between anonymous asynchronous and personal private synchronous mediums, or in variations that include online and offline communications/interactions.

Ambiguous loss refers to uncertainty without finality or resolution that remains unclear. Ghosting creates ambiguity and uncertainty in the ghostee wherein they are unable to achieve closure after the indirect breakup. Ambiguity freezes the grief process (Boss 2007). Ambiguous loss was previously conceptualized as physical absence with psychological presence or psychological absence with physical presence (Boss 2007); ghosting now enables physical and psychological absence with technological presence. Parties involved in a relationship hold one or more presences across technological social mediums and platforms. When non-initiators are ghosted, the presence of their former romantic partner remains visible on social media, which does not allow for closure of the ghostee. Rather, the ghostees experience a distressing circumstance upon realizing that initiators simply have opted out without directly indicating intentions. Ghosters continue to be visible through technology, communicate on social media, and continue to engage on social networking sites—and yet they choose not to be physically and psychologically connected to the non-initiator, even if only to provide closure through coping and grieving (even in minimal or superficial relations).

Ghosting creates an unfinished script for the ghostee. Thus, the relationship script between partners is in a state of ambiguity. Future encounters are built from relationship experiences and craft upcoming communication and behaviors; therefore, non-initiators should be mindful of their encounters and proactively and retrospectively reflect on their interactions. Sometimes initiators may forewarn that they desire to exit the relationship, and rather than directly confront, they choose to indirectly forewarn inevitability of the upcoming ghosting. Non-initiators should consider their previous actions when ghosted, since most relationship participants have experienced ghosting from the initiator and non-initiator role (LeFebvre et al. 2017). Through relational experiences, particularly as mobile dating apps become more conventional, individuals will create memory structures (Bower, Black, and Turner 1979) and should reflect upon the memories when similar future incidents occur. Uncertainty surrounding the dissolution process, or lack thereof, leaves more questions than answers. As more research examines ghosting, I argue that entering into future relationships may be difficult for ghostees who have hesitancy in how to "naturally" behave from previous ghosting that may have been internalized without adequate information about the closure. Research should examine the short- and long-term effects of uncertainty and ambiguity promoted from singular and multiple ghosting occurrences, and how these experiences affect accounting and relational grave-dressing/resurrection processes.

PRACTICAL SUGGESTIONS

Ghosting is a form of rejection, and as such it may cause uncertainty and at times be painful. As we have articulated in this chapter, dissolution can be emotionally distressing regardless of who initiates the breakup (Eastwick et al. 2008). Ghosting does not provide any cues or guidelines for the initiators surrounding the guilt (Eastwick et al. 2008), or responses and uncertainty for non-initiators on how to react, since they do not always know why initiators are not responding. We offer practical advice for initiators and non-initiators to consider before making hasty relationship decisions.

For initiators, direct and timely dissolution strategies are recommended for initiating partners, even for individuals utilizing asynchronous, and private or one-on-one technologies. Individuals who directly confront their partner face-to-face should consider how to alleviate uncertainty rather than prolong it for non-initiators. Initiators have often also experienced ghosting as non-initiators (LeFebvre et al. 2017), so they are aware of the implications for both. Therefore, ghosters may feel guilty, but they should not feel remorseful about their decision to end any relationship; however, they should attempt to empathize with the non-initiators. Specifically initiators might consider utilizing strategies that: (1) reflect pre-existing relationship patterns (e.g., positive memories, negativity between partners, and holistic relationship behaviors) (Sprecher, Zimmerman and Abrahams 2010), (2) realize how they would like to feel during and after the breakup (e.g., relief or regret), and (3) show empathy for how they would like their partner to feel during and after the breakup (e.g., sad, hurt). Utilizing ghosting provides an ambiguous message; therefore, initiators should think about their personal, partner, and relationship consequences of their action or inactions.

Non-initiators must respond to inaction or a disappearance from their partner. The indirect strategies leave the non-initiator or ghostee without closure in the relationship dissolution process. As a consequence, questions surrounding the disappearance or ambiguity may arise for the non-initiator, such that ghostees may wonder: Why did I become the victim of this rejection? What caused the sudden quiet treatment? What did I do to cause this? What is wrong with him/her? What is wrong with me? Why was I not able to read the situation? and other questions that surround uncertainty, ambiguity, and relationship and/or self-worth. Since relationship dissolution can be distressing, for initiators and especially non-initiators, individuals should communicate to their social network or trained personnel about their concerns. Seeking social support is commonly reported during and after romantic dissolution, and it is positively correlated with recovery and adjustment (Frazier and Cook 1993); therefore, acknowledging and engaging in coping with rejection will aid in recovery from dissolution (Harvey and Karpinski 2016).

FUTURE DIRECTIONS

This chapter offers a definition for ghosting as unilateral ceasing communication (temporarily or permanently) in an effort to withdraw access to individual(s) prompting relationship dissolution (suddenly or gradually) commonly enacted via one or more technological medium(s). *Ghosting* is a colloquial term that offers ample opportunity for exploration to understand this technologically associated relational dissolution enigma. I offer three future directions that explore medium interactivity, message and medium awareness and paradoxes, and channel selections.

Ghosting may spark uncertainty and ambiguity for the ghoster, since indirect and self-oriented actions are the least caring and compassionate forms of relationship dissolution (Sprecher, Zimmerman, and Abrahams 2010). Direct and other-oriented strategies are the kindest and most compassionate, and they are perceived more often with a positive valence in comparison to indirect strategies, such as ghosting. When exploring ghosting, future scholarship should consider how the medium and the message configure and interplay with each other, as well as the interaction between impersonal, interpersonal, or hyperpersonal communication (Carr and Hayes 2015). Emergent social media platforms afford a sense of interactivity where each party may perceive the relationship in differing ways, leading to disparate views of the relationship. One may feel it is an interpersonal exchange while the other perceives it as a relationship. Therefore, scholars should determine how the perceived interactivity emerged as well as the contextual exchanges between parties that led them to opt for indirect technological dissolution strategies.

Additionally, future scholarship should investigate the interplay between medium and message. For instance, the medium in which communication (e.g., online or offline) was evoked may suggest that impersonal interactions and relationships that commenced on social media may have parties who easily accept that this medium is customary for any relational exchange, whether initiation, maintenance, or dissolution. As such, partners may perceive closeness based on their conventional mediums utilized, allow any interpersonal action as commonplace, and not consider how the medium may influence, or impact the message. The medium may be the modifier of the message (Ledbetter 2014), in that ghosters choose to enact the dissolution and disappear through technology since they consider the richness evoked through that medium reflects their regard for the partner and/or relationship.

Furthermore, future research should explore which mediums and how the sequence of channel choices influences ghosting in technological settings. For instance, interpersonal communication channels and their associated or perceived technological affordances differ in their ability to convey or offer ambiguity and clarity (O'Sullivan 2000). Specifically, researchers have explored initiation processes and determined that relationship development, maintenance, and dissolution based on online, multimodal contexts, or modality switching, or shifting interactions from one communication channel to another influence development (McEwan and Zanolla 2013; Ramirez and Zhang 2007). The channel, or medium selection, should be examined as a means for understanding how selecting a channel from the available emergent technological repertoires is appropriate and effective for the specific interaction of dissolution. The number of channels used before an offline meeting significantly predicts greater intimacy, composure, and social orientation (Ramirez et al. 2015), so researchers must further explore which mediums and their affordances are preferred for initiators and non-initiator channel selection. Since people utilize communication technologies to self-regulate information and maximize rewards or minimize costs, researchers should investigate how the threat of self-presentation presents alternative strategies that manifest as ghosting. Self-presentation in various mediums may alter preferred mediated channels affordances, and the associated costs or consequences for partners, relationships, and current and future networking sites and media.

CONCLUSION

Romantic breakup can prove emotionally painful and is frequently cited among life's most distressing psychological events (Kendler et al. 2003). Now the affordances offered by technologies can be used to dissolve relationships. As technology brings us more access and accessibility, ghosting showcases that technology can also be utilized to distance and terminate our communication and relationships. With the advent of emerging technologies, access to potential partners increases and, simultaneously, ways to dissolve relationships.

This chapter informs the exploration of relational disengagement through the ghosting phenomena that occurs when partners disappear or cease communication in relationships via emerging technologies. Indirect dissolution strategies involving self-oriented avoidance are not new; however, the manner in which they are enacted is newly conceptualized due to emerging technologies. One such newly labeled phenomenon is ghosting. The inability to communicate disinterest or dissatisfaction causes partners to decrease communication or disappear, which has prompted this chapter to investigate and identify the ghosting phenomenon and the variations that occur online and through mobile dating venues. The relationship dissolution process involves vanishing first without notice online or through mobile mediums, which involves less complicated strategies for initiators, all while simultaneously compounding the ambiguity and rejection for non-initiators.

Conceptualizing the ghosting phenomena demonstrates evolving social media realms that impact romantic relationship processes adapting to emerging technologies. This chapter produces an essential exploratory basis of ghosting, the unexplored popular disengagement phenomenon, prevalent in contemporary romantic relationship development. Ghosting comprises an initiator enacting ghosting, the non-initiator realizing the relationship's end, and his/her partner disappearing without a trace as a phantom lover into the virtual cosmos.

RECOMMENDED READINGS

Baxter, Leslie A. "Trajectories of Relationship Disengagement." *Journal of Social and Personal Relationships* 1, no. 1 (1984): 29–48. doi:10.1177/0265407584011003.

Ledbetter, Andrew W. (2014). "The Past and Future of Technology in Interpersonal Communication Theory and Research." *Communication Studies* 65, no. 4 (2014): 456–59. doi:10.1080/10510974.2014.927298.

LeFebvre, Leah, Kate Blackburn, and Nicholas Brody. "Navigating Romantic Relationships on Facebook: Extending the Relationship Dissolution Model to Social Networking Environments." *Journal of Social and Personal Relationships* 32, no. 1 (2014): 78–98. doi:10.1177/0265407514524848.

LeFebvre, Leah E., Ryan Rasner, Shelby Garstad, Aleksander Wilms, Callie Parrish, Brianne Brasher, Cindi Coal, Emily Cornell, Shelby Johnsen, Madison Klopfer, Kasey Lara, Giavanna Marquez, Chris Miller, Shannon Monaghan, Robin Morrison, Cassie Niles, Samantha T. Ramlo, Breanna M. Walsh, Kaylee J. Williams, and "It's Not Me, It's Definitely You: Conceptualizing the Ghosting Phenomenon in Emerging Adult Relationships." *Journal of Social and Personal Relationships* (under review).

Regan, Pamela C. *The Mating Game: A Primer on Love, Sex, and Marriage* (3rd ed.). Los Angeles, CA: Sage Publications, 2017.

Sprecher, Susan, Corinne Zimmerman, and Erin M. Abrahams. "Choosing Compassionate Strategies to End a Relationship." *Social Psychology* 41, no. 2 (2010): 66–75. doi:10.1027/1864-9335/a000010.

REFERENCES

Abelson, Robert P. 1981. "Psychological Status of the Script Concept." *American Psychologist* 36 (7): 715–29. doi:10.1037/0003-066x.36.7.715.

Battaglia, Dina M., Francis D. Richard, Darcee L. Datteri, and Charles G. Lord. 1998. "Breaking Up Is (Relatively) Easy to Do: A Script for the Dissolution of Close Relationships." *Journal of Social and Personal Relationships* 15 (6): 829–45. doi:10.1177/0265407598156007.

Baxter, Leslie A. 1985. "Accomplishing Relationship Disengagement." In *Understanding Personal Relationships: An Interdisciplinary Approach*, by Steve Duck and Daniel Perlman. London: SAGE Publications.

———. 1984. "Trajectories of Relationship Disengagement." *Journal of Social and Personal Relationships* 1 (1): 29–48. doi:10.1177/0265407584011003.

———. 1982. "Strategies for Ending Relationships: Two Studies." *Western Journal of Speech Communication* 46 (3): 223–41. doi:10.1080/10570318209374082.

———. 1979. "Self-Disclosure As A Relationship Disengagement Strategy: An Exploratory Investigation." *Human Communication Research* 5 (3): 215–22. doi:10.1111/j.1468-2958.1979.tb00635.x.

Boss, Pauline. 2007. "Ambiguous Loss Theory: Challenges for Scholars and Practitioners." *Family Relations* 56: 105–11.

Bower, Gordon H., John B. Black, and Terrence J. Turner. 1979. "Scripts in Memory for Text." *Cognitive Psychology* 11(2): 177–220. doi:10.1016/0010-0285(79)90009-4.

Carr, Caleb T., and Rebecca A. Hayes. 2015. "Social Media: Defining, Developing, and Divining." *Atlantic Journal of Communication* 23 (1): 46–65. doi:10.1080/15456870.2015.972282.

Crotty, Nora. 2014. "Generation Ghost: The Facts Behind the Slow Fade." *Elle*. Accessed September 30, 2016. http://www.elle.com/life-love/sex-relationships/advice/a12787/girls-ghosting-relationships/.

Dailey, Rene M., Leah LeFebvre, Brittani Crook, and Nicholas Brody. 2016. "Relational Uncertainty and Communication in On-Again/Off-Again Romantic Relationships: Assessing Changes and Patterns Across Recalled Turning Points." *Western Journal of Communication* 80 (3): 239–63. doi:10.1080/10570314.2015.1094123.

Doering, Jan. 2010. "Face, Accounts, and Schemes in the Context of Relationship Breakups." *Symbolic Interaction* 33 (1): 71–95. doi:10.1525/si.2010.33.1.71.

Duck, Steve. 1994. *Meaningful Relationships: Talking, Sense, and Relating*. Thousand Oaks, CA: Sage Publications.

Eastman, Ari. July 16, 2015. 10 People Open Up About Why They Ghosted In A Relationship." Thought Catalogue. Accessed October 2, 2016. http://thoughtcatalog.com/ari-eastman/2015/07/10-people-open-up-about-why-they-ghosted-in-a-relationship/.

Eastwick, Paul W., Eli J. Finkel, Tamar Krishnamurti, and George Loewenstein. 2008. "Mispredicting Distress Following Romantic Breakup: Revealing the Time Course of the Affective Forecasting Error." *Journal of Experimental Social Psychology* 44 (3): 800–807. doi:10.1016/j.jesp.2007.07.001.

Fisher, Kendall. March 29, 2016. "Charlize Theron Talks Sean Penn Split: I Wasn't 'Ghosting' Him." Accessed June 29, 2016. http://www.msn.com/en-us/movies/celebrity/charlize-theron-talks-sean-penn-split-i-wasnt-ghosting-him/ar-BBr4qN3?li=BBnb7Kz.

Frazier, Patricia A., and Stephen W. Cook. 1993. "Correlates of Distress Following Heterosexual Relationship Dissolution." *Journal of Social and Personal Relationships* 10 (1): 55–67. doi:10.1177/0265407593101004.

Gershon, Ilana. 2010. *The Breakup 2.0: Disconnecting over New Media*. Ithaca, NY: Cornell University Press.

Hansen-Bundy, Benjy. 2016. "How to Handle Ghosting Like a Gentleman." *GQ*. Accessed June 29, 2016. http://www.gq.com/story/ghosting-guide.

Harvey, Abby B., and Andrew Karpinski. 2016. "The Impact of Social Constraints on Adjustment Following a Relationship Breakup." *Personal Relationships* 23 (3): 396–408. doi:10.1111/pere.12132.

Hill, Charles T., Zick Rubin, and Letitia Anne Peplau. 1976. "Breakups Before Marriage: The End of 103 Affairs." *Journal of Social Issues* 32 (1): 147–68. doi:10.1111/j.1540-4560.1976.tb02485.x.

Kendler, Kenneth S. John M. Hettema, Frank Butera, Charles O. Gardner, Carol A. Prescott. 2003. "Life Event Dimensions of Loss, Humiliation, Entrapment, and Danger in the Prediction of Onsets of Major Depression and Generalized Anxiety." *Archives of General Psychiatry* 60 (8): 789–96. doi:10.1001/archpsyc.60.8.789.

Ledbetter, Andrew W. 2014. "The Past and Future of Technology in Interpersonal Communication Theory and Research." *Communication Studies* 65 (4): 456–59. doi:10.1080/10510974.2014.927298.

LeFebvre, Leah, Kate. Blackburn, and Nicholas Brody. 2015. "Navigating Romantic Relationships on Facebook: Extending the Relationship Dissolution Model to Social Networking Environments." *Journal of Social and Personal Relationships* 32 (1): 78–98. doi:10.1177/0265407514524848.

LeFebvre, Leah E., Ryan Rasner, Shelby Garstad, Aleksander Wilms, Callie Parrish, Brianne Brasher, Cindi Coal, Emily Cornell, Shelby Johnsen, Madison Klopfer, Kasey Lara, Giavanna Marquez, Chris Miller, Shannon Monaghan, Robin Morrison, Cassie Niles, Samantha Ramlo, Breanna Walsh, Kaylee Williams. 2017. "It's Not Me, It's Definitely You: Conceptualizing the Ghosting Phenomenon in Emerging Adult Relationships." Paper presented at the Western States Communication Association Conference in Salt Lake City, Utah.

McEwan, B., and David Zanolla. 2013. "When Online Meets Offline: A Field Investigation of Modality Switching." *Computers in Human Behavior* 29 (4): 1565–71. http://dx.doi.org/10.1016/j.chb.2013.01.020.

O'Brien, Sara Ashley. September 24, 2015. "And Then I Never Heard From Him Again: The Awful Rise of Ghosting." *The Date Report*. Accessed June 30, 2016. http://www.thedatereport.com/dating/advice/and-then-i-never-heard-from-him-again-the-awful-rise-of-ghosting/.

O'Sullivan, Patrick B. 2000. "What You Don't Know Won't Hurt Me: Impression Management Functions of Communication Channels in Relationships." *Human Communication Research* 26 (3): doi:10.1111/j.1468-2958.2000.tb00763.x.

Ramirez, Artemio, Erin M. Sumner, Christina Fleuriet, and Megan Cole. 2015. "When Online Dating Partners Meet Offline: The Effect of Modality Switching on Relational Communication Between Online Daters." *Journal of Computer-Mediated Communication* 20 (1): 99–114. doi:10.1111/jcc4.12101.

Ramirez, Artemio, and Shuangyue Zhang. 2007. "When Online Meets Offline: The Effect of Modality Switching on Relational Communication." *Communication Monographs* 74 (3): 287–310. doi:10.1080/03637750701543493.

Regan, Pamela C. 2017. *The Mating Game: A Primer on Love, Sex, and Marriage* (3rd ed.). Los Angeles, CA: Sage.

Samakow, Jessica. October 30, 2014. "'Ghosting:' The 21st-Century Dating Problem Everyone Talks About, But No One Knows How To Deal With." *Huffington Post*. Accessed June 29, 2016.http://www.huffingtonpost.com/2014/10/30/ghosting-dating-_n_6028958.html.

Safronova, Valeriya. 2015. "Exes Explain Ghosting, the Ultimate Silent Treatment." *New York Times*. Accessed June 29, 2016.http://www.nytimes.com/2015/06/26/fashion/exes-explain-ghosting-the-ultimate-silent-treatment.html.

Sciortino, Karley. 2015. "Breathless: To Ghost or Not to Ghost?" *Vogue*. Accessed June 29, 2016. http://www.vogue.com/13379566/breathless-karley-sciortino-ghosting/.

Smith, Aaron, and Monica Anderson. 2016. "5 Facts about Online Dating." *Pew Research Center RSS*. N.p. Web. 26 Sept. 2016.

Sprecher, Susan, Corinne Zimmerman, and Erin M. Abrahams. 2010. "Choosing Compassionate Strategies to End a Relationship." *Social Psychology* 41 (2): 66–75. doi:10.1027/1864-9335/a000010.

Sprecher, S., C. Zimmerman, and B. Fehr. 2014. "The Influence of Compassionate Love on Strategies Used to End a Relationship." *Journal of Social and Personal Relationships* 31 (5): 697–705. doi:10.1177/0265407513517958.

Stanley, Scott M., Galena K. Rhoades, and Frank D. Fincham. 2011. "Understanding Romantic Relationship among Emerging Adults: The Significant Roles of Cohabitation and Ambiguity." In *Romantic Relationships in Emerging Adulthood*, ed. Frank D. Fincham and Ming Cui, by Scott M. Stanley. Cambridge: Cambridge University Press.

Starks, Kaitlin M. 2007. "Bye Bye Love: Computer-mediated Communication and Relational Dissolution." *Texas Speech Communication Journal* 32 (1): 11–20.

Stevenson, Verity. 2016. "Ghosting in the Modern Dating World—*Toronto Star Touch*." *Toronto Star Touch*. Accessed October 03, 2016. http://startouch.thestar.com/screens/4d7bbdd3-8564-4748-bc02-29b8a47fdb78丨_0.html.

Veksler, Alice E., and Michaela D. E. Meyer. 2014. "Identity Management in Interpersonal Relationships: Contextualizing Communication as Central to Research on Emerging Adulthood." *Emerging Adulthood* 2 (4): 243–45. doi:10.1177/2167696814558061.

Weisskirch, Robert S., and Raquel Delevi. 2013. "Attachment Style and Conflict Resolution Skills Predicting Technology Use in Relationship Dissolution." *Computers in Human Behavior* 29(6): 2530–34. doi:10.1016/j.chb.2013.06.027.

Whitbourne, Susan K. June 20, 2015. "The Most Compassionate Way to End a Relationship." *Psychology Today*. Accessed June 29, 2016. https://www.psychologytoday.com/blog/fulfillment-any-age/201506/the-most-compassionate-way-end-relationship.

Wilmot, William W., Donal A. Carbaugh, and Leslie A. Baxter. 1985. "Communicative Strategies Used to Terminate Romantic Relationships." *Western Journal of Speech Communication* 49 (3): 204–16. doi:10.1080/10570318509374195.

Zimmerman, Corinne. 2009. "Dissolution of Relationships, Breakup Strategies." In *Encyclopedia of Human Relationships*, by Harry T. Reis and Susan Sprecher. Thousand Oaks, CA: Sage Publications.

FIFTEEN

Post-Dissolution Surveillance on Social Networking Sites

Nicholas Brody, Leah E. LeFebvre, and Kate G. Blackburn

This chapter examines the relational and individual processes individuals undergo following the dissolution of their romantic relationships. Specifically, this chapter explains and expands on conceptual models for understanding and exploring the breakup process. In the past, these models have mostly been used to investigate offline and face-to-face behaviors as they occur after a breakup. The present chapter builds on recent research by extending these models to better understand post-breakup behavior in online and, in particular, social networking environments. We explore how social networking sites (SNS) have altered and/or complicated the post-dissolution processes. Specifically, we investigate one relatively frequent behavior—surveillance of a former partner following a breakup.

This chapter has several goals. First, we explore how models of relational dissolution can be extended to understand online behavior following a breakup. Second, we explain how technology such as SNS affect the breakup process and investigate why surveillance is a particularly notable behavior. Third, we further explain surveillance by investigating the relational, emotional, and personality factors that are associated with increased surveillance behaviors following a breakup. We report the findings of two studies that investigate predictors of post-dissolution surveillance. Finally, we synthesize these findings within the aforementioned models of relational dissolution, and call for future scholarship that investigates the role of relational memory in these processes.

RELATIONSHIP DISSOLUTION MODELS

The accessibility of information on SNS influences relationship development and aids in relationship maintenance over time. Researchers have been challenged to examine how online behaviors reflect progression through the various stages of relationships, including breakups and post-dissolution processes (Walther 1996). Relationship dissolution models characterize breaking up as a normative lifecycle process. As such, two frequently cited communication conceptual models include the relationship de-escalation and relationship dissolution approaches (Duck 1992; Knapp 1978; Knapp and Vangelisti 2010; Rollie and Duck 2006). These models emphasize the communicative and psychological processes that people experience in order to end and begin new romantic relationships.

Relationship De-escalation Model

Knapp's model of relational development provides a framework for understanding how relationships grow toward (i.e., escalation) and away from (i.e., de-escalation) intimacy. Specifically, relationship de-escalation explores how relationships dissolve from intimacy through five stages: *differentiating, circumscribing, stagnating, avoiding,* and *terminating* (Knapp 1978; Knapp and Vangelisti 2010). *Differentiating* encompasses one or more partners attempting to reestablish or regain their individuality, rather than their relational identity, and as partners reassure more independence. *Circumscribing* finds the relationship communication deteriorating as partners constrict their communication, both in the quality and quantity of communication. *Stagnation* represents that the relationship embodies a shell of the former relationship. Partners may share a similar space; however, they do not share themselves with each other and rather are closed off and communication is stilted. *Avoiding* removes the physical connection and closes off communication channels. Partners take active steps to refrain from contact with each other. Lastly, *terminating* represents the end of the relationship and romantic communication. Most relationships do not experience all stages of dissolution, nor do they always happen in this order. This model provides a foundation for understanding the normative patterns, and sequent behavioral and communicative changes that occur as partnerships end.

Relationship Dissolution Model

Duck's relational dissolution model emphasizes psychological states and communication patterns individuals experience throughout the relationship breakup processes (Duck 1983; Rollie and Duck 2006). The model argues that the relationship dissolution model is a process that individual partners experience as they move through five processes: *intrapsychic, dyadic, social, grave-dressing,* and *resurrection,* occurring over variable time periods. The *intrapsychic* process focuses on the partner as an internal desire by one or both partners that stems from an individualistic reflection about the state of the relationship. The *dyadic* process focuses on the relationship and transpires when the two partners discuss their problems or reservations about the relationship, calling to question and potentially jeopardizing the future or redefinition of the relationship. Partners can choose to dissolve, repair, or postpone the relationship. The *social process* occurs after one or both partners have decided to terminate the relationship, and news of the breakup is communicated to outside parties. Social processes entitle partners to the means to create and distribute public stories about their particular version of the relationship dissolution. This process focuses on facing the social and public consequences of publicizing the decision to family, friends, and acquaintances, and it unfolds as account(s) of the relationship dissolution are made public among an individual's network members (Duck 1982). The outcome of the social process is to publicly acknowledge the separation and move into *grave-dressing,* where individuals focus on tidying up the accounts representing explanations for past actions and events (Sorenson 1993). Lastly, the newer model included the *resurrection* process, which focuses on the potential lessons learned from the previous relationship as individuals prepare for future romantic relationships (Rollie and Duck 2006). This process communicates that individuals are ready to start anew and re-enter the dating world. This model outlines the ability to comprehend both the psychological considerations and ensuing relational behaviors that address individual, dyadic, and social networking through all the processes.

These conceptual models were originally developed to understand face-to-face interpersonal relationship processes. However, the romantic relationship landscape is now multimodal, which in turn has somewhat transformed how relationships develop and dissolve.

Relational De-escalation and Dissolution on Social Networking Sites

The conceptual models for understanding the underlying thoughts and ideas that guide the process of relationship dissolution are likely affected by SNS. Recently, researchers began studying how SNS, specifically Facebook, may alter these models. Previous studies (e.g., Fox, Warber and Makstaller; LeFebvre, Blackburn, and Brody 2015; Tong 2013) explored how post-dissolution processes are changing in line with the rapidly increasing rate of SNS adoption (e.g., Facebook has over 1.71 billion monthly active users worldwide) (Smith 2016). The prevalent use of Facebook makes this SNS a natural context to study how users share and gather information about their relationships, and provides an opportune venue for understanding behavior following a breakup. SNS afford the visibility of public or private information presented online, and can include sharing information about romantic interpersonal relationships (Fox and Moreland 2015). In these previous studies, individuals observed their romantic partners' online actions during the breakup, and throughout the dissolution process. By investigating these processes in online environments, this chapter strengthens the understanding of the scope of the relational features and processes stipulated by the models, while also extending the original models to include technological affordances.

HOW SNS COMPLICATE THE DISSOLUTION PROCESS

Social networking sites provide a wide array of features that enable users to form and sustain interpersonal relationships. These mediated contexts typically allow users to maintain personal profiles, store digital artifacts, and share personal information. Additionally, SNS provide a platform for users to interact with the profiles and archives sustained by others in their network. SNS lend themselves to gathering information about friends and maintaining social bonds between users (Ellison, Steinfeld, and Lampe 2007; Lampe, Ellison, and Steinfeld 2006). Commonly, this includes sharing information about their romantic relationships. Users can readily access and identify current relationship statuses on these sites—going *Facebook official* to signal to others the seriousness of the romance and altering elements of their profile as part of the recovery process after a breakup (Fox, Warber, and Makstaller 2013; LeFebvre, Blackburn, and Brody 2015). Indeed, a body of emerging scholarship documented the various ways in which people use SNS in their romantic relationships (e.g., Zhao, Sosik, and Cosley 2012).

One behavior, *surveillance*, is of particular relevance because it exemplifies how SNS have changed the breakup process. Consider that both relationship dissolution models emphasized several social aspects of the breakup process. For instance, the relationship de-escalation model described the circumscribing and avoiding stages of breakups, in which partners begin to reduce and, ultimately, completely cut off contact with their partner. SNS users' undertaking of these processes becomes increasingly difficult as access to social information about a partner is easily available, both passively (i.e., seeing comments made by an previous partner on someone else's post; seeing a status update by an ex) or actively (i.e., opening up an ex's profile and viewing their recent activities). Similarly, the relationship dissolution model outlined the grave-dressing process of relational dissolution, in which individuals create an explanation and account for the breakup and come to terms with the reasons underlying the end of the relationship. Again, easy access to information about previous partners can complicate this process, as individuals are forced to reconcile their memories of the relationship with a steady stream of up-to-date information about their former relationship and partner. While stalking behavior certainly occurred prior to the advent of SNS (Spitzberg and Cupach 2007), clearly technology has expanded opportunities for engaging in surveillance of previous romantic partners.

Surveillance and Romantic Relationships

Interpersonal electronic surveillance (IES), or in colloquial terminology, *creeping* or *stalking* (often used interchangeably) describe mediated contexts of surveillance behaviors. Specifically, IES characterizes strategies or behaviors individuals use over communication technologies to gain awareness of another user, or multiple users' online, offline, or multimodal behaviors (Tokunaga 2011). Scholarship indicates that IES behaviors provided individuals with the opportunity to track others and is often seen as a normative behavior (Lampe, Ellison, and Steinfeld; Tokunaga 2011). The design and features of SNS allows and encourages varying levels of surveillance in interpersonal relationships. For instance, IES enabled individuals to observe their previous partners' behavior, and their partners' social network as they progressed through the relationship dissolution process (LeFebvre, Blackburn, and Brody 2014). IES is not just an information gathering technique; in some circumstances it can be negative to the breakup recovery process. For example, people experienced a delayed recovery after a breakup if they engaged in IES (Marshall et al. 2013).

People engage in IES to gather information about another person through viewing status updates, photos, and wall/timeline posts. IES can foster obsessive relational intrusion, might prolong rumination on the breakup, and delays the recovery process. (LeFebvre, Blackburn, and Brody 2014). Studies have examined the relational characteristics that might be associated with IES, particularly related to the post-breakup time period (Tokunaga 2015). Additionally, researchers previously explored the way current and previous partners monitored Facebook to learn about the activities of their previous partners (Marshall et al. 2013). Other research examined users recounting their desire to creep on previous partner's Facebook to gain information about their partners and relationship statuses (LeFebvre, Blackburn, and Brody 2015). Moreover, individuals who use Facebook for IES post-breakup experience increased distress (Lucaks and Quaan Haase 2015). To better understand the relational and emotional factors that precede IES, the following hypotheses are proposed.

Breakup Initiator

An individual's initiator role (i.e., whether someone initiated a breakup or was broken up with) affects a variety of breakup outcomes (Doering 2010). Initiators experienced a different orientation to the dissolution process than non-initiators (Aronson, Wilson, and Akert 2005). These studies indicated that those who initiated the breakup often experience fewer regrets, more positive emotions about their relationship role, and more satisfaction in subsequent dissolution processes. Applying this research to SNS, one study found that non-initiators were more likely to engage in IES (Tong 2013). This study extends research by exploring whether the breakup initiator role was associated with surveillance behavior beyond the norm. Since the initiator and the non-initiator experience breakup outcomes differently, the following is proposed:

> H1: *Breakup initiators will report lower levels of IES behavior than non-initiators.*

Negative Emotion

Experiencing a romantic breakup can be one of life's most distressing psychological events, associated with emotional and physical health consequences (Kender et al. 2003). The relational dissolution model argues that people experience negative emotions such as resentment during breakups, and those feelings, in turn, affect communication activity (Rollie and Duck 2006). Breakups are often rife with negative emotions, including anger, sadness, and guilt (Guerrero and Anderson 2001). Non-initiators experience more negative emotion, particularly immediately following the breakup (Sprecher 1994). Negative emotion may mediate the role between breakup initiator and IES. The desire to seek out information based on negative emotion may drive and possibly increase IES behaviors. Several negative emotions have been found to predict stalking behaviors, although this association has not been directly tested in online environments (Davis, Ace, and Andra 2000). To better understand some of the underlying mechanisms as to why individuals may engage in increased surveillance following a breakup, the following is proposed:

> H2: *The relationship between initiator role and IES behaviors will be mediated by negative emotion.*

Rumination

Relationship rumination—or repetitive, obsessive thoughts about a relationship—may also influence IES. Rejection often leads to rumination, and rumination is commonly associated with relational intrusion behaviors and stalking (Spitzberg et al. 2014). Rumination may lead to disproportionate and intrusive thinking about previous events or persons (Nolen-Hoeksema 1998). Since the non-initiator role (i.e., being rejected by a romantic partner) might lead to rumination, which in turn may lead to increased IES behaviors, the following is proposed:

H3: The relationship between initiator role and IES behaviors will be mediated by rumination.

STUDY 1

Participants

Participants (N = 270) were students at a large southwestern university. This study drew from a collegiate sample because 70 percent of college students will experience a breakup (Knox, Zusman, and Nieves 1998) and they represent the largest user FB demographic (Duggan and Smith 2013). Participation criteria included: having recently been in a relationship lasting at least one month, experiencing a breakup of that relationship (within the previous twenty-four months), and that both relational partners had Facebook accounts. Participants (N = 99) that did not meet these criteria were removed from the sample. The final sample included 171 participants. Participants were 42.1 percent male and 51.5 percent female, and 6.4 percent declined to answer. The average age was 19.4 (SD = 1.59). The average relationship duration was 12.6 months (SD = 12.8) and the couples had been broken up for an average of 10.9 months (SD = 7.52). On average, participants reported using Facebook approximately 94.99 minutes per day (SD = 176.06; Mdn = 60). Participants estimated how many friends overlapped with friends of their former relationship partner (M = 149.59, SD = 195; Mdn = 60). Approximately 39.2 percent were currently in a new romantic relationship.

Measurements

IES Behaviors

A list of surveillance-related behaviors were created based on previous qualitative scholarship (LeFebvre, Blackburn, and Brody 2015). Participants were asked to consider whether or not they had engaged in the behavior during the breakup using a dichotomous measure (yes/no). If participants responded yes, they then reported on a 1 (*Not much*) to 5 (*Very much*) Likert-type scale as to the extent to which they engaged in the behavior *beyond their normal usage* (M = 2.68, SD = 1.07). See Table 15.1 for the items and the number of respondents who reported engaging in each behavior. In contrast to previous work on surveillance, this approach treats surveillance as a dynamic rather than a static behavior. Since most participants probably participate in some baseline level of surveillance, this approach reported on any changes in surveillance during the breakup process.

Breakup Initiator

A dichotomous variable asked who initiated the relationship (e.g., self or partner). Previous relationship termination research found that those who experience relationship termination might not accurately report the initiator. Therefore, mutual initiations were not measured, since there are commonly misperceptions about mutual initiations (Metts, Cupach, and Bejlovec 1989; Sprecher 1994). Participants indicated 67.7 percent self- and 33.3 percent partner-initiation.

Negative Emotion

Participants were asked about the intensity of negative affect they experienced during the breakup (Thomas and Diener 1990). This Likert-type scale asked participants to report the extent to which they were: *unhappy, depressed, anxious, frustrated, worried, hostile,* and *angry* during their breakup, from 1 (*Slightly*) to 5 (*Extremely*) ($M = 2.67$, $SD = .90$, $\alpha = .84$).

Rumination

The Relationship Preoccupation Scale was used to measure preoccupied rumination (Davis, Shaver and Vernon 2003). These nine Likert-type

Table 15.1. Extent of Engagement in Facebook Surveillance Behaviors

	Engaged in Behavior			Usage Beyond Normal
	Yes	No	Do not use	*M* (*SD*)
I viewed my former partner's Facebook wall	136	29	5	3 (1.27)
I viewed my former partner's photos	112	53	5	2.9 (1.3)
I viewed mutual friends' Facebook walls	73	93	4	2.5 (1.28)
I viewed the photo albums of others	58	107	5	2.3 (1.29)
I viewed the accounts of my former partner's exclusive friends	47	116	7	2.9 (1.2)
I attempted to log in to my former partner's Facebook account	14	149	7	2.9 (1.41)
I attempted to "friend" friends of my partner	9	159	6	2.8 (1.04)

Note: If participants reported they engaged in a behavior, they also reported the extent to which they did so beyond normal.

scale statements asked participants to respond regarding their focus on the lost relationship (e.g., *I have trouble thinking about anything but my last partner*) on a 1 (*Not at all like me*) to 7 (*Very much like me*) (*M* = 1.98, *SD* = .94, α = .87).

Facebook Intensity

Because previous research has demonstrated that the Facebook intensity usage can predict IES behavior, intensity was measured as a control (Ellison, Steinfeld, and Lampe 2007). Six statements (e.g., *Facebook is part of my everyday activity*) were rated on a five-point Likert scale, from 1 (*Strongly disagree*) to 5 (*Strongly agree*). This scale proved reliable (*M* = 3.13, *SD* = .95, α = .85).

Results

Most participants reported engaging in partner IES behaviors during their breakup. The most common was: *I viewed my former partner's Facebook wall*, while the least common behavior was: *I attempted to "friend" friends of my partner.* Roughly 15 percent of participants reported engaging in five or more IES behaviors, and 90 percent of participants reported engaging in at least one IES behavior (see Table 15.1).

Breakup Initiator

The first hypothesis predicted that a person role in initiating the breakup would predict the extent to which participants went beyond their normal usage. This hypothesis was tested using hierarchical regression. Previous research suggested sex (e.g., Muise, Christofides, and Desmarais), Facebook intensity, and frequency of use are related to IES behaviors (Tokunaga 2015); thus, the following items were also entered in the first step as control variables: sex (0 = male, 1 = female), Facebook intensity, and minutes of Facebook use per day. The initiator role variable was dummy coded (0 = initiator, 1 = non-initiator) and entered in the second step.

The overall *F*-test indicated that the model significantly predicted IES beyond normal usage, adjusted R^2 = .08, $F(4, 131)$ = 3.72, $p < .01$. The participant sex control variable was significant, $b = -.18$, $t = 2.13$, $p < .05$, indicating that women were more likely to undertake surveillance than men. The initiator role variable was significant, $b = .22$, $t = 2.50$, $p < .05$, indicating that individuals reporting on non-initiated breakups (i.e., their partner was the initiator) enacted more IES than individuals reporting on self-initiated relationship breakup. Hypothesis 1 was supported.

Negative Emotion and Rumination as Mediators

The second and third hypotheses predicted that the relationship between the initiator role and IES behaviors would be mediated by negative emotion (*H2*) and rumination (*H3*). These predictions were tested using the SPSS *Process* macro, which utilizes a resampling mediation procedure (bootstrapping) (Preacher and Hayes 2008). The negative emotion composite variable and control over breakup were entered as parallel mediators of the relationship between initiator role and IES behaviors. The initiator role was dummy coded.

Figure 15.1 illustrates the mediation procedure, which utilized 5,000 bias-corrected bootstrapped samples, and displays the results. Effects were considered significant if the upper and lower bounds of the 95 percent confidence interval do not overlap with 0.

Hypothesis 2 was supported—negative emotion mediated the relationship between the initiator role and IES. Breakup initiator role related to negative emotion (non-initiators experienced more negative emotion), which, in turn, predicted IES (high levels of negative emotion positively related to surveillance behavior). Rumination did not mediate the relationship between initiator role and IES behaviors. The initiator role was not associated with rumination, although rumination directly related to IES behaviors. Hypothesis 3 was not supported.

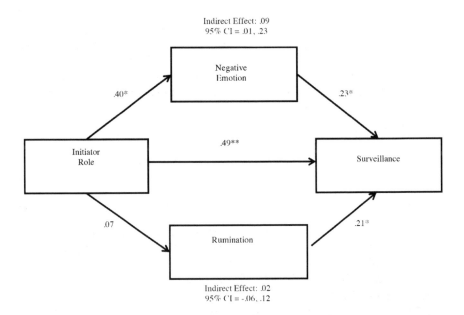

Figure 15.1.   Mediating role of negative emotion and rumination. Note: Model Total R2 = .15**. * p < .05, **p < .01

Study 1 Implications

Online behaviors can reflect the tumultuous social and psychological changes individuals experience when relationships end (LeFebvre, Blackburn, and Brody 2015). These processes are represented on SNS in various ways, including distancing and monitoring the behaviors of a previous partner (Tong 2013). Since previous research demonstrated that IES is a normative behavior on Facebook, this study explored IES behaviors on Facebook following a breakup. The present results indicated that individuals who were broken up with engaged in higher levels of IES. However, negative emotion mediated that relationship, such that those who were broken up with experienced more negative emotion, and in turn engaged in higher levels of IES on their previous partners. Although rumination did not mediate the relationship, individuals who reported higher levels of rumination also engaged in more IES of their previous partners.

Overall, these results build on existing literature that examines emotional and relational predictors of both online and offline surveillance. For instance, this research corresponds with findings that non-initiators engage in more surveillance (e.g., Tong 2013), but added nuance to those results by showing the mediating role of negative emotion. Negative emotion has been shown to relate to offline stalking behavior (Davis, Ace, and Andra 2000), and these findings reveal a similar pattern in SNS environments.

To further elucidate the predictors of IES in the SNS environment, Study 2 investigates the relationship between personality and IES. Although research has examined the role of personality on identity management in SNS environments (Eftekhar, Fullwood, and Morris 2014), as well as the personality profile of men who stalk their previous partners following the end of a relationship (Kamphuis, Emmelkamp, and de Vries 2004), to our knowledge no research has examined the role of personality in predicting post-breakup IES.

RQ: What personality factors predict the use of IES following a breakup?

STUDY 2

Participants

Data were collected as part of a larger study of 363 undergraduate students exploring relational behaviors in SNS environments. Similar to Study 1, college students were chosen, as they frequently experience breakups and they are frequent Facebook users (Knox, Zusman, and Nieves 1998; Duggan and Smith 2013). For the present study, the 174 participants reported on a partner with whom they had recently terminated a relationship. These participants had not yet begun a new relationship, and the breakup must have occurred within the previous two years. Participants' relationships had ended an average of 8.69 months (SD = 8.53) prior to completing the present study. One hundred and twenty-three of the participants were female (70.7 percent), and 51 were male (29.3 percent). The average age was 20.59 (SD = 2.85). The average relationship duration prior to the breakup was 13.3 months (SD = 14.95).

Measurements

Surveillance

As part of a larger measure of relational behaviors on SNS, participants completed a six-item measure of their surveillance behavior of their ex-partner on Facebook. Sample items included *I view my partner's past timeline photos* and *I view my partner's Facebook account.* Participants responded on a on a 1 (*Never*) to 5 (*Always*) Likert-type scale. Reliability was high (M = 2.49; SD = .92; α = .92).

Personality and Facebook Intensity

Participants completed the Ten-Item Personality Inventory (i.e., TIPI), which is a shortened version of the Big Five personality inventory (Gosling, Rentfrow, and Swann 2003). The TIPI contains two items each to assess extraversion (e.g., *I see myself as extraverted, enthusiastic*), agreeableness (e.g., *I see myself as sympathetic, warm*), conscientiousness (e.g., *I see myself as dependable, self-disciplined*), neuroticism (e.g., *I see myself as disorganized, careless*), and openness to experience (e.g., *I see myself as open to new experiences, complex*). The same items reported in Study 1 were used to measure Facebook intensity. This scale again proved reliable (M = 3.40, SD = .93, α = .90).

Results

The research question was addressed using hierarchical regression. The overall regression was significant, adjusted R^2 = .20, $F(7, 162)$ = 6.89, p < .001. The first step contained the control variables—a dummy-coded variable for participant sex (1 = male; 0 = female) and the Facebook intensity variable. Both sex (β = -.35, t = 3.10, p < .001) and Facebook intensity (β = .31, t = 4.29, p < .001) significantly predicted surveillance behavior. Similar to Study 1, men were less likely to engage in IES than women, and intensity of Facebook use was positively associated with more IES behavior.

The second step contained the five personality factors—extraversion, agreeableness, conscientiousness, neuroticism, and openness to experience. The addition of the personality factors significantly improved prediction of IES, R^2 change = .08, $F(5, 155)$ = 3.29, p < .01. Specifically, conscientiousness (β = -.17, t = 2.30, $p < .05$), neuroticism (β = .17, t = 2.27, $p <$ .05), and openness to experience (β = .19, t = 2.32, $p < .05$) each related to IES. Results suggest that more conscientiousness participants were less likely to surveil their previous partners, but more neurotic and open participants were more likely to engage in IES on their previous partners.

Study 2 Implications

Study 2 highlighted how personality may play a role in surveillance. For example, people that tend to be high on openness may be more likely to seek out information about their partner. One reason could be that these people have a proclivity to seek out information that is related to their self-identity more so than those people who may not be as open (McCrae and Oliver 1992). Additionally, the results showed that people who scored higher on neuroticism are more likely to engage in surveillance. People that scored high on neuroticism tend to express strong emotions (e.g., depression) more so than people who score lower on neuroticism (McCrae and Oliver 1992). These results hint that certain personalities may predict how some individuals engage in surveillance, and provide more insight into the predictors of surveillance behavior. The following section further explores the implications of these findings.

GENERAL DISCUSSION

The present study sought to further elucidate the role of technology and SNS in the relational dissolution process by exploring the relational and dispositional predictors and mediators of surveillance behavior following a breakup. Results indicate that people's role in the breakup—whether they initiated the breakup or were broken up with—relates to whether or not they engage in IES following dissolution. Specifically, non-initiators were more likely to engage in IES of their previous partner. However, that association was mediated by negative emotion. In other words, being broken up with related to higher levels of negative emotion, which in turn predicted surveillance behavior. Moreover, individuals enact surveillance based on individual factors. Specifically, personality characteristics were also associated with surveillance. Neuroticism and openness to experience were each positively related to IES, and conscientiousness was negatively related to IES.

Relationship Characteristics and Emotion

Initiator Role and Negative Emotion

Initiator role was associated with IES, and the relationship was mediated by negative emotion. Non-initiators tended to experience more negative emotion and in turn surveilled their previous partner. Experiencing relational dissolution is associated with intense negative emotion (Kender et al. 2003), particularly for non-initiators (Sprecher 1994), and negative emotion can lead to increased offline stalking behavior during a breakup (Davis, Ace, and Andra). The results extend these findings to illustrate how people process breakups online as they attempt to manage negative emotions.

This study establishes a clear mediating role of negative emotion, and future research should test for serial mediation from initiator role to other variables—such as relational uncertainty—to negative emotion to IES. By monitoring the previous partners' SNS presence, individuals can unobtrusively stay aware of their partners. Future research should examine specific behaviors connected to surveillance and negative emotion.

Rumination

Researchers have found that people ruminate in two distinct ways—as a proactive coping mechanism to help people come to terms with the ending of a relationship, and as a method to recall relationship experiences with regret (Saffrey and Ehrenberd 2007). Given that technology can provide access to these past relationship experiences, there is the possibility that people have additional rumination resources. For instance, some research suggests that people high in Facebook rumination may experience higher long-term depression levels—when people looked at their previous partner's online profile, they had higher long-term depression levels than people who did not view it (Tran 2012). Surprisingly, results did not show that rumination mediated the relationship between initiator role and IES—although rumination was a direct predictor of IES. Perhaps the complex nature of breakups provides the opportunity for rumination to occur for both relationship partners. Previous research has suggested that rumination and IES might delay recovery and adjustment following a breakup (LeFebvre, Blackburn, and Brody 2015). Future research should examine this more specifically, and further explore how rumination and negative emotion might be affected by the stage of the breakup process.

These results shed light on the breakup process on Facebook—in particular, the findings reveal some relational and emotional predictors and mediators of online surveillance. However, as part of the larger goal, to investigate how surveillance functions within relationships, we also explored the dispositional predictors of surveillance. The second study built on these findings by reporting on dispositional, personality-based predictors of post-breakup surveillance.

Individual Characteristics and Personality

Study 2 examined the personality-related predictors of IES, and found that conscientiousness was negatively related to IES, whereas neuroticism and openness to experience were positively related to IES. These findings built on past research that showed that people's personality traits are linked to how they manage their online presence (Eftekhar, Fullwood, and Morris 2014), indicating that extraverts tend to have more friends in their social network, as well as more photo uploads, compared to other people. In addition, these studies provided evidence that people who score high on neuroticism created more photo albums compared to other personality types. Furthermore, prior research indicated that personality traits such as extraversion and openness are positively related to SNS use (Correa, Hinsley, and Gil de Zúñiga 2010). One study showed that higher levels of neuroticism were associated with how people use social outlets (e.g., chat rooms) (Hamburger and Ben-Artzi 2000). In particular, men who scored high on neuroticism used more information services compared to those men who scored lower on neuroticism. Other research found that neurotic people also tend to engage in instant messaging more often than others (Ehrenberg et al. 2008). Researchers have speculated that one reason people high on neuroticism seek out social interaction and information online is to bolster social support. Overall, these results indicated that neurotic and open individuals may be more active technology users, and it appears that pattern carries over into the use of IES following a breakup.

In addition, research into the personality profile of offline stalkers following a breakup noted that they tended to score lower on conscientiousness and emotional stability (the inverse of neuroticism) (Kamphuis, Emmelkamp, de Vries 2004). Overall, these findings demonstrated that personality indeed influences how people actively manage their online presence and levels of social interaction. Future research should examine a broader set of personality features and examine differences between offline stalking, online IES, and multimodal operations. For instance, an analysis of ten studies on stalking behavior indicated that preoccupied attachment might play a role (Meloy 1996). Other research found a link between anxious attachment and increased Facebook use; however, the role of attachment on IES is less clear (Oldmeadow, Quinn, and Kowert 2013). Overall, the results suggest that IES is not just driven by relational or emotional factors, but also the personality profile of the partner.

Sex Differences

This chapter did not set out to directly examine sex; however, when examining the control variables in both studies, a relationship between sex and IES existed. Similar to past IES research, females were more likely to engage in IES than males (Muise, Christofides, and Desmarais 2009). Additionally, researchers have found that females are more likely to report jealousy over Facebook activity than males (McAndrew and Shah 2013). A plethora of research has investigated differences between males and females in relation to infidelity and relational dissolution, and this study suggests similar patterns emerge in examining IES behaviors (Shackelford, Buss, Bennett 2002).

Contributions to Models of Relational Dissolution

These findings provide insight into the predictors of IES and deeper understanding of the relational dissolution process. Major relational dissolution models note the importance of social processes in ending a relationship. Social media and networking sites allow for individuals to continue to actively or passively monitor their former partners, which can delay the circumscribing, avoiding, and terminating stages as described by the relational de-escalation model. Individuals' personality, emotional state, and role in the breakup lead some people to continue passively or actively monitor their ex-partners from afar, which might delay or even completely negate the ability of a partner to completely terminate the relationship. The present findings allow us to better understand how people move through the breakup process when still connected to their previous partner via technology.

Moreover, the role of negative emotion as a mediator between breakup role and IES parallels the important role of emotion during the intrapsychic phase of the breakup, which is centralized on the inner thoughts of relational partners as they try to make sense of the dissolution (Rollie and Duck 2006). When people end a relationship, they must make sense of how and why the relationship ended, and as a result, they have to reorganize their memories of the relationship (Duck and Sants 1983). A byproduct of the current research exposes how these relationship memories may be changed by technology. Continuing to monitor their previous partners can re-expose individuals to events, experiences, and/or emotions associated with the relationship.

Mere exposure, a social phenomenon, has been defined as the way people perceive people, places, and things the more they are exposed to them. Studies have shown that the more people are exposed to these targets, the more positively they will view them (Serenko and Bontis 2011; Zajonc 1968). Yet, other research indicated that exposure may lead people to recall people, places, and things more negatively (Meier and Gray 2014). Therefore, when analyzing IES, researchers and practitioners should consider how repeated exposure, or overexposure, may influence the way people positively or negatively perceive themselves and the world around them.

Future research should consider how the mere exposure to these relationship artifacts changes the dissolution model. In particular, researchers may want to examine how different levels of exposure to relationship artifacts may delay the recovery process. Researchers cannot only study the social media and networking behaviors of people undergoing the dissolution process, but they can also begin to examine how mere exposure may influence people's memories of their relationship by studying how they recall tangible and intangible artifacts. Overall, future scholarship can broaden the focus of the present study to examine how continued exposure to virtual artifacts following a breakup may influence people's memories, behaviors, and emotions, and ultimately their adjustment to the end of a relationship.

Limitations

The current studies have several limitations. For instance, findings are correlational in nature. IES behavior affects emotion and rumination, but it may be that emotion and rumination affect IES behavior. Future studies should use experimental procedures to further test the direction of the effect and casual sequence. The present studies also used a convenience sample of college students, many of whom were reporting on relationships they were in as adolescents or emerging adults. A broader sample that includes participants going through a divorce (rather than a breakup) could provide more information on how the nature of the relationship influences online and surveillance behavior. Finally, the present chapter examined surveillance within Facebook, specifically. Although it is likely that these findings can be extrapolated to other social media sites, researchers should test similar predictions in a broader set of social networking and media contexts.

CONCLUSION

This chapter had two goals. First, we explored how models of relational dissolution can be extended to understand online behavior following a breakup, further extending relational dissolution to SNS platforms. We reported the findings of two studies examining predictors of post-dissolution surveillance. We extended these relational dissolution models to showcase how technology may reshape how people behave when experiencing the end of a relationship, given the ability to continue to observe previous partners post-breakup.

Moreover, this chapter captures information about how personality and relational factors—such as whether an individual was the breakup initiator—may use technology differently. The results reveal how these behaviors influence relationship processes and influence how people internalize and recreate perceptions of relational events, such as breakups. Thus, our studies call attention to the broad consequences of technology use related to how people create and process memories. The studies reported in this chapter explore how SNS affect people's behaviors during the end of a relationship. Overall, this chapter explains how relational, emotional, and personality factors predict the extent to which people engage in IES, and reveals how traditional relationship models can be extended to better understand the impact of SNS on romantic relationships.

REFERENCES

Aronson Elliot, Timothy D. Wilson, and Robin M. Akert. 2005. *Social Psychology*, 5th ed. Upper Saddle River, NJ: Prentice Hall.

Correa, Teresa, Amber W. Hinsley, and Homero Gil de Zúñiga. 2010. "Who Interacts on the Web?: The Intersection of Users' Personality and Social Media Use." *Computers in Human Behavior* 26 (2): 247–53. http://dx.doi.org/10.1016/j.chb.2009.09.003.

Davis, Keith E., April Ace, and Michelle Andra. 2000. "Stalking Perpetrators and Psychological Maltreatment of Partners: Anger-Jealousy, Attachment Insecurity, Need For Control, and Break-up Context." *Violence and Victims* 15 (4): 407–25.

Davis, Deborah, Phillip R. Shaver, and Michael L. Vernon. 2003. "Physical, Emotional, and Behavioral Reactions to Breaking Up: The Roles of Gender, Age, Emotional Involvement, and Attachment Style." *Personality and Social Psychology Bulletin* 29 (7): 871–84. doi:10.1177/0146167203029007006.

Doering, Jan. 2010. "Face, Accounts, and Schemes in the Context of Relationship Breakups." *Symbolic Interaction* 33 (1): 71–95. doi:10.1525/si.2010.33.1.71.

Duck, Steve D. 1982. "A Topography of Relationship Disengagement and Dissolution." In *Personal Relationship: Vol. 4. Dissolving Personal Relationships*, 1–30. Vol. 4. London: Academic Press.

Duck, Steve W., and Harriet Sants. 1983. "On the Origin of the Specious: Are Personal Relationships Really Interpersonal States?" *Journal of Social and Clinical Psychology* 1: 27–41. doi:10.1521/jscp.1983.1.1.27.

Duggan, Maeve, and Aaron Smith. 2013. "Social Media Update 2013." *Pew Research Center*. Accessed August 5, 2016. http://www.pewinternet.org/files/2014/01/Social_Networking_2013.pdf.

Eftekhar, Aazr, Chris Fullwood, and Neil Morris. 2014. "Capturing Personality from Facebook Photos and Photo-Related Activities: How Much Exposure Do You Need?" *Computers in Human Behavior* 37: 162–70. http://dx.doi.org/10.1016/j.chb.2014.04.048.

Ehrenberg, Alexandra, Suzanna Juckes, Katherine M. White, and Shari P. Walsh. 2008. "Personality and self-esteem as predictors of young people's technology use." *Cyberpsychology & Behavior* 11, no. 6 (2008): 739–41. doi:10.1089/cpb.2008.0030.

Ellison, Nicole, Charles Steinfield, and Cliff Lampe. 2007. "The Benefits of Facebook 'Friends': Social Capital and College Students' Use of Online Social Networks Sites." *Journal of Computer-Mediated Communication* 12: 1143–68. doi:10.1111/j.1083-6101.2007.00367.x.

Fox, Jesse, and Jennifer J. Moreland. 2015. "The Dark Side of Social Networking Sites: An Exploration of the Relational and Psychological Stressors Associated with Facebook Use and Affordances." *Computers in Human Behavior* 45: 168–76. doi:10.1016/j.chb.2014.11.083.

Fox, Jesse, and Katie M. Warber. 2013. "Romantic Relationship Development in the Age of Facebook: An Exploratory Study of Emerging Adults' Perceptions, Motives, and Behaviors." *Cyberpsychology, Behavior, and Social Networking* 16: 3–7. doi:10.1089/cyber.2012.0288.

Fox, Jesse, Katie. M. Warber, and Dana. C. Makstaller. 2013. "The Role of Facebook in Romantic Relationship Development: An Exploration of Knapp's Relational Stage Model." *Journal of Social and Personal Relationships* 30: 771–94. doi:10.1177/0265407512468370.

Guerrero, Laura K., and Peter A. Anderson. 2001. "Emotion in Close Relationships," in *Close Relationships: A Sourcebook*, ed. Clyde A. Hendrick, Susan S. Hendrick, 171–83. Thousand Oaks, CA: Sage.

Gosling, Samuel D., Peter J. Rentfrow, and William B. Swann. 2003. "A Very Brief Measure of the Big-Five Personality Domains." *Journal of Research in Personality* 37: 504–28. doi:10.1016/S0092-6566(03)00046-1.

Hamburger, Yair Amichai, and Elisheva Ben-Artzi. 2000. "The Relationship Between Extraversion and Neuroticism and the Different Uses of the Internet." *Computers in Human Behavior* 16: 441–49. doi:10.1016/S0747-5632(00)00017-0.

Kamphuis, Jan H., Paul M. Emmelkamp, and Vivian de Vries. 2004. "Informant Personality Descriptions of Postintimate Stalkers Using the Five Factor Profile." *Journal of Personality Assessment* 82: 169–78. http://dx.doi.org/10.1207/s15327752jpa8202_5.

Kendler, Kenneth S., John M. Hettema, Frank Butera, Charles O. Gardner, and Carol A. Prescott. 2003. "Life Event Dimensions of Loss, Humiliation, Entrapment, and Danger in the Prediction of Onsets of Major Depression and Generalized Anxiety." *Archives of General Psychiatry* 60: 789. doi:10.1001/archpsyc.60.8.789.

Knapp, Mark L. 1978. *Social intercourse: From greeting to goodbye*. Boston: Allyn & Bacon.

Knapp, Mark L., and Anita L. Vangelisti. 2010. *Interpersonal Communication and Human Relationships*. Vol. 6. Boston: Pearson.

Knox, David, M. Zusman, and W. Nieves. 1998. "What I Did for Love: Risky Behavior of College Students in Love." *College Student Journal* 32: 203–5.

Lampe, Cliff, Nicole Ellison, and Charles Steinfield. 2006. "A Face (book) in the Crowd: Social Searching vs. Social Browsing." In *Proceedings of the 2006 20th Anniversary Conference on Computer Supported Cooperative Work*, 167–70. ACM.

LeFebvre, Leah, Kate Blackburn, and Nicholas Brody. 2014. "Navigating Romantic Relationships on Facebook: Extending the Relationship Dissolution Model to Social Networking Environments." *Journal of Social and Personal Relationships* 32: 78–98. doi:10.1177/0265407514524848.

Lukacs, Veronika, and Anabel Quan-Haase. 2015. "Romantic Breakups on Facebook: New Scales for Studying Post-Breakup Behaviors, Digital Distress, and Surveillance." *Information, Communication, and Society* 18: 492–508. doi:10.1080/1369118X.2015.1008540.

Marshall, Tara C. 2012. "Facebook Surveillance of Former Romantic Partners: Associations with Postbreakup Recovery and Personal Growth." *Cyberpsychology, Behavior, and Social Networking* 15: 521–26. doi:10.1089/cyber.2012.0125.

Marshall Tara C., Kathrine Bejanyan, Gaia Di Castro, and Ruth A. Lee. 2013. "Attachment Styles as Predictors of Facebook-Related Jealousy and Surveillance in Romantic Relationships." *Personal Relationships* 20: 1–22. doi:10.1111/j.1475-6811.2011.01393.x.

McAndrew, Francis T., and Sahil S. Shah. 2013. "Sex Differences in Jealousy over Facebook Activity." *Computers in Human Behavior* 29: 2603–6. doi:10.1016/j.chb.2013.06.030.

McCrae, Robert R., and Oliver P. John. 1992. "An Introduction to the Five-Factor Model and Its Applications." *Journal of Personality* 60: 175–215. doi:10.1016/j.chb.2009.09.003.

Meier, Evelyn, and James Gray. 2014. "Facebook Photo Activity Associated with Body Image Disturbance in Adolescent Girls." *Cyberpscyhology, Behavior, and Social Networking* 17: 199–206. doi:10.1089/cyber.2013.0305.

Meloy, J. Reid. 1996. "Stalking (Obsessional Following): A Review of Some Preliminary Studies." *Aggression and Violent Behavior* 1: 147–62.

Metts, Sandra, William R. Cupach, and Richard A. Bejlovec. 1989. "'I Love You Too Much To Ever Start Liking You': Redefining Romantic Relationships." *Journal of Social and Personal Relationships* 6: 259–74. doi:10.1177/0265407589063002.

Muise, Amy, Emily Christofides, and Serge Desmarais. 2009. "More Information Than You Ever Wanted: Does Facebook Bring Out the Green-Eyed Monster of Jealousy?" *Cyberpsychology, Behavior, and Social Networking* 12: 441–44. doi:10.1089/cpb.2008.0263.

Nolen-Hoeksema, Susan. 1998. "The Other End of the Continuum: The Costs of Rumination." *Psychological Inquiry* 9: 216–19. doi:10.1207/s15327965pli0903_5.

Oldmeadow, Julian A., Sally Quinn, and Rachel Kowert. 2013. "Attachment Style, Social Skills, and Facebook Use Amongst Adults." *Computers in Human Behavior* 29: 1142–49. doi:10.1016/j.chb.2012.10.006.

Preacher, Kristopher J., and Andrew F. Hayes. 2008. "Asymptotic and Resampling Strategies for Assessing and Comparing Indirect Effects in Multiple Mediator Models." *Behavior Research Methods* 40: 879–91. doi:10.3758/BRM.40.3.879.

Rollie, Stephanie S. and Steve W. Duck. 2006. "Divorce and Dissolution of Romantic Relationships: Stage Models and Their Limitations." In *Handbook of Divorce and Relationship Dissolution*, ed. S. W. Duck, 223–40. Mahwah, NJ: Lawrence Erlbaum Associates.

Saffrey, Colleen, and Marion Ehrenberd. 2007. "When Thinking Hurts: Attachment, Rumination, and Postrelationship Adjustment." *Personal Relationships* 14: 351–68. doi:10.1111/j.1475-6811.2007.00160.x.

Serenko, Alexander, and Nick Bontis. 2011. "What's Familiar is Excellent: The Impact of Exposure Effect on Perceived Journal Quality." *Journal of Informetrics* 5: 219–23. doi:10.1016/j.joi.2010.07.005.

Shackelford, Todd K., David M. Buss, and Kevin Bennett. 2002. "Forgiveness or Breakup: Sex Differences in Responses to a Partner's Infidelity." *Cognition & Emotion* 16: 299–307. doi:10.1080/02699930143000202.

Smith, Craig. Last modified August 29, 2016. *Facebook Statistics and Facts* (August 2016). http://expandedramblings.com/index.php/by-the-numbers-17-amazing-facebook-stats/.

Sorenson, Kelly A., Shauna. M. Russell, Daniel. J. Harkness, and John. H. Harvey. 1993. "Account-Making Confiding, and Coping with the Ending of a Close Relationship." *Journal of Social Behavior and Personality* 8: 73–86.

Sprecher, Susan. 1994. "Two Sides to the Breakup of Dating Relationships." *Personal Relationships* 1: 199–222. doi:10.1111/j.1475-6811.1994.tb00062.x.

Spitzberg, Brian H., and William R. Cupach. 2007. "The State of the Art of Stalking: Taking Stock of the Emerging Literature." *Aggression and Violent Behavior* 12: 64–86. doi:10.1016/j.avb.2006.05.001.

Spitzberg, Brian H., William. R. Cupach, Annegret F. Hannawa, and John P. Crowley. 2014. "A Preliminary Test of a Relational Goal Pursuit Theory of Obsessive Relational Intrusion and Stalking." *Studies in Communication Sciences* 14: 29–36. doi:10.1016/j.scoms.2014.03.007.

Thomas, David L., and Ed Diener. 1990. "Memory accuracy in the recall of emotions." *Journal of Personality and Social Psychology* 59: 291. doi:10.1037/0022-3514.59.2.291.

Tokunaga, Robert S. 2011. "Social Networking Site or Social Surveillance Site? Understanding the Use of Interpersonal Electronic Surveillance in Romantic Relationships." *Computers in Human Behavior* 27: 705–13. doi:10.1016/j.chb.2010.08.014.

Tokunaga, Robert S. 2015. "Interpersonal Surveillance Over Social Network Sites: Applying a Theory of Negative Relational Maintenance and the Investment Model." *Journal of Social and Personal Relationships* 33: 171–90. doi:10.1177/0265407514568749.

Tong, Stephanie. T. 2013. "Facebook Use During Relationship Termination: Uncertainty Reduction and Surveillance." *Cyberpsychology, Behavior, and Social Networking* 16: 788–93. doi:10.1089/cyber.2012.0549.

Tran, Tanya B. 2012. "Rumination and Emotional Adjustment: The Role of Social Networking Sites." University of Miami, University of Miami Scholarly Repository.

Walther, Joseph B. 1996. "Computer-Mediated Communication: Impersonal, Interpersonal, and Hyperpersonal Interaction." *Communication Research* 23: 3–43. doi:10.1177/009365096023001001.

Zajonc, Robert B. 1969. "Attitudinal Effects of Mere Exposure." *Journal of Personality and Social Psychology* 9: 1–27. doi:10.1037/h0025848.

Zhao, Xuan, Victoria Schwanda Sosik, and Dan Cosley. 2012. "It's Complicated: How Romantic Partners Use Facebook." Paper presented at the annual SIGCHI Conference on Human Factors in Computing Systems, Austin, Texas, May 5–10, 2012.

V

Conclusion

SIXTEEN

Future Directions for Swiping Right

The Impact of Technology on Modern Dating

V. Santiago Arias, Narissra M. Punyanunt-Carter, and Jason S. Wrench

The presence of computer-mediated communication technologies (CMC) has become ubiquitous (Levy 2015); for example, the population from 8 to 18 years old consumes 10.45 hours of CMC daily (Rideout, Foehr, and Roberts 2010). Interestingly, the adoption of smartphone technology has been widespread: There are more than 2,500 models of smartphones, 2 million apps, and 7 billion users; considering that the world population is around 6.8 billion, this means that there is almost one smartphone for every individual in the world (Berger 2015). Thus, derived from this widespread technological adoption, one conclusion can be certainly drawn: The boundaries between "mass" and "personal" communication scholarship are no longer tenable (Perloff 2013; Pfau 2008), because the formation of fundamental interpersonal relationships is highly mediated through technology. Indeed, one in five marriages is currently sparked online (Finkel, Eastwick, Reis, and Sprecher 2012; Sprecher 2014), and, not surprisingly, in 2012, a new online dating app exclusively available for iOS and Android smartphones devices took over the cyberdating market: Tinder.

Tinder is one of the most popular apps among people from 18 to 30 years old (Bertoni 2014; Sumter, Vandenbosch, and Ligtenberg 2017); 30 million people use Tinder, which is estimated to make more than 15 million matches daily (i.e., fourteen matches per second) among about 1.2 billion profiles (Bertoni 2014b). The rapid stampede of cyberdating in general results from a combination of online dating matching–software, pervasive access to personal computers, GPS technology, and its massive dissemination through social networks diffusion effects and mass media advertisement (Finkel et. al. 2012), which was also exponentially enhanced with the actual adoption of smartphone technology (Cecere, Corrocher, and Battaglia, 2015). In consequence, Tinder is in the eye of an academic and popular storm: For some analysts, the app has a reputation of being a hook-up app (Hoffman, 2015) because it promotes virtual affairs (*Hollywood Reporter* July 2015), whereas for others scholars: "Tinder should not be seen as merely a fun hook up without any strings attached, but as a new way for emerging adults to initiate committed romantic relationships" (Sumter et al. 2017, 67). However, before understanding media effects or deciding that this app is just a venue for romantic initiation, the characteristics of audience involvement such as motivation and selectivity should be addressed at first place (Rubin 2009). In fact, individuals are making "actual" romantic decisions in the online dating context (Sprecher 2014), and then virtual contexts should be understood as actual communication contexts (Lister et al. 2009); for example, in political communication scholarship, Bennet and Iyengar (2008) suggest the importance of recognition of individuals' subjective aspects of individuals while engaged in the CMC consumption in order to extend the understanding of experimental findings linked to actual communication conditions. Therefore, here is the relevance for this study to analyze users' expectations and motives to further the comprehension on Tinder to foresee any potential risk of future media dependency, because when needs and motives instigate narrow information-seeking strategies while using a given media outlet, this generates dependency (Rubin and Windahl 1986), which also "leads to other attitudinal or behavioral effects and feeds back to alter other relationships in the society" (Rubin 2009).

Online dating is a CMC technology to facilitate romantic initiation (Finkel et al. 2012). Finkel et al. (2012) delineate online dating functioning on the basis of its three main features: (1) access to a vast number of profiles,[1] which gives users a false perception of having more chances to succeed,[2] (2) a convenient and discreet communication channel to initiate contact, and (3) a romantic compatibility-matching algorithm to pair potential romantic candidates. Moreover, Quiroz (2013) suggests that these OD features were substantially enhanced by merging with the fast development of hand-held devices[3] and satellite app[4] technology, transforming OD into "location-based dating"[5] (Quiroz 2013). As a result, online dating's burgeoning popularity is often explained through the massive effects of social networks and increased access to technology, both of which were not available during previous computer dating or video dating (Finkel et al. 2012). The smartphone innovation with GPS technology made cyberdating very appealing.

Notwithstanding, this innovation is not "simply" an advancement of hardware modality; indeed, the type of CMC device or platform has a forceful impact on users' perceptions of the interactivity experience. Xie and Newhagen (2014) compared the effects of interface proximity in three media platforms (i.e., desktop, laptop, and hand-held devices), while participants received university emergency alerts. Findings suggest that hand-held devices (i.e., iPads and smartphones) significantly enhance more the feelings associated with these alerts (i.e., anxiety in this specific study) compared to the other type of devices; thus, it was shown that interface proximity moderates users' perceptions of the interactivity experience in a given mediated task. On top of this idea, it can be inferred that Tinder enhances the online dating experience more than other apps because of its particular exclusivity for smartphone technology; thus, the distance between users and the dating event is minimal. Certainly, it will not be surprising to infer that the decision of Tinder (as a company) to choose smartphone technology as its sole platform was purposely to intensify the online dating experience.

Although Tinder is particularly well-suited for smartphones that allows users to quickly look at pictures, most previous and other cyberdating platforms are similarly structured (Rosen, Cheever, Cummings, and Felt 2008; Finkel et al. 2012; Sprecher 2014): Users post a photograph and provide personal information and other relevant demographic information about themselves. Tantamount to the typical combination of visual and textual information of users as the main structure of online dating software configuration, the most used theoretical framework for research on this subject has been the hyperpersonal model: "[T]he hyperpersonal CMC model (Walther 1996) posits that CMC users take advantage of the interface and channel characteristics that CMC offers in a dynamic fashion in order to enhance their relational outcomes" (Walther 2007, 2540). Affordances refers to the properties of the perceived environment that provide possibilities for actions (Lu and Cheng 2013), and this concept is primordial for CMC use because the design of a given technological product should respond to the question about how that product can help users "afford" a given experience (Pucillo and Cascini 2014). For the particular case of online dating, such CMC affordances are described by Walther (1996, 2007) as follows: (a) editability lined up with malleability to transmit messages, (b) unlimited time to construct and edit those messages thereafter, and (c) physical isolation from the receiver. Therefore, these medium characteristics allow users to hide any nonverbal and verbal cues that may jeopardize relationship goals where users execute control on visual and textual information while interacting. In consequence, the overall CMC affordances instigate users to reallocate cognitive resources to message composition (Walther 2007) for managing impression behavior where, in addition to this, the physical isolation prompts anonymity and makes users experience more disinhibition while interacting

(Walther 2007; Lapidot-Lefter, and Barak 2012). In other words, "[. . .] social evaluations [. . .] are not impeded by messy hair, lack of makeup, or normal imperfections" (Walther 1996, 20), so then it is more appealing for individuals to use this technology for first impression formations.

As a direct denouement of the suitability of this model for online dating, research findings yield results on users' self-presentation and self-disclosure communication strategies in CMC interactions (e.g., Tidwell, and Walther 2002; Gibbs, Ellison, and Chi-Hui 2011; Rosen et al. 2008). Indeed, Segrin and Flora (2011) report that much of the research has focused on how impressions are managed online, especially with regard to self-disclosure, and how people vary in their use and dependence on technology for dating. Perhaps because of the high stakes involved in creating a positive impression, roughly one-third of photos on online dating profiles are rated by independent judges as "not accurate" (Hancock and Toma 2009). Women's photos are less accurate than males, either because the photo shows them at a younger age or because it has been retouched in some way. Nonetheless, on the one hand, physical attractiveness is one of the features most unclear in online dating profiles (Turner and Hunt 2014); albeit, on the other hand, it is rated as the most important aspect in online dating than the traditional "old-fashioned" face-to-face (FtF) dating (Rosen et al. 2008).

Other online dating forums rely heavily on written profiles that are often a mix of reality and an ideal presentation of oneself (Yurchisin, Watchravesringkan, and McCabe 2005), and these forums have not become as popular as Tinder did in terms of number of users and the rapidness in which it got that popular. In this study, the first messages users get from another person report that they prefer low levels of self-disclosure at first, but are drawn to descriptions and messages containing high emotion words like "exciting" and "wonderful" as opposed to less emotional words like "fine." This happens because emotion has been largely found to be a main moderator of media effects in terms of its impact on individuals' increasing attention, which also explains the persuasive nature of any given media (Nabi 2009). On the other hand, Tinder differs from other online forums by encouraging less self-disclosure before any FtF contact. Ramirez et al. (2015) investigated the association between the amount of time spent online before meeting the potential candidate in real life and the motivation to meet the person FtF. Although their investigation did not include analysis of Tinder usage, they found that the more time daters spent on the online platform, the less motivation they had to meet the other person face-to-face, because it dampened the perceptions of closeness.

While using Tinder, users primarily swipe pictures, and this mechanic for use momentarily rules out the textual element from the online dating experience. This is crucially important, because the way in which users communicate with other online daters is contingent upon the way the site is set up (Whitty 2008); in other words, interface design and boundaries play the leading role in individuals' communication behavior in CMC settings. Secondly, it seems that as more an online dating interface emulates the naturalness of users' experience of first impression formation in FTF settings, the more it gets popular.

Nonverbal research on interpersonal relationship formation indicates that physical attractiveness is what actually motivates individuals for initial approach at large (Richmond, McCroskey, and Hickson 2007), and even more for romantic initiation: The level of physical attractiveness is a better predictor for initial encounters than psychological traits (Tidwell, Eastwick, and Finkel 2012). Not surprisingly, the same pattern is present in online dating, but in an even more pronounced fashion: Whitty (2008) conducted a qualitative study to understand how individuals present themselves on an online dating site, as well as their judgments on how others present themselves on this site. Sixty online daters (e.g., thirty men and thirty women) were interviewed for this research; the findings suggested that participants consistently placed a supreme importance on posting an outstanding personal picture over any other personal characteristic. Then, she found that what really triggers contact initiation in cyberdating is individuals' attractiveness with no significant differences between genders; this is surprising nonetheless, because physical attractiveness has been found to be a larger predictor to make the decision for contact initiation more for men than women (Deyo et al. 2011).

Therefore, in a given online dating setting in which the visual aspect is the most salient aspect, where the space for negotiation of textual meanings is reduced to its minimal condition possible, such as on Tinder, then the analysis of users' expectations and motives becomes more critical because: first, the selection and use of a given media, and the communication behavior displayed in CMC context is goal-directed, purposive, and motivated (Rubin 2009), and only these elements are at hand; on top of this idea, the reduced amount of textual information does not give enough space to apply the hyperpersonal model to understand users' communication strategies, but expectation and motives instead. Additionally, structural differences, or the way in which information can be accessed and set in play an important role in users' communication behavior, as Whitty (2008) suggested earlier.

STRUCTURAL DIFFERENCES IN DIFFERENT ONLINE DATING PLATFORMS

While previous online dating sites and apps ask users to create in-depth personal profiles, Tinder has innovated online dating by providing users with a seemingly endless selection of photos of potential mates without the need to answer questionnaires or forms (Bertoni 2014c). It is inferred that the algorithm of the app links users' contacts from Facebook profiles to provide photographs of potential romantic candidates. After solely looking at photos of potential mates, users swipe right if they like a person and left if they do not (Bertoni 2014d). If both parties like each other, the platform provides a parallel interface to send messages to one another to decide whether to meet in person or exchange personal contact information.

In an attempt to understand why users immerse themselves in Tinder, Sumter and colleagues (2017) conducted a study to analyze users' motivations. Findings suggest that (a) "love" motivation was stronger than "casual sex" motivation, (b) male users showed a higher motivation for casual sex than females, (c) users engage through Tinder because of the ease of communication through this app where men feel to be more benefited, (d) in terms of self-validation there were no significant differences between genders, and (e) users who also immersed themselves in Tinder because of the thrill of excitement were those individuals with higher levels of sensation seeking use it more. This study concludes that "Tinder goes beyond the hook up culture" (74). This asseveration contests Finkel and colleagues' (2012) argument about online dating as an unable CMC platform to guarantee successful romantic partnering, since: first, online dating algorithms are based on criteria of psychological similarity, compatibility, or a combination of both, but there is no substantial empirical evidence to suggest that homophily assure successful romantic outcomes; additionally, since these algorithms are proprietary of dating companies and they do not release for academic examination, online dating services cannot be the subject of further scholarly examination (Finkel et al. 2012; Toma 2015). Therefore, it seems too early for the present study to make such a claim, and scholarly work needs to dig more into individuals' intentions encompassed in relationship expectations and communication motives to avoid conclusions that end up supporting online dating business rather than extending theory.

FUTURE DIRECTIONS

It is obvious that more work needs to be done in this area. This book provides a foundation for scholars to learn and reflect. Moreover, the information provided in this text stimulates ideas for future directions and research.

Future research will need to analyze the impact of technology on romantic relationships. What impact do online romantic relationships have on levels of satisfaction and relational outcomes? How are perceptions different depending on age, race, gender, and other demographic variables? In addition, how do different people use technology to find romance? Why would someone use technology to find romantic relationships?

As mentioned earlier, the analysis of Tinder on this matter is important due to its specific differences in software configuration (i.e., swiping faces) and platform exclusivity (i.e., smartphones) compared to other online dating services. Tinder is noted for prompting a quick progression to face-to-face interaction. Tinder avoids in-depth written profiles; photos appear to be especially crucial. Tinder's interface architecture and its modus operandi perhaps suits better to human perception of forming impressions based on physical appearance assessment (Arias and Punyanunt-Carter 2016). And, being as emotions the driving force for humans to adapt to situational conditions that are externalized as intentions, an examination of the relationship expectations and communication motives along with the communication nature of online dating is paramount. Thus, future research should look at specific platform uses and configurations on romantic relationship attraction, development, and expectations. Why is Tinder so successful and so popular? What other dating apps are comparable? What can improve the online dating experience?

It would be interesting to see how technology affects our interpersonal communication and how it differs from our online communication. Several suitors may be successful in face-to-face interactions, but they may not be successful in online interactions. What characteristics make a person competent in online dating and romantic relationship development? What characteristics make a person effective in online dating situations? Further, how do scholars define *competent* and *effective* in this particular situation? Are there any cultural factors that come into play?

All in all, there is still more research that needs to be conducted in this area. Several scholars have started the process in understanding theories and behaviors in online dating situations. However, as we have seen, these trends have changed over time, and technology is constantly changing to meet the needs and desires of its users. Throughout this book, we have tried to provide a basic understanding of the different aspects of online dating and romantic relationship development. We hope that you will hopefully "swipe right" to the opportunities that lie before you in the future.

NOTES

1. This false impression refers to the endowed progress effect (see Nunez and Dreze, 2006), which refers to when individuals are provided with artificial advancement to perform a given task, the task is reframed in a way such that goal completion is redirected to persistence, giving a false perception of completion.

2. In addition, the decision field theory shows that as the number of choices increases, the quality of decisions decreases (see, for a review, Jessup, Veinott, Todd, and Busemeyer, 2009).

3. *Hand-held devices* refers to any kind of electronic communication devices that can be used anywhere at any time, such as tablets, smartphones, androids, etc. (Xie and Newhagen, 2014).

4. The term *app* is shorthand for "application"; apps constitute software that can be run on any electronic device, which also may include GPS technology (Quiroz, 2013).

5. Thus, in addition to the three main features, the new version of online dating provides potential candidates' profiles to users on the basis of users' location and proximity convenience.

REFERENCES

Aida, Yukie. 1993. "Communication Apprehension and Power Strategies in Marital Relationships." *Communication Reports* 6: 116–11.

Adler, Ronald B., Lawrence B. Rosenfeld, and Russel F. Proctor II. 2015. *Interplay: The Process of Interpersonal Communication,* 13th ed. New York: Oxford Press.

Anderson, Traci L., and Tara M. Emmers-Sommer. 2006. "Predictors of Relationship Satisfaction in Online Romantic Relationships." *Communication Studies* 57, no. 2: 153–72.

Baker, Alan L., and Joe Ayres. 1994. "The Effect of Apprehensive Behavior on Communication Apprehension and Interpersonal Attraction." *Communication Research Reports* 11, no. 1: 45–51.

Aydm, Betül, and Serkan Volkan San. 2011 "Internet Addiction among Adolescents: The Role of Self-Esteem." *Procedia-Social and Behavioral Sciences* 1: 3500–3505.

Bandura, Albert. 2001. "Social Cognitive Theory: An Agentic Perspective." *Annual Review of Psychology* 52, no. 1: 1–26.

Baxter, Holly. "Tinder is the Dating App with Many Matches but no Spark." *NewStateman,* retrieved from http://www.newstatesman.com/society/2013/11/many-matches-no-spark EBSCO*host* (accessed December 1, 2016).

Bercovici, Jeff. 2014. "No, Tinder Is Not Worth $5 Billion." *Forbes.Com*, April 11.

Berscheid, Ellen, William Graziano, Thomas Monson, and Marshall Dermer. 1976. "Outcome Dependency: Attention, Attribution, and Attraction." *Journal of Personality and Social Psychology* 34, no. 5: 978.

Bertoni, Steven. 2014. "Sex, Lies and iPhone." *Forbes* 194, no. 7: 112–22, November 14.

———. 2015. "Tinder CEO Sean Rad: From Boss, Booted, And Back." *Forbes.com*, October 9. *Business Source Complete*, EBSCO*host* (accessed December 1, 2016).

———. 2014. "Tinder Swipes Right to Revenue, Will Add Premium Service in November." *Forbes.com*: 27, October 20. *Business Source Complete*, EBSCO*host* (accessed December 1, 2016).

Borrajo, E., M. Gámez-Guadix, and E. Calvete. 2015. "Cyber Dating Abuse: Prevalence, Context, and Relationship with Offline Dating Aggression." *Psychological reports* 116, no. 2: 565–85.

Brennen, Bonnie. 2012. *Qualitative research methods for media studies*. New York: Routledge.

Bucy, Erik P. 2004. "Interactivity in Society: Locating an Elusive Concept." *The Information Society* 20, no. 5: 373–83.

Buss, David M., and David P. Schmitt. 1993. "Sexual Strategies Theory: An Evolutionary Perspective on Human Mating." *Psychological Review* 100, no. 2: 204–32.

Byrne, Donn, Charles R. Ervin, and John Lamberth. 1970. "Continuity Between the Experimental Study of Attraction and Real-Life Computer Dating." *Journal of Personality and Social Psychology* 16, no. 1: 157–65.

Campbell, Scott W. 2015. "Mobile Communication and Network Privatism: A Literature Review of the Implications for Diverse, Weak, and New Ties." *Review of Communication Research* 3, no. 1: 1–21.

Carroll, Jason S., Brian Willoughby, Sarah Badger, Larry J. Nelson, Carolyn McNamara Barry, and Stephanie D. Madsen. 2007. "So Close, Yet So Far Away: The Impact of Varying Marital Horizons on Emerging Adulthood." *Journal of Adolescent Research* 22, no. 3: 219–47.

Carstensen, Laura L. 1993. "Motivation for Social Contact Across the Life Span: A Theory of Socioemotional Selectivity." In *Nebraska Symposium on Motivation*, vol. 40, 209–54.

Carstensen, Laura L. 1995. "Evidence for a Life-Span Theory of Socioemotional Selectivity." *Current Directions in Psychological Science* 4, no. 5: 151–56.

Cherlin, Andrew J. 2010. "Demographic Trends in the United States: A Review of Research in the 2000s." *Journal of Marriage and Family* 72, no. 3: 403–19.

Clemens, Chris, David Atkin, and Archana Krishnan. 2015. "The Influence of Biological and Personality Traits on Gratifications Obtained Through Online Dating Websites." *Computers in Human Behavior* 49: 120–29.

Crandall, Beth, Gary A. Klein, and Robert R. Hoffman. 2006. *Working Minds: A Practitioner's Guide to Cognitive Task Analysis*. Cambridge, MA: MIT Press.

Cohen, Jacob. 1992. "A Power Primer." *Psychological Bulletin* 112, no. 1: 155.

Douglas, William. 1991. "Expectations About Initial Interaction: An Examination of the Effects of Global Uncertainty." *Human Communication Research* 17, no. 3: 355–84.

Duhachek, Adam, Shuoyang Zhang, and Shanker Krishnan. 2007. "Anticipated Group Interaction: Coping with Valence Asymmetries in Attitude Shift." *Journal of Consumer Research* 34, no. 3: 395–405.

Dutton, Donald G., and Arthur P. Aron. 1974. "Some Evidence for Heightened Sexual Attraction Under Conditions of High Anxiety." *Journal of Personality and Social Psychology* 30, no. 4: 510–17.

Eastwick, Paul W., and Lucy L. Hunt. 2014. "Relational mate value: Consensus and uniqueness in romantic evaluations." *Journal of Personality and Social Psychology* 106, no. 5: 728–51. doi: 10.1037/a0035884.

Finkel, Eli J., Paul W. Eastwick, Benjamin R. Karney, Harry T. Reis, and Susan Sprecher. 2012. "Online Dating: A Critical Analysis from the Perspective of Psychological Science." *Psychological Science in the Public Interest* 13, no. 1: 3–66.

Gaertner, Samuel L., Mary C. Rust, John F. Dovidio, Betty A. Bachman, and Phyllis A. Anastasio (1996). "The Contact Hypothesis: The Role of a Common Ingroup Identity on Reducing Intergroup Bias Among Majority and Minority Group Members." In *What's social about social cognition? Research on Socially Shared Cognition in Small Groups*, ed. Judith L. Nye and Aaron M. Brower, 230–360. Newbury Park, CA: Sage.

Gaver, William W. 1991. "Technology affordances." In *Proceedings of the SIGCHI conference on Human factors in computing systems*, 79–84.

Gerlich, R. Nicholas, Kristina Drumheller, and Jeffry Babb. 2015. "App Consumption: An Exploratory Analysis of the Uses & Gratifications of Mobile Apps." *Academy of Marketing Studies Journal* 19, no. 1: 69–79.

Gibbs, Jennifer L., Nicole B. Ellison, and Rebecca D. Heino. 2006. "Self-Presentation in Online Personals: The Role of Anticipated Future Interaction, Self-Disclosure, and Perceived Success in Internet Dating." *Communication Research* 33, no. 2: 152–77.

Guadagno, Rosanna E., Bradley M. Okdie, and Sara A. Kruse. 2012. "Dating Deception: Gender, Online Dating, and Exaggerated Self-Presentation." *Computers in Human Behavior* 28, no. 2: 642–47.

Hancock, Jeffrey T., and Catalina L. Toma. 2009. "Putting Your Best Face Forward: The Accuracy of Online Dating Photographs." *Journal of Communication* 59, no. 2: 367–86.

Heeter, Carrie. 2000. "Interactivity in the Context of Designed Experiences." *Journal of Interactive Advertising* 1, no. 1: 3–14.

Hefner, Veronica, and Julie Kahn. 2014. "An Experiment Investigating the Links Among Online Dating Profile Attractiveness, Ideal Endorsement, and Romantic Media." *Computers in Human Behavior* 37: 9–17.

Heino, Rebecca D., Nicole B. Ellison, and Jennifer L. Gibbs. 2010. "Relation-Shopping: Investigating the Market Metaphor in Online Dating." *Journal of Social and Personal Relationships* 27, no. 4: 427–47.

High, Andrew C., and Scott E. Caplan. 2009. "Social Anxiety and Computer-Mediated Communication During Initial Interactions: Implications for the Hyperpersonal Perspective." *Computers in Human Behavior* 25, no. 2: 475–82.

Hoffman, D. (2015). "How Old People Took Over Tinder." HuffPostStyle.com. Retrieved from http://www.huffingtonpost.com/damona-hoffman/how-old-people-took-over-tinder_b_6626524.html.

Hunt, Lucy L., Paul W. Eastwick, and Eli J. Finkel. 2015. "Leveling the Playing Field: Longer Acquaintance Predicts Reduced Assortative Mating on Attractiveness." *Psychological Science.* doi: 10.1177/0956797615579273.

Jessup, Ryan K., Elizabeth S. Veinott, Peter M. Todd, and Jerome R. Busemeyer. 2009. "Leaving the Store Empty-Handed: Testing Explanations for the Too-Much-Choice Effect Using Decision Field Theory." *Psychology & Marketing* 26, no. 3: 299–320.

Kang, Tanya, and Lindsay H. Hoffman. 2011. "Why Would You Decide to Use an Online Dating Site? Factors That Lead to Online Dating." *Communication Research Reports* 28, no. 3: 205–13.

Kotlyar, Igor, and Dan Ariely. 2013. "The Effect of Nonverbal Cues on Relationship Formation." *Computers in Human Behavior* 29, no. 3: 544–51.

Levy, Karen E. C. 2015. "Intimate Surveillance." *Idaho Law Review* 51, no. 3: 679–93.

Lo, Shao-Kang, Ai-Yun Hsieh, and Yu-Ping Chiu. 2013. "Contradictory Deceptive Behavior in Online Dating." *Computers in Human Behavior* 29, no. 4: 1755–62.

Loveless, Miles, William G. Powers, and William Jordan. 2008. "Dating Partner Communication Apprehension, Self-Disclosure, And the First Big Fight." *Human Communication* 11, no. 2: 231–39.

Nunes, Joseph C., and Xavier Drèze. 2006. "The Endowed Progress Effect: How Artificial Advancement Increases Effort." *Journal of Consumer Research* 32, no. 4: 504–12.

Quiroz, Pamela Anne. 2013. "From Finding the Perfect Love Online to Satellite Dating and 'Loving-the-One-You're Near': A Look at Grindr, Skout, Plenty of Fish, Meet Moi, Zoosk and Assisted Serendipity." *Humanity & Society* 37, no. 2: 181–85. doi: 10.1177/0160597613481727.

Ramirez, Artemio, Christina Fleuriet, and Megan Cole. 2015. "When Online Dating Partners Meet Offline: The Effect of Modality Switching on Relational Communication Between Online Daters." *Journal of Computer-Mediated Communication* 20, no. 1: 99–114.

Riggio, Heidi R., Dana A. Weiser, Ann Marie Valenzuela, P. Priscilla Lui, Roberto Montes, and Julie Heuer. 2013. "Self-Efficacy in Romantic Relationships: Prediction of Relationship Attitudes and Outcomes." *The Journal of Social Psychology* 153, no. 6: 629–50.

Rosen, Larry D., Nancy A. Cheever, Cheyenne Cummings, and Julie Felt. 2008. "The Impact of Emotionality and Self-Disclosure on Online Dating Versus Traditional Dating." *Computers in Human Behavior* 24, no. 5: 2124–57.

Sassler, Sharon. 2010. "Partnering across the life course: Sex, relationships, and mate selection." *Journal of Marriage and Family* 72, no. 3: 557–75. doi: 10.1111/j.1741-3737.2010.00718.x.

Speilberger, Charles D. 1966. *Anxiety and Behavior.* New York. Academic Press.

Stephure, Robert J., Susan D. Boon, Stacey L. MacKinnon, and Vicki L. Deveau. 2009. "Internet Initiated Relationships: Associations Between Age and Involvement in Online Dating." *Journal of Computer-Mediated Communication* 14, no. 3: 658–81.

Stevens, Sarah B., and Tracy L. Morris. 2007. "College Dating and Social Anxiety: Using the Internet as a Means of Connecting to Others." *CyberPsychology & Behavior* 10, no. 5: 680–88.

Thornton, Arland, and Linda Young-DeMarco. 2001. "Four Decades of Trends in Attitudes Toward Family Issues in the United States: The 1960s Through the 1990s." *Journal of Marriage and Family* 63, no. 4: 1009–37.

Tidwell, Natasha D., Paul W. Eastwick, and Eli J. Finkel. 2013. "Perceived, Not Actual, Similarity Predicts Initial Attraction in a Live Romantic Context: Evidence from the Speed-Dating Paradigm." *Personal Relationships* 20, no. 2: 199–215.

Turner, Mark, and Natalie Hunt. 2014. "What Does Your Profile Picture Say About You? The Accuracy of Thin-Slice Personality Judgments from Social Networking Sites Made at Zero-Acquaintance." In *International Conference on Social Computing and Social Media*, 506–16. New York: Springer International Publishing.

Uecker, Jeremy E. 2008. "Religion, Pledging, and the Premarital Sexual Behavior of Married Young Adults." *Journal of Marriage and Family* 70, no. 3: 728–44.

Walther, Joseph B. 2007. "Selective Self-Presentation in Computer-Mediated Communication: Hyperpersonal Dimensions of Technology, Language, and Cognition." *Computers in Human Behavior* 23, no. 5: 2538–57.

Whitty, Monica T. 2008. "Revealing the 'Real' Me, Searching for the 'Actual' You: Presentations of Self on an Internet Dating Site." *Computers in Human Behavior* 24, no. 4: 1707–23.

Yurchisin, Jennifer, Kittichai Watchravesringkan, and Deborah Brown McCabe. 2005. "An Exploration of Identity Re-Creation in the Context of Internet Dating." *Social Behavior and Personality* 33, no. 8: 735–50.

Zhang, S. and S. Krishnan. 2007. "Anticipated Group Interaction: Coping with Valence Asymmetries in Attitude Shift." *Journal of Consumer Research* 34: 395–405. doi: 0093-5301/2007/3403-0013.

Index

About the Editors and Contributors

V. Santiago Arias is a doctorate student of the PhD program in Media & Communication at Texas Tech University. In his first semester, he afforded to publish two scholarly articles. He usually teaches courses of Spanish as a second language, business and professional communication, and interpersonal communication and CMC. His research interests focus on interactivity and online dating, Hispanic media, and agenda setting. His work has been published in *Communication Research Trends* and *Communication Education*.

Megan Bassick is a PhD student and director of graduate teaching assistants for an introductory communication course at the University of Oklahoma. She regularly teaches courses on introductory communication, public speaking, and interpersonal communication. Her research interests include the dark side of intimate relationships, rumors, serial arguments, long-distance relationships, friends with benefits, dissolution of intimate relationships, and the use of communication technologies in intimate relationships. She has co-authored a book chapter in *Contexts of the Dark Side of Communication* and a journal article in the *Electronic Journal of Communication*.

Jennifer L. Bevan (PhD, University of Georgia, 2003) is a professor in the School of Communication and director of the Health and Strategic Communication MS program at Chapman University in Orange, California. Her research and teaching interests center upon interpersonal and health communication within close relationships. Dr. Bevan's publications include over fifty peer-reviewed or invited scholarly articles and book chapters appearing in such journals as *Human Communication Research*, *Communication Research*, *Communication Monographs*, and *Computers in Human Behavior*. Her first book, *The Communication of Jealousy*, was honored with multiple national and international awards, including the National Communication Association's 2014 Diamond Anniversary Book Award and the International Association for Relationship Research's 2016 Book Award.

Kate G. Blackburn (PhD, University of Texas at Austin) is an Oak Ridge Institute for Science and Education Post-Doctoral Fellow in the Department of Psychology at the University of Texas at Austin. Inspired by word-counting analytical methods, she uses computerized text analysis software on large quantities of online data to explore the perceptual and behavioral processes of language use reflected in people's stories and social interactions. Some of her research has examined language use in breakup stories, food themes communicated within online communities, relational behaviors on social networking sites, and deceptive health messages related to absenteeism. This research appears in the *Journal of Social and Personal Relationships*, the *Journal of Language and Social Psychology*, and *Health Communication*.

Derek R. Blackwell (PhD, University of Pennsylvania, 2014) is an assistant professor in the Department of Languages and Communication at Prairie View A&M University. He teaches courses on media literacy, media industries and professions, and digital media. His research focuses on the impact of new digital tools on romantic relationships, with topics ranging from the design of online dating sites, to the role of social networking sites in romantic relationships, to the ways new technologies complicate understandings of infidelity. Dr. Blackwell's work has been published in *Social Sciences*, the *Journal of Communications Media Studies*, and *Digital Media 2: Transformations in Human Communication*.

Eryn Bostwick (MA, University of Oklahoma) is a PhD student in the Department of Communication at the University of Oklahoma. Her research interests include family communication, relational conflict, and the intersection of media and relationships.

Nicholas Brody (PhD, University of Texas at Austin) is an assistant professor of communication studies at the University of Puget Sound. His research explores the interplay of mediated communication and personal relationships, and he teaches classes in online communication, communication theory, quantitative research methods, and relational communication. His recent research has examined bystander intevention during cyberbullying incidents, relational maintenance via text messaging, social networking site use during breakups, language use in breakup accounts, and communication in on-again/off-again relationships. This research appears in *Communication Monographs*, the *Journal of Social and Personal Relationships*, the *Journal of Language and Social Psychology*, *Personal Relationships*, *Computers in Human Behavior*, and *Social Media + Society*.

John P. Caughlin (PhD, University of Texas at Austin, 1997) is a professor in the Department of Communication at the University of Illinois. He studies communication in families and other close relationships, including the interconnections between online and offline communication. He has published more than sixty-five articles or chapters in outlets including *Human Communication Research, Communication Monographs*, and *Journal of Social and Personal Relationships*. He is a fellow of the International Association for Relationship Research and has received the Bernard

Brommel Award for Outstanding Scholarship or Distinguished Service in Family Communication from the National Communication Association.

Gina Masullo Chen (PhD, Syracuse University, 2012) is an assistant professor in the school of journalism at the University of Texas at Austin. She spent twenty years as a newspaper reporter and editor before becoming an academic. She teaches courses in journalism skills and in gender as it relates to news. Her research focuses on online conversations on social media platforms, and she has a particular interest in both uncivil debate and how gender intersects in this process. She is co-editor of *Scandal in a Digital Age* (2016/Palgrave Macmillan) and author of *Online Incivility & Public Debate: Nasty Talk* (forthcoming in 2017/Palgrave Macmillan). Her research has been published in academic journals, including *Communication Research, Computers in Human Behavior, Mass Communication and Society, Journalism Practice,* and *New Media & Society.*

Jonathan D. D'Angelo is a PhD candidate in the Department of Communication Arts at the University of Wisconsin–Madison. His research focuses on the social and psychological impact of communication technologies with a focus on health and relational outcomes. He holds an MA in communication from Ohio State University and a MAEd from the University of Michigan.

Jayson L. Dibble (PhD, Michigan State University, 2008) is an associate professor in the department of communication at Hope College. He regularly teaches courses on interpersonal communication, communication and relationships, and persuasion. His research specialties include interpersonal communication, personal relationships, non-traditional dating and sex relationships, breaking bad news, persuasion, and social scientific research methods. Dr. Dibble has authored or co-authored several journal articles and book chapters on these topics, and his work has been published in *Human Communication Research, Communication Research, Computers in Human Behavior,* and *Psychological Assessment.*

Jesse Fox (PhD, Stanford University) is an assistant professor in the School of Communication at Ohio State University and director of the Virtual Environment, Communication Technology, and Online Research (VECTOR) Lab. Her research interests include technologically mediated communication in relationships, experiences of women and LGBTQ+ individuals online, and persuasive virtual environments, particularly in the contexts of health and environmental communication. Her work has appeared in journals including *Journal of Communication, Communication Research, New Media & Society, Media Psychology, Journal of Computer-Mediated Communication,* and *Human-Computer Interaction.* You can see more of her work at her website, http://commfox.org.

Jessica Frampton (MA, Clemson University, 2015) is a PhD student in the School of Communication at Ohio State University. Her primary research interest concerns the media's role in threat perception and information management, particularly in the context of romantic relationships.

Jennifer Huemmer is a doctoral candidate at Texas Tech University. Her research examines media as a process of meaning construction that is interpreted, negotiated, and resisted through the actions and interactions of individuals and communities. Specifically, she investigates these processes as they occur at the intersection of gender and religious identities.

Amy Janan Johnson (PhD, Michigan State University, 1999) is a professor in the Department of Communication at the University of Oklahoma. She teaches classes in the areas of interpersonal communication, family communication, conflict, and statistics. Her research focuses on long-distance relationships, friendships, stepfamilies, and interpersonal argument. She has published in such venues as *Communication Monographs*, *Communication Yearbook*, *Journal of Computer-Mediated Communication*, and *Journal of Social and Personal Relationships*.

Brianna L. Lane (PhD, University of Oklahoma, 2015) is an assistant professor in the Department of Communication at Christopher Newport University. Her research and teaching interests include interpersonal communication within electronically mediated contexts. Her main line of research examines impression formation from online identity claims. Additionally, Dr. Lane has conducted research regarding social support on social networking sites and the effects of cell phone use in romantic relationships. She has also worked on a research team that created a video game designed to reduce intelligence analysts' reliance on cognitive biases. Dr. Lane teaches courses in interpersonal communication, communication and technology, advanced relational communication, and research methods.

Leah E. LeFebvre (PhD, University of Texas at Austin, 2014) is an assistant professor in the Department of Communication & Journalism at the University of Wyoming, where she teaches courses in interpersonal and relational communication, communication technology, communication theory, and research methodology. Her research focuses on romantic relationships and emerging technologies, or the interplay of communication, technology, and healthy behavior. She also explores meaning-making through narration and storytelling processes that inform, reinforce, and reshape relationships during initiation, conflict, and dissolution. Her research appears in such major journals as: *The Journal of Social and Personal Relationships*, *Communication Monographs*, *Social Media + Society*, *Journal of Applied Communication Research*, *Health Communication*, *Communication Education*, *The Journal of Language and Social Psychology*, and *Cyberpsychology, Behavior, and Social Networking*.

Hinda Mandell, PhD, is an assistant professor in the School of Communication at RIT in New York. She is the co-editor of the book *Scandal in a Digital Age* (Palgrave Macmillan, 2016), and the author of the forthcoming book, *Sex Scandals, Gender, and Power in Contemporary American Politics* (Praeger). She researches news coverage of scandals, and her essays on the topic have appeared in the *Los Angeles Times, Chicago Tribune, USA Today, Boston Herald, Palm Beach Post, Politico*, and in academic journals, including *Women's Studies in Communication, Visual Communication Quarterly*, and *Explorations in Media Ecology*. Mandell is a regular contributor to Cognoscenti, the commentary site for Boston's NPR station, and a contributor to the *Huffington Post*. Her website is omghinda.com, and she's on Twitter: @hindamandell

Terri Manley (MA, California State University, Fullerton, 2012) is currently pursuing a PhD at Texas Tech University, with an expected graduation date of May 2018. Terri teaches within the public relations college and regularly teaches courses on digital and social media, public relations strategies, and writing. She studies media and communication with a specialty in strategic communication, posing questions about new media, culture, and motivations. Her six years' public relations field experience helps inform her research within the strategic communication field, and it continues to strengthen her research questions and agenda. Terri is specifically interested in the impact of new media branding efforts on culture and motivations for using new media. Currently, Terri is examining dating applications and individual experiences as influenced by cultural beliefs and values.

Paromita Pain is a doctoral candidate in journalism at the University of Texas at Austin, expecting to graduate in August 2017. Her research focuses on alternate media, diversity studies, and global journalism practices. Her doctoral dissertation aims to extend the theoretical applications of citizen journalism, agenda setting, and development communication by triangulating both qualitative and quantitative methods. Her research has been published in refereed journals like the *Journalism and Mass Communication Educator, Journalism Studies, Journalism Practice and Media Asia*. She has published various book chapters on the intersection of gender and social media besides looking into areas of online commenting and uncivil behavior and its impact on journalistic practices. Besides presenting over twenty-five papers at annual ICA, AEJMC, ISOJ, and IAMCR conferences, she has won awards as well.

Cameron W. Piercy (MA, University of Oklahoma, 2011) is an assistant professor in the Department of Management at the University of Central Missouri. He teaches courses in business/organizational communication and computer-mediated communication. His research focuses on organizational communication, network dynamics, and computer-mediated communication. His research has been published in *Computers in Human Behavior, Communication Research,* and in the *Proceedings of Lecture Notes in Computer Science.*

Narissra M. Punyanunt-Carter (PhD, Kent State University) is an associate professor of communication studies at Texas Tech University in Lubbock, Texas. She teaches the basic interpersonal communication course. Her research areas include mass media effects, father-daughter communication, mentoring, advisor-advisee relationships, family studies, religious communication, humor, and interpersonal communication. She has published over forty articles that have appeared in several peer-reviewed journals, such as *Communication Research Reports, Southern Journal of Communication,* and *Journal of Intercultural Communication Research.* She has published numerous instructional ancillaries and materials. She is also a coauthor of *Organizational Communication: Theory, Research, and Practice* (2014, Flat World Knowledge).

Dr. Nathian Shae Rodriguez specializes in critical-cultural and digital media studies. He grew up in Balmorhea, Texas, and was valedictorian of his graduating class. He attended the University of Texas of the Permian Basin, where he received a BA in mass communication. He went on to receive a masters of journalism and mass communication with a concentration in public relations from Kent State University and a PhD from Texas Tech University. His research focuses on minority representation in media, specifically LGBTQ and Latinx portrayals and identity negotiation, as well as pop culture, identity, radio broadcasting, and issues of masculinity. He has ten years or professional radio experience as on-air talent, sales, promotions, and social media marketing.

Liesel Sharabi (PhD, University of Illinois at Urbana-Champaign, 2015) is an assistant professor in the Department of Communication Studies at West Virginia University. Much of her research explores how communication technologies are used in interpersonal relationships. She primarily teaches courses in interpersonal communication, computer-mediated communication, and communication research methods. Her work has appeared in edited volumes and peer-reviewed journals, such as *Communication Monographs, Journal of Communication, Journal of Social and Personal Relationships,* and *Personal Relationships.*

Hua Su (PhD, University of Iowa, 2015) is an assistant professor in the Department of Journalism and Communication at Beijing Language and Culture University, China. She regularly teaches courses in media and civilization, intercultural communication, and social media and networked communication. Her research specialties include mediated relationships, media history, and intercultural communication. Dr. Su has recently published journal articles on romantic relationships and their connections with old and new media in *Media, Culture & Society* and *Interactions*.

Catalina L. Toma is an associate professor in the Department of Communication Arts at the University of Wisconsin–Madison. Her research examines how people understand and relate to one another when interacting through new communication technologies. She focuses on how relational processes such as self-presentation, impression formation, deception, trust, and emotional well-being are shaped by the affordances and limitations of computer-mediated environments.

Jason S. Wrench (EdD, West Virginia University) is an associate professor and chair of the Communication Department at the State University of New York at New Paltz. Dr. Wrench specializes in workplace learning and performance, or the intersection of instructional communication and organizational communication. His varied research interests include workplace learning and human performance improvement, computer-mediated communication, empirical research methods, family communication, humor, risk/crisis communication, and supervisor-subordinate interactions. Dr. Wrench regularly consults with individuals and organizations on workplace communication and as a professional speech coach for senior executives. Dr. Wrench has published numerous books on a variety of communication topics: *Intercultural Communication: Power in Context, Communication, Affect, and Learning in the Classroom* (2000, Tapestry Press), *Principles of Public Speaking* (2003, The College Network), *Human Communication in Everyday Life: Explanations and Applications* (2008, Allyn & Bacon), *Quantitative Research Methods for Communication: A Hands-On Approach* (2008, 2013, 2016, Oxford University Press), *The Directory of Communication Related Mental Measures* (2010, National Communication Association), *Stand Up, Speak Out: The Practice and Ethics of Public Speaking* (2011, Flat World Knowledge), *Communication Apprehension, Avoidance, and Effectiveness* (2013, Allyn & Bacon), *Organizational Communication: Theory, Research, and Practice* (2014, Flat World Knowledge), and *Training and Development: The Intersection of Communication and Talent Development in the Modern Workplace* (2014, Kendall Hunt). Dr. Wrench is also the editor of three books on the subject of organizational communication: *Casing Organizational Communication* (2011, Kendall Hunt), *Workplace Communication for the 21st Century: Tools and Strategies that Impact the Bottom Line: Vol. 1. Internal Workplace Communication, Vol. 2. External Workplace Communication* (2013, both with Praeger), *Casing Public Relations* (2014, Kendall Hunt), and *Casing Sport Communication* (2015, Kendall Hunt). Dr. Wrench has also published over thirty peer-reviewed articles in a wide range of journals. Dr. Wrench served as the president of the Eastern Communication Association from 2016–2017.